RITUALISM DETHRONED

AND THE

TRUE CHURCH FOUND;

OR,

THE DIVINE LIFE IN ALL THE CHRISTIAN AGES MOST REVEALED IN THOSE CHURCHES AND "MARTYRS OF JESUS"

THAT HAVE WITNESSED AGAINST A

CEREMONIAL AND SACRAMENTAL LAW.

(A PLEA FOR CHRISTIAN LIBERTY, CHRISTIAN UNION, AND THE HIGHER CHRISTIAN LIFE.)

BY

REV. WILLIAM B. ORVIS,

AUTHOR OF "CHRIST COMING IN HIS KINGDOM;" FORMERLY EDITOR OF "PEOPLE'S PREACHER AND CHRISTIAN ERA;" "WESTERN INDEPENDENT," ETC.

"Blotting out the handwriting of ordinances, which was against us."
"How shall not the ministration of the Spirit be rather glorious?"
"For we, being many, are one bread and one body."
"One Lord, one faith, one baptism . . . even as ye are called in one hope of your calling."
"The flesh profiteth nothing: the words that I speak unto you, they are spirit, and they are life."

265
Or 9r

PHILADELPHIA:

HENRY LONGSTRETH,

738 SANSOM STREET.

1875.

1401693

CONTENTS.

PRELIMINARY—THE OUTLOOK.

THIS work is written in the hope that it may aid in lessening the too frequent and too manifest idolatrous attachments to rituals, and in the re-enthronement of Christ as the SANCTIFIER of His Church, and the LIGHT and LIFE of the world.

It is written specially in the hope that a day will dawn when the pretentious claims of a CEREMONIAL LAW will cease, and the long-enduring custom of building sects upon conformities or non-conformities in orders and rites will have come to an end. That the Millennial peace and glory of Zion will not be marred by rivalries and contentions about baptisms and other external rites and ceremonies of the churches, is the inmost conviction of nearly all who love Christ and desire the complete triumph of His cause. That "ordinances," so-called, will not hold as high a place in the esteem of Christ's spiritual flock as they do now, is the concession of many who insist that they are *now* filling, by divine appointment, a needful place in the economy of the Church. They concede that when that which is perfect is come, that which is but symbolic, and not intrinsic, or essentially life-giving, may pass away.

The writer's early education was in the Baptist Church. He was inducted thereinto by immersion, in the spring season of 1837, in Franklin county, New York. A year later, while at Oberlin, Ohio, the writer is fully conscious that for the first time God opened his eyes to see that he had never "passed from death unto life" spiritually, and being equally sure that in June of 1838 the spiritual sight was given, and a newness of life in Christ, and a spiritual baptism all un-

known before, the query at once arose : "Am I baptized
with believers' baptism in accordance with the Baptist
faith ?"

I answered *No*. Yet having the soul made alive, and " illu-
mined " by the Holy Spirit ; and realizing the unearthly and unutterable joy and glory of Christ, revealed within, I shuddered
at the thought of again stooping to the cold watery element,
as though I must needs be in bondage thereto in order to
stand accepted in Christ, who had already accepted me, as
the Holy Spirit witnessed with my spirit, in a manner all un-
thought and unhoped for before ; causing me to adore and
wonder at that " matchless grace," which wonder of redeeming love, I believed, though unrecognized by sects on earth,
would be an amazement in heaven forever. Nearly two years
later I saw in an argument for the union of all the saints (as
an obstacle to which, every one knows, that water baptism
stands pre-eminent), the suggestion that Paul's " one baptism "
(Eph. iv. 5) must be the baptism of the Spirit, else we have
two baptisms, viz. : that of water, and also that of the Spirit,
since the essential baptism of the Spirit, certainly, must not
be given up. This was a seed-thought ; and falling upon
my heart, already prepared by the querying about my Master's will, and the Spirit's teaching before alluded to, it has
taken root and grown into the tree exhibited in this volume,
and in convictions more intense than I dare hope to impress
upon others.

The writer had, ere this, however, found a fold consonant
with his enlarged views and Christian sympathies, in the
church at Oberlin, which stood for twenty-one years as the
embodiment of the " unity of the saints," no other church
having been planted there in that period. And many there
were that, during this time, came from the East, and the West,
and the North, and the South, of Congregationalists, and
Methodists, and Presbyterians, and Baptists, and Churchmen,
and Quakers, and sat down in their " one fold," under their
" one (earthly) shepherd," Prof. Finney, their beloved pastor

(whom God hath honored in the calling of many thousands into his kingdom), and enlisted with them in work for Christ. And through all this thrice septennary of years, no discourse was preached from that pulpit to show that any Christian believer should attach himself to this or that denomination rather than another, but a constant preaching of Christ, and a full salvation for all through Him.

Moreover, the writer, in a conversation with Prof. Finney, proposed the question : "Should a member of the Society of Friends, recognising the importance of church organization and labor, as they do, yet objecting to water baptism, ask to be admitted to your church, *i. e.*, that of which you are pastor, would you receive him without the baptism?" Prof. Finney promptly replied, "I without hesitation answer YES."

And when before a Congregational Council, at Lenox, in Northern Ohio, for ordination, some years later, although the writer frankly stated that he recognized no New Testament "ordinances" to be binding as a ritual law, these having been "blotted out" by the cross of Christ, it was made no bar to his receiving ordination, and he has never known of its being a bar to his work, as a minister of Christ in the church of his choice. He (like Paul in circumcising Timothy) places all rituals upon the basis of mere church authority and expediency; and is willing to accord to each church, the Baptist and the Friends, equally and alike, the right to order its externals in accordance with its best wisdom, and conscientious convictions of law and right. If, however, any church adopts a regime which seems to freeze its charity, or mar its loveliness, and is designed to impeach all others, who may be equally acceptable in God's sight, and thus the peace, unity and beauty of Zion is marred, those thus "set at nought" by their brethren may protest, and in the Spirit of Jesus endeavor both by precept and example to "show a more excellent way."

That the hitherto unending controversy respecting "ordinances" and sacraments has been an unqualified disgrace to the Christian Church, both in the inception of the ritualistic ideas, and in their extension in the later centuries, it would be impossible to deny. And the manner in which all counter querying has been excluded, and even the knowledge of the non-ritualistic churches and their testimony, both in the past and present, has been suppressed or prevented, is far from an honorable and candid exhibit of the historic records. Excepting NEANDER (a converted Jew) the popular Church historians have only traced church history in the ritualistic lines, and Neander has obliviated much of the non-ritualistic history in the two generations immediately succeeding the apostles, or, at least, only taught it by inference, as our record will show.

What historian has given a full and frank history of that Spiritual Church of Christ, in which God has manifestly dwelt, and the baptism of the Holy Ghost has been its characteristic feature and outline?—where the higher life of faith, love, and consecration to Christ, death to sin, and the endurance of persecutions for Christ's sake, have been constantly exhibited? Had this unwritten history been written it would have eclipsed their water-baptisms by a better baptism, and would have shown how the church that has walked in the Spirit, and has been taught of God, has understood the Master's teachings, and their mission to the nations. It would have ever thrown (during the earlier ages) the supreme honor upon the non-baptizers and non-ritualists, upon whom, it would be seen, God has so continually set his seal of approbation by clothing them with holiness as a robe, and enduing them with power from on high. Had the complete history been written it would have been seen that ritualists and baptizers have full oft unchurched Christ himself, and that they have very extensively dethroned Christ as an atoning sacrifice and Saviour, through their widely prevalent doctrine of baptismal regeneration. They have unchurched Christ by making water-baptism a door into their folds, thus rejecting very many with whom Christ has manifestly dwelt, because they rejected the baptism of water. Thus their churches have been folds, not for Christians simply, but for *baptized* Christians, or baptized professors of Christ, which is quite another thing than a fold for Christians because they are such.

These ritualists have been as carnal in their interpretation of the words of Christ: "Go ye, therefore, and teach all nations, baptizing them," etc., as the Jews were in interpreting Christ's proposal to give "His flesh for the life of the world," or, the disciples in understanding the "leaven of the Pharisees," or, the "meat which Christ ate, which they knew not of." And it is doubtful whether, with the amount of "tares" that have grown from the use of the external (Jewish) baptism, the good that is derived from its use, even approximately, compensates for the loss of moral and spiritual power thereby occasioned, and is continued to this day. It has, moreover, been hidden from later ages, that the fathers of the Christian Church seldom referred to Christ, as authority for their ritualistic baptism, when they practised it; and perhaps never used the formula found in Matt. xxviii. 19, but connected the practice of baptism with the Jewish idea of a priesthood, "laver," the anointing oil, etc., and many of them, with the continuance of circumcision itself, which latter was not considered complete until the *purification* from blood had cleansed the circumcised individual. It has too often been hidden, also, in later centuries, that the Christian worshippers of the early centuries never thought of the eucharistic supper but, either as a "feast of love," or "charity," or as the continuance of the *Pascha*, or *Jewish Passover*, with a remembrance of Christ superadded. The *Christian* Church at first grew out of the *Jewish*, and its baptisms and Passover were by many engrafted upon the Christian Church. The unutterable retinue of mummeries and vagaries connected with baptism and other rites, as seen in all lapsed and apostate churches, and in some not so far lapsed, has never been shown to be other than the natural out-growth of an exotic, yet assumed indigenous ritual law, blinding the eyes of those who might have been true worshippers, to what God accepts as true worship.

If it has required a thousand volumes, and all the Papal and Sacramentarian teachers of the past, to define and guide to the right observance of ritual baptism and the eucharist, and enforce their claims, may it not require *one volume*, of the size here exhibited, to expose the assumptions and false reasonings of their votaries, to unravel the confused net-work in which they appear to be snared; and to extricate them from the meshes in which, for centuries, they have seemed to be hopelessly plunged? Let it not seem strange that it requires the piling of demonstration upon demonstration, like the heaving of Pelion upon Ossa, in mountain height, just to lift the eye of the sectarist and ritualist above the smoke-clouds of the contest, and the dense fogs that seem to envelop them relative to this subject. Yet, as Bayliss says, " Little by little the smoke of the long strife is disappearing, and we may hope that erewhile the royal form of eternal and universal truth shall be revealed, and all these hitherto contending hosts shall unite in its coronation; even now, through the rifts of the smoke, we get an occasional glimpse of the monarch." May he soon stand fully revealed in the sunlight of God's glory, the true exaltation of Christ as Redeemer, and the illumination of the Holy Ghost. To enkindle hope of this result, be it remembered that truth has many allies; that every conflict between two errorists affords some vantage ground for the truth-seeker to stand upon, perhaps all unseen before, and furnishes so much ammunition and artillery for truth's advance upon the strongholds of either error, that any one, finding the truth, having followed the gleamings of light seen through the spray, may use it in error's final over-throw. Thus have we taken the ritualistic assaults and defences as they tilt the one against the other, and thus learning their weak and defenceless positions, we are enabled oft to condemn them out of their own mouths, as well as out of the Word of Inspiration. We have not confined our analytic crucible to the teachings of merely (so-called) High Church ritualists (that we leave to another occasion and another sphere); in this work we strike deeper, and take into view the more pervasive forms of ritualism, as entrenched under the pretentious name of *sacraments;* and have traced this record of ritualism and non-ritualism, through collateral periods of history; endeavoring to set forth as clearly as practicable the differing points evolved by each. While we admit that ritualists have oft taught much religious truth, and that the ritualistic churches have been marked by various shades and degrees of superstitious attachment to rites and sacraments, and that the dissidents from the Papal ritualism did not always attain full-orbed views of the Christian system, and the fulness of the divine life in Christ; yet we have ever found that the church, in proportion as it was ritualistic, has lost sight of Christ, and a full salvation through Him; and in proportion as it was non-ritualistic, has it sought to honor Christ, and attain this full salvation in Him. That some of the non-ritualists may have unduly disparaged the institutes of Moses, as compared with the Gospels, and the clearer and more spiritual light of the New Testament, we will not deny; but generally, they were pre-eminent in their attachment to the Scriptures, and in their zeal for their spread among men; and all, holding that Christ was divine, by the union of the divine and human nature in one, though differing as to the time when this incomprehensible union took place, they ever deemed Jesus the Christ, a Divine Redeemer and Saviour, through the blood of atonement and sacrifice; and thus have ever put to the blush those who have virtually and undeniably taken Christ's work from Him by attributing a saving power to sacraments administered by the puny agency of man. Thus have the non-ritualists ever maintained, in the main, that faith and love, and obedience to the moral law, which all admit to be *essential* Christian characteristics, while nearly all the jars, and schisms, and apostasies have manifestly grown out of an undue attachment to sacraments and rituals which are certainly non-saving; yet have bewitched the nominal church just in proportion as it has departed from Christ.

In the chapter, devoted to the analytical dissecting of the ritualistic teachers, we have found them very successfully annihilating each other, and oft, as conclusively annihilating their own scheme, by their utter inconsistency of premises and conclusion, as when Dr. Wall, having searched all ante-Christian and later history to prove his theory of infant-baptism as belonging by right to the birthright members of Christian households, yet virtually denies the historic fact of its later *application to the birthright members of the Jewish Church !*

This work is issued at an era when most Protestant churches find themselves in the practice of certain rites and ceremonies called "*ordinances*," and assuming the authority therefor to be "from heaven," they essay to bind them upon all Christians even to the end; (albeit, there is no approach to an end of the debates among themselves respecting the circumstantials thereof;) yet, as stated, an inquiry respecting their origin and authority is frowned upon, and the worthless questions of *how, when,* and *where,* have been almost the only queries allowed respecting them.

On these frivolous questions sects shoot off from sects, each rearing a new banner for the defence of its interpretation of a *ritual law,* and not for an illustration of the sanctifying power of the Gospel, and that life of holiness which the baptism of the Holy Ghost secures; nor for recovering the tarnished honor of Christ, thus set at nought by a false trust in a ritual; nor for a more consistent and perfect manifestation of unrestricted Christian love. It has seemed to escape the notice of these champions of sacraments and rites, that no superior holiness or moral virtue, or *moral heroism,* has been attained by themselves or their followers; yet have they not ceased to seek the final entl ronement of their sacramentarian idol among men, and to be willing to count as dross, and throw away the *baptism of the Spirit,* and all its fulness of spiritual life for man, only to retain their cold and lifeless form of baptizing with water. Meanwhile, the customs of religious people in the observance of "ordinances" have been as variable as the wind and tide, and as various as the ever-coming retinue of sects.

We have long been pressed with the conviction, that our ritualistic historians had largely ignored the anti-ritualistic record, or defaced it with unwarrantable charges of heresy; just as in our day, they have sometimes ignored in their *Evangelical Alliances*, or otherwise misrepresented, the *Society of Friends*; and our record will clearly show that we were not mistaken in our surmise. Indeed, the most grateful part of our work has been, in searching out and vindicating by unquestionable testimony the record of early and later anti-ritualists. We have assuredly found these, in all the ages, the light and life of the church and the world; and without their light the true church could scarcely have been found at all in some of the early and middle ages.

If the long-enduring sacramental customs of the church (parts of it) be adduced to sanction such customs, we have adduced as long-enduring anti-sacramentarian customs of the most spiritual portion of the church, to countervail it. Nor does long-enduring tradition or custom prove a law. The Jews have for *three thousand years* looked for a Messiah yet to come; is He, therefore, yet *to come?*

We would that our own reading in the search of the early records could have been as extensive as that of a NEANDER, or a DALE, whose records we have freely used, however, and that with the personal consent of the latter, seen face to face; and we may say, that the later and very extensive researches of the latter have still more confirmed the positions and conclusions we had before reached.

Would any one suggest, that it betokens undue confidence in the writer to hope to sustain his positions in the face of a ritualistic Christendom, he answers, it is God himself that commands, "LET THERE BE LIGHT!" and the writer has but done his duty in writing as he has. With God alone he leaves all the consequences, either to the writer, or to the church that

Christ has purchased with a great price; or to a hungering and thirsting world of immortal beings, needing something more satisfying and heavenly than the empty and hollow rites that occupy so much of the attention of bewildered millions.

Remember that *sacraments* are no more holy than their participants are; the term "holy" is altogether misplaced when given to the ceremony. And these ceremonies are as really open to inquiry as the customs of the Jews were, or of the present celibate clergy of Rome, or the non-celibate clergy of Russia or of England, or of any other land.

God himself is not so holy, but he delights in being more perfectly known.

The writer questions not any church's abstract right to an avowed *church* custom; he has a right to question, and does question, their propriety in certain cases, but more especially their claim when they arrogate the sanction of Divine authority.

He would not loosen the organic bonds of any fold, provided Christ be received and not rejected therefrom; and he has observed that the Pedobaptist and the Quaker, who both teach birthright membership in their folds, have each a strong hold on the birthright members; the latter, however, more potent for good, perhaps, than the former; so that it is not in the baptism that the moral strength abides.

And the writer having been one of them, is fully aware that the Baptist church will sooner accept his position of *no law for baptism*, or for church union through baptism, than assent to the claim that aught else than immersion in water is ritual baptism. Those who ask Baptists to forego their demand for immersion, simply ask them to forego baptism entirely, and we only ask of other denominations the same that they ask of the Baptists.

Any impeachment of the writer's motives will fall harmless at his feet, since God alone is the Supreme Judge, and he is willing to refer the motive to His tribunal; and realizing already, the ineffable melody as of a "harp" from heaven in his soul, as he presses on in the preparation of the work, poor would be the exchange for the favor of any sect or body of Christians, or even of all united in one. He only asks that his record and proofs be read with candor and kindness, the same that he has ever attempted to exercise toward all in the preparation of the work.

It has been deemed best to give *conceded and determinate principles*, the first place in our plan. The *origin* and various uses of the term the second place. Then the correction of very general false impressions relative thereto, by setting forth the true *Christian baptism*. Succeeding this, will follow the *historical outline* of the conflict between the Pauline and Judaic, or ritualistic and non-ritualistic tendencies in the early Christian ages. The argument adverse to *sacramentarian and ritualistic* claims to be continued by continuing the record of the long line of non-ritualists and non-sacramentarians, which record extends through all the Christian ages to the present time: to close with chapters presenting such refutation of sacramentarian claims, and such testimonies as the most spiritual and eminent Christians have penned from time to time. Being ever ready to correct a mistaken record on any point of fact or doctrine, and, also, ready to answer for any of the positions here taken, the writer submits the work, the result of inquiries pushed through at least one-third of a century, to a public that needs not the "forms of godliness," but the power thereof; not a "name to live" through mere external conformities, but the heaven-bestowed blessing of ETERNAL SALVATION.

RITUALISM DETHRONED,

AND THE

TRUE CHURCH FOUND.

CHAPTER I.

CONCEDED AND DETERMINATE PRINCIPLES.

GOD ACCEPTS NOT THE FORM.

GOD never accepted any man for his appearance, his liturgy, or his ritual observance.

The kingdom of God never consisted in "meats and drinks," or "divers baptisms," but in "righteousness, peace and joy in the Holy Ghost."

Lip service, and forms of religious worship, have ever been of small account in the divine economy.

Yet, on no subject has the Christian Church, in many of its divisions, been more bewildered than on this.

These have thought that God has given some sacred function to the ceremony, and is very jealous for its maintenance—and touching this, they manifest much zeal for God, but it is questionable whether it be "according to knowledge."

In some portions of Christendom, ritualism and ecclesiasticism are overshadowing the professed Christian Church to an extent that might well cause solicitude on the part of all who wait to see the kingdom of God come, not in word only, but in power, and who are assured that it is *essentially* a spiritual kingdom, and not a form of external worship.

2   17

CHRISTIANITY ADAPTED TO UNIVERSAL ACCEPTANCE, AND TO THE UNIFICATION OF ALL.

Christianity, as a system, is one of ethics, and has in it nothing provincial, nothing schismatic, nothing merely temporary, or local; but is the transcendent and universal religion. It is God's moral legation, sent alike to *all* nations, and destined to pervade all nations, and, therefore, adapted alike to all. Its laws and principles are as apposite and appropriate in the torrid as in the frigid zones—on the bleak mountains of Greenland, as by the crystal fountains and lakes of Palestine—in the waterless deserts of Africa, as on the shores of the Jordan or the sea of Galilee. Everywhere, in all climates, circumstances, or conditions of men, in sickness or in health, in vigor or in infirmity, to the Jew and to the Gentile, Christianity is from the beginning and forever the same. It requires nothing that cannot in all this variety of circumstances be equally rendered by each and all. And this, because its whole law is fulfilled in this one word, LOVE.

In its genius and DESIGN, it differs from all other religions—since all others *are distinguished* by their rituals—and their rituals may be said to inhere in the systems, so that the rituals *are but the exponents of the systems.* Such was Judaism, Magianism, Mahometanism, Paganism,—and such the Papacy of to-day.

But Christianity is as full-orbed and complete without a ritual as with it; the same to the slave as to the freeman— to the Puritan, enjoying in full his dear-bought religious heritage, as to the prisoner in his cell—to the exile, banished and precluded from all human society, as to the punctilious worshipper at some thronged and frequented fane. It matters not of what age, race, color, or clime; of what philosophy, school, or sect. Christianity knows none of these distinctions. Like an ocean tide overflowing pools, it wipes them all out; knowing no external lines of demarcation, no boundaries even of dogma or creed, or characteristic, save such as necessarily evince an inward purity of heart; for its boundaries (like the unseen land) are all internal and not external; its identification is *the spirit of man swayed by the law of love!*

Christianity, the *love* that sent Christ to do and suffer for man, was born in heaven, before ever the "world was," or the nations had a name or a place, or any mode of "worshipping the Father," "of whom are all things;" and was the same in essence before Abraham or Moses, or a ritual law was known—as it has been since *a ritual law has passed away.* The same in essence to those apostles that preached and practised Judaism, as to the Apostle Paul, the apostle of the Gentiles, that *did not preach nor practise Judaism.* The same to the early non-ritualistic Christians, as to those half-blinded by the later apostatizing ritualism of the Papacy; the same to those who possessed its spirit in the dark middle ages, as in the future millennial glory of Zion; the same in the past and future of the Church on earth, as in the eternal light and harmony of heaven. *Love,* the same everywhere, and in all ages, and all worlds, is the ultimate of Christianity, and *is the fulfilling of the law.*

The Infinite Father looks with equal eye upon all modes of sincere approach to Him, that are in harmony with equal love and good-will to man! He beholds with equal eye each of the diverse sects that truly "know His name," Himself knowing none of them by the names men have given them, but simply by the registry of heaven, as engraved on the tablet of His infinite heart of love! He concerns not Himself with human disputes about modes of worship, forms of church organization, or ritual observances; He is as high above these as heaven is above the earth, or God's thoughts above man's. He is only solicitous that the true spirit of penitence, love and worship be found, and He is as well pleased with the one worshipper as the other. He wills that the individual members of all folds should walk in wisdom toward them that are without; in love and harmony with all that are within, and in sanctified fellowship one with another. The history of the Church shows that He has never marked any distinctive fold as the exclusive recipient of His favor; He has in turn prospered them all, as their purity or steadfastness in the saving faith would permit; and all alike have been made participants of many of the richest blessings of His grace. Thus has He sealed with His own signet, Gentile and Jew, Waldensian and Catharist, Reformed Episcopalian and Reformed Covenanter, the Independent and the Presbyterian, the Baptist, Methodist and Quaker, the Evangelical Lutheran, and the Moravian, each and all, and ten thousand times ten thousand more, who have received His forgiving smile and benediction; and their work has been crowned with distinguishing marks of the Divine favor. Oft have they been honored with unusual success in turning men from sin to holiness; and which of them in turn has not at intervals shown incipient marks of backsliding, spiritual imbecility and threatened decay?

But this Divine impartiality evinces that it is the spiritual and holy Church, the Christ-like individual, that God accepts, whatever be their creed, their liturgy, their ceremonial observance, or non-observance of ceremony, or their manner of worshipping the God of truth, love, and holiness. Hence we see that CHRISTIANITY POSITIVELY APPERTAINS TO THE INTERNAL, the heart-worship, and not to the external. This that is internal is all that therein can be *positive*, unceasing and invariable. Christianity is, and must be, in the nature of things, *a spiritual religion*. Its seat and subject is the *inner man!* It is not "in the letter," but "in the spirit." Nothing outward or extrinsic strictly belongs to it. Its precepts and commands, each and all, inculcate principles, or the spread of principles to the heart-renovation, or spiritual regeneration of man. Whatever is an attribute or element of benevolence is an element of Christianity, and naught else is or can be. The *moral law* and the *Christian law* are simply synonymous terms. That law is co-eternal with God, and as universal as the universe; Jesus Christ was its embodiment, the teacher, the exemplifier of this universal law. Contingent, local, temporary, or circumstantial laws may grow out of, and be the demand of this universal law in its specific application; but be it remembered that all these are *circumstantial* and *contingent*, and not inherent in Christianity, nor commensurate with it, and have no other binding force than the circumstances which created their necessity. The circumstances of God's people in Palestine once demanded a Ceremonial Law, and that law was instituted, and inhered in a system we now term *Judaism;* but Christianity knows no such ceremonial law, no more than it knows the ceremonies of pagan worship which were cotemporary with Judaism. *Christ,* the Teacher and Redeemer of all, broke down all these ceremonial walls of partition.

THE GENIUS OF CHRISTIANITY OPPOSED TO A CEREMONIAL LAW.

Its genius of universal adaptability forbids its being encumbered with such a law. Its catholicity and demand for unity forbid its being jeopardized by such a law. It is not supposable or admissible that its All-seeing Founder would consent to jeopardize its unity or catholicity by such a law. The Judaic ritual was designed to be restrictive and local in its application. Its ceremonial was peculiar to one people, and was required of none but the lineage of Abraham. It was appointed *for the purpose* of distinguishing one nation from all others. It was, therefore, *provincial* in its design. The design of Christianity is directly the opposite of this, viz.: to unify all nations. Christianity neither can be known by any external and arbitrary sign, nor does it allow of the attempt to be thus known. It does not *define*, and how preposterous to assert that it *appoints* a ritual! True, Christianity requires wisdom in the use of means and measures, because wisdom is an attribute and manifestation of benevolence; but the measures themselves are not such attributes, nor necessarily the exponents of benevolence. Good-will is *the only law,* all else must remain contingent. Yet reason affirms that the law of love requires the use of every appropriate means to secure the great ends of benevolence, without placing the benevolent actor under bondage to any of them. The example of Jesus Christ and his apostles, who used in freedom all customary methods, and yet in the end held themselves in bondage to none, substantiates this inference. No mode or measure casually adapted to secure the great objects of benevolence, can be erected into a positive institution, an unremissible and unceasing ordinance, as this would externalize the Christian system, causing it to resemble permanently the temporary and local system of Judaism, or he Papacy. It would destroy at once its distinctive features of spirituality, universality, catholicity, and intrinsic excellence and perfection. Christianity calls, regenerates, sanctifies, and saves men as individuals by their own faith, and not by any intervention of a human absolution, or administration of rites. A full obedience to its claims is rendered when the attributes of benevolence are possessed and manifested, without any submission to a ceremonial law. That which secures the heavenly mind, and prepares the soul for the heaven to come, is all that is obligatory upon the Christian believer here. Every well-informed writer upon the evidences of regeneration, and the Christian graces, will very correctly delineate the genuine attributes and manifestations of benevolence. They are very distinctly drawn out in Christ's Sermon on the Mount; in 1 Cor. xiii.; in Gal. vi.; also in modern uninspired treatises, such as "Edwards on the Gracious Affections," "Alleine on True Conversion," and "Finney on Regeneration," and on "Sanctification." The latter writer specifies some forty or more of the attributes, as Love, Mercy, Faith, Patience, Purity, Zeal, etc., all of which undeniably inhere in the spirit of benevolence, or Christian love; yet not one of them requires or includes obedience to a ceremonial law, while each and all imply obedience to every moral duty enjoined in the moral law. Nor does any truly spiritual mind look to any ceremonial obedience for proof of the spiritual regeneration of any man. Not even a bodily exercise in the external form of prayer, or praise, or exhortation, however intrinsically fit these may be, at suitable times, is regarded as the ever-required exponent of love to God and man, and the invariable manifestation of true piety. Yet, how much more fit that these should be erected into an *ordinance* as "ordained of God" by an assumed inflexible law, than those arbitrary rites, so oft thus magnified in the eyes of men? For, deprecate and protest as you will, if you teach that men have not given full proof of repentance, and have not "fulfilled all (moral) righteousness," until they have put on some form of external obedience, you have, to their view, raised that *ritual* to the dignity of a moral law, and have created in the mind of the novitiate the impression that something very nearly connected with salvation is hinged upon their proper observance of the arbitrary ceremonial. Hence a superstitious reverence for the ceremonial is engendered, as every reader knows, for it is everywhere seen. They deem that their *moral* state is *not quite* pleasing to heaven until they have bowed to some form of ceremonial obedience!

Yet if there be no ritual law enjoining upon each Christian believer a form of preaching, of prayer, of praise, of worship, as there is not, while all these are intrinsically adapted to the Christian life and work, how much less should there be a law enjoining that which has no intrinsic merit? Shall there, then, be a law enjoining *sacraments*, or *ceremonies of worship*, the intrinsic value of which is at least questionable?

What is Following Christ?

So in regard to *following Christ*. The externalized conception is not only infinitely far from Christ's intent in the command, "Follow me," but it is almost infinitely low and unworthy of the Christian's thought. Men, claiming to be sage religious teachers, talk of following Christ "down the banks of Jordan," as though this were an excellent thing, and very pleasing to Christ himself. If so, why not go to the Jordan (as Mahomet enjoined his followers to go a pilgrimage to Mecca), and there follow Christ down the banks of Jordan? You would thus *very literally* be a follower of Christ. We will not say that it would prove you spiritually one! You would much more consistently give proof of being truly in spirit a follower of Christ by visiting the sick, clothing the naked, relieving the distresses of the poor, the orphan and the widow, and seeking to assuage the cup of life's sorrow everywhere? You are not "made under the (Jewish) law," that you need to be *purified* (baptized) into the priesthood: you are, if regenerated, already a "king and priest" to God; and you may, without waiting for any priest (as John was) to lead you down "Jordan's banks," or to any altar, or shrine, bring your soul, and your offering direct to Christ, and to His suffering poor, assured that you will be abundantly accepted without any canonical interposition of any earthly mediator or administrator of rites.

If you think there is any excellence or virtue in following Christ in the external form, why not be circumcised, and eat the Passover; why not recline at your meals as Jesus reclined, and sleep upon such a mattress as did He? If a minister of Christ, why not commence your sermon without a text, oft, and without a song or prayer in form, and preach chiefly in the open air? If a young man, why not work at the same trade for life, and eat and drink similar food, and clothe yourself with similar raiment? How amazing the infatuation reached by centuries of bigoted and superstitious teaching, filling the imagination of otherwise earnest Christians with the conceit that a *ceremonial* likeness to, or imitation of Christ, is aught that Christ requires! Hence the endless inquiry after the manner of some of His bodily acts, and a zealous effort to attain to a full conformity thereto! Whole denominations of Christians are continually slumping into this pit. Should not Christ's ministers have sufficient spiritual discernment to warn their flocks of the danger and folly of this? A mechanical obedience is not what Christ seeks, but the daily obedience of love. "What and if ye shall see the Son of Man ascend up where he was before? It is the spirit that quickeneth! The flesh profiteth nothing!" And should you follow Christ, bodily toward heaven, as the builders of Babel did, for a little way, would that be of any avail? Suppose you follow Christ down the banks of Jordan and are *there* baptized precisely as he was, are you the better for it? Or is any one else the better or happier for your act?

JUDAISM REQUIRED NO BODILY IMITATION.

Even under the strict Jewish ritual law there was no effort to *imitate one another* in their ceremonial performances. Whom did Moses imitate when he took the hyssop branch, with scarlet wool, and dipping it in blood and water, sprinkled (baptized) all the people? You say he was the mediator of that covenant, and the founder of the ritual law. Yes; but what priest ever sought precisely to imitate Moses? Can one be named? Moreover, most of the purifyings under the law were self-administered, at least in part. Did they ever seek to imitate one another? When they washed (baptized) themselves, and bathed their flesh, as so oft, they evidently did as we of modern times do,—they used water with the hand, or with other means of appliance, to secure the bodily cleansing that they sought, having reference only to the result and not to the method of attaining it. No superstitious reverence was paid to *a method* then; that was left to those who fail to understand the spirituality of the Christian Dispensation.

This superstitious homage to rites is left for those who fail to see that it is not possible for a *spiritual dispensation* to require an external ritual, a ceremonial routine, a mere bodily exercise, or bodily imitation one of another, or of some earlier prototype;—who have also failed to see that if Jewish priests followed Moses the Mediator of the Old Covenant, in baptiz-

ing typically, we, ministers of Christ, may follow Christ,
the Mediator of the New Covenant, who certainly did not
baptize typically.   The *determinate* principle is this: we may
forget what Christ did as "under the law," either in respect
to circumcision, baptism, sacrifice, or Passover, which all was
done that He might be fully accepted of the Jews, to obviate
all ceremonial objections, and that those " under the law"
might hear the call, and be "redeemed;" and we may follow
Christ " in the regeneration," or what Paul calls " the reformation," not in the oldness of the letter, but in that spiritual
worship which the "Father seeks," and which requires no
ritual or temple service either at Jerusalem or Samaria; no
altars red with blood of beasts, nor *purifyings* with human
hands, either in Jordan, Enon, or Bethabara.

The Judaic Economy a Rudimentary School.

The Judaic economy given by pattern and instruction received in the "holy mount," was rudimentary in its nature;
a school for catechumens, taught by diagrams, rather than *a
law* for those matured in the knowledge of God, and the way
of salvation.   Those diagrams could scarcely claim the authority of positive law; they were simply prescribed methods of
instruction, and *never* reached the altitude, nor wore the
aspect of *sacraments;* nor were they ever called by that name
in all the ages of the Mosaic ritual.   Did Moses or a prophet
ever reprehend the people of Israel because they had neglected
their external purifications?   Nay, they were but too fond of
placing their chief reliance on these.   And in every age it
has required the constant vigilance of the spiritual-minded to
withhold the mass of worshippers from such a vain trust,
where the ritual has been in use at all.   But after the lapse
into idolatry of which Israel in Egypt was guilty, a ritual,
innocent in itself, and less imposing in pomp and circumstance than that of the idolatrous nations, to which also a
proper significance might be given, was "added," Paul says,

because of "transgressions," until the "seed should come," unto whom was the "promise" of being the inheritor of the "purchased possession," through His one great sacrificial offering and atonement for man. Of this great work of the great Redeemer, all Jewish sacrifices and baptisms were simply typical emblems and foreshadowings. They served in lieu of the antitype itself, the purpose of suggestive symbols of the real atoning sacrifice, and the real baptism which Messiah should enjoin and secure in the purifying of their hearts.* Through these, in the then state of need, moral lessons might be taught, and influences thereby exerted to withhold a half-reformed people from yielding to the constant temptation to idolatry. But when the fulfilment or antitype of all these had come, and was seen and known of all, to keep the type before them still, would have been like keeping the taper burning after the sun has arisen with all his effulgence of light. How can any Christian deny this?

---

* Alluding to the difference between the Abrahamic and the Mosaic covenants, Rev. F. G. Hibbard says: "The reader will see that the ceremonial law was not the *Church Charter* under the former dispensation, but only the temporary discipline and system of elemental instruction under which Jehovah placed the Church for a season. The ceremonial law and the Abrahamic covenant are not to be confounded. . . . . In the covenant of Abraham 'all nations' were to be blessed. It contained the gospel to the Gentiles (Gal. iii. 8) as well as to the Jews. On the contrary, the institutes of Moses were rather adapted to a high spirit of *nationality*, and I may say, *exclusiveness*, among the Jews. One grand design of the ceremonial law was to secure the distinct preservation of the Jewish people until Christ should come. To these ends, the inexorable ritual of Moses was well adapted. Thus a 'middle wall of partition' was kept up between Jews and Gentiles, and a *complete separation* preserved. . . The ceremonial law is abolished, but the covenant of Abraham is established in Christ." Now *the* marvel of the ages is, that those who thus can write respecting the difference between a dispensation whose *characteristic*, as they affirm, is a ceremonial law, and one whose *characteristic* is, that it is spiritual, and has no ceremonial law, do not see that it would not be to the breaking down of "partition walls" to annul one ceremonial law, and then immediately establish another, a law of baptisms, which was assuredly a part of the former ceremonial law.

HIBBARD, the Methodist writer on Baptism, p. 28, well says :

"These external ceremonies and symbols originated and assisted their first conceptions of truth; afterward came the long line of illustrious prophets, endowed with supernatural penetration and wisdom, and expounded more fully the spiritual sense of the 'law,' lifting the mind of the nation (the Jewish) through another ascending grade of divine knowledge. And when, finally, by these external means the *principles* of theology were fully communicated; when the Jews had so associated with other nations by commerce and travel, but especially by colonizing themselves everywhere, so as to incorporate their elemental ideas of religion into other languages, and in some sense to transfuse their own principles into pagan systems of philosophy and religion; when the human mind became thus in a measure prepared, when the fulness of time had come, 'God sent forth his own Son,' the great Teacher, to *abolish* the elemental system, to mature those conceptions of truth, and to complete the illumination of the human mind. . . . These elemental principles once mastered by the mind, they could be easily taken and applied to various subjects at will, while the *external machinery*, which was the means of imparting them, *could be dispensed with*. The people of God need be 'no longer under a school-master,' they could now 'leave the first principles of the doctrine of Christ, and go on unto perfection.' . . . All our abstract ideas are derived primarily through the outward senses; hence all *primary words* in all original languages, *though many of them* now *stand for abstract ideas*, originally represented sensible objects."

See also DALE on origin of *Baptisma* and *Baptistes*.

The above reasoning of Dr. Hibbard is eminently correct and clear, and it may be remarked that this logic covers the *whole* ceremonial and ritual law of the Jews, which, moreover, originated not as a law, but was employed by Moses *as a means of moral instruction*, and so continued by the Levites as a *picture lesson* for study, rather than as a blind allegiance to a statutory law. What did the Jehovah ever require of Israel, or any other nation, but to "do justly, to love mercy, and to walk humbly with God."

The very need of the type then, was the evidence not only of their estrangement from the knowledge of God, but also, that the perfect dispensation of fulfilled prophecy and promise, by the revelation of the all-efficient atonement, baptizer, and Saviour, had not yet come. These rituals were but sentinels, placed all the way to keep and point the way of the *coming*

One; and in the nature of the case, when He comes, these sentinels may stand aside.

Ritualists have monstrously perverted the words of hortation to Moses on Sinai: "See that thou make all things according to the pattern shown thee in the mount;" as though we were *now* to build an external tabernacle, as Moses then was directed to do.

Such a charge was pertinent, and carefully observed by Moses, as head of that "ministration," and lawgiver and mediator of the old covenant. But no such pattern of external things was given by Jesus on Calvary; but rather the nailing of Himself and the old dispensation to the cross, that not the symbol and type should point darkly to the "kingdom of heaven;" but the glorious antitype should, in its fulness be enjoyed, filling the whole moral horizon with the blessed illumination of the *new dispensation,* the "kingdom of heaven" already come. Is there any truth more clearly stated in the whole New Testament, and especially in the Epistles to the Hebrews and to the Gentile churches? We say, the vision that Moses saw in the mount related to the tabernacle which should be constructed in the wilderness by human hands; which, Paul tells us, was the figure or symbol of the "true tabernacle," which is not built with human hands, but which "God pitches and not man."

What pattern, as co-worker with God, is man to follow here, but the pattern of the cross?

We have no wilderness tabernacle now; of course, we need none of its accompaniments, none of its sacrifices, baptisms, oblations; all these belonged to that external tabernacle, which is now removed and superseded by the heavenly, where Christ "forever" pleads His one "offering," and where the Holy Spirit which He sends is forever the Purifier (Sanctifier), and every sanctified soul is God's temple. Has not Jesus entered into the "true tabernacle," and into the holy of holies (to which also He freely invites us), there to sprinkle the mercy-seat with the blood of the everlasting covenant, having *obtained* eternal redemption for us?

Do *we* need now to offer expiatory sacrifices? Are we now (or ever) spiritually cleansed by the waters of baptism? or do we need the cold external element, when the true spiritual life has come? Christ's baptism (of suffering, and of the Holy Anointing) now baptizes us. Do we need more than this? The blood of "atonement" is now our sanctifier. Also,

> "That blood atones for all our race,
>   And sprinkles now the throne of grace."

It is true that even in the old dispensation, he only that had clean hands and a pure heart (unstained by sin) was accepted in God's "holy hill," and in the "most holy place!" Their outward circumcision was not accepted in lieu of the "circumcision of the heart." Should the annoying *concision* continue forever? Better that God should form our frames as He would have them at first. That ceremony, like every other, was for a local and temporary object. That attained, God never desired "vain oblations," nor "sacrifices" rather than "judgment, mercy, and the love of God." The moral end; the fruits of righteousness, was all He ever sought, through these or without them. "What doth the Lord require of thee, but to do justly, to love mercy, and to walk humbly with thy God?" The ceremonial was to be used during that "ministration" for such moral end. Yet so ineffectual did it prove, that it was called the "ministration of death" (see 2 Cor. iii.); and also, "of the letter that killeth," rather than "of the Spirit that giveth life." Hence Christ "disannulled the commandment" (in the type or letter), "going before," to introduce a more perfect ministration "of the Spirit." Not only is there an intrinsic inability and inaptitude in a ceremonial to purify the soul, but all historic evidence is against the claim of rituals to be successfully serviceable in this work. They can only serve as piers or breakwaters against what is worse. Alternating reformations and backslidings was the record of the Jewish nation after the Mosaic ritual was given, until the nation was well-nigh apostatized from God again. The Greek Church ritualists, and the Papal ritualists have afforded no better record. And what is the record of millions called Protestant: as the High Church Episcopal, the Lutheran, and the ritualistic "Reformation" of Alexander Campbell in this respect? Is it any better?

Yet since the Mosaic ritual was disannulled, without a present definitive ritual law, how many myriads of arrogant claims to exemplify and correctly expound a New Testament *ritual law* have been made?

ASSUMPTIONS OF INFALLIBILITY.

"All men think all men mortal but themselves," was the pertinent saying of Dr. Young, alluding to the too common conception of human frailty, and the brevity of life. So may it be as truly said, "All men think all men fallible but themselves," specially in judging of theologic and revealed truth, and Church claims—and in all reasonings relative to a ceremonial law. The English prelate, contesting the claims of the Pope at Rome, boldly and very justly announces: " I hold that if any man be infallible, *I* am the man!" This is the heart-language of every independent thinker, who nevertheless may be perfectly honest and unassuming in his search after all advancing light, and walking in all the light already attained. Truth is beautiful, and all radiant with glory to such an earnest and appropriating spirit.

That mind *is* infallible in the sense of being incessant in its reaches after truth; also in the fact of its constantly adding to its store new truth, and also in constantly looking at the old in a new and beautified light.

Such a state of mind, moreover, will assuredly be found acceptable to God; and ever approved in its aims and moral affections, yet ever fallible when compared with infinite wisdom itself.

Effort to find the Infallible Church.

The effort to find the infallible church, composed of fallible men, is an effort to find immaculateness in a body which is not in any individual of that body. And the effort to detect the heaven-sanctioned church by its ritual, is as absurd as an effort to find a righteous man by looking at his dwelling, or the contour of his countenance.

The true spirit of worship usually manifests itself in some external form—yet not always, for there may be a thankful or a praying spirit that never manifests itself in forms, as there may be an obedient spirit that has never yet had the opportunity of manifesting itself in the outward act.

Church organization itself is but an expression of the spirit of life from God in its members—*i. e.*, if it be a true church of God—it thus manifests the intent of its members to serve God, and worship Him in accordance with the degree of divine illumination given, and the best exercise of reason and judgment attainable. The illumination from God pertains to the spirit of worship and service; man's reason and judgment select the mode that seems most in accordance with antecedents, or with the object in view. When men assume that God has given to the Christian Church, or continues in the Christian Church a prescribed ritual in any respect, they engraft both Judaism and Popery upon the Christian Church, and make it a hot-bed of contentions and strifes about that which intrinsically profits nothing, and which Jehovah never valued for its own sake. Every church must worship, if it worship in the sight of men, after some form; but the large-hearted and enlightened Christian never stamps divinity upon his formula or ritual, or assumes that his brother man is less acceptable to God on account of his differing ritual.

Who is the Ritualist?

The Ritualist is the man that claims divine authority for the specific rituals of his Church; and excludes all others, measurably, at least, from heaven's favor, in his own esteem, on account of their divergences from his model. He may discover the same assuming spirit in others respecting their rites, and may denounce them as sectarists and bigots for this cause; but he never has discovered it to be bigotry and a spirit of ritualistic worship in himself. Thus by changing a word of our starting aphorism, we may say, "All men think all men bigots but themselves," or ritualists, as the case may be. And there is no cure for this ritualism, but to strike at its base, and admit that all that appertains to an organic Church, save the spirit of life from God, which constitutes its members one in spirit with Christ, is human, and of no more binding authority than anything else that is human, that good men may prescribe or approve.

How to find the True Church.

Suppose the organic body, non-organic, just as the Holy Spirit leaves each individual when renovated in heart, before any human, or church action or labor is attempted; there you have all that is strictly divine in the church. All else is the result of human wisdom or *un*wisdom moved by benevolent intent.

The Divine Life takes the Mould of Circumstances.

The divine life in the human soul takes form according to circumstances—according to the primal ideas of each nation, tribe or individual, moulded by education and antecedent example. In other words, this divine life takes the form of the mould in which it is run—and how oft is that mould or form, by each individual, through human weakness, deemed almost or quite as sacred and indispensable as the divine life itself!

Few rise so near the primal source of divine life—the Sun of Righteousness, as to see that it is the same "light that lighteth" all, or to see over the walls that divide them from others; and discern the light on the other side. Hence men

3

value their own forms, and see all excellence in them, just in proportion to their distance from God, and their distance in heart affections from their fellow-men.

Hence the too prevalent ritualism of churches and their bigotries of sect and creed. Yet each pities his neighbor as a ritualist, and is prone to congratulate himself that he has escaped that folly, or at least that he certainly has found God's appointed rites, for obedience to which God looks very complacently upon him. Thus the Independent pities the ritualism of the Low Church, and the Low Church, in turn, pities the ritualism of the High Church, and the High Church pities the Puseyite and the Papist for the same cause. The High Church historian is so blinded by his ritualism that he cannot give a fair and unbiassed history of his Low Church brethren, or of Quakers and Independents. And even the Independent and the Presbyterian, while proposing to write creeds that will embrace "all evangelical Christians," will, perhaps, utterly ignore the Friends, the Moravians, or the Plymouth Brethren, each manifesting the spirit of Christian love and missionary zeal that many larger bodies of Christians (those that ignore them for example) would do well to imitate. Who can show a church creed, written of man, that will embrace "all evangelical Christians?" Even those called *union creeds* are usually assuming and divisive in certain directions: showing that the writers have not God's eyesight, and God's expansive charity toward all that truly love Him. If aught beyond the Christian spirit were really and wholly of God, *i. e.*, if church organization were as divine as is the new birth to holiness, dare we suppose that God would organize churches on a basis that would exclude one soul that Christ's blood had cleansed? Surely not.

CHRIST ORGANIZED NO CHURCH.

Christ did not organize his followers into a denomination called after his name; but, up to the time of His crucifixion, left them in the Jewish organization, yet purposing ere while to extend the call far beyond the Jewish fold. Nor did he engraft Judaism, or the ceremonial law, upon Christianity, nor prescribe any ritual, which would have been both incongruous, and an unspeakable embarrassment to the new faith ; but used the ritual then current—otherwise He would have added a new (Jewish) sect to those before existing. He aimed rather to bring the ritual into disesteem, and lay open an area for an *undivided fold,* composed of all the diverse nations, whose "One Lord, one faith, one baptism," should cement them as one forever.

By the opposite assumption of an external polity, or ritual engrafted upon the Church by its founder, many Christian philosophers (and some who are not Christians) are enabled to deal damaging blows against the *assumed* churches, and their self-elected umpires of theology and polity in Christendom. Nothing has dishonored the church more than these assumptions and canonical pretensions of great, and oft good men, whose arrogance in this direction, however, tends to divide the fold of Christ, and is ever in violation of a true catholicity.

Who hath made thee a judge, or umpire of the question : *Where is the true Church?* these acute philosophers may well ask the rival claimants of that honor. Is your charter direct from heaven, to the exclusion of your brother Christian who evidently has the signet of heaven as well as thee? The true Christian knows that the true church of Christ must embrace "whosoever feareth God and worketh righteousness," whatever polities or rituals they embrace and observe, or whether they make use of any at all, or not. Yet from the Papist to the Puseyite, and from the Puseyite to the Independent and the Baptist, each assumes his *order* and his *ritual* to be the alone heaven-approved, and the only one to be accepted and approved of men. And they may as well claim heaven's exclusive approval of their ritual, as to claim its appointment of heaven at all ! The proof of the one is as clear as the proof of the other.

These Christian philosophers do not criticise and abjure the *principles* of the Christian system, only the ritualisms and superstitions of the leaders and champions of the Christian faith. The bigotry and infatuation of exalting conventionalities above the spirit of life, as seen in the humblest of Christ's friends, is, by them, scanned with philosophic and philanthropic eye, very much to the disparagement of those champions of the generic faith. If, therefore, the church of Christ cannot be saved from the narrow, canting, and uncatholic prejudices of archbishops, bishops, and doctors of divinity, it must ever stand vastly depreciated in the estimation of all true Christian philanthropists, and true church reformers.

A theology that eschews world-wide charity because of any divergence of creed or ritual, and eschews absolute catholicity, patterns after the false Romanistic Catholicity, and limps at every step in its work, and is, in principle, no better under the Protestant name, than is the Greek Church patriarchal prelacy, or the Papacy of the Roman Church, and the prelacy of the High Church episcopacy. For this self-assuming lack of charity, on the part of a self-assumed priesthood, is but acting the Pope with one's own conscience, and an attempt to act the dogmatism of Popes over the consciences and intelligence of all others.

How Rituals are used.

Rituals, may be, and are used mainly to give power to a priesthood, or a canonical enclosure of assumed saints, to dominate over God's heritage, and bring weak and uninstructed consciences in subjection—to keep up sect-boundaries, and win and hold honest yet superstitious believers in denominational folds—almost, or quite, assuming thereby to open or shut the door of heaven to men. Yes, they are made the "keys of the Kingdom," opening or shutting its pearly gates, and giving or withholding the canonical passport to all the blessings within. They assume to stand in Christ's place, with *ex cathedrâ* power to receive or cast away, to approbate and retain, or exorcise, and anathematize, according to the varying conceits of diversely educated and fallible men. Before heaven we must arraign them as having usurped Christ's place over men's consciences, and as having supplanted Christian love, and blinded the eye to the behests of true gospel charity, and the peremptory demands of the moral law.

And this, not by a perversion of a ritual law, but by a *turning aside to a ritual law*, which "yoke of bondage," and seed of schism, "neither we nor our fathers have ever been able to bear;" and which Jesus Christ, the great Head of the church, never imposed upon his followers. HE never gave to His church wisdom and understanding adequate to be of one mind respecting a ritual law, and it is impeaching His official dignity, as "Head over all to the church," to impute to Him the authorship of a law that can never be defined, and clearly understood and obeyed.

For the love of Christ's sake, therefore, and for His divine honor, we protest against erecting the inquisition of some *positional* or *ceremonial* test thus to exclude or make bigots of untaught Christian brethren.

If you would unite all the Christians of a place in an organic union, it must be done on the simple basis of the unity of Christian love in each believer's heart—not on the basis of a like understanding of any ritual law, or any other incident or form, that, either in the past or future, may be connected with the organic action of Christians.

FOR WHAT OBJECTS CHRISTIANS MAY UNITE.

Christians may unite and form organic churches for either of three purposes—or for all combined, viz: 1. For purposes of religious instruction only, and then they may co-operate with any and all who will seek the same end—even if they be but catechumens in Christ's school, not even claiming to have an experimental knowledge of the way of salvation. This is the Methodistic and Friends' plan. 2. They may organize for the promotion of some specific reform, that pertains to the advance of Christ's kingdom and the lasting welfare of man ; and in this case they are required to receive only those who desire to give their influence to that specific branch of reform, and they are not exclusive, nor do they violate Christian love, if they do not receive all Christians, even, to their fold, and their ranks. They only require those who would enlist in that particular form of warfare. They do not thereby necessarily disown, or disparage the work of those who are engaged in other departments of the great cause. 3. They may organize for the exemplification of the true Christian spirit, and the full extent of Christian charity. In this case they are bound to receive all that are adjudged to be Christians, who desire their fellowship, rejecting none of these for any cause ; and receiving none that lack the evidence of the Christian spirit and life.

Touching the second object specified above, anti-slavery Christians were often found organized for the promotion of that specific reform ; and this they did even with a design of rejecting and disowning those professed Christians who were pro-slavery, or neutral on the subject. And they were, no doubt, justified in this course, whatever charity may have affirmed of some who were thus rejected. It was a method of administering needful Christian rebuke for public and glaring sin, in obedience to the behest, " Thou shalt in any wise rebuke thy brother, and not suffer sin upon him." But for Christians to differ respecting a ritual law is infinitely far from proving any sin against either party, as all must admit, yet those who make any ritual a test or boundary of fellowship, do so, we think, invariably with the implication that all that reject their test ought to have been in fellowship with them by receiving and adopting their ritual. Here is where their dogmatism and their Popery stand revealed.

LET RITUALISTS DO JUSTICE TO EACH OTHER.

Instead of looking upon their organizations as called for,

in order to accomplish specific objects, as harmonious branches of the one common church of Christ, how many of the diverse organizations have assumed that their own particular branch *is the only canonical church of Christ ?*

Nearly all build upon the assumption that some ritual is *the door* into the church fold, and have each, of course, assumed that their own ritual, or polity, is the only one that is canonical, or heaven ordained.

And each impeaches the other for want of conformity to the divine pattern or model " shown in the mount!" And, perhaps, each will accuse the other of being exclusive because themselves are rejected from their fellowship for nonconformity in rituals, not heeding the palpable fact that themselves are rejecting some others on precisely the same grounds. Baptists reject Pedo-Baptists for noncomformity in rituals, and the Pedo-Baptists are not slow to censure their bigotry in so doing. Nevertheless, these Pedo-Baptists have not discovered that they are rejecting one branch of the Church at least, the Quakers, for the same reason, and that themselves refuse to receive unbaptized believers into their folds. Baptists and Pedo-Baptists are therefore planting themselves upon the same ritualistic basis. So each has a ceremonial law. Christian ministers oft read in Paul's epistles, and expound his teachings respecting the abolition of the ceremonial law, not perceiving that most of these ministers are really in bondage to a ceremonial law as grievous as any that Paul declaimed against. The Jews had a ceremonial law, they say, almost commiserating their pupilage under these " rudiments." So have you, my rite-bound brother, a ceremonial law, and you are as much in bondage to it as they ever were.

WEAR NON-RITUALISTIC GLASSES.

Now, why not wear glasses that will enable you to see yourselves as others see you, and such as a true Christian freedom from rituals, and true Christian union require ? Nor be afraid to march straight up to a difficulty, and look full in the face, your own inconsistency! That is what true Christian magnanimity requires. God hath not given thee all wisdom as yet, and wisdom will not die with thee. Be willing to see the full sweep of a radical, levelling principle, though it lay thy shibboleths all low as others. Time was when rituals were not, and time will be when the false idea of their sanctity will pass away. The idea of their sanctity is naught but *sacramentarianism*, and remember that the true worship of God existed before these rituals had place, and brought them into being, and hence we may infer that the true worship of God may exist after they have ceased to ensnare and pervert the consciences of men, or have any part in God's true worship. If the true spirit of worship has in time past induced varying rituals, such spirit of worship in fallible men will continue to vary them, until all shall have passed away, or be entirely changed.

IDOLS AND DIVISIVE WALLS MUST FALL.

Rituals must cease to be made into idols before which befooled men bow themselves, honoring them more than they do their Christian brethren, and they must cease to be made into partition walls, or they must surely be obliterated. Judaism was appointed by God, but it failed ever to make the comers thereunto perfect, and it became a great snare, being substituted for spiritual religion, and a true worship of God. So God " found fault with it," and Christ " took it out of the way," save, as is seen, an imperfect church is found still clinging to shreds of it.

An abuse of that which, in its time is good in part, may be a just cause for its utter disuse. A correct idea of religion may not be able to supplant a perversion or superstition otherwise. Judaism was, in part, good, but came to stand in the way of the union of Jewish and Gentile Christians; hence the necessity for its removal. It became a partition wall. Christ took away the enmity occasioned by those "ordinances," innocent in themselves. And if Christ has abolished the "law of commandments, contained in ordinances," you, who hold yourselves and the Christian Church subject to ordinances, are "teaching for doctrines the commandments of men," and abusing God thereby, by substituting an idol in the place of God; a ritual law in the place of the moral law of love to God and man;—thus you make God an infinite trifler in teaching that He has given a worthless, yea, an injurious law, yet that He prizes it more highly than your love to Him and to your brother man.*

* The danger of placing a ritual law in the place of the moral law, and arrogating the Divine sanction for "commandments of men," is illustrated by what Rev. John Hall, D.D., of New York, says of the Papal Church turning aside to the Popish institution of the *Confessional*. Alluding to what Père Hyacinthe had said respecting it, Dr. Hall continues:

"Now the Rev. Father laments that the men turn away, as a rule, from religion; and the women, 'essentially religious, loving, suffering,' 'sympathetic,' unable to 'be solitary in their religion' must (the men having abdicated) 'go to the confessional.' This, it will be observed, is a return—and something more—from the Scripture ground to necessity. If the Scripture *obliges* the priest to hear confession and absolve, he needs no apologetic plea like this.

"Now we submit a question at this point, and with profound respect ask to it the Rev. Father's attention.

"Set up two similar institutions side by side, one simply divine, the other, however well meant and in itself unobjectionable, but human, and does not all experience show that the divine will be deserted for the human? Set up with the Lord's Day holidays for religious uses, and they supersede the Lord's Day. Set up the Church and traditions beside the Scriptures, and they supersede the Scriptures. Set up the Supreme Pontiff along with Christ, and the Supreme Pontiff supersedes Him. Set up the human priesthood and the great High Priest is put out of view. The list might be easily enlarged. It is the old story of King Ahaz, in 2 Kings xvi.—fancying an altar he saw at Damascus, then sending the pattern of it to Urijah, then setting it up beside God's altar, then of approaching *it*, and then offering thereon; and how he dealt with God's true ordinances the reader can study for himself. Precisely so God set up the priesthood of the family, which Father Hyacinthe honors, and the absence of which he deplores among Roman Catholics. Rome set up her priesthood beside it. The usual result has followed. Man's fixture is preferred by man to God's. If the priesthood of the family is to be restored over Roman Catholic Christendom, it is to be by the abandonment of the Church's priesthood. Let Christ's ministers in all love and tenderness preach Christ in

UNSANCTIFIED SOULS LIVE IN THE SHELL OF RELIGION.

Blind, unsanctified zeal feeds and prides itself on the husks and shell of religion; and as the chameleon and other living creatures wear the color of that upon which they brood, so do these sticklers for the shell assume the variegated colors these shells reflect upon them. When they quote Christ's words spoken to Moses under a typical law, "See that thou make all things according to the pattern shown in the mount," they forget that Jesus gave no ritualistic pattern save the Mosaic; neither on the Mount of Olives nor Mount Moriah, nor Calvary, save the pattern there, of suffering to the death to "draw all men unto Him." And Himself has said respecting all earthly shrines and rituals: "Neither in this mountain (of Samaria), nor at Jerusalem, shall men worship the Father, but they that worship Him (henceforth) are to worship him in spirit and in truth," and not according to the letter or form. Christ worshipped according to the law given on Sinai, but we have come to a better mountain, even to "Mount Zion, and to the heavenly Jerusalem," and to a better covenant than that remembered by a ritual law—a covenant which, according to the promise, made under the old, is written in the heart—which "stands not in meats and drinks and divers baptisms,

---

public and in private, and declare remission of sins to every believer in him; let them come as near to men and women, and men as much as women, as human hearts can approach one another; but let them forego the claim to the Lord's unparticipated work, the forgiveness of sins; and, with the removal of the human rival, the true scriptural priesthood of the family will, under the balanced and symmetrical teaching of divine truth, be regained, to the great good of men and to the glory of God."

Modern opponents of SECRET SOCIETIES oft allude to their use of man-made rites as a reason for their being discountenanced, since such rites thus employed tend to the disparagement of those that are God-given. These opponents of rites of human invention, would do well to bear in mind that *saints* are not known by their rites, but by the "fruits of the Spirit" which they bear. Moreover, the Christian Church has been on the chase after the *God-given* rites for 1900 years, and seem no nearer reaching the end of the search than when they first began.

and carnal ordinances," but in the power of the Holy Ghost revealed in the souls of believers.

Yet towering walls of bigotry and sect are built around rituals, called "ordinances," and "sacraments," like the flaming sword around the tree of life, lest any man come, and eat and live. Ostensibly the wall is built, lest the sacrament be defiled, or its sanctity be trampled on, which mockery of pretence if there be amazement in heaven, surely all heaven stands amazed at such exclusion and sacrifice of souls, for whom Christ died, for the sake of saving a dead form—a ritual! which thus proves a curse to all who so idolize it.

God is not afraid of any man's harming a rite, whether he observe it or not, if only his heart be right toward God and man. God *is* solicitous that we have pure and loving hearts. He is opposed to our neglect of the sacraments of truth and love, and righteousness. Benevolent Christian labor, considering the poor, and doing good to others, is a much better sacrament in God's sight, than eating bread or drinking wine, or performing sprinklings or ablutions in a steepled sanctuary.

WHEN SACRAMENTS MAY BE NECESSARY.

Customs, and the superstitions in which men are educated, may render sacraments needful, as it was needful for Paul to circumcise Timothy "for the sake of the Jews," among whom he was about to take him as a Christian teacher, but it was Jewish superstition that was thus subserved, not any Christian law, save the general law of good will. Some know no other door to the Church, than by the use of rituals; they have been so taught, and *their* consciences require their observance, and they scarce could feel at rest in any neglect of them. So the Papist as conscientiously says mass, and counts beads, and crosses himself, all sanctimoniously, because he has been so taught.

So the Jew still eats his Passover, and Mahometan dervishes howl their worship or incantations by the hour. Ritualists, that think to be purified, or made meet for the Church, or in any way to do God service by the waters of baptism, are just as wise as the above, and no wiser. And each and all are necessary for man's good only as a matter of conscience, based on personal persuasion in the mind of each.

Our Divine Father is not half as solicitous to continue Judaistic, Papal, Mahometan, or even Protestant rituals, as are their human devotees. With the purifying of man's heart, and his devotion to works of love and righteousness, God's revealed will terminates. This, from the beginning, would have satisfied Him: "Shall not the uncircumcision, which is by nature, if it fulfil the law (the moral law), judge thee who by the letter and circumcision dost transgress the law (the law of love)?" So God would spiritually purify and unite the Christian Church, and he that has this spiritual purifying and union with Christ and His people, shall evermore judge those that have the outward purifying or baptism, and yet have not true union with Christ and all His people.

"Israel after the flesh," with all its ritual, is ever judged by "Israel after the Spirit." Many saints before the law (the ritual law) was given could judge those who (afterward) "by the letter and circumcision did transgress the law."

The outward baptism doth not offend God, if therewith its administrator and receiver doth not for that cause reject and "set at naught his brother for whom Christ died;" but when he does, his baptism is an offence unto God. His baptism is made un-baptism, either in letter or spirit. God is willing to bless baptizers (with water), i. e., to endure long with their ritualism, if they will still love and save men, otherwise He will spew their baptisms out of His mouth. He is as willing to bless non-baptizers (with water) if they love and save men, for they have equally fulfilled the law with those that baptize.

Dost thou think that God has commanded all saints to join some Church that has a ritualistic door, and to pass through that door? If so, which is the Church? Is it the Congregational Church? or the Baptist Church? or the Presbyterian

Church? or the Episcopal Church? or the Methodist Church? or which of the forty or fifty extant *orders* of the Protestant Church? or the Greek, the Lutheran, or the Papal Churches? If Paul were to return to earth, which would he decide to be the *canonical* Church? Or Jesus, the Great Head of all churches? Perhaps, He would select (elect) *your* church, and *your* baptism, and meekly inform all the others that they were not acceptable in His sight. Thinkest thou this, O vain man and bigot? Perhaps, He would place Himself restrictively in the German Reformed Church, or the Moravian, or the Friends, or among the Plymouth Brethren? Then what would your boastedly huge denominations say and do? *We think* that He elects even now, as individuals, all those in every organization, who serve Him with a loving heart, and a single eye. And He sanctions the election these make of the different folds in which *they* choose to worship Him. He doth not quench the smoking flax anywhere, nor break the heart that trusts Him.

The above-named different folds and organizations are all necessary, it seems, in order to enfold and employ all the workers for Christ, and to exhibit their varied conceptions of polity and duty; and their varied rituals are all needful and obligatory, simply because the adherents of these various schemes are so instructed, and, therefore, so assume, and for no other reason whatever! "Conscience, I say," says Paul, "not thine own, but of the other; for why is my liberty judged of another man's conscience?" *

And these varied churches are all canonical, if baptized with Christ's Spirit, and doing Christ's work, and for no other reason whatever.

The true Idea of the Church.

The definition some give to the term *Church* is utterly sacramentarian and false. That is, "It is an organized body

---

* Will the child, born and educated by Puritans, be aught else than a Puritan, as a general law? "The disciple is as his master." This truth enforces upon spiritual Christians the duty of "teaching all nations" and educating the world aright.

of Christians, united for the purpose of maintaining Gospel ordinances." *   *Ordinances*, they make the door into the organization.   Does the organization exist for the sake of the door?   And it is pure assumption, we have seen, that the Church of Christ is made by *ordinances*—*i. e.*, those that are technically so called.   If you say *institutions* of the Gospel, rather than ordinances, we make no demurrer, for all the organized modes of benevolent labor are *institutions* of the Gospel.   These comprehend all the ministries and offices of the Church—all the charities, and societies, and benevolent channels through which the Church acts.   And many of these benevolent and Christian agencies, which, however, are not called Churches, much more nearly exhibit the mind of Christ, and His blessed work, than many that *are* called churches.

The Young Men's Christian Associations, for example, composed of individuals adhering to the different (so called) churches of our large towns and cities, oft much more nearly represent Christ's ideal of what His own Church should be and do, than the bodies to which they confess allegiance as

---

* Hibbard, a recent Methodist writer, thus defines a *visible Church :*

1. "A congregation of persons who hold those cardinal doctrines of the Bible which are necessary to make a person wise unto salvation.

2. "They worship God according to His own will and directions, written or otherwise expressed.

3. "They are distinguished by the world at large by a particular mark, or sign, appointed by God as a token of their fidelity to Him, and of the Divine favor to them."

In regard to the first definition, we insist that "devils" themselves, and millions of "whited sepulchres" on earth, hold the "cardinal doctrines" necessary to salvation.

In regard to the second definition, viz: "They worship God according to His written or otherwise expressed will," we have to say that God has "written" no formula for "worship," and that "forms of worship" are no proof of a Church of Christ.

And as to the third, be it remembered, that no external "mark," or "sign," is any proof, whatever, of God's favor to man or of man's fidelity to God.

Our Shepherd doth not mark His sheep in that way !

His seal, and signet, is the Holy Spirit given ;—the evidence, *the "fruits of the Spirit."*

churches; albeit they celebrate no ordinances, and introduce to their membership by no rituals.

So Missionary Societies, Christian Commissions, and Christian Unions, which are working for Christ and seeking to extend the knowledge of His name, are as really Churches of Christ, as those bodies, more compact, which have gained the appellation of churches, in the dialect of men. The Friends' organizations can be called societies or churches, while eschewing rituals and a ceremonial law; why not those that do not eschew them, but do not use them in their corporate capacity? Does not custom blind the eyes of most of us to the essential nature of things?

We stated that there were three objects Christians might propose as the aim of an organization to be called a church: 1. A union of Christians and their friends, for the purpose of receiving religious instruction. Such a body among Congregationalists and Presbyterians is called a Society, in *which* their churches inhere, constituting a part of the Society, and mainly directing its movements. This body, we perceive, is wider than the Church—as now technically understood—but it is precisely the form in which Jesus Christ left his followers at His crucifixion. The use of "ordinances" belongs not to such a Society as universally admitted. 2. The second purpose, as stated, for which a church might exist, is to press on some reform, or rebuke (so-called) church organizations for non-fealty to Christ's law of love, or purity. These, it is perceived, must necessarily be narrower in their fellowship than the whole sweep of the denominational churches; since their very existence is designed oft to erect a standard that shall be a living reproof of those that are remiss, and this they usually propose to do, in part, through the sacramentarian regard for rituals, so common in Christendom; and herein their assumed sacraments may be of some use.

3. The third purpose of organization, named, viz.; the union of Christians, as such, for Christian fellowship, watch-care, worship and labors; and this is the ostensible purpose of most

evangelical churches, and many of them hold that this fellowship should be as wide as Christ's true spiritual fold. Yet
very few, if any of these denominations have reached thus
far, we have seen; but most of them have erected barriers in
the form of rituals, in the way of the universality of such
fellowship. These barriers were not designed to be placed as
barriers, but as evidences of supposed fealty to Christ; nevertheless they do exist as barriers, and must so remain, as long
as the sacredness of rituals is maintained.

EXTENT OF VISIBLE FELLOWSHIP.

Our view of the extent of Christian fellowship is, that it
should be as wide as Christ's spiritual fold, and that this spiritual fold is to be known, not by any adoption of, or consent
to outward rites and symbols, nor by laboring in the same
organization, but by the spirit of penitence, humility and
grace, together with the works of faith and labors of love
which are exhibited. Thus hear the *Advance* commenting on
Papal discussions, resulting from the German and Austrian
revolt from the decisions of the late Council at Rome. It says:

"All high-churchism is finding its position untenable. The Church of
Christ is not mere form; it rises superior to Congregationalism, to Presbyteri-
anism, to Episcopacy, and to Papacy. Paul said, 'The kingdom of God is
not in word but in power.' Look for 'the power,' and you will find 'the
kingdom.' Pure doctrine, pure worship, pure living, resulting in sinners
converted, and saints edified, evidence the presence of the true Church, and
the actual reigning of the King in His kingdom."

There you have it, and we know that these tests are not
restricted within any denominational lines, nor to Dissenting
or Protestant, or National or State churches, but in every
nation, community, polity and sect, "He that feareth God
and worketh righteousness, is (equally) accepted of Him."

We insist, therefore, that no question of organization or
ritual shall come in to make weight on the question of Christian
fellowship, but every man, everywhere, shall be recognized and
actually received on the bare question of Christian character,
totally irrespective of all other issues.

And let the broad principle be recognized that Christians of any fold are under no more obligation to observe sacraments, or initiate by certain rites, than they are to carry diagrams into a church to illustrate a discourse, or to wash themselves in the midst of a discourse to illustrate spiritual purifying. Religious teachers may do these things if they choose, but to teach that they are so taught of God, is simply to confound Christianity with Judaism, and to supplant the moral law by a ceremonial law.

The sacramental, or ritualistic idea of the Church, will forever narrow the boundaries of Christian fellowship and influence, while the idea that bases the Church on catholic love and Christian work as its bond and object, ever enlarges the boundaries of Christian fellowship, and tends to increase Christian love and zeal for every benevolent work. The conception that the Church is for work and not for a sacramental glorying in each other and in one's self, expands the heart, until it takes in every Temperance Society, every Anti-slavery Society, every Missionary Society, Young Men's Christian Association, Christian Commission, Bethel Society, Magdalen Society, Revival Effort, etc., as part and parcel of the Church and its working power, and its true exponent, pointing directly to where the Church is, and who are its members, rather than any eating bread or drinking wine together, or performing ablutions and baptisms from the days of John the Baptizer (the Purifier), until now. These best illustrate Christianity.

WHAT SACRAMENTAL CHURCHES ARE BUILT UPON.

The sacramental churches are built on conceit and prejudices, and evidence a perverted idea of what God wills and prizes, like the Jews' legalism and bondage to Moses in Christ's day (when the "vail was on their hearts"), and like the Papal idea of the Church to-day; and the Coptic, Armenian, and Greek Churches, each and all seeing *the Church* only in the shell or rind of its ritual, not in any spirit of life

4

from Christ in their own souls. Even the prophets of old denounced this conception of the Church; see Isaiah i. 11–17: "To what purpose is the multitude of your sacrifices unto me? ... Your new moons and your appointed feasts my soul hateth: they are a trouble unto me; I am weary to bear them." Is not God as "weary to bear" the baptisms and sacramental "feasts" of to-day, which are continually being put in Christ's stead, and made barriers to Christian love, and put in place of the "cleanness" of the heart and works of love and mercy? May we not now, as properly as then, say to the sects: "Wash you; make you clean; put away the evil of your doings; ... cease to do evil, learn to do well ... judge the fatherless; plead for the widow," etc. Micah sets this matter forth in words of unmistakable import; see Micah vi. 6–13: "Wherewith shall I come before the Lord, and bow myself before the high God? Shall I come before him with burnt offerings" (sacraments)? etc. "He hath showed thee, O man, what is good; and what doth the Lord require of thee, but to love mercy," etc.

SACRAMENTARIANISM IS TO WANE.

The sacramentarian churches are all to evanish before the rising light and power of a true spiritual Church, just as Protestantism, which is less sacramentarian than the Papacy, is supplanting the Papacy, and is reforming the Coptic, Greek, and Armenian Churches. As this sacramentarianism decreases, love and holiness will increase. Christ's baptism of the Spirit is demonstratively purifying and uniting, while ritual baptism and all sacramentarianism is as demonstratively the reverse. Eating Christ's body by faith in Him who is invisible (the bread from heaven), demonstratively gives life, while eating sacraments (bread of earthly elements), as demonstratively gives self-complacency, a censorious spirit, and divisive, and a false idea of the work and will of Christ.

As Christ said, "The hour is coming when neither in the mountain of Samaria, nor in Jerusalem shall men worship the

Father," so the hour is coming, as the *American Baptist* (a New York periodical) admits, when men shall neither immerse nor sprinkle, and call it baptism, or in obedience to a baptismal law. "In the Millennium," that journal says, "all these baptisms may be done away." If so, and we admit it, how much holier and how much nearer the Millennium ought we to be, before we begin in good earnest, to lay aside these un-Millennial rituals and incumbrances? Will not the true Millennial doctrine and work, by a truly Millennial Church, more swiftly advance the Millennium than one that insists on holding the Church in bondage to the law of ceremonials, and to that which is a stumbling-stone to all the churches?

If ritualism is unfitted to the Millennium, it is unfitted to that which is the preparatory work, the advance steps to the Millennium. The Millennium is to be no new dispensation, but the consummation of this; hence nothing that is of divine appointment for the Christian Dispensation can be supplanted by the rising light and supernal glory of the Millennium.

ERROR DIES SLOWLY—TIME TRIES SYSTEMS.

Men will drink in and retain fallacies and error for whole generations, which will require whole generations of wearisome and earnest endeavor to remove. When will the fogs of Judaism be dissipated from the Jewish mind, and from the minds of Judaizing Christians? When will Paganistic superstitions die? When will the doctrine of baptismal regeneration die out of the Papal and Lutheran Churches, and the Greek ,and Armenian Churches? The long dominion of such superstition and errors does not sanctify them nor make them truth. And the puerile logic of church-founders and defenders, and the defenders of ritualistic superstition is for a marvel to those who ask a semblance of proof of the thing asserted. For example, Dr. Hopkins, in his "Christian Instructor," a manual prepared for the doctrinal instruction of the earlier classes in college; as a part of the

evidence of a change of the Sabbath from the seventh to the
first day of the week, urges the fact that the early Christians
for a series of years observed both the seventh and the first
days of the week as sacred days, or Sabbaths; and in the
sequel rested upon the first as *the* Sabbath. Now the historic fact is undoubted, and also that some Judaizers much
longer retained the seventh day Sabbath than other Christians; but what connection this logic has with the proof of
a divine appointment of the change of the day, who can see?

We believe in the first day Christian Sabbath; but had we
not other proof of the propriety of its observance, we should
deem the proof entirely wanting. Dr. Hopkins, if we mistake
not, employs precisely similar logic in proof of the substitution
of baptism in the Christian Church, for the circumcision of the
Jewish Church: "They were contemporaneously observed for
a series of years; and finally, baptism supplanted the Jewish
circumcision." And *it is assumed* that this must have been
done by the Divine direction.

Conceding that the Church has Divine teaching in the
spiritual life, and wisdom from above in her work of love, we
nevertheless repudiate the Episcopal and Papal claim of
authority from God to establish *ordinances, laws, and liturgies.*
Circumcision and baptism were contemporaneous through all
the Jewish history, and in the Christian ages circumcision
might have waned and baptism taken its place, without *assuming* a Divine warrant therefor; and the conceit that water-
baptism, as practised by Christians, differs in spirit, end, or
aim, from water-baptism practised by Jews, is an assumption
wholly gratuitous.

And did not circumcision come to an end (among Jewish
Christians) largely on account of the Jewish national death?
And were not the Jewish "divers baptisms" largely revived
a century later, by Judaizing Christians, and that after
Paul had delivered the Gentile Churches, to a great extent,
from the bondage of *ordinances?* In the proper place we
shall see this to be the truth of the case.

To have a ritual (baptism) called "Christian" take the place of "divers baptisms" called Jewish, we shall see was never Paul's aim. But it was his aim to leave the Christian Church in Gentile lands unfettered by a divisive, restrictive, and cumbersome ritual. Paul taught that "circumcision availeth nothing,"—not that baptism "avails" in its place.

He taught that the true baptism is the spiritual baptism *into Christ,* and not a baptism by water that leaves its subjects as far from Christ as they were before.

Others have assayed to prove pedo-baptism (since it was a Jewish custom), from the fact that there is nothing *forbidding it* in the New Testament.

We have never read a prohibition of wearing white robes, counting beads, or saying prayers for the dead. Are these Papal customs, therefore, of Divine appointment?

Yet whole generations, and even whole centuries of Christian teachers will confuse themselves by such logic, and Church creeds, and ecclesiastical systems are based thereon. And if a writer or speaker will strike at such logic and such systems and creeds, why, he "takes away our gods, and what have we more?"

Nevertheless, time tries all creeds and systems; and the out-working evil from an evil cause, the creaking and tottering, where foundations are rotten or disjointed, evinces, in due time, the need of a surer foundation taking the place of the effete. Judaism did not make the " comers " thereunto perfect ; nor have the Papal, Greek, and Armenian rituals. They have all, as systems, been weighed in the balances and found wanting. " By their fruits (the fruits of Sodom) ye shall know them."

Pure and spiritual religion dies out under their baleful and degenerating influence. So in many of the Protestant sects, as evidenced by the High Church Ritualists, and those sticklers for water-baptism, who build sects and communions on an adherence to the rite of immersion, thus making one cold, lifeless ceremony the end of the law for love, fellowship, and communion in the household of faith.

CHAPTER II.

ORIGIN AND IMPORT OF BAPTISM.

SCRIPTURE ARGUMENT.

WE (who wholly eschew church ritualism) propose to leave those forms of ritualism which hold the High Church Episcopacies in thraldom, since the dissenting religious press and pulpits are amply exposing them, and to address ourselves to the work of criticising the more widely disseminated ritualism of the prevalent sects (by which they are continued as sects, without Bible warrant), and whereby Christian love is restrained, and the higher plane of Christian life and fellowship in Christian labor is prevented; and there is much waste of effort and means in building up that which must ultimately be torn down.

We propose to deduce from Scripture teaching and the logic of the case, that *ordinances*, by Protestants so called, are simply borrowed Judaisms, undefined as to time and manner in the early Christian Church (being pre-defined only by the law of Moses), contingent as to observance in the early church, and received from, and ranked with the other ceremonies of the prior dispensation; and therefore are not *positive institutions*, nor of any binding force in the Christian Church. That moral expediency, or temporary utility, then and now, among those who have received a Jewish or ritual training, is the only reason why they need be observed at all. And the same with respect to any other form or rite. If we succeed, we shall have established the position that there is *no ceremonial law in the Christian Dispensation.*

54

Now, let no sectarian be alarmed at this proposition, for the writer was also " a Pharisee of the Pharisees," " made under the law " of ritualism—a Baptist of the " straitest sect " and " regular order," coming with all the credentials of baptism, and ordination, and theological parchments, and of ritual observances according to the appointed order of sect worshipping—"an Hebrew of the Hebrews," touching the ceremonial law. But all these he now counts loss for Christ and truth, and boldly takes the ground that the Christian Dispensation knows *no ordinances, or ritual law.*

WHY PRECISELY TWO SACRAMENTS AND NO MORE?

A strange and mysterious fact may be observed in relation to the attitude of Protestant Churches, viz.: that rejecting all other rites, symbols, types or means of grace as " ordained " by Divine appointment and authority, they fasten upon two undefined and ambiguous symbols as of special and enduring obligation in the Christian Church. These are *Baptism* and the *Eucharistic Feast.* No such positive law is claimed requiring all Christians to preach, or pray, or sing, or visit the sick and anoint them with oil, or wash the feet of the saints in their assemblies, or to worship after any prescribed model. Yet all these, save the " washing," may be truly useful and indispensable as Christian duties ; but these *Protest*-ants have affixed the seal of sacredness to the arbitrary signs that can claim no intrinsic necessity or essential utility, and claim for them the express authority of the Great Head of the Church.

The Papists, on the other hand, against whom these Protestants protest, affirm the ordinances or sacraments to be seven! And we presume that the Greek, and Armenian, and Coptic and Nestorian Churches, virtually recognize the same number. Now where is the reason for this ritualizing, or sacramentarianism being carried so far as to two positive ordinances, and why, if these be conceded, go no further ? Is the New Testament silent respecting any other ceremony or ritual ? By no means. Others are not mentioned as oft, perhaps, but certainly are as positively and really enjoined. By what rule do these champions of a ritual New Testament law admit some to be obligatory and reject others? Come, thou ritualist, bring forth thy "strong reasons!"

PROTESTANT SACRAMENTS BUT SUBSIDIZED JEWISH RITES.

Besides, the two rites (sacraments) that Protestants have assumed to be incumbent and unceasing, were both cotemporaneous with, and perpetuated through the whole Jewish economy.

What are they, then, but subsidized Jewish rites? exotics, sought to be grafted forever on the Christian system? The Passover Feast is known to be Jewish, which the Christian Eucharist but perpetuates. And Dr. Wall, in his "History of Baptism," has demonstrated the same respecting water-baptism. It is perfectly certain that it is first introduced into the New Testament record by no prescriptive law, but historically. Hence it is as certain that it came from, and was a "rudiment" or constituent element of the ritual dispensation just closing as the New Testament record is opened. It is just as certain that *all* the *purifyings* of the Jews were called *baptisms* by the early Christian teachers as that they were practised at all. They were also a part of the Jewish ritual law. (See Heb. ix. 1, 8, 9, 10.)

"Then verily the first covenant had also ordinances of Divine service, and a worldly sanctuary. . . . . The Holy Ghost this signifying that the way into the holiest of all was *not yet made manifest*, while as the first tabernacle was yet standing; . . . . which was a figure for the time then present, &c., ... which stood only in meats and drinks and *divers baptisms* and carnal ordinances, imposed on them till the time of reformation."

Now the "time of reformation" is under the Dispensation of Christ. (See 13, 14 v.)

"For if the blood of bulls and of goats and the ashes of a heifer" (elements by which some of the former baptisms were administered) "sprinkling the unclean, sanctified to the purifying of the flesh; how much more shall the blood of Christ, who, through the eternal Spirit, offered himself without spot to God, purge" (i. e. *purify*,) "your conscience from dead works" (sinful works) "to serve the living God."

So the 10th chapter continues the theme. (See 4, 9, 10 and 14 v.)

"For it is not possible that the blood of bulls and of goats" (*elements used in former baptisms*) "should take away sins. . . . . Then said he, Lo, I come to do thy will, O God!" [*God's will is our sanctification!*] "By the which will we are sanctified by the offering of the body of Jesus Christ" (*not by ritual baptism*) "once for all. For by *one offering* He hath perfected forever them that are sanctified."

SYNONYMS OF BAPTISM.

Now Alexander Campbell and Pres. E. Beecher inform us, that in Christ's day *baptism*, and *purification*, and the *New Birth*, or *Regeneration*, and *Sanctification*, and Dr. Dale adds, *Merging into Christ*, were all synonymous terms. If so, they are all attained by Christ's one offering, accepted by faith, and not by any "carnal ordinances," for these were only to endure "till the time of reformation," *i. e.*, until Christ's effectual offering should commence its saving work.

And mark, this offering of Christ "once," this shedding of His own blood, in contrast with the inefficiency of the blood of bulls and goats, shall "forever purge the conscience of those sprinkled (baptized) thereby," "for it speaketh better" (more effectual and enduring) "things than that of Abel." See Hebrews xii. 24: "For we are come to Jesus, the Mediator of the *new covenant*, and to the blood of sprinkling that speaketh better things than that of Abel," who offered the first sacrifice that God ever accepted.

Now, this "blood of sprinkling" to which "we are come," is shed only once for all time,—not yearly, as under the law— *i. e.*, the old covenant; hence this baptism (of Christ's blood), received not by any human administrator, but by faith, purifies the conscience from sin, and "perfects forever those sanctified thereby." If such be not Paul's reasoning concerning the baptism of the Old Dispensation as contrasted with the "one baptism" of the New, we have failed to comprehend it. Mark vii. 2-5, 8, and John iii. 25, 26, will abundantly show that the Jewish cleansings, or purifyings, were called baptisms. Mark says, "For the Pharisees and all the Jews except they wash" (*nipto*, to wash) "their hands oft, eat not, holding the traditions of the elders. And when they come from the market, except they wash" (*baptizo* here used as a synonym of *nipto*) "they eat not. And many other things there be, which they have received to hold, as the washing" (*baptizing* here used) "of cups and pots, brazen vessels and beds." *Klinōn* (Gr.) here evidently refers to *beds*, which like all other domestic furniture and utensils the Jews punctiliously, and very superstitiously, oft purified, lest some ceremonial uncleanness therefrom might defile them. Thus they carefully baptized ("made clean") the "outside of their cups and platters," while their own inward man was "full of all uncleanness."

So by John (iii. 25) we learn that there arose a dispute about "purifying" between John's disciples and the Jews. And the next verse informs us that this was about "baptism." Thus we learn that John's baptism (with water) was a continuing of the purifyings of the Jews. And Christ's disciples, before the law dispensation ended, and ere the Gentiles were called, continued the same. And many Christians, a century or two later, who should be called mongrels, half Jew and half Christian, sacramentized these daily ablutions, calling them baptisms; hence arose in the second century the sect called *Emero-Baptists*, i. e., *daily baptizers*, which Ambrose designates when he says, "For what else *in this daily sacrament* do we teach except that sin is drowned," (alluding to the deluge,) "and error destroyed; while piety and innocence remain safe."

We may have occasion to allude to these again. So the "daily breaking of bread," mentioned in Acts ii., as succeeding the spiritual awakening on the day of Pentecost, was evidently a merging of the many feasts of the Jews (the Jews observed ten national festivals), into one "feast of love," or "breaking of bread" with, and thus showing fellowship with the poor, by the more wealthy early Christians; and we have marvelled that there had not arisen a sacramentizing sect of "daily bread-breakers," as we have now several that "break the bread" every Lord's Day.

ORIGIN OF BAPTISM.

Learning from Paul, Hebrews ix. 10, that the Jews practised "divers baptisms;" and from Mark vii. 2–8, that some of these, self-imposed, or otherwise, were practised daily, and from John iii. 25, 26, that the purifyings of the Jews were called baptisms; and from the record of John's (the Baptizer's) introduction to the Jewish nation, as recorded in Matthew iii., that he was in continuance of a custom well understood, since just prior to his work no baptismal law is recorded as having been given; we are led to the inquiry, where and when did the law for baptism originate? Like the sombre shadows that rested over certain terminal points in Mirza's vision, so the dense shades that, either from ignorance or design, have been suffered to rest upon the origin of baptism, have stood largely in the way of deluded ritualists, that they did not see, and could not see the error of their impressions respecting its origin, and hence were held unaware of the fact that they were in bondage to a Jewish, and not to a Christian law. Let ritualistic baptizers not be unaware of the fact that baptisms, in all the ages through which any records reach, were practised as much before the Christian era, as since, and that by heathen nations as well as Jews; and by the Jews, as the Christian era approached, with as much superstition and addenda of diverse ceremonies, perhaps, as now among the Papists: See Mark vii., and the Jewish Rabbis' accounts of baptismal ceremonies.

In truth every heathen nation had a law of baptisms as well as the Jews, and this, in connection with their religious worships and festivities. Says Robinson, a Baptist historian:

"Purifying by water is of the highest antiquity; anterior to Judaism itself. The Romans, Greeks, Hebrews, Egyptians, Etruscans, Ethiopians, Druids and

Celts practised it. And all other people of whom any knowledge has come
down to the present time."

They practised it "before, *i. e.*, preparatory to, worship or sacrifices, and also preparatory to initiation into the mysteries.
Holy water was kept in the temples of the gods for these
purposes." See p. 272. See also his account of their modes
of purification, their baptisteries, etc. He also says, that
the Ethiopians (after becoming Christians) "rebaptize annually in commemoration of Christ's baptism, and also *circumcise their children, male and female, on the* eighth day." P. 368.
He also speaks of some who "baptize by fire, or in fire." P. 364.*

Carrying the history down the track of time, he finds Mahometans disputing as hard about baptism (its mode) as
Christians do. He quotes the Persian and Turkish bigots,
who baptize their hands and arms (as see Mark vii. above,
respecting the Jews), and these Mahometans, in constant and
fierce disputes, resulting in rival sects, on the question whether
they shall wash *up* or *down*, i. e., whether they shall begin at
the wrist and wash upward, or begin at the elbow and wash
downward. The question appears to be about as sublime, of
as much moral efficacy, and as hotly contested, as whether they
shall immerse, pour, or sprinkle in Christian baptism. Perhaps
the two collateral contests will about as soon come to an end.

But history records no such dispute about the real ritual
law of the Jews. The Divine Lawgiver, who, through Moses,
prescribed it, so defined it, that there has been none occasion of a war about their ceremonials among the Jewish temple worshippers. Presumptively, this should be so from
the outset of their observance to the end. A law, to be a
law, must not be ambiguous. (See ceremonial law as given by
Moses, specially in Exodus and Leviticus.) What bearing
should this self-evident truth have in the mind of our Chris-

---

* Let this statement of Dr. Robinson lift the veil especially from those Baptist (immersionist) ritualists who have been so willing to remain in ignorance of the fact that baptism preceded the mission of John (Christ's forerunner), and was practised at least through all the Jewish ages. This obscurity
respecting the origin of baptism is not to the honor of those teachers that
place so much stress upon the ritual.

tian sects which are in antagonism on the subject of baptisms;
resulting in, perhaps, a thousand differing sects on that issue
alone; and, perhaps, four times that number of differing views
and teachings on the subject?

But having found the Jewish baptisms a part of the Old
Testament economy (in Paul to the Hebrews), we propose to show when and where these baptisms had their origin.

CUSTOM AND NOT LAW ORIGINATED BAPTISM.

We have said that the record of baptisms is introduced in
the New Testament without a prescriptive law. It is precisely
so in the Old Testament, showing that Robinson's testimony
respecting the ancient prevalence of baptism applied to the
Jews as well as to all other nations—and showing that a
physical and social as well as moral effect was sought. Their
baths and ablutions were evidently a sort of climatic necessity,
and were turned to the account of religion by all the Asiatic
nations of antiquity.

And mark, Paul, in Heb. ix., in referring to the "divers baptisms" practised by the Hebrews, and especially as practised by
Moses, their great law-giver, cites us to the very first instance
of baptism as recorded in the Old Testament. (See Ex. xxiv.)
Here Moses first declares God's words: "Moses came and told
the people all the words of the Lord, and all the judgments:"
and the people vowed obedience and allegiance; just as is now
done on professing faith in Christ. (See vs. 3 and 6.)

"And all the people answered with one voice and said, All the words which
the Lord hath said we will do!" Do our modern candidates for church membership do more than this? v. 6: "And Moses took half of the blood" (i. e.
of the oxen; see v. 5), "and put it in basins; and half of the blood he
sprinkled on the altar;" vs. 7 and 8: "And he took the book of the covenant,
and read in the audience of the people;" (just as our churches do.) "And
they said, All that the Lord hath said we will do, and be obedient."

"And Moses took the blood, and sprinkled it on the people, and said, Behold
the blood of the covenant, which the Lord hath made with you concerning all
these words."

So in Heb. ix. 19.

"When Moses had spoken every precept to all the people, according to the
law, ... he sprinkled both the book and all the people."

This sprinkling of the book and the people was, therefore, the first of the "divers baptisms" alluded to in Heb. ix. 10, which, however, did not make those that did the service "perfect as pertaining to the conscience."

In Ex. xxix. and xxx., we have the first prescriptive law for baptisms in any form (and also for the holy anointing or chrism), which baptisms were first appointed for the priests, and afterward, in various forms, extended to all the people. (See Ex. xxix. 4, 12, 16, 21.)

"And Aaron, and his sons, thou shalt bring unto the door of the tabernacle of the congregation, and shalt wash them with water." (Compare with Mark vii. 8, quoted above.) Verse 12: "And thou shalt take of the blood of the bullock, and put it upon the horns of the altar with thy finger, and pour all the blood beside the bottom of the altar." Verse 16: "And thou shalt slay the ram, and thou shall take his blood and sprinkle it round about upon the altar." Verse 21: "And thou shalt take of the blood that is upon the altar, and of the anointing oil, and sprinkle it upon Aaron, and upon his garments, and upon his sons, and upon the garments of his sons with him: and *he shall be hallowed*, and his garments, and his sons, and his sons' garments with him."

(See also ch. xxx. 17–21.)

"And the Lord spake unto Moses, saying, Thou shalt make a laver of brass, and his foot also of brass, to wash withal; and thou shalt put it between the tabernacle of the congregation and the altar, and thou shalt put water therein. For Aaron and his sons shall wash their hands and their feet thereat. When they go into the tabernacle of the congregation, they shall wash with water, that they die not; or when they come near to the altar to minister, to burn offerings made by fire unto the Lord: so shall they wash their hands and their feet, that they die not; and it shall be a statute forever to them, even to him and to his seed throughout their generations."

Thus, in the 29th chapter of Exodus, we have the prescription for the baptism into the priesthood, by Moses, the founder of the tabernacle service, and in chap. xxx., the law for the self-baptism of Aaron and his sons while engaged in the temple service. The latter part of the 30th chapter of Exodus gives instructions for preparing the holy anointing oil, alluded to more than once in the New Testament, and which was a type of that "unction from the Holy One," or "anointing" which the Apostle John speaks of in the 2nd chapter of his first epistle, and synonymous with the baptism of the Holy Ghost;

see 1 John ii. 20, 27 : "But ye have an unction from the Holy One. . . . But the anointing which ye have received of Him abideth in you." The above, with the context of the passages cited, is all the law on the subject of baptisms and purifyings found in Exodus.

In Leviticus xi., xii., xiii., xiv. and xv., are various laws for purification, which Paul refers to in Heb. ix., and which, as Robinson says of the heathen nations (that they all had baptismal purifyings), so more especially did the Hebrews, as we thus find. The law for the purifying from unclean beasts; for the purifying of women after childbirth; for the purifying of lepers, or those who had touched them; and for the purifying of those afflicted with issues, and those who touched them; and those who had touched a dead body, is recorded in these chapters.

In Leviticus xvi., is the law of atonement, which also required different baptisms for cleansing. (See vs. 4, 14, 15, 16, 18, 19, 24.)

"He (Aaron) shall put on the holy linen coat . . . . and with the linen mitre shall he be attired; these are holy garments, therefore shall he wash his flesh in water, and so put them on. . . . . And he shall take of the blood of the bullock, and sprinkle it with his finger upon the mercy seat eastward, and before the mercy seat shall he sprinkle of the blood with his finger seven times. . . And he shall sprinkle of the blood upon the (altar) with his finger seven times, and cleanse it, and hallow it from the uncleanness of the children of Israel." See Heb. ix. 21, 22. "Then shall he kill the goat of the sin-offering, that is for the people, and bring his blood within the vail . . . . and sprinkle it upon the mercy seat, and before the mercy seat. And he shall make an atonement for the holy place, *because of the* uncleanness of the children of Israel; and because of their transgressions in all their sins. 24th : "And he shall wash his flesh with water in the holy place, and put on his garments and come forth and offer his burnt-offering and the burnt-offering of the people, and make an atonement for himself and for the people ! " *

---

* DR. WALL quotes Ex. xix. 10, and Num. xv. 14, 15, as passages that all the Jews recognize as requiring baptism, of Jews and of strangers. So all passages requiring them to be clean when they eat the Passover or worship before Jehovah, as Gen. xxxv. 2, and Lev. xi. 25, 28, 40; xiv. 8, 47; Num. xix. 10, 21; xxxi. 24.

The Jews affirm that the command "Be clean and wash your garments,"

Thus have we gone through the Mosaic law of baptisms, for purifying; and, be it remembered, that Paul, in Heb. ix. must have alluded to these, for he could have alluded to none other, for no law of Moses marks out any other. And these purifyings (baptisms) might all be self-administered, save those consecrating the priests to their work. These required a canonical succession of administration, yet was this rule oft violated by Israel and Judah's kings, in later ages, who "took of the lowest of the people," for priests, because of the defection of the Levitical priesthood, or the contempt these kings would show to the Aaronic line.* In these last citations, of sprinklings for atonement and washing with water, we discern the purport of the frequent language of the New Testament, connecting baptism with the remission of sins. "Arise and be baptized," says Ananias to Paul, "and wash away thy sins." Such was the typical mode of cleansing in all the Jewish Dispensation; and Ananias had not yet escaped from Judaism. So Aaron and his sons were to wash their

---

means "purify (baptize) yourselves." They assert that circumcision was given in Egypt (see Ex. xii. 48), and sacrifice and baptism in the wilderness. So the Talmud says : " Israel does not enter into covenant but by these three things, circumcision, baptism and a peace offering; and all proselytes in like manner, one law shall be for all."

So Cyprian (a ritualist), seeking to engraft water-baptism on the Christian Church, says, " The Jews had already, and a very long time ago, the baptism of the law and of Moses, and were now to be baptized in the name of Jesus Christ." From viewing Christ as the greater, came the conceit also, that John's baptism was not sufficient, but those baptized unto (or by) John must also be baptized unto Jesus Christ (see Acts xix. 1–7). So Basil compares the baptisms of Moses, of John, and of Christ. " The baptism of Moses," Basil says, " required sacrifices to be joined with it ; " and days of separation— the baptism of John had none of these incumbrances, yet was it far transcended by the baptism of Christ ; " For," he says in another place, "they (i. e. the Arians), baptized with water, *but Christ baptized with the Spirit.*"

* So their Passovers were observed by each family without intervention of priests ; every man was a "king and priest" before God in the first founding of the Israelitish Theocracy. No prestige, power or patronage was given to the Jewish priesthood as special administrators of rites; either of circumcision, baptism or Passover. The priest had no monopoly of these.

hands and their feet at the laver of brass. In Christ's day this custom of washing the feet was extended to others than the priests, and that with Christ's approval, as a token of humility: see John xiii. But it has never been considered an ordinance of the New Dispensation; yet it was an "ordinance" of the Old Dispensation. It was one of the "divers baptisms." And mark, these baptisms were few if any of them *dippings;* they were either washings with the hand (with the *pugme,* fist, as it reads in the original of Mark vii. 3); or sprinklings and affusions.* When Moses purified the people, he "took the blood of calves and of goats, with water;" and using scarlet wool (*i. e.,* wool purified with blood), and hyssop branches, "he sprinkled both the book and all the people:" see Heb. ix. 19. Moses in purifying Aaron and his sons dipped the tip of his finger in the purifying element (as Pedo-Baptists now do), and applied it to the recipient of baptism, as directed in Ex. xxix. 20, 21. The whole process is most specifically defined by Moses in his instructions on the subject, thus being totally the reverse of the New Testament indefiniteness on the subject. When the priests or others baptized themselves, they of course did as we do, and, as Mark says the Jews did, taking one hand, or both, to apply the water to the part to be purified. So the Mahometans, the one sect washing upward to the elbow, and the other washing downward from the elbow, each dipping only the hand, and applying the lifted water to the part to be cleansed. Yet both the dipping and

---

* *Baptizo* is found but twice in the Septuagint (only gradually did it take its place as a synonym of *katharizo*—to purify), viz: in 2 Kings v. 4, and Isaiah xxi. 4. In the first of these instances it is most manifestly used in the sense to *purify*—to be cleansed from *leprosy*; and in the second place (Isaiah xxi. 4), evidently refers to an inundation or whelming with fear.

Bapto is found eighteen times in the Old Testament; and perhaps in every instance in connection with the Jewish purifyings, and is correctly translated *dip,* which dipping is of something used in purifying (baptizing); but in no instance refers to the object baptized, but to *a part of the process*—as a dipping of the finger in water to sprinkle (or purify) another object; see Exodus, xii. 22: Leviticus iv. 17; and xiv. 14–18.

the affusion, as we know, will cleanse the flesh. And the flesh is all that is cleansed by the ritual baptisms. When God purifies (baptizes) by the Spirit, He pours it from on high.

PRETENSIONS OF THE BAPTISTS.

We cannot well refrain from noticing here the arrogant pretensions of the Baptists and their defence of restricted communion on the ground of having with them the whole truth on the subject of baptism. Alluding to a Baptist author, who had (as he claimed) demonstrated that immersion alone was baptism, the *American Baptist* discourses thus :

" It is well that we should have these defences of our faith for the silencing of cavillers, and yet we have often thought that such a multiplicity of labor to prove that immersion alone is baptism, was only wasting powder. The fact is, that so far as reason and argument can settle any question, this question has been settled long ago. It is a question no longer. No man, with any degree of sincerity and candor, can read the works that have been written without seeing that it is what Professor Stuart pronounced it, ' *a case made out.*' In the early part of this controversy, when the whole subject was overspread with the dust and traditions of Popery, light was needed, and men entered into the discussion on both sides, with the sincere desire of obtaining that light. Pedo-Baptist ministers buckled on their armor in defence of a time-honored practice, and in cases too numerous to be mentioned, were not ashamed, on discovering their error, to confess it, and become the champions of a creed they had opposed. But that day has gone by. There is no such spirit of honest inquiry now. We cannot expect to convert the world to Baptist sentiments by proving that they are true. People of the present generation are not influenced by argument. They go by instinct; they are moved by passion, by prejudice, by a thousand subtle influences of which they themselves are scarcely sensible. Where shall we find the community that worships truth alone, and consequently is impressible by reason and argument? We must, therefore, meet this baptismal question in some other way, if we wish to convert the Christian world to what we believe to be the primitive practice. We must adapt ourselves to the different phases of mind we would influence. We must go back to the simple question of facts, and address ourselves to the underlying obstacles which prevent those facts from having their legitimate influence.

" We must not forget that our opponents are of two distinct classes. In the first, there is a disregard of principle that renders effort useless. We can do nothing with a man who has no innate love for truth, such as would lead him to make all sacrifices for its upholding. We might as well beat the air as to combat opponents of this stamp. There is a prior work to be done with them. The religious foundation itself is to be laid."

So some of us are not Baptists, because we are so uncandid and untruth-loving that we will not listen to the arguments that have so oft demonstrated to Baptist understandings that immersion in water alone is baptism—a point so clear to them that they can scarcely stretch their charity so far as to see how any honest inquirer after truth can deny it—and even so clear that an eminent Pedo-Baptist professor is constrained to admit that it is a *"case made out!"* They, therefore, find in our *caprices* and *prejudices*, with the bias of a false education, and " a thousand subtle influences," the ground of our dereliction from the peculiar Baptist tenets.

They, therefore, deeply feel the need of *our change of heart.* Alas, for the slow-rolling wheels of progress toward the conversion of Christendom to Baptist sentiment!

If, however, this Baptist critic had reversed his artillery, and assured all the world that it is vain to attempt to convert the Baptists from their ritualistic bondage and worship, by showing that the most of their teachings on the subject are intrinsically false and only assumed—contradicting, as they do, the history of the origin of baptisms, and its nature—he would have come much nearer the truth, and might have done his Baptist brethren some good.

In former numbers of the *Church Union* we have presented the admissions of the *American Baptist* upon these two points, viz.: In the first place, admitting that the last dispensation of God's kingdom here is to know *no ritual law*, which last dispensation it would be difficult for any to show is not the present; and second, that there is no New Testament law placing communion as the sequel to baptism. Nevertheless, the Baptists hold the (so-called) sacraments in strict abeyance to a denominational interest, sacrificing all that is dear and precious in Christian fellowship thereto.

Let us, however, premise that both the severe strictures quoted above and the admissions were occasioned by the pressure of a growing demand among the laity of the Baptist Church for open communion, which demand is not lessened by the roar all the way across the Atlantic, as of many waters, and of mighty thunderings, from the great mass of Baptist churches there, with Spurgeon, Noel, Carson, and Robert Hall at their head, demanding that the Baptist Church in America shall imitate the Baptists in England in granting unrestricted fellowship and communion-fellowship with their fellow-Christians of all the evangelical denominations. Instead of listening to these demands, however, the Baptist editors, ministers and leaders here have been assiduously endeavoring to divert the attention of the Baptists of America from this pressure by a fiercer cry against other denominations, because they will not at this juncture give up their conscientious and as evidently Scriptural views of baptism, and adopt those of the Baptist Church.

They seem disposed to raise the loudest clamor upon this point, as they are manifestly about being compelled to succumb to the force of a liberalizing public sentiment, and a conscience enlightened by more consistent interpretations of the word of God on the subject of rituals, opening the way for a more expanded Christian charity. This outcry for a denominational badge and watchword at this juncture, and the effort to "strengthen the stakes" (if not to lengthen the cords) of sectarian exclusiveness, may well be resembled to an effort which we may suppose certain Jewish priests, at the dawn of Christ's day, may have made to proselyte all other Jews to a certain mode or peculiarity of performing the rite of circumcision—prescribing that it be done with certain consecrated instruments, and by certain canonical administrators—whom they, *par excellence*, should name, that the work might all be *in their hands*—not foreseeing, except by an inward premonition, perhaps, how soon the breath of God, through His Son Jesus Christ, would sweep the whole away.

WHAT THE BAPTISTS HAVE ASSUMED.

The arguments not only of Baptists, but all other ritualists, who deem themselves under a law of water baptism, have been pure assumptions. We have seen that baptisms were not introduced even in the Old Testament record at first in the form of a law, but as a historic record of what Moses did in purifying the people, and also Aaron and his sons, and introducing the priesthood and temple service. *Afterward* this whole service was *regulated* by law, the baptisms among the rest. Well, in the New Testament these same baptisms, if any of a ceremonial kind, are introduced in the same manner in the record of John, and some of the disciples of Christ, before the Great Commission given by our Saviour just prior to his ascension, afforded the Christian Church what it now claims as a law for baptisms. John, the forerunner of Christ, came in the wilderness of Judea, typically *purifying* and preparing a people unto the coming of the Messiah. This he himself declares. See Matthew 3rd chapter: "In those days came John the *Purifier*," (*Baptist* is the word in our version, which is neither the Greek word anglicized nor translated). The word "*Baptistes*," as in Greek, if anglicized, would be *Baptizer*, and if translated as Drs. E. Beecher and Dale have abundantly shown, would be *Purifier*. Not that the word *Baptizo* (Greek) has no other sense than *purify*, but it has this sense when used in connection with the Jewish ceremonial law.

THE BAPTISTS ARE WITNESSES.

The Baptists will attest this, for this sense of the word is too common and too palpable to be gainsayed.

We have already quoted Dr. Robinson's testimony on the subject; but the testimony of Dr. Conant, the great champion of, and chief worker in the AMERICAN BIBLE UNION—an association whose specific work has been to give the world a translation, or version of the Bible, with the word *Baptizo* translated *immerse*—is still more to the point. In his work entitled "*Baptizein*," which form of the verb is the Greek Infinitive of *Baptizo*; by numerous quotations from the Christian Fathers, and interlocutory comments of his own, he has

shown how commonly the purifyings of the ancient Hebrews
were, by these Fathers, called *baptisms*.   On p. 122 he says:

"The idea of *cleansing*, associated with the Christian rite of immersion in
water, naturally suggested comparison with the Jewish rites of purification,
especially by water; hence, the Christian Fathers treat these ritual purifications as types foreshadowing the grace to be imparted through the Christian
rite."

On p. 126 he quotes John of Damascus as saying:

"He (Christ) is baptized, not as himself needing cleansing, but appropriating my cleansing, that He may whelm sin and bury all the old Adam in the
water."

Discoursing on Baptism, he (John) says again:

"By water every one unclean, according to the law, is cleansed, even the
garments themselves being washed with water. . . . And almost all things,
according to the law, are cleansed with water."

So, on p. 129, Dr. C. himself says:

"From the idea of *cleansing* associated with immersion in water, they call
Christ's expiatory death a *baptism*, not only as an expression of overwhelming
suffering, but also because by it He cleansed from sin."

So he quotes Chrysostom as calling it "a *baptism;* because
by it he cleansed the world."   So he calls martyrdom (p. 130)
"a baptism by blood," ascribing to it "the same cleansing
efficacy as to literal immersion in water."   On p. 132, he
quotes Athanasius as teaching thus:

"Three immersions (baptisms), purgative of all sin whatever, God has
bestowed on the nature of man: I mean that of water; and again, that by the
witness of one's own blood; and, thirdly, that by tears, in which, also, the harlot was cleansed."

Now we have cited the above, (as we might many more
from the same work,) not as proving the writer's assumption
of *immersion* as the meaning of *baptism ;* nor, that in order for
baptism to be ritually performed, there must be *three* immersions of the same candidate, as Athanasius and the early
Christians required; nor, that the baptism by *tears* or *sufferings*
and martyrdom were immersions at all, or with water at all,
but to show that in their view all these baptisms of the Jews

and of a later time, *by water, by blood, by sufferings and tears,* were *purifications,* as all these writers admit. This substantiates our position, and is the point at which we here aim.

MEANING OF THE WORD "BAPTISMA" AND ITS COGNATES.

Dr. J. W. Dale's recent work on "Baptism" (3 vols., with a fourth prepared, but not issued) presents the most exhaustive treatise (or treatises) on the philology and etymology of the word yet furnished by any writer—more complete than is furnished by all other writers combined. This is affirmed without fear of question on the part of any who will examine his work.

In his treatise on "Classic Baptism" (the first in the series), his investigations have resulted in the conclusion thus announced:—p. 354:

"The master-key to the interpretation of *Baptizo* is CONDITION,—condition characterized by completeness, with or without physical envelopment. WHATEVER IS CAPABLE OF THOROUGHLY CHANGING THE CHARACTER, STATE OR CONDITION OF ANY OBJECT IS CAPABLE OF BAPTIZING THAT OBJECT; AND BY SUCH CHANGE OF CHARACTER, STATE OR CONDITION DOES IN FACT BAPTIZE IT."

And Dr. Dale further states:

"There is *no form of act inherent in Baptizo.* The conception that any word expressive of condition can be self-limited as to the form of the act or agency effecting such condition, is an error."

He further states:

"Baptism is a myriad-sided word, adjusting itself to the most diverse cases. It has no form of act of its own; it asks for none; it accepts, indifferently, of any, of all, competent to meet its demand—*change of condition.* It demands a complete change of condition, physical, intellectual, moral, or ceremonial; and accepts of any agency, physical or spiritual, competent to the task. Controversy (in the past) has set toward the proof or disproof of certain acts—*to dip, to plunge,* on one side; *to sprinkle, to pour,* on the other. The controversy has proved to be both unsatisfactory and interminable.* It would continue to be so if prolonged through three thousand years instead of three hundred."

---

*Aye, not only interminable, but in its worthlessness "a horrible disgrace to the Christian Church," as the Baptist minister in New York city said—because all others had not adopted his immersion views!

It is only about three hundred years since the question of *mode* has been controverted by the churches. Dr. D. has thus demonstrated, by philological induction, through an almost exhaustive examination of the ancient Greek writers,—which philological investigation must hold the empire even over the lexicons, for only by such philological research are lexicons made—that neither is *Baptizo* a word of mode, nor a word confined in its scope and use to secular, earthly or material things; that the agency, element or mode is not known by the simple use of the word itself, but that it expresses *condition*, which may be the result of a "myriad" different agencies, modes of action, and receiving or effecting elements.*

He says "*Bapto*," the root whence *Baptizo* comes, signifies, primarily, *to dip*, and hence, logically, to dye, stain, tinge, or color, as derived senses of the word. And if this word were used relative to religious things at all, (as it is not,) it must take the logically derived sense, *i. e.*, a change of character, a new color or hue given to the character. *Baptizo*, its derivative and intensive, is applied to moral and spiritual things, almost times without number; and philology shows that it is thus

---

* In "Classic Baptism," Dr. D. has traced the word *Baptismos* and its cognates to the causative agencies (and modes of action of course), suggested by the following record among others not here specified. See Johannic Bap. 237. 1. Baptism of wine, a drunken condition. 2. Baptism of war, a desolated condition. 3. Baptism of care, an anxious condition. 4. Baptism of trouble, a harassed condition. 5. Baptism of passion, an excited condition. 6. Baptism of grief, a sorrowful condition. 7. Baptism of ignorance, an unenlightened condition. 8. Baptism of wickedness, a depraved condition. 9. Baptism of taxes, an oppressed condition. 10. Baptism of debts, a bankrupt condition. 11. Baptism of mental labor, an imbecile condition. 12. Baptism of questions, a bewildered condition. 13. Baptism of disease, a sickly condition. 14. Baptism of Magian arts, a superstitious condition. 15. Baptism of poverty, an impoverished condition. 16. Baptism of a drug, a somnolent condition. 17. Baptism of pleasure, a joyous condition. 18. Baptism of fright, an alarmed condition. 19. Baptism of surprise, a startled condition. 20. Baptism of *heifer ashes, a ceremonially pure condition.* 21. Baptism of mersion or submerging, a whelmed condition.—Twenty examples against one (the latter), in favor of a variety of meanings, and of non-physical as well as physical applications of the word.

used with reference to a permanent change of moral character or condition. The *terminus ad quem* of the word never designates a mode of doing this, or the agency, but the result, the changed condition,—whether it be *imbued, purified, regenerated, consecrated to, merged into*, etc., etc., or other resultant and abiding condition of the soul or mind. The Greek dative of agency (by or with), either expressed by the force of the dative itself, or by a preposition with the accusative, of termination or result, is usually the grammatical relation of *Baptizo* in all Greek sentences. This dative agency may be the Holy Spirit, fire, flood, water, blood, ashes, tears, sufferings, martyrdom, a flaming sword, a sea, a cloud, wine, dew, etc., etc.; and is found nearly as oft used where water is not, and cannot be a concomitant or element or agent, as where it is.

In all moral and religious uses of the word, Dr. D. shows that no water is to be inferred from the use of the word, unless water be specified directly or in the context. He also shows that the intent or meaning of the word never terminates on the use of water—that there is not in all the Greek language any such expression as baptizing into water—but even if water be used, or is implied, it is only as *the means* of securing *another* result, viz. a (*purified*) state or condition—a *whelmed* state,—a *mersed* or *merged* state, etc. JUDAIC BAPTISM, he assures us, was a symbolic *purifying* by water, or ashes, or blood, as required in the Mosaic law, and rehearsed Hebrews 9th; while JOHN'S BAPTISM was more, a *baptism into repentance* itself, of which the use of water might be a sign, but was not the real baptism. John's commission was to preach the *baptism*, i. e., the *doctrine* or *duty* of *repentance*—and he really performed his work had he never baptized (or purified) with water at all. God's command did not rest on the sign, but on the terminal object of his commission, *repentance*—the "*baptism of repentance.*" Of the Greek words *Baptisma metanoias*, correctly rendered *baptism of repentance*, he assures us that the former word—

"1. Is never met with in the classics. 2. Its use originates in the Scriptures, in which it is never used with a *physical* defining adjunct. 3. It is never employed in Patristic writings to denote a simple physical mersion, but a controlling moral influence." See Johannic Bap., p. 239.

Dr. D. further asserts that the Baptist new version of this phrase, "*immersion of repentance*," is without meaning, or if taken as elliptical and paraphrased, as they are wont, it eviscerates and annuls the force of Scripture language.

It is not, he says, a baptism which makes a mere "profession of repentance," but a baptism of *repentance*, that *secures* the *remission of sins*. "*Immersion* in water," says Dr. D., "expresses only the condition of an object resting in repose in the water." Is it meant that John preached that "men and women" must occupy such a condition? Certainly that is most heroic doctrine! And what of "repentance?"

"This also is eviscerated of its life, and we convert the repentance of inspiration into a *profession* of repentance. And what of 'remission of sins?' The immersion of 'men and women' in water making 'profession' of repentance, *never reaches unto 'remission of sins*,'—that is Campbellism—but true soul-repentance will avail unto the 'remission of sins.'"

Dr. D. hints that—

"Some would shrink from contradicting John by making that baptism outward which he declares is inward and soul-renewing, and would shrink from transforming *Baptisma* into an immersion in which there is no immersion, but only an evanescent dipping, which divorces *Baptisma* from *metanoias*, and establishes an unlawful union with water; which takes away *metanoias* and gives us in its stead an empty 'profession;' which denies thus what John affirms, and treads down every word of this Scripture by a mangled rending of its members from their living relations."

He adds:

"I am disposed to gather up the torn fragments that they may be restored to their divinely appointed relations, and to accept of them, just as the Holy Spirit has given them, without any attempt at rewriting in order to make them square with a theory."

And there are Baptist writers, not a few, who candidly admit what Dr. D. claims, and thus give these words respecting John's baptism their full force. Says Professor Ripley, an eminent Baptist commentator, (on Acts xviii. 25):

"The *Baptism of John* is here put for all the ministry of John the Baptist, and all the doctrine he taught. . . . We received the *doctrine* which John the Baptist taught."

So Professor Hackett on same passage, says:

"Knowing only the baptism of John ... since John, however, taught that the Saviour was about to appear, and that *repentance*, faith in Him, and holiness were necessary to salvation ... Apollos could be said, with entire truth, to be instructed in the way of the Lord."

The *Christian Standard* (Baptist), also says:

"This phrase, '*Baptism of John*,' is to be taken for the *doctrine* of this great herald of Jesus."

JOHN'S REAL BAPTISM NOT WATER-BAPTISM—DR. DALE'S VIEW.

Discoursing further on the phrase *Baptisma metanoias*, as defining John's baptism, Dr. D. remarks:

"If 'faith' and 'sin' can produce such changed conditions of the soul as are denoted by 'righteousness,' ('righteousness of faith,') on the one hand, and 'deceit,' ('deceitfulness of sin,') on the other, there can be no embarrassment in attributing to 'repentance' the office of changing the condition of the soul in that thorough manner indicated by *Baptisma*."

And the subjective genitive in Greek, he insists, lawfully defines its connected noun. Thus we have *baptisma puros*, baptism of fire; *baptisma aimatos*, baptism of blood; *baptisma dakroūn*, baptism of tears; *baptisma marturōn*, baptism of martyrdom, etc. So we have "*lavacrum fidei*, the washing of faith; *lavacrum penitentiæ*, the washing of repentance. In all these, he says:

"The genitive adjunct defines and establishes the baptism or washing; and in no instance is the baptism or washing within a physical element. The reference is only to a condition of the soul."

But Dr. D. pertinently inquires:

"Does any one in alarm ask, 'Do you mean to deny that water was used by John in administering baptism?' I mean (he says) to deny just what the word of God denies; and to affirm just what the word of God affirms. I mean to be very jealous for that excellent glory claimed by our Baptist brethren, of sternly adhering to the very word of God; and, therefore, to follow very humbly and very adoringly (as otherwise knowing nothing) the very words which the Holy Ghost teacheth. And in doing so I mean to distinguish just so much and no more as the Holy Spirit distinguishes between the baptism which John preached, in which there was no water, and the ritual baptism which John administered in which there was water. John's mission did not consist in the administration of a ritual ordinance, ... John was not sent to administer a ritual water-baptism, but was sent to preach repentance baptism, just as Paul 'was not sent to baptize, but to preach the gospel' (1 Cor. i. 17). The phrase *Baptisma metanoias*,' means nothing more nor less than a pervading and controlling penitential condition of the soul. This was what John was commissioned to preach, and this was what he did preach, Mark, Luke, Peter, and Paul being witnesses. He both denies that he was sent to administer water-baptism, as his ministry, and affirms that his mission was to preach repentance baptism, when he refuses water-baptism to the Pharisee and Sadducee, and calls them to repentance baptism, to be evidenced by its appropriate fruits."

This last remark of Dr. Dale is a sufficient reply to his own concession in one place, that—

"John's mission did include the administration of a rite, in which water, as a symbol, appeared, illustrative of and lending force to that repentance baptism, in the preaching of which (*water not entering into it*) his mission did so preeminently consist, that it is even used by the Holy Spirit to characterize it."

John's purifying with water was simply a continuation of the office of the Levite, or Jewish priest. Bating this slight concession to ritualistic teachers, Dr. D. reasons otherwise correctly.*

---

* Indeed Dr. D. on another page recognizes the Levitical character of John's ministry and external baptism; thus, p. 275: "Water, then, may appear in John's ritual baptism as fulfilling an office which such ritual baptism demands, and which (as in the record) reads, 'I indeed baptize you with water,'—*en hudati eis metanoian*. The exigency of the case (as a Jewish priest) requires the presence of water as a symbol agency. Water has a symbol power; it can symbolize the purifying nature of 'repentance,' and the purified condition consequent upon remission of sins, and the purifying power of the atoning 'blood of the Lamb,' but it cannot give repentance nor remit sins." He also quotes Professor *J. H. Goodwin*, "Notes on Mark," (London, 1869,) who says: "John was both a prophet and a priest. As prophet he preached, and as priest he used a rite of purification similar to those used by the priests. All purifications with water, and all in which *one person acted on another* were by sprinkling or affusion. These, and only these were appointed by the law, and were called baptisms (Heb. ix. 10). The same term which is used for the *rite* is also used for the *reality* of which it is an emblem. As there was a circumcision of the body, so there was a circumcision of the mind. The baptism which was the subject of John's preaching, and which was *for* the remission of sins, was that of the mind. Justin Martyr speaks of the cleansing of repentance, and of the knowledge of God, and declares this to be the only baptism which can purify the person. And he asks, 'Of what use is that baptism which cleanses the flesh and the body only?'"

Matthew (iii. 1–12) most abundantly confirms Dr. D.'s position respecting the real mission of John:

"In those days came John the Baptist, preaching in the wilderness of Judea, and saying, REPENT YE."

He did not preach saying, "Be baptized in water." Till Christ's post-resurrection appearance on Olivet, no claim is made by any one that a command for ritual baptism is found in the New Testament, and we shall allow Dr. Dale and other "able ministers of the New Testament" to deal with that final commission of our ascending Lord.

Here we wish to hear Dr. D. a little further respecting John's baptism. On p. 252 ("Johannic Baptism"), he writes.:

"Whether Mark and Luke unite in stating merely the fact of John's preaching, or Mark be accepted as stating both the fact of John's ritually baptizing, and also preaching the 'baptism of repentance into the remission of sins,' we have a broad distinction made, tacitly in the one case, and expressly in the other, between the preaching and baptizing. That John did ritually baptize is unquestionable. *That his oral addresses consisted in the proclamation of a ritual baptism, and a call upon the people to receive such baptism,* is (in view of the nature of his mission) a simple absurdity. But all inspired writers unite in testifying that the grand feature of John's ministry was the *preaching a* BAPTISM; that baptism, then, could not have been a water-baptism, but must have been, as we are expressly told, a REPENTANCE *baptism.*"

Now hear Dr. D.'s concession to ritualistic teaching again, which, however, he himself refutes every time ; p. 253 :

"There is a ritual baptism pertaining to Christianity, but, whatever the theory may teach upon the matter, *neither Paul, nor any other minister of Christ, was ever sent to preach a ritual baptism.* The Christian commission is to preach Christ and his baptism (who never baptized with water) . . . . and the man of whose ministry it can be justly said, his preaching is the preaching of a ritual ordinance, cannot be one of those whom Christ has sent to preach the gospel."

Now on what authority does Dr. D. assert that "there is a ritual baptism pertaining to Christianity?" yet, which "no minister of Christ was ever sent to preach?" Has he cited us to any law for it? Nay, nor will he! He finds a ritual baptism *existing* among Christians, and that is all the

law there is to be found. We shall yet have his own testimony further to this ; p. 253 :

"Inasmuch as the ministry of the Forerunner is evermore described as the
preaching of the 'baptism of repentance,' the 'baptism of repentance into
the remission of sins,' it follows just as certainly, as that there was no ab-
surdly incongruous relationship between the preaching of John and the preparation of the way of the Lord, that ritual baptism was not the theme of the
preaching of him who was 'filled with the Holy Ghost from his mother's
womb,' and who entered upon his work 'in the spirit and power of Elias,'
to 'prepare the way of the Lord, and *to give the knowledge of salvation unto
his people.'*"

Analyzing the "New Version" translation of this passage,
issued by the Baptist Union, which is as follows : " preaching
the immersion of repentance *unto* the remission of sins," and
Mr. Campbell's version, " immersion *in water* into the remission of sins," Dr. D. remarks :

"The translation of *eis* in connection with immersion by *unto* is something
remarkable for Baptists.   There is not a single case outside the Scriptures in
which, in such relation, they translate *eis* by '*unto*.'   The proper translation,
as shown by the character of the Greek verb, is *into*.   Up to this point the
Baptist theory has insisted on this in the most imperative manner.   This
principle has not been disregarded here, and their universal practice discarded
without some strong reason. What that strong reason is, is sufficiently obvious.
A translation here, in harmony with their translation of the preposition, in
every case of classic baptism, would cut up their theory (of water-baptism) by
the roots.   Our translation of the preposition, even with their 'immersion,'
makes an end of their theory.   Try it : 'He preached the immersion of repentance *into the remission of sins*.'   Then the 'immersion' is not into *water*,
but into the '*remission* of sins,' and of necessity the baptism cannot be physical.   '*Into* the remission of sins,' states a truth under a proper interpretation
of 'baptism of repentance,' but 'immersion (in water) unto the remission of
sins,' states, on its face, an untruth, ruinous to the Gospel, and to the soul that
confides in it."

But Dr. D. apologizes for the Baptist translation of *eis*
"*unto*" in this case only—in connection with baptism—by
attributing it not to a design of perverting the Word of God ;
but to the pressure of their mistaken conception of the meaning of *baptizo* ; he says :

"When they came to this passage they reasoned thus : '*Baptismos* must be
translated *immersion*, but if we translate *eis*, as we have always insisted it

should be translated, *into*, we take away *water* from our "immersion" by giving to it a purely ideal element, which would ruin our doctrine; ' and as our doctrine cannot be wrong, *eis* here cannot mean *into*, *therefore*, we are justified in translating it *unto*. And it will be better to confront the self-contradiction in our translations than to abandon a baptism into WATER for a baptism *into* REMISSION OF SINS."

We will not take the space to continue Dr. D.'s scathing analysis of the Baptist translation here, and the reason for it, and also Mr. Campbell's doubling the preposition and interpolating *water* in order to get his ritualism into the text; but press directly to Dr. Dale's summing up of the argument, or rather his announcement of the conclusion :

"I say, then, that *Baptisma metanoias eis aphesin amartiōn* is a complete statement needing no addition, and that it is the fullest and most vividly distinct statement of the distinguishing characteristics of John's preaching to be found anywhere in the Scriptures. The meaning of *baptisma* has been sufficiently established, both philologically and by usage. There is not a particle of evidence that it does ever, in the Scriptures, *enter into physical relations*. And so far as my examination goes, *it is never used in physics* out of the Scriptures."*

What now is the sentiment of the whole ? "John preached the *baptism of repentance into the remission of sins*,—*i. e.*, John preached a *thorough change in the condition of the soul to be effected by repentance, and to be accompanied by the forgiveness of sins*, pointing out the Coming One, already in their midst, exclaiming: '*Behold the Lamb of God that taketh away the sin of the world.*'

"Is this preaching so unsound, or so unintelligible, that *it must be converted into water dipping before it can be received ?* "

We say *Amen* to this reasoning of Dr. D.

HEAR DR. DALE'S CONCLUSIONS.

"*Johannic baptism is a spiritual condition of the soul, a 'baptism into repentance,' 'into the remission of sins,'* which *condition* of repentance and of remission (is not momentary), has no self-termination, and is the work of the Holy Ghost. *This is Johannic baptism in its reality.*

"This same baptism . . . . exhibited in symbol by the application of pure water to the persons in a ritual ordinance, is Johannic baptism in its shadow.

---

* *Baptismos* is the word used by religious and secular writers where physical purifying is intended.

John's (real) baptism is a new baptism. 'Baptism into repentance,' and 'baptism into water,' are, as to their nature, as far removed from each other as is pole from pole."

We had not dared to hope for an ally as strong in the result of research as Dr. Dale, who would so boldly deny a ritualistic law for baptism with water, and especially in the case of John, who really lived "under the law," and to whom we had conceded more of the ritual in his commission than does Dr. D. But Dr. D. bases his argument on that moral sense of the word *baptisma* which we, for many years, had been fully persuaded was the underlying sense, as used in the New Testament; hence, we see no way of evading the result of his research. Of course the Christian era does not go back on this record to a ritualism exceeding that of John's day, and Dr. D. sees this as clearly.

PRIMARY AND SECONDARY USE OF WORDS.

The primary use of all words and language pertains to things seen and temporal. When the human mind soars high enough to talk about things mental, moral and spiritual, the language before framed, endowed with an added mental, spiritual, or moral sense, is oft used to save the coining of new words for every variety of sentiment or meaning.

Thus the word *day* is first applied to that period of time that succeeds the night. Its moral, religious, and symbolic use is known to all Scripture readers. If you please to call this the secondary meaning, or derived meaning, none will object, but the derived sense is just as full-orbed and prolifi and intelligible as the primary, and just as needful. So the word *heaven* was first applied to the concave above the earth, then to the moral and spiritual realm where the righteous dwell, and this latter sense, or use of the word, is infinitely more momentous than the other.

So with the word baptism and all its synonyms—wash, cleanse, sanctify, purify, regenerate, merge into, disciple, etc. —the primary sense of them all was carnal and outward, but when God would bring a moral and spiritual kingdom to light, and adumbrate it to the mind of man, destined for, and aspiring to immortality, all these terms are appropriated to that spiritual cleansing and renewal, which alone fits man for a blessed immortality. Who shall say that the latter, the moral sense or application of these terms, is not the more pregnant and momentous? Ay, as heaven is higher than the earth? Why drag, if possible, these terms down to the level of the earthly and the carnal, rather than, after the pattern of prophets, and all inspired men, essay with them by these very terms to lift men up to the saving power, to the true life and all that is holy and heavenly?

The Baptism sought by the Old Dispensation.

The baptism really sought, even under the Old Dispensation, was spiritual, as we have seen; for God never exalted *forms* in place of this, and only allowed the spiritual things to be symbolized in an age, and among a people, that needed the diagram in their rudimentary state. And when the symbol that aided the faith of some had usurped the place of the substance in the many, as the idol had taken the place of God in the heathen mind; God " found fault with it," and " abolished " it. If the symbol code of the Old Testament be not annulled, no ceremonial law has been annulled.

What the Great Reformation sought.

That the Great Reformation, under John, Christ, and apostles, sought to substitute the moral and spiritual for the ceremonial and external, and this with respect to baptism, as well as sacrifices, temple worship, oblations, feasts, etc., the following considerations must evince:

1. Spiritual heart-worship was sought *in place of* that which was external.

2. The use of *baptisma*, as derived from the secondary, or moral sense of the word *baptizo* rather than *baptismos*, the

6

word used by secular writers, and this so oft with its synonyms and parallelisms, *convert, regenerate, remit sins, cleanse, wash, sanctify, save, shall be saved*, etc., cumulatively tends to establish the same truth.

3. The Patristic writers so oft using the term in a spiritual sense, and spiritualizing so many typical events, as baptisms that were not external baptisms, but by them were made continually to point to the spiritual baptism, or purifying of the heart, points in the same direction.

There is almost no end to these allusions, and spiritual interpretations of the prior acts of the patriarchs and prophets, and the historic records of the Old Testament. In Judaic Bap., p. 134 :

TERTULLIAN, in commenting upon the scene described in Gen. i. 2, where the Spirit of God is said to have hovered over chaos, says :

"Whereby also may be recognized the prime nature of baptism .... foreshown by a figure, that the Spirit of God, which from the beginning was upborne above the waters *would transform the imbued.* The holy was borne above the holy, as *that which here received sanctity from that upborne* .... so the nature of the waters was sanctified by the Holy, and itself received the power to sanctify."

This teaches correctly that all true baptism must be originally derived from the Holy Spirit. With Tertullian's borrowed conceit, that thus the Holy Spirit imparted power to the inert material element of water to purify the soul, we need have nothing in common.

AMBROSE, speaking of the flaming sword that was placed at the east of Eden to "keep the way of the tree of life," says, p. 223 :

"Sin began and baptism began ; by which they might be purified who desired to return. .... Who is it that baptizes by this fire ? ... He, of whom John says, 'He shall baptize with the Holy Spirit and fire.' .... Then shall come the Great Baptizer (for so I call him, as Gabriel called him), Luke i. 32, saying, 'He shall be Great,' he will see many standing before the entrance of Paradise, he will wave the sword turning every way, he will say to those on the right hand, 'Enter into my kingdom;' so every one of us burned (purified) by that sword, not consumed, having entered into the delights of Paradise, may give thanks to his Lord, saying, Thou hast brought us into rest."

This, then, was a baptism that saved. So ORIGEN, p. 224, says:

"Therefore the Saviour brings both sword and fire, and BAPTIZES THOSE THINGS WHICH could not be purged by the purification of the Holy Spirit."

So, alluding to a coal of fire being laid upon the lips of Isaiah (Isa. vi. 5–7), AMBROSE says:

"Read the commandments of the Law and you will find it written, ' *Whosoever shall touch the dead becomes defiled,* (Num. xvii. 11). Therefore we need purgation, because we have touched the dead. . . . We all touch the dead, for who will boast that he keeps his heart pure, or who will dare to say that he is clean from sins? . . . Hence, immediately one of the Seraphim came down and touched his (Isaiah's) lips with a coal and cleansed his unclean lips."

The connection of the above shows that Ambrose was speaking of the many baptisms known under the Law, for he says "Baptism is not one," but many.

So EUSEBIUS says, p. 241:

"Serenus, who after the endurance of great torments is said to have been beheaded, and of women, Herais, yet a catechumen (*i. e.* unbaptized), received that baptism which is by fire, and departed out of this life."

Thus JUSTIN MARTYR, commenting on Isa. i. 16, 17, "Wash you, make you clean," etc., points out to Trypho, the Jew, the difference between the true baptism and that baptism with water which the Jews practised. He says:

"Through the washing of repentance and of the knowledge of God, which was established on account of the transgression of the people of God, as Isaiah declares, we have believed and made known that this very baptism, which he fore-announced, is the *only one able to cleanse the repenting ;* this is the water of life. But the cisterns which you (Jews) have dug out for yourselves are broken and are useless to you. *For of what use is that baptism which cleanses the flesh and the body only ?* BAPTIZE THE SOUL FROM ANGER AND FROM COVETOUSNESS, AND FROM ENVY, AND FROM HATE, AND BEHOLD THE BODY IS PURE."

So JEROME, on the same text, " *Wash ye, be clean,*" says:

"Instead of former victims and burnt-offerings, and the fat of fed beasts, and the blood of bulls and of goats . . . . the religion of the Gospel pleases *me,* that ye may be baptized by my (Christ's) blood, through the washing of regeneration, which alone can take away sins."

BASIL, quoting Isa. iv. 4:

"When the Lord shall have washed away the filth of the daughters of Zion, and shall have purged the blood of Jerusalem by the spirit of judgment and the spirit of burning," says: "Perhaps, there are three meanings of baptism, purification from defilement, regeneration by the Spirit, and trial by the fire of judgment, so that the washing (v. 4) is to be understood in reference to the removal of sin now, but by 'the spirit of judgment and by the spirit of burning,' the reference is to the trial by fire in the future world."

Thus by every citation from the Fathers in expounding the Scriptures, and by a penetrating survey of the Scripture language of the New Testament, respecting that baptism which steps beyond the Jewish, we see how far short of a full and complete comprehension of its meaning all ritualists have fallen. God is not a ritualist—inspiration does not teach ritualism—but a spiritual condition as high above aught that rituals can secure as heaven is higher than the earth.

There are almost as many symbol baptisms spoken of by the Fathers, where water could form no element or adjunct, as where it is. Whatever had the effect of introducing the subject into a new and abiding condition, is said by the ancients to baptize that subject. Thus, by the Mosaic Law, the sprinkling of blood, the sprinkling of heifer ashes, the sprinkling of water, and laving with water, were equally agencies employed in introducing the subject into a ceremonially pure condition, and that ceremonially pure condition is called baptism. So God's placing the flaming sword at Eden's gate, and touching Isaiah's lips with a coal of fire, and sufferings, and martyrdom, are supposed to have the same effect, and are as fitly called *baptisms.* * The waters of Marah (Ex. xv. 23) are

---

* "The Seleucians taught that baptism is not to be received by water, and substituted a mode of baptism with fire."

"Valentinus re-baptized those who had only received water-baptism, conferring on them the baptism of fire." (Well, fire will purify the flesh.)

"The *Ascodrutæ,* a branch of the Valentinians, rejected the use of all symbols and sacraments." (2d Century.)

"Clemens Alexandrinus remarked on the proverb, 'Be not pure in the laver,

purified by a tree thrown into them, and this is called a *baptism* of the waters : they remained in a *baptized state.* So Ambrose assures us, and in speaking upon this very point he assures us that there were many (so-called) external baptisms in his day, and even which are not real baptisms, because they result not in a purified condition. He says :

"There are many kinds of baptisms, but the Apostle announces *one* baptism. There are baptisms of the Gentiles, but they are not baptisms. They are washings, they cannot be baptisms. The body is washed ; *sin is not washed away.* There were baptisms of the Jews, some unnecessary, others in figure. . . . . Moses cast the wood into the fountain, and the water which before was bitter grew sweet. . . . That is bitter which cannot take away sin. Water, therefore, is bitter, but *when thou shalt have received the cross of Christ, and the heavenly sacrament, it becomes sweet and pleasant.*"

To Ambrose's view, then, nothing was baptism that did not remove sin.

And in further proof that an element of the Great Reformation under John, Christ and apostles, was the effort to substitute the moral for the external sense of baptism, we adduce also this fact—While it is true that the Fathers of the second century did, many of them, recognize the true baptism as internal and spiritual—it is also true that near the close of this century some lapsed toward the carnal and outward conception of it, yet ever used the term *baptism* as a synonym of regenerate, renew, sanctify, or merge into Christ, and as securing salvation. Thus showing that by Christ and the apostles they had been instructed respecting the *saving baptism* only, and that the Church when drawn toward Christ and his teachings (and Paul's), retreated from the Jewish and outward view, but when unduly influenced by Judaism and the borrowed ideas of heathenism, lapsed into a trust in externals again.

---

but in the mind,'—"I suppose an exact and firm repentance is a sufficient purification ; judging and considering ourselves for the deeds we have done, cleansing the mind from sensual affections and former sins ; " p. 461.

The Fathers never used Baptism as a Symbol.

But the Patrists never relapsed into that form of Judaism which regarded baptism as a *type* or *symbol* of purifying, as our modern theologians assume, but as *conversion* or *regeneration* itself; evincing that they had mistaken the efficacious agency in the work (the Holy Spirit), and were conceiving of some magical or divinely imparted power in *water* to regenerate the soul.   Tertullian discourses at large upon the pervading and efficacious agency of water in nature's operations, and then, very incongruously infers its efficacy in renewing man morally and spiritually.   He says (as quoted before):

" So the nature of the waters was sanctified by the Holy (Spirit) that brooded upon the waters, and itself received the power to sanctify." *

This " sanctifying" of the waters of baptism was erewhile assigned to the officiating priest or administrator ; and hence early grew up, in the Western Church especially, this prime element of the Papacy—*baptismal regeneration.*

From the internal baptism taught by Christ and apostles, they swung over wholly to the external.   Protestant sects of our day have abridged the Patristic error, by swinging back only to the Jewish idea of a typical or symbol baptism.   Yet many of the Fathers disowned and denied the saving power of ritual baptism.   As saith Jerome:

---

* So Cyril says : " If anyone desires to know why grace is given by means of water, and not by means of any other of the elements ; searching the divine Scriptures he will find out.   For water is some great thing, the best of the four visible elements of the world.   Heaven is the dwelling-place of angels, but the heavens are of the waters.   The earth is the home of men, but the earth is of the waters.   Before everything of the things which were made during the creation of the six days, the Spirit of God was upborne above the water.   Water was the beginning of the world, and the Jordan was the beginning of the Gospels."

Such a confounding of things natural and things spiritual was not uncommon among the Fathers, especially when ritualistic ideas began to steal upon them, and a hierarchy sought to lift up itself by this means.   The crudeness of their philosophic views is also patent to the most cursory reader.

"The bodies of infants stained with blood, are washed as soon as born. So also spiritual birth needs the *salutary washing*. The heathen practise many washings in their mysteries, but do not wash into salvation. So not only of heretics, but of those connected with the church, who do not receive with full faith the salutary baptism. They receive the water, but do not receive the Spirit; as Simon the Magician, who was baptized, indeed, with water, but by no means baptized into salvation."

And ORIGEN says—alluding to the laver where the sons of Aaron were to wash their hands and feet:

"The word of the precept, truly, with the feet, orders the washing with *internal water*, announcing figuratively the sacrament (saving power) of baptism."

And CLEMENS says:

"Be pure, not by *washing*, but by thinking."

AMBROSE, also says:

"We are renewed by the regeneration of washing—we are renewed by the effusion of the Holy Spirit."

Quoting Ps. li. 2–7, he adds:

"'Thou shalt sprinkle me with hyssop, and I shall be clean.' *He is rightly renewed who is changed from the darkness of sin into the light of virtue and grace!* . . . Rejoice, O heavens, and be glad, O earth, because of those who are about to be sprinkled with hyssop, and to be purified by the spiritual hyssop, through the power of Him, who, in His suffering, drank from the hyssop and the reed."

JEROME, also, quoting Ezekiel xxxvi. 25:

"'And I will pour out (or sprinkle) upon you clean water,' . . So that upon the believing, and those converted, I will pour out the clean water of saving baptism, and I will cleanse them from their abominations and from all their errors, with which they have been possessed, and I will give to them a new heart, that they may believe upon the Son of God."

HILARY says:

"But sprinkling, according to the law, was the cleansing of sin through faith, purifying the people by the sprinkling of blood (Ps. l. 9), a sacrament of the future sprinkling by the blood of the Lord, faith, meanwhile, supplementing the blood of the legal sacrifice."

DIDYMUS of Alexandria writes:

"And the very image of baptism (pillar of cloud and fire) both continually illuminated and saved all Israel, as Paul wrote (1 Cor. x. 1, 2), and as Ezekiel prophesied: 'I will sprinkle clean water upon you, and ye shall be clean from all your sins.' And David says, 'Sprinkle me with hyssop and I shall be clean.'"

CYRIL of Jerusalem is no less specific concerning the baptism that saves:

"Thou seest the power of baptism—Be of good courage, O Jerusalem, the Lord will take away all thine iniquities. The Lord will wash away the uncleanness of his sons and daughters by the spirit of judgment and the spirit of burning; He will sprinkle upon you clean water, and ye shall be purified from all your sin."

And we find JUSTIN MARTYR, actually eschewing both ritual circumcision and baptism for the sake of the spiritual. He asks:

"What, then, is the word of circumcision to me, having received testimony from God? What need is there of that baptism (with water) to one baptized by the Holy Spirit?"

CYRIL calls spiritual baptism a circumcision:

"Therefore by the likeness of the faith of Abraham we come into adoption. And then, after faith, like to him, we receive the spiritual seal, being circumcised through washing by the Holy Spirit."

Joshua is said to have circumcised Israel with a second circumcision by knives of stone. Origen and Justin Martyr compare this to the saving baptism. JUSTIN says:

"He is said to have circumcised the people with a second circumcision, which was an announcement of this circumcision with which Jesus Christ himself circumcises us from stones and other idols."

ORIGEN says:

"But since Christ came, and gave us the second circumcision by the baptism of regeneration, and purged our souls, we have cast away all these things, and in their stead have received the answer of a good conscience in the Lord. Then, by the second circumcision, the reproaches of Egypt have been taken away from us, and the vices of our sins have been purged."

BAPTISM BY BLOOD.

CYPRIAN says:

"The baptism of a public confession and of blood may avail for salvation. . . . The Lord declares in the Gospel, that those baptized by His blood and passion, are sanctified and attain the grace of the divine promise; when He speaks to the thief, believing and trusting in the very passion, and promises that he shall be with Him in Paradise."

THEOPHYLACT says:

"He (Christ) calls His death a baptism, as being a purging of us all."

TERTULLIAN says:

"These two baptisms he shed forth from the wound of His pierced side."

Did he shed forth an *immersion?* Nay, but the water of salvation, and the blood that atones!

BASIL says:

"The blood of the lamb (by Israel slain) is a type of the blood of Christ."

ORIGEN says:

"That we may die, washed by our own blood, for it is the baptism of blood only which makes us purer than the baptism of water made us."

DIDYMUS of Alexandria gives us this remarkable testimony to the sufficiency of the spiritual baptism, and much more of the baptism of blood (or martyrdom) without water, to sanctify and save:

"But without being born again by baptism through the Spirit of God, and sealed by sanctification and made his temple, no one can partake of the heavenly blessings, although his life should be found *in other respects blameless.* However they who have *attained martyrdom before baptism*, being cleansed by their own blood, are thus made to live by the Spirit of God."

And even CYPRIAN, with all his later zeal for infant salvation by water-baptism, is constrained to admit that a martyr's death is the best baptism. He asks:

"Can the power of baptism be greater or better than *confession*, than *martyrdom*, when one confesses Christ before men, and is baptized by his own blood?"

So, BASIL, one of the early Fathers of note, says:

"There are some who, in striving for piety, have undergone death for Christ, in reality, not in semblance, needing, for salvation, nothing of the water symbols, being baptized by their own blood."

CYRIL, also, assures us:

"The Saviour calls martyrdom baptism, saying, 'Can ye drink of the cup that I drink of, and be baptized with the baptism that I am baptized with?'"

Speaking of John the Forerunner, who baptized our Lord, John of Damascus says:

> "John was baptized by *putting his hand upon the divine head,* and by his own blood."

SPIRITUAL BAPTISM HUMANLY ADMINISTERED.

And this idea of baptism became very common, as we shall find many cases where a *simple laying on of the hand* was called baptism, but more generally called *consolamentum,* or spiritual baptism—since in thus laying on the hand the Holy Spirit was invoked—and claimed to be conferred by those thus laying on the hands, after the pattern of the apostles as mentioned in Acts viii. 18; vi. 6; xix. 6. Dr. DALE says:

> "The old Greeks did not hesitate, very freely, to speak of baptism as effected by *the touch of the hand* without water-using, a simple formula of invocation or consecration."

FIRMILIAN says:

> "Paul baptized those who had been baptized by John (before the Holy Spirit had been sent by the Lord) again, by spiritual baptism, and put his hand upon them that they might receive the Holy Ghost."

And, as though Christ had been baptized of John in the same manner, HIPPOLYTUS says:

> "He bowed his head to be baptized by John."

JEWISH PURIFYINGS NOT RESTRICTED TO THE USE OF WATER.

We have already cited the Jewish and Patristic use of the term *fire-baptism.* And, summing up, we find that the Jewish writers and Christian Fathers used the term baptism to signify a *religious purification* or *merging into Christian life,* as oft where water was not the regimen or element, as where it was. Dr. Dale, in summing up his treatise on " Judaic Baptism," says:

> "*The number of facts embraced in the investigation* (of the question) *is not less than fifty, and the number of times in which the Greek word* (baptizo) *in one form or another appears is more than three times fifty.* These facts," he adds, "are all taken from Jewish sources, from writings both inspired and uninspired. Ten Jewish writers (here cited) employ the word in application to their re-

figious rites, and to matters apart from religion. Christian writers, with one consent, interpret these facts of Jewish religious history as cases of baptism. The time embraced by the usage of this word by Jewish writers, in application to their religious rites, extends through several centuries."

Dr. D. not only affirms that these baptisms were usually SPRINKLINGS either of *water, blood, or ashes* (if physical baptisms), but concludes thus :

"JUDAIC BAPTISM *is a condition of* CEREMONIAL PURIFICATION *effected by the* WASHING *of the hands or feet; by the* SPRINKLING *of sacrificial blood, or heifer ashes ; by the* POURING *upon of water ; by the touch of a coal of fire ; by the* WAVING *of a flaming sword ; and by divers other modes and agencies, dependent in no wise upon any form of act, or covering of the object."*

Dr. D. further asserts that the word *baptizo* is so oft used both in classic and inspired writings (but especially the latter), where no physical element is implied, that the presence of the physical element must be proved, and never gratuitously assumed. He adds : "There is no such language to be met with as baptism into water." And he affirms, that when water was used by the Jews, it was a symbol agency, merely ; the real baptism was the supposed resultant purification. This attained resultant *condition* is what is called *baptism*—a momentary act never. The Baptist idea, he affirms, that *baptizo* means *to dip*, that is, "to put an object within, and withdrawing it out of a fluid element," is pre-eminently baseless :

"*Baptizo makes demand for a condition of intusposition* without regard to the manner of its accomplishment; and no momentary introduction and removal is possible without destroying the life of the word."

This, he affirms, is both its classic and religious use :

"The secondary (or religious) use of the word is as clearly as it is exclusively based on an indefinitely *prolonged continuance of condition in contradistinction from one that is momentary and evanescent.* . . . The baptism preached by John was a baptism (*eis metanoian*) *into repentance* without removal; elsewhere termed (*eis aphesin amartiōn*) *into remission of sins,* without removal from that state. These baptisms are intensely real, thorough and abiding changes in the condition of the soul."—Johannic Bap., p. 308.

If the reasoning of Dr. D be correct (and we see no way to evade it), we discover what unutterably unworthy views of baptism nearly all who baptize with water have entertained ;

and how, by the utter degradation of this word *baptizo* and its
derivative *baptisma*, they have dethroned a great moral truth
of revelation, and put in the place of it a worthless shell, a
shadow—a freezing and love-crucifying ceremonial.   Dr. D.
quotes from the Fathers such accounts of the baptism of
Christ by John as lead himself to doubt whether John's baptism of Christ was aught more than the *consolamentum, or laying on of hands* on the Redeemer's head; through which, as in
the sequel it is recorded, the Holy Spirit in its ineffable fulness descended upon Him.   He claims that Mark i. 9, is the
only passage that by Greek usage apparently militates against
this view (Matthew being as reconcilable with it as with the
Baptist theory), and he quotes Jerome, and Gregory Thauma-
turgus, and many others, as giving the same interpretation to
Mark i. 9, as himself.

They read it thus: "Jesus comes (*eis*) *unto* the Jordan to
be baptized."   And Hippolytus, describing the baptism, says,
"He (Christ) bowed his head to be baptized by John," *i. e.*,
that John might lay his hands thereon.

Gregory dilates upon the theme thus—representing John
as saying:

"How shall I touch thy undefiled head? How shall *I stretch out my right
hand over thee* who hast stretched out the heavens as a curtain, and established the earth upon the waters? How shall I stretch out my servile fingers
over thy divine head? How shall I wash the spotless and the sinless? How
shall I *enlighten the light?* How shall I *offer prayer for thee* who dost receive
the prayers of those who know thee not? In baptizing others I baptize into
thy name, that they may believe on thee coming with glory; baptizing thee
of whom shall I make mention? Into whose name shall I baptize thee?
Into the name of the Father? but thou hast all the Father in thyself! or into
the name of the Son? but there is none other beside thee, the Son of God! or
into the name of the Holy Ghost? but He is of the same nature with thee, in
everything united with thee—of the same will, of the same mind, of the same
power, of the same honor, and with thee receives worship from all! Baptize,
therefore, if thou wilt, O Lord, baptize me the baptizer! Make me whom
thou hast caused to be born, *to be born again!* Stretch out thy dread right
hand which thou hast prepared for thyself, and *crown by thy touch my head*,
that, forerunner of thy kingdom, and crowned like a forerunner, I may preach
to sinners, crying unto them, 'Behold the Lamb of God which taketh away the
sin of the world.'"

Jesus is represented as answering:

"'Lend me *thy right hand*, O Baptist, for the present ministration. . . . . Take hold of my head which the Seraphim worship. Baptize me who am about to baptize them that believe by *water*, and *Spirit* and *fire;* by water, which is able to wash away the filth of sin; by Spirit, which is able to make the earthly Spiritual; by fire, consuming by nature the thorns of transgression.' The Baptist having heard these things, stretching out his trembling right hand, *baptized the Lord*."

Now, why should Gregory in the above mean literal water, any more than he means literal fire? for both are mentioned. And the whole scene as presented, precisely resembles every account we have of those who rejected water-baptism, and with *laying on of hands*, invoked the descent of the Holy Ghost upon their initiates. Not that we doubt that John did at times use the symbol of water, as a priest of the Jewish faith, but his baptism was infinitely more portentous and real than any such ceremonial could be. Justin Martyr says that John dwelt near the Jordan, perhaps "beyond Jordan," as one evangelist has it—and thither the people thronged to be roused and thrilled by the energy of his appeals—and even the Jews, by thousands, to be purified by the "baptism of repentance into the remission of sins." And Dr. Dale reiterates:

"Matthew's 'REPENT!' and Mark's and Luke's '*Baptism of repentance into the remission of sins*,' and John's 'Behold the Lamb of God that taketh away the sin of the world,' have all alike the same amount of water in them; that is to say, just as much as may be found in the burned out craters of the moon. The verb *baptizo*, and the noun *baptisma*, as used in the history of John's baptism, have no more to do with the quantity or the manner of using the water employed in his symbol rite than has the multiplication table to do with the amount or manner of using Rothschild's wealth. Let these words mean what they may, they have no more control, in the relations in which they stand, over the use of water, than a sleeping infant has over the earth's diurnal revolution."

Dr. D., alluding to some that Augustine mentions, who literally baptized with fire, by burning the right ear, says:

"If this baptism was to be by real fire, then these heretics did not err much in employing *bona fide* fire, instead of referring it to the fire of Pentecost, as do our Baptist friends. Moreover, the reasoning by which they seek to justify a *dipping* into water, as a substitute for *baptism in water*, viz. because such a baptism would drown, is equally apologetic for those Seleucians,—for fire baptism will burn up. If, to escape drowning, baptism may be converted into a dipping, then to escape burning up, baptism may be converted into a cauterization of the ear. It is no less a heresy to convert Bible baptism into water dipping, than it is to convert baptism 'by the Holy Ghost and fire' into a burning of the right lobe of the ear. .... Of the two heresies, that of the fire Baptists is the less; for there is no evidence that they regarded the fire as appointed to be the element within which the baptism was to take place, but only as a symbol; while the water Baptists declare that water is that within which the baptism is commanded to take place. They say, that God does clearly and imperatively demand a baptism in water. If they are right as to God's command, they are wrong as to their obedience. .... Dipping into water is no more Patristic baptism, than is the dipping of white linen in spring water, the same as covering that same white linen in a purple dye, and leaving it there. Every Patrist that ever lived would reject, at a word, the notion that a dipping into water was, or was of the essence of, Christian baptism. Use it in whatever form they may, they do universally use it in the faith *that it is filled with the influence of the Holy Ghost, and so, has power, as a means, to baptize the soul:* which soul-baptism, thoroughly changing its condition by the remission of sins, was, in their view, *Christian baptism.* Therefore, they could and did baptize, as absolutely and as literally, the dying by sprinkling as the living by covering."

Dr. D., in pushing this investigation into the ulterior premises, furnished by Greek usage, in "Johannic Baptism," p. 235, says:

"If it be insisted upon, that John's commission *Baptizein en hudati* refers to the execution of a physical baptism, the element of the baptism being water, and the verb used in its primary literal sense, then it is as certain as that Greek is Greek, that John was commissioned to drown every person whom he baptized. Not only does not the Greek word ever take out of the *condition* in which it once places its object, and not only is this the Greek word employed expressly to denote the drowning of men (see abundant citations on another page), but in accordance with the Baptist interpretation itself, the result of John's baptism was *to leave his disciples resting within the water;* as the *Baptist Quarterly* for April, 1869, p. 142, says, '*Baptizo* never does take its subject out of the water.' Whether, then, we look at this commission of John through a classic, a Hellenistic, or Patristic medium, there is an imperative arrest of that interpretation which would command John to baptize men and women in water."

Water is not the receiving element of the baptism, but simply an adjunct symbol—sometimes used;—"repentance" and "remission of sins" is the receiving element, the terminal point, and attained condition.

Mistaking on this one point, see the endless confusion of ideas respecting baptism, and the utter lack of discrimination between those Scripture passages which allude to a ritual, and those which speak of the internal and spiritual baptism only. Even Baptists can publish a tract from which such a summary as the following may be copied verbatim. See "Johannic Baptism," p. 218.

"Baptism."

1. " The word *baptism* is Greek, and signifies a dipping.
2. " There is but one baptism, for Paul so says, Eph. iv. 5.
3. " That one baptism is water; so says Peter, Acts x. 4.
4. " This one baptism in water, is a *burial;* Rom. vi. 4; Col. ii. 12.
5. " A man is not in Christ before he is baptized, for we are plainly taught that we must be *baptized* INTO HIM ; Gal. iii. 27.
6. " Baptism is for the *remission of sins* that are past; Acts ii. 38.
7. " Baptism, like all God's commands, is essential to salvation; 1 Peter iii. 21."

The italicizing and emphasizing is from the tract itself. And when such a tract can be sent out by a body of Christians styling themselves evangelical, it is time for a Philip to inquire: "Understandest thou what thou readest?" And for an "Ezra" or a Dale to give the sense of the word. In the above extract is seen both ritualism and sacramentarianism, without qualification. The following from Alexander Campbell can be no more so, based also, as it is, upon the mere physical or external sense of the word *baptizo :*

" Baptism is for the remission of sins, to give us through repentance and faith, *a solemn pledge and assurance of pardon;* any other baptism *is a human invention.* ' He that believeth and is baptized shall be saved,' associates faith and baptism as antecedents, whose consequent is salvation. The apostles in their epistles allude to baptism as a symbol of moral purification, a washing away of sin in a figure, declarative of a true and real remission of sin, *a formal and definite release of the conscience from the feeling of guilt, and all its condemnating power. Baptism was for the true, real, and formal remission of sins,* through faith in the Messiah, and a genuine repentance toward God. . . . . Not that there is anything in the mere element of water, or in the act, or in the administrator, or in the formula, but all its virtue and efficacy is in the faith and intelligence of him that receives it. 'Baptism doth save us.' To him that believeth and repenteth of his sins, and to none else, then, we may safely say, 'Be baptized for the remission of your sins,' and it will surely be granted by the Lord, and enjoyed by the subject, with an assurance and an evidence which the word and ordinances of the Lord alone can bestow."

None that approve the teaching of Alexander Campbell will say, that in the above extract we have not presented as fair, complete, and concise a statement of those teachings as could be given, and that in his own words. And we must admit that the chief impression made upon our mind, while copying it, is that of the astounding moral bewilderment of an otherwise acute reasoner and genuine scholar. As another has remarked:

"The body of his reasoning upon this subject contains statements which in their relations to each other are so indefinite, so ambiguous, so incongruous, and so irreconcilable, that the conviction is forced upon the mind that the writer is painfully struggling to establish harmony between admitted vital truth, and the pernicious error of sadly misinterpreted texts of Scripture."

We will admit that he conceives of the design and results of baptism (the external) as did many of the Fathers of the third century, viz., as exclusively "*for the remission of sins.*" But *he ought not* to have drunk in their superstitious conceit, that God had *hallowed* the waters of all the earth that they might exert a saving power in baptism. Nor ought he to assume that a divine command for an external act imparts to that act a saving power. God commanded circumcision, yet thousands in all ages have been saved without circumcision, and thousands and tens of thousands of the circumcised have been lost. Cornelius and his household were not circumcised—yet the law of circumcision had not yet been formally abrogated—and they were saved. The external act must ever have some ulterior end short of absolute soul-salvation—it may be a means—but the surrender of the heart to God alone attains salvation by whatever means induced. And see how oft Mr. C. admits and then denies this truth in the extract above. Note first the utter incongruity of making a sinner's act, or

any saint's act, "a solemn pledge and assurance of pardon."
What monster of iniquity may not have a "solemn pledge,
and assurance of pardon," if a bodily act of his own gives it?
Again, "it is a *symbol* of moral purification—a washing away
of sin in a figure." All this is very well. But hear the
sequel,—"*declarative of a true and real remission of sins.*"
Then, forsooth the sinner, by consenting that an administrator (the absolver) may plunge him in the water, *thereby declares his own sins remitted*—thereby furnishes himself with a
"solemn pledge and assurance of pardon"—ay, attains the
"true, real, and formal remission of sins!"—of which he enjoys "an evidence and assurance which the word and ordinances of the Lord alone can bestow." Now we scarcely
know how to characterize, as we think merited, such a sub-
version, and perversion of the teachings of God's word as to
the way of salvation, and especially as to the baptism
that saves. No wonder that Mr. C. himself alludes to an
"imaginary incongruity between the means and the end."
But list! At times Mr. C. will state other and connected
terms or conditions of salvation,—and thus, by a sort of meta-
physical mysticism seek to cover his bold and bald ritualism—gyrating like one on a rotary platform, that he may
seem to face one way while his scheme faces the other way:
thus "to him that *believeth and repenteth* of his sins, *and to
none else*, then, we may safely say, 'Be baptized for the remission of your sins.'" And *he assures* us that it will surely be
granted by the Lord, and we may enjoy such assurance as the
word and ordinances of the Lord only can bestow. Now we
tell Mr. C. and all his followers, that "To him that believeth
and repenteth of his sins," *without Mr. C.'s water baptism*, GOD
WILL GRANT AN ASSURANCE OF PARDON AND REMISSION OF
SINS INFINITELY ABOVE MR. C.'S COLD COGNIZANCE OF A RIT-
UAL OBEDIENCE, as taught by the mere letter of the "word,"
and the "handwriting of ordinances,"—even "OUR CON-
SCIENCE IN THE HOLY GHOST BEARING WITNESS, and giving
the peace of God which passeth all understanding"—even

7

"joy unspeakable and full of glory." This is heaven, higher
than the human consciousness merely, of having performed a
ritual act, and this *may be had without the assumed act.**
Hence Mr. C.'s interpretation of the baptism that is connected
with the remission of sins is radically false, and strikes a fatal
blow at Christianity itself. Yet would he have his adherents
distinctively called "Christians"—thus asking all who maintain the true faith to libel Christianity, by giving up the
name to a mere pretender—one that robs the atonement of
Christ of its alone saving efficacy, and rejects thus the "head-
stone of the corner" of the Christian's hope, and rejects the
alone sanctifying efficacy of the Holy Spirit.

Well says Dr. D.:

"It is Mr. C., and not John, the Forerunner, that has put water into that
baptisma of John. The President of Bethany has embarrassed himself, and
imperilled others by a misunderstanding of that great announcement of John,
the 'baptism of repentance for the remission of sins.' When the error shall
have been corrected, and the true announcement of the Holy Ghost, through
the Forerunner, is allowed to be made, of a baptism, not into water, but into
the remission of sins; effected not by a human administrator, but by the Holy
Spirit working through repentance, then human error will be eliminated *and
the pure truth of God will be revealed.*"

---

* Yet Mr. C. will ever affirm that *faith* and *repentance* are insufficient without baptism (in water) to transfer the soul to the *renewed* state—to the kingdom and light of God. This putting *faith* and *repentance* as antecedents, then,
is a mere make-shift or tortuosity—an evasion—for the turning point, the
transferring act, after all, is *baptism* in his scheme, disguise, appendage, and
ruse it as he may. As well might he say that birth and the use of reason are
adjuncts, for they are indispensable, but neither birth, nor reason, nor faith,
nor repentance with him constitutes the new man, but *baptism.*

CHAPTER III.

WHAT IS CHRISTIAN BAPTISM?

WE have now reached a point where it may be proper to attempt an answer to the question: "What is *Christian Baptism* as taught in the word of God?"

We shall answer it very briefly in our own words, having, on pp. 71–81, given Dr. Dale's definition of *Classic Baptism*, of *Johannic Baptism*, and of *Judaic Baptism*, to which we concede, asking thereunto the attention of every reader. We shall answer the query, and quote two or three corroborative authors (one that we have largely quoted already), and then proceed to a definition such as philology demands, followed by certain strictures, which will lead the way to the close of the present theme, and to the survey of the non-ritualistic historic record. To declare it, then, CHRISTIAN BAPTISM *is simply a* BAPTISM INTO CHRIST; nothing more, nothing less.

If a recognition of the three that "bear record in heaven," the "Father, Son, and Holy Ghost," be more than recognizing our "oneness" in the "Sonship" of Christ, then *Christian baptism* in its highest and most complete sense, is *a baptism into the Father, Son, and Holy Ghost.*

In truth, to define the word (both the verb *baptizo*, and the noun *baptisma*) in harmony with New Testament usage, which is in perfect harmony with the classical primary and secondary meaning of the word, we shall discover that a physical or external sense is there rarely attributable to it, or if it be, it is only by inference or allusion, and not the direct and palpable intent of the word. Dr. D. says that *baptisma* is never found in the New Testament in a complementary relation with water. The following are the only relations where it occurs when speaking of John's baptism : 1. *Baptisma autou* (his baptism). 2. *Baptisma Ioannou* (John's baptism). 3. *Baptisma ekerusse* (baptism preached). 4. *Baptisma metanoias ekerusse* (baptism of repentance preached). 5. *Baptisma metanoias ebaptise* (baptism of repentance baptized). 6. *Baptisma metanoias eis aphesin amartiôn kerussòn* (preaching the baptism of repentance into the remission of sins). Dr. Dale says :

> "In all these limiting adjuncts water fails to make an appearance." "There is not a particle of evidence conjoining *'o Baptistes* (the Baptizer) with a physical complementary element." "*Merger*, the corresponding word, derived from *mergo*, through *merge*, presents in its usage the most absolute evidence of divorce from physical relations."

Merge is a law term designating the drowning, sinking, absorption, or extinguishment of one estate in another. The Christian baptism designates the merging, sinking, or absorption of one person in another—*i. e.*, making their spirit, cause, and interest, *one !* We may define, then, in strict harmony with classic, Judaic and Johannic usage :

> BAPTIZO (the verb), 1, *to merge into*, as to "baptize into Christ," to *merge* into Christ ; 2, *to consecrate* or *transfer allegiance to*, as, "baptized unto Moses," allegiance transferred to Moses ; 3, *to induct* or *interpose*, to come into a vital union with ; as Christ says, "Abide in me and I in you ;" 4, *to renew, convert*, or *regenerate*, through this vital union of the One all pure, with one that was impure : Hence, 5, *to purify, sanctify, cleanse, remit sin, wash, hallow*, etc. We have quoted in the foregoing pages, in full measure, these words used as synonyms of *baptize*. 6, *to anoint, imbue, endow, fill with the Spirit, endue with power from on high, fill with the fulness of God*, etc., as, "Ye shall be baptized with the Holy Ghost," "Behold, I send the promise of my Father upon you," "Receive ye the Holy Ghost," etc.

These definitions are borne out by the manifest New Testament aim and usage. That a ritual purifying of the Jews is also alluded to in the New Testament, in several passages, we question not ; but this *not being Christian baptism*, does not properly come into the list of definitions.

We will also briefly define the noun *baptisma*, as used in the New Testament, prefacing the remark that *baptismos* is used in a few cases, confessedly referring to the Jewish ritual baptisms; but never, seemingly, ever commanding or commending them in a single epistle, either to Jews or Gentiles. The proper New Testament word, then, we define thus:

BAPTISMA, 1, *a saved condition*, as, "baptism doth also now save us," 1 Pet. iii. 21; 2, *a merged or intusposed condition*, as, "As many as have been baptized into Christ, have put on Christ;" 3, *a doctrine that points the way of salvation*, as "The baptism of John, was it from heaven, or of men?" 4, *the cross of suffering, or martyrdom*, as, "I have a baptism to be baptized with," etc. Christ alluding to the coming agony and ministry of the cross. 5, *a renewed or regenerated condition*, as "The baptism of repentance into the remission of sins;" 6, *a purified or endowed condition*, as "But ye are washed, but ye are sanctified, but ye are justified in the name of the Lord Jesus, and by the Spirit of our God," "But ye have an unction from the Holy One," "The Holy Ghost fell on all them that heard the word."

Dr. E. Beecher's Testimony.

To the definitions above given tends the whole work of Rev. E. Beecher, D.D., entitled "Baptizo; its Import and Modes." Dr. B. has virtually taken the word out of the category of a question of modes, or of one of mere physical relations and inquiries, by attempting to establish for the word the generic sense of *purify*, which attempt, however, partially failed, because of the inadequacy of the word *purify*, or any other one word, to meet the whole scope of the Greek usage of the term *baptizo*. He did, however, establish that sense of the word, and that in moral as well as physical relations—as palpably in the one as the other—from the Jewish usage—from the New Testament—from the Christian Fathers—and from Greek writers and lexicographers. And if the fundamental position of Dr. B., in his work, be correct thus far, that it ceases to be *a question of mode* as to immersion, or pouring, or sprinkling, and becomes one of typical or real *cleansing* or *purification*, by whatever agency or mode attained; then, so far, his interpretation harmonizes with Dr. Dale, and with our own definitions.

His inductive reasoning corroborates Dr. Dale's interpretation of *Judaic baptism*, but fails to meet fully the question of *Christian baptism*. Christian baptism, in the New Testament, includes more fully the conception of a *merging into Christ*, than of a *purifying* by Christ. And to this not only agrees the Great Commission (Matt. xxviii. 19); but Rom. vi. 3–10; Col. ii. 12, and 1 Cor. xii. 13, will accept of nothing short of the *merging into Christ*. The term *purify* is altogether inept and inadequate in expounding these passages. Dr. B. labored through many pages to show that these passages could not be forced to a ritual and modal interpretation, but found it rather awkward and tame to say, "We are buried with Christ by *purification*," whereas the other, the Christian definition—We are *merged into Christ*, secures not only the *purification*, but all else that appertains to the fulness of the Christian life, for thereby we come to *live in Christ*.

Dr. B., in a personal conversation with the writer, some years since, admitted that in the Great Commission, "*Go ye and teach all nations, baptizing them*," etc., the word, if rendered *purify*, as he would render it, may, as properly, and perhaps, more in harmony with the intent of the commission, be understood in the moral and not physical sense. He thus recognizes the fact that *the great work* of the Church is to morally *purify* the nations. And, in a letter replying to the writer's letter of inquiry, some years later (in 1868), Dr. B. cites from the earliest Greek lexicographers, definitions of *baptizo*, which, bating one ritual allusion, harmonize with Dr. Dale's and our own anti-ritual definitions in full.[*] We quote from the letter alluded to:

"The lexicons relating to *baptizo* are those of ZONARAS and PHAVORINUS. These two agree in definition, and omit altogether the idea *to immerse*, etc. They give the religious, the ecclesiastical sense of the word. They define it in Greek, which translated is as follows: '*BAPTIZO, the remission of sins by water and the Spirit. The unspeakable forgiveness of sins. The loosing of the bands (of sin) granted by the love of God towards man.*' This is equivalent to sacrificial purification. They add, what is equivalent to moral purification : '*The voluntary ordering of a new life according to the will of God. The releasing or recovery of the soul for that which is better,*' *i.e.* holiness.

"These lexicons do not give *purify* expressly as the sense of *baptizo*, but they give the equivalents of sacrificial and moral purification. BASIL *the Great* defines Baptism as Purification.

"Yours fraternally,

"EDWARD BEECHER."

Even the cursory reader of the above will not fail to see that whatever symbol of water may have been used in baptism, the lexicographers named did not gather from the teachings of the Church, or from inspiration, the conception of baptism as anything short of real spiritual regeneration.

Many of the lexicographers of a later and modern date have, evidently, been largely influenced in their definitions by the intense ritualism into which the Greek, Roman, Lutheran and English Churches have relapsed. A philological research, like those of Drs. Beecher and Dale, absolutely outweighs them all. Like scientists, they chiefly keep themselves to the external sense, and classic use of the word, admitting as an exception only the ritualistic religious sense.* It was not their work to inquire after a religious use of it, which even the carnal and lapsed cotemporary religionists had failed to discern.†

---

* Their definitions are inadequate to meet the exigences of classic usage, as Dr. Dale has abundantly shown.

† Yet they all give the religious ritual or moral sense of *purify, cleanse,* or *wash,* in their definition of the word.

Parkhurst's " Greek Dictionary " defines BAPTIZO, *to wash with water,* in token of purification from sin.

Greenfield defines it, " In New Testament, *to wash, to perform ablution, to cleanse,*" etc.

Ainsworth defines thus, " *To baptise is to wash any one in the sacred baptismal font, or to sprinkle on them the consecrated waters.*"

This definition is evidently drawn wholly from the customs of the Greek and Roman Churches of to-day.

Wahl (Robinson's translation) renders *baptizo,* first *to wash, to perform ablution, to cleanse,* etc. (over.)

Remember, all the prophets and apostles found it necessary to turn the attention of an apostate world to that spiritual, internal and *eternal* kingdom which was so dimly apprehended by the carnal mind.

Dr. J. W. Dale's Testimony.

It remains but to elicit the testimony of Dr. Dale to the correctness of the definition we have given to *Christian baptism.*

As we said, Dr. D.'s finishing volume, expressly upon that theme, is not yet issued. But we have recently had the plea-

---

Stephanus gives *baptizo* the import, first, of *immersion*, then of *cleansing* or *washing.*

Scapula, Passor, and *Suidas* give not only the above, but the more general meanings, *wetting, washing, purging, cleansing.*

Verillong says, " *Baptizo* in Greek, the same as *lavo* in Latin, properly speaking, signifies nothing except washing." Meagre, indeed, had been his inquiries on the subject.

Prof. Stuart was somewhat more nearly correct, when he says, " *In the Bible,* it signifies *to wash in the literal sense.*" This is true of Mark vii., and a few other cases.

Trelcatius.—" *Baptism,* according to the etymology of it, signifies any kind of ablution or cleansing."

Doederline.—" The power of the word *baptizo* is expressed in *washing,* or *performing ablution.*"

Bonaventura.—" *Baptizo,* in Greek, signifies as much as *lavo* in Latin, *i. e.,* to *wash.*"

Maldonat.—" With the Greeks *baptizo* signifies *to dip, to wash, to wash oft.*"

The above lexicographers seem to give the *early* Greek secular sense, and the *modern* religious use of the word. As to the dipping, *Attersol* says, " Dipping into water is not necessary to the being of the sacrament."

Dr. John P. Campbell says, " *Christian baptism is a washing with water,* in the name of the Father, Son, and Holy Ghost."

It cannot be a moral or spiritual cleaning, then ? Note the unseemly dogmatism of lexicographers and bewildered Scripture expounders.

Dr. Wall.—" *Baptizo,* in Scripture, signifies *to wash* in general." And adds, " The sense of a Scripture word is not to be taken from the use of it in secular authors, but from the use of it in the Scriptures."

Very well, let the research be thorough and unbiassed, and the result be at least self-consistent.

sure of scanning an epitome of the work, in the form of a
lecture, delivered before the Philadelphia Synod, which, by a
vote of the Synod, was specially prepared for the press and is
now printed.   The extract we make is from the closing paragraphs of the lecture, which, as every reader will see, not only
fully sustains our definitions, but strengthens and confirms them,
as we humbly claim, beyond the reach of cavil or hurtful
criticism.   Dr. Dale's philological and logical processes by
which he has reached this conclusion respecting the nature of
Christian baptism, and the exegesis of Matt. xxviii. 19, have
received the most cordial and unmeasured approval of nearly
every religious journal in the land (save those of the Baptists),
and of all the prominent theological professors (save those
excepted above), and, perhaps, of not less than a hundred of
the doctors of divinity, pastors of the most prominent churches
in the land.*   The extract is exegetical of Matt. xxviii. 19.

---

* Specimen of the notices and commendations of Dr. Dale's volumes on the
Baptismal question.

"A most masterly philological discussion."
Prof. J. C. Moffat, of Princeton Theological Seminary.

"The ablest treatise on the subject in the English language."
Central Presbyterian.

"Logic of Chillingworth, wit of Pascal."—*N. Y. Evangelist.*

"It comes in like Blucher at Waterloo."—*Congregational Review.*

"Nothing we know of in our language to compare with it."—*W. Ch. Ad.*

"It is not simply a new *book*, it is a new *work*, and one of extraordinary
ability and originality. Proof is carried to the point of actual demonstration."
Western Presbyterian.

"It embodies an immense amount of research and learning."—*Bishop Lee.*

Of "Judaic Baptism," hear scholars :

"Thorough,—Candid,—Conclusive."—*Prof. Packard*, Ep.

"Thorough—Exhaustive—Convincing."—*Prof. Lindsey*, Meth. Ep.

"Learned—Thorough—Decisive."—*Prof. Pond*, Congl.

Of "Johannic Baptism," hear scholars :

"Happy and successful vindication of the truth."
Prof. J. T. Cooper, Presb.

"Will meet with the cordial approbation of the whole Christian Church."
Prof. W. S. Plummer, Presb.

"The author's investigations are singularly far-reaching, exhaustive, and
satisfactory."—*Prof. Schmucker*, D.D., Lutheran. (over.)

Exegesis (*in brief*) of Matt. XXVIII. 19.

"Observe that the command is to make disciples of all nations. . . . . But discipleship under any teacher is represented as baptism into that teacher. Therefore, Paul asks of those who would be his disciples, 'Were ye baptized into Paul?' The Jews said, 'Ye are Christ's disciples, but we are Moses' disciples,' and they refused to be baptized into Christ while they and their fathers were baptized into Moses.

"There is, then, no rational ground to doubt, 1. That the nations were to be made disciples of Christ.

"2. That the discipleship involved baptism into Christ.

"3. That, inasmuch as discipleship of Christ requires repentance and faith, this baptism into Christ is such baptism as is effected by the Holy Ghost.

"4. That if any ritual baptism be associated with the real baptism, then the rite can only symbolize the reality. There is an *absolute necessity* for this baptism of the nations into Christ as antecedent and preparative, and also *causative* of the ulterior baptism into the Father, Son, and Holy Ghost. The Lord Jesus Christ teaches in the most absolute and universal terms, 'No man cometh to the Father but by me.' It is utterly subversive of all the teachings of Scripture to hold that a sinner can be baptized into the Father, Son, and Holy Ghost, without first being baptized into a crucified Redeemer. The Lord Jesus says, 'I am the way; no man cometh to the Father but by me.' Where remission of sins is, we have 'boldness to enter into the holiest by the blood of Jesus, by a new

---

"This appeal to usage must settle the controversy, if anything can."

Prof. Packard.

"You are doing a great and good work, both for Scripture exegesis, and for settling on irrefragable grounds, *the meaning* of this long discussed word."

Prof. B. M. Smith, Hampden Sydney College.

"You have invested this discussion with fresh interest and increased light. *Baptisma* has not, in my judgment, *any physical usage in the New Testament.*"

Prof. J. W. Beecher, Auburn Theol. Sem.

"I have marvelled at your patience in stopping against the 'immersionists' every actual, probable, possible, *imaginary, improbable, and impossible* hole, and when you had proved a point ninety-nine times, still proving it the hundreth, lest your work be not quite complete."— — a Professor of Greek.

"Ought to secure you the gratitude of the whole Christian Church."

Pres. W. Lord, D.D.

and living way; having our hearts sprinkled from an evil conscience, and our bodies washed with pure water.' Unto God in his holiness the sinner in his pollution cannot come. Unto God, in Christ, the 'Lamb of God that taketh away the sin of the world,' the sinner, in all his guilt, *may come*, MUST COME! When the sinner has come to Christ—has been 'baptized into Him'—'baptized into the remission of sins'—has been invested with His 'fulfilment of all righteousness,' then, and only then, is he prepared to be led by the Mediator between God and man, along the 'new and living way,' by which he can be received by God in His holiness, and be qualified for the ultimate baptism which is forever, even forever and ever, '*into the name of the Father, Son, and Holy Ghost.*'

"Thus this wondrous baptism, which is the consummation of the work of redemption, is indissolubly joined with *the baptism of the cross*, and could have no existence without it.

"Our general conclusion is, that all baptisms of the Bible, Old Testament and New Testament, originate in, and are only to be expounded by the baptism of the cross,—the Lamb of God, spotless under temptation, suffering, drinking the cup, even unto death, to purify our souls and unite us to God."

We will but add the

TESTIMONY OF WM. J. ALLINSON,

for many years editor of the *Friend's Review*, Phila., Pa. He reasons thus:

"This command (Matt. xxviii. 19) was very extensive, comprehending *all nations*; and all nations, save the Jews, were heathen, not having a true knowledge of Father, Son, or Spirit, of course, not of Triune Deity as expressed by this comprehensive phrase. Considering the universality of the command, which included not merely the countries of Asia and Europe, but our undiscovered continent, and the shivering denizens of the frozen north and south, and those Central African regions which civilized foot *even yet* has never pressed; considering this, and the wide range of meaning of the word *baptize*, is it a forced or unfair construction to infer that they were to teach all nations, *introducing* or *initiating* them, into a true knowledge of the true God? An impossible command would not be given. A nation, as such, could not, *in the ceremonial sense of the word*, be baptized. It was not possible for those to whom the command was given, thus to reach and to dip or sprinkle each individual of each nation ; but where man had penetrated before, some disciple, led by the Spirit, might find his way, *commissioned to sow seminal truth,* and so to teach as to introduce, to initiate the knowledge of the living God, of his Son, of the Holy Spirit, and of *the plan of salvation.* . . It is popularly taken for granted that this word 'baptizing' is to be received in a ceremonial sense." [Our Lord taught of moral, not physical things.] "Thus He calls himself 'the vine,' 'the door,' 'the bread of life,' etc.; and oft when He speaks of *water* explains that He is not to be understood literally. When His words were too literally taken He shows His sense of the dulness of His hearers: 'How is it that ye do not understand?' In the vague, indefinite literal sense of the word *baptize,* it may mean wash, purge, sprinkle, pour, immerse, stain, ornament, apply, overwhelm, etc., but in a theologic sense, it were rank heresy to deny the proposition that there is but 'ONE BAPTISM.' What that is, and what it is not, we find clearly established ; and in the text under review, there is no naming of water. It were begging the question to place it there (if it were there I should claim for it its theologic sense) ; no command to use any outward rite or type ; but the promise of the true Baptizer immediately follows : 'Lo, I am with you always,' etc.*

---

* Nor is there in the New Testament a case of the use of the word *baptizo,* or *baptize,* with *eis* following, and this joined with *water* as the terminal element. Whether water be assumed to be an instrumental agent, or no, in any case, *it is not that whereinto any one is said to be baptized.* Take every case (every differing one) in the New Testament, and this will at once be seen :

Matt. iii. 11, "Baptize (*eis*) into repentance."

Mark i. 4, "Baptize (*eis*) into remission of sins." Also, Acts ii. 38.

Matt. xxviii. 19, "Baptizing (*eis*) into the name of the Father."

Acts viii. 16, "Baptized (*eis*) into the name of the Lord Jesus."

Acts xix. 3, "Baptized, then, (*eis*) into what?"

Acts xix. 3, "Baptized (*eis*) into John's baptism."

Rom. vi. 3, "Baptized (*eis*) into Jesus Christ."

Rom. vi. 3, "Baptized (*eis*) into his death." Also, Rom. vi. 4.

1 Cor. i. 13, "Baptized (*eis*) into the name of Paul."

1 Cor. i. 16, "Baptized (*eis*) into my own name."

1 Cor. x. 2, "Baptized (*eis*) into Moses."

1 Cor. xii. 13, "Baptized (*eis*) into one body."

Gal. iii. 27, "Baptized (*eis*) into Christ."

Mark, no Greek passage in the New Testament, or elsewhere, can be found which reads :

"*Baptizo eis*" (into) water.

"*Baptizo eis*" (into) blood.

"Then they are told to 'teach, baptizing' (not *teach and baptize* as two distinct things), which must mean, preaching only under the Divine influence, the Holy Spirit, the One Baptism shall accompany the word preached, carrying it to the souls of the hearers with convicting power, 'purifying their hearts by faith.' Teaching under holy inspiration was to be *the Spirit's act through an instrument*, and the 'One Baptism,' the Spirit's act direct, was to accompany, and unto God should be all the glory. . . . Peter, an apostle, was, by simultaneous revelation to himself and to Cornelius, required to go to a company of *Gentiles* and teach baptizingly. The words of his teaching were given to him by the Spirit, and the baptism was given to them by the Spirit. To confirm the fact so that there could be no gainsaying, it was *visibly conferred*. Peter told the Church the astonishing story : 'As I began to speak the Holy Ghost fell on them, as on us at the beginning. Then I remembered the word of the Lord, how that he said, John, indeed, baptized with water, but ye shall be baptized with the Holy Ghost.' What matters it to us, that Peter, not yet fully enfranchised from the old law, began to think of applying to them another baptism, which, in the efficacious sense, was no baptism at all ? The converts were Gentiles—converted to a new religion ; the Jews habitually marked every such step by a symbolic washing." [It was much that Peter could overlook their non-circumcision even ;] yet "placing them on a par with Jewish converts, he cried out, 'Who can forbid water, that these should not be purified (baptized), seeing they have received the Holy Ghost as well as we ? '"

A *Christian* Gentile might well ask, what is this that Peter now proposes to add to the purifying and anointing they had already received by the mighty effusion of the Holy Ghost ? But we may not continue this phase of the argument.

"*Baptizo eis*" (into) wine.

"*Baptizo eis*" (into) fire.

"*Baptizo eis*" (into) tears.

"*Baptizo eis*" (into) martyrdom, etc.

Yet baptism by means of all these is oft found in Greek writers.

The above are all the cases where *baptizo* is followed by *eis*, unless it be a repetend of these ; and it is perfectly evident that the *ritual* makes no appearance in most of them, either as to a human administrator, or a physical element ; thus demonstrating that the term *baptizo* itself *in no case* determines either the agent or element employed.

THE TERM BAPTIZE COMPREHENSIVE IN CHRIST'S DAY.

He is a poor student of the Bible who has not come to see that in Christ's day the word *baptize* had attained a prolific sense, branching out as we have defined it (and as Dr. Dale its classic use; see pp. 71–81); and that the agency is no more to be assumed to be water than it is to be assumed to be blood, or fire, or tears, or ashes, or the Holy Spirit. It would be more congruous with the New Testament aim to assume both *water* and *baptism* to be used in a *spiritual sense*, than the opposite—yet the immediate theme and context must determine even this—largely judged, however, by the nature of things. Alexander Campbell is right when he says that *baptize* in the New Testament is synonymous with *convert, regenerate, renew, sanctify, disciple*, etc. But it must ever be understood in the moral, and not ceremonial sense, when thus synonymous. The *baptized* were those who had transferred their allegiance from Satan to Christ, and were received into the brotherhood of the pure, the sanctified. Material water, whether used or not, was wholly neutral in the matter. A ritual administrator, or a priestly interference had nothing to do with it; but preaching Christ "with the Holy Ghost sent down from heaven," had all to do with it.

He is, moreover, a poor student of the New Testament who does not see that therein the whole ritual, or ceremonial law of the Old Testament is set aside as cumbersome, and as a thing of nought to the Christian Church. And if any writer will point us to where a ritual law is re-established in the same Testament, marking its form and outline, to the intent that it may be practically apprehended as *thus far from God and no farther*, and just to what extent (when, where and how) the will of Christ, the Great Head of the *Christian Church*, would have us interested in it, we will meekly and thankfully sit at his feet and learn. But the New Testament law, to meet our conception of law, must not continue to leave the subject, both in the main point, and in its adjuncts, in a labyrinth of conjecture.*

How writers stumble—Rev. E. B. Turner criticised.

As a specimen of how men reason well and reason ill on the subject of rituals, or a ritual law, so that like the snake, you cannot tell whether he is "going out or coming back," I will quote a few sentences from a discourse of Rev. E. B. Turner, formerly pastor of Congregational Church, Morris, Ills. The theme he entitles, "*Forms not Religion*." He makes out his case well, but for the blundering and inconsistent admissions silted in far too oft. He affirms correctly that the Jewish converts to Christ were ever disposed to manifest an unyielding and bigoted spirit toward the Gentiles, and that

---

* Ritualists say respecting baptism, "God commands us to perform *an act*, a well-defined act, *i. e.*, to *dip* or *plunge*." Dale asks, "which, dip, or plunge?" To plunge leaves the body immersed—to dip, the opposite—removing the body again from the element into which it was plunged. But emersion is not in the meaning of the word *plunge* or *merse*, as Dr. Conant admits. Now, is that *the* act that God commands to be performed upon all believers?—sad doom, as the reward of the simplicity of faith!—or, simply to have the convert dipped into water, or sprinkled with water,—is that the highest thought (or thought at all) of the "High and Lofty One that inhabiteth eternity?" If baptism ever symbolized purification, or was simply the public act of consecration or profession of faith, which is it that God seeks, the *real* purification, or symbol? The *real* consecration or the outward expression of it in an act, that the hypocrite can perform as well as the Christian? Is not the baptism *of tears*, i. e., *of repentance*, to be succeeded by the baptism of the Holy Spirit and fire, sufficient? The baptism of tears (repentance) *purifies*. The baptism of the Holy Spirit *really purifies*. The baptism of fire (suffering and martyrdom) purifies. "Resisting unto blood against sin," *i. e.*, *baptism of blood*, purifies. Water baptism, at best, is the weakest and least efficacious of any of them, and utterly worthless without the others as adjuncts. Why need the ceremony and the substance both? It is like a man carrying a candle, that shone well at night, along with him into the noonday sunlight. Does God ask you to keep the candle after the sunlight has come? Then the Romish farce of burning candles by day may please Him? God told Moses to purify the priests of Israel—a *definite act*— and to build a tabernacle in the wilderness for them—every act *definite*; is that the tabernacle, and are those the purifications (baptisms) of to-day? "Tell me ye that desire to be under the law, do ye not hear the law?" Gal. iv. 21.

mainly with respect to their observance of the Mosaic rites. And he adds (p 3):

" This tendency to lay great stress on the outward forms of religion . . . has existed in every age. The ranks of Christ's followers have in every age been rent asunder by strife and contention, and her strength greatly weakened by it. . . . Under the Jewish dispensation, religion was embodied in forms. . . . Though they were but types and shadows, they had all the importance of things essential and real until the great antitype should appear."

This is altogether *too legal* a view of the case. But mark what follows:

" Since these have had their fulfilment in the coming of the Messiah, they have lost their significance and importance. All that remains of them are the essential truths which they shadow forth. No part of the Mosaic religion was designed to be perpetuated but its principles. Her forms and ceremonies having now become of no importance, have become obsolete. . . . The entire absence of any prescribed forms in the New Testament indicate it. If any particular external modes of exemplifying and perpetuating the doctrines of the Gospel had been designed, would they not have been the subject of express instruction? Of what use are principles, which cannot, through defect of the means of applying them, be made of practical utility? And if any fixed forms were i tnded to be established, and to be made perpetual in all countries and ages, is it probable that we should be left without any written formularies on the subject? Who will undertake to show that there are any such formularies in the New Testament? Who will say that they are so clearly defined that 'he who runneth may read?'"

Thus far this writer reasons well. But read the next sentence:

" The various duties of religion are those (in the New Testament) enjoined, and *certain ordinances* are made obligatory, but where are the prescribed forms of worship?"

Now, does not this writer see that the everlasting incertitude, the bone of contention, the apple of discord, is thrown into this one short sentence? What has been the bone of contention in all ages but ORDINANCES? And if ordinances are "made obligatory," then let this writer give the form and outline, lest all he says about indefiniteness come against himself. Moses was *very* specific in outlining " ordinances." He adds:

" So far as He (Christ) observed any rites or ceremonies, He conformed to the customs of the country, without even suggesting any alterations or setting up any peculiar forms of his own."

Very good! Then He took the ceremonial law as He found it—as we have before said; and made no changes in it, and said nothing about establishing any other. The writer still continues:

" We find no prescribed forms in the teachings of the Apostles and the practice of the primitive churches. . . . Churches were formed in places remote from one another, and composed of individuals of diverse habits and education. Converts were received into the Church, wherever and whenever they gave evidence of a change of heart."

All good: but see the ritualism that is still in the mind of this writer crop out; read on:

" The *rites of religion* were administered in various places and evidently in various ways" [and why not add: or left unadministered?]. " They were baptized in the house and out of it, by the river side and the running brook, where there was ' much water' and where ' there was *no* water.' " [Sure !]

He adds:

" Let any one undertake to find the prescribed mode in so many words, and he will soon be convinced that all this hue and cry about forms has not the slightest encouragement in the Bible."

But, my brother, if God commands the forms, and makes them "obligatory," then the "hue and cry" has a large amount of "encouragement in the Bible," and the question as to the *mode* is ever made a very important one. We have not in this way got rid of the strifes about the " law" (ritual law), in the least degree. We have not moved one step toward it. What one says is baptism, for example, or the eucharist, another says is not. Thus the question is forever to be mooted.

See the writer's inconsistency in the following sentence by itself:

" It (the Bible) requires every individual to repent and be baptized, but prescribes no form."

Is not the baptism the writer alludes to here, a " form?"

8

He does not allude to a moral or spiritual baptism; albeit, we have no doubt Christ does, in the passages whence this writer infers his duty of observing the *form*.

Such concessions to a ritual, Judaic law, weaken the whole fabric of this discourse. It puts the convert to Christ, in every instance, on the inquiry as to how that *requirement* is to be met. It must be so, if he would intelligently obey. Hence the whole question as between Baptists and Pedo-Baptists, and other ritualists, comes up continually; and no answer can be given unless you go back to the old Jewish law, and assume it to be still in force. In concluding our strictures upon this writer, we only ask why did he not apply his own rule, when he says, on p. 14:

"Whatever principles you find revealed in the Scriptures, adhere to with all firmness; do not consider the *practices of Christ or his disciples as necessarily of binding force, unless they are accompanied with an express precept*. When you find a 'thus saith the Lord' for any particular mode, then accept it, and submit to it with all honesty. But, where God has not spoken, do not do injustice to your own minds, nor degrade the cause of our holy religion by striving to make yourselves wiser than the Scriptures. While you have your own opinion as to the particular forms, etc., be willing that others should enjoy theirs. Let no contracted or bigoted spirit keep your sympathies and affections within the pale of a single sect: adopt no theories that will prevent others from the cordial reciprocation of your Christian affection. Remember that the kingkom of God is not meat and drink, but righteousness and peace, and joy in the Holy Ghost."

Very well put, brother! So Paul exhorted both the Jewish and Gentile converts when he tore in pieces and set aside the Jewish ritual law.

New Testament Record merely historical.

We are now prepared to continue our exhibit of the manner the subject of baptism has been introduced into the New Testament. We discover it to be, as before stated, only historically, without any pre-existing New Testament law on the subject; which also shows that if afterward it were erected into the form of law it would be but an *ex post facto* law—as our lawyers term it—in John's case, and therefore would not, by any means, prove a special divine appointment of this rite for the New Testament.

To prove that John had a divine command to baptize (save such as the Jewish priests all had), is not possible ; to prove a New Testament law on the subject, that law must have been revealed to men. When Jesus asks the Jews, therefore, as to the baptism of John, whether it were "from heaven or of men?" he only refers to his *ministration*, or his heralding of the Messiah, and pre-announcement of Christ's immediate coming and work.

John came as a *purifier* (reformer) to herald the coming of Christ, to prepare the hearts of multitudes to receive Christ by turning their attention to Him, and consecrating them to Him—using only the forms of purifying the priesthood were then using.

John was a priest of the law, and the son of a priest. His father Zechariah was a priest of the "course of Abia" (Luke i. 5), and John was therefore executing his office in due order. True he was a great reformer, and preacher of repentance with unusual unction and demonstration of the Spirit, as Samuel and Elijah, and Jeremiah and Malachi had been before him. But John, and even Christ, whose work succeeded John's in point of time, mainly, were both "made under the law," as Paul says in Gal. iv. 4. True, Christ tells us that the "law and the prophets were until John," since then "the kingdom of God is preached, and every man presseth into it." But Daniel and Zechariah preached also the kingdom of God ; while John preached it only as "at hand," even as did Christ in all his labors before His crucifixion. The "vail of the temple" and the vail of the law were rent asunder in Christ's crucifixion ; so theologians generally tell us : (see 2 Cor. iii.). In every record or notice of John's ministry, therefore, we may expect to find the term *baptism* or *baptize* used in the sense of *purify;* when the allusion is made to the symbolic baptism of water, just as the antitype baptism of the Spirit really purifies.

So, by the context, we shall see the word will bear to be rendered in each case.

Let us, then, quote the New Testament record giving the word the rendering that the context and the subject matter in each case seem to require, yet transcribing *baptize* untranslated where no word in English will render it. (Matt. iii.)

"In those days came John the *Purifier*, preaching in the wilderness of Judea, and saying : Repent ye, for the kingdom of heaven is at hand . . . Prepare ye the way of the Lord, make his paths straight . . . Then went out to him Jerusalem and all Judea, and all the region round about Jordan, and were *purified* of him in Jordan, *confessing their sins*. But, when he saw many of the Pharisees and Sadducees come to his *purifying*, he said unto them, O generation of vipers, who hath warned you to flee from the wrath to come ? Bring forth, therefore, fruits meet for repentance !" [*i. e.* put away your sins ; for this baptism of water but symbolizes that *purifying* which you need.] "I, indeed, *purify* you with water unto repentance ; but he that cometh after me is mightier than I, whose shoes I am not worthy (not pure enough) to bear. He shall *purify* you with the Holy Ghost and with fire." [The Holy Spirit and fire are mighty purifying elements.] "Whose fan is in his hand, and he will throughly *purge* his floor, etc." [Thus the idea of purifying by various terms is kept up by the context.] "Then cometh Jesus from Galilee to Jordan unto John to be *purified* of him. But John forbade him, saying ; I have need to be *purified* by thee, and comest thou to me ? And Jesus answering said unto him : Suffer it to be so now, for thus it becometh us to fulfil all righteousness. Then he suffered him. And Jesus, when he was *purified*, went up straightway out of the water. . . . And lo, a voice from heaven, saying : This is my beloved Son, in whom I am well pleased."

Thus the *purifying* and consecration of Christ to the priesthood by John, gave Christ the legal authority He needed to be acceptable to the Jews ; and Christ now, also, received heaven's signet, by the sealing power of the Holy Spirit being shed freely and "without measure" upon Him.

The above record is rehearsed in the other evangelists more or less fully of course, with no differing sense of the term *baptism* or its cognates. It may simply be said that, in each case, referring to John or his work, where "*John the Baptist*" is found, it should be rendered *John the Purifier ;* and the *baptism* of John should be the *purifying or preaching* of John.

In Matt. xx. 22, Mark x. 38, 39, and Luke xii. 50, Jesus

uses the term *baptism* evidently more fully in the sacrificial sense (as Dr. Beecher deems it), *to suffer* or to be whelmed with suffering, alluding to the coming agony of the cross, and the climax of the work of atonement. Christ replies to the woman that asked great honor for her sons: "Are ye able to drink of the cup that I shall drink of, and to be baptized with the baptism that I am baptized with?" We may render the answer, (and of course the same word in the question, also) thus: "Ye shall drink indeed of my cup, and be *whelmed* with the anguish that I am *whelmed* with." Jesus in both question and reply assuredly alludes to that hour when His soul should be overwhelmed with anguish, as in Gethsemane; and also when on the cross, His body should be crushed to death with the inward anguish of the soul, consequent on the hidings of His Father's face, and the tortures men were allowed to inflict upon His body. No moral effect (as purifying) was needed in His case, but it was endured for others' purifying; and hence, the sacrificial idea is conveyed, and Christ longs to endure it for others' sakes.

The earliest use of the Greek word *baptizo* did convey the sense of whelm, merge, inundate, or submerge under some overpowering influence that should end one condition, estate or interest by merging it into another; hence, as we shall see, comes the highest *Christian* sense of the phrase to *baptize into Christ*. But as moral purification is the result of this, and also is needful to stand in God's favor; and, as the external and internal purifying harmonize in the generic idea, Jewish writers call the *Jewish rites* of cleansing by the symbolic term *purify*. These Jewish purifications were seldom or never by whelming or immersing the object to be purified in water, but by some form of washing, sprinkling or ablution. The Greeks, in their religious rites, did more oft immerse.*

---

* Yet Socrates, the Greek philosopher, 400 years before Christ, speaks of "a celebrated font, out of which water is poured from above on the baptized person."

If, then, you make immersion, as a religious rite, antedate Christ's day, you make it of heathen origin; and Dr. Robinson, the Baptist historian, says that all the ancient nations baptized and had baptisteries for that purpose. No Christian of our day will contend for the transfer of the whole Mosaic ritual to the Christian dispensation; yet all Pedo-Baptists are practising their baptisms after the model of certain parts of the Mosaic ritual; and the Baptist churches, after a model that the Mosaic ritual will allow, yet really of Gentile origin. When we find nearly or quite all those that practised immersion in the third century after Christ using almost invariably trine immersion, and almost invariably baptizing the candidates naked, we see that much of their baptismal ceremony must have come from the heathen nations. Nor did Jesus adopt and institute by law the heathen baptisms—or the Jewish even.

To be followers of Christ, is not, as we have seen, to mimic any bodily act of His, or any ceremonial of that age—such a conceit is infinitely unworthy and degrading—but it is to love as He loved, and to possess the spirit of God as He possessed it. John the symbolic *purifier* makes a clear distinction between his own *symbolic* and Christ's *real* purification.

Are we to suppose that Christ annulled this distinction, and re-entailed on His Church John's baptism; or one that, in the nature of things, could be no better—being also a ritual, but only called by another name? Christ gave us many hints that He would set aside the Jewish economy, rituals and all; and Paul abundantly teaches us that He did. (See Letters to Pres. Finney, Letter viii.)

Paul taught in direct precept, on this subject, what Christ only taught in principle. Christ's words mean much when He says (John xvi. 12): "I have many things to say unto you, but ye cannot bear them now." After His crucifixion and ascension, enlightened by the Holy Spirit, they could much better understand the spiritual things of the New Covenant (even its baptism) than they could while Christ was with them in body, and under the Jewish law. But He gave them clear hints that Judaism would pass away when He says:

"The hour is coming, when neither in this mountain (of Samaria), nor at Jerusalem shall men worship the Father, . . . but the hour cometh when the true worshippers shall worship the Father in Spirit and in truth; for the Father seeketh such to worship Him."—John iv. 21–23.

So also when He says:

"The flesh profiteth nothing, the words that I speak unto you, they are spirit and they are life."

In such passages Jesus teaches the spiritual *vs.* the ritual nature of the New Dispensation.

Jesus never practised ritual baptism, *i. e.*, never administered it, as Moses did and, Dr. D. says, never used the word *baptize* or *baptism* in a ritual sense. Christ was Priest of the "true tabernacle," Paul says in Hebrews ix., and the Mediator of the New Covenant "written in the heart," not in types and symbols, nor on tables of stone. His baptism is doubtless in harmony with His priesthood, as was that of Moses. The word *baptizo* itself, according to Dr. E. Beecher and A. Campbell, being synonymous (see "Synonyms of Baptism") with *purify, sanctify, regenerate, convert, cleanse, renew*, etc, we may more fitly give the moral sense to the word as used by our Saviour, than the ritual one.

How Christ used the term Baptism.

Christ alludes to John's baptism (referring to his doctrine), in some instances, and to John himself as a great prophet, but pronounces the "least in the kingdom of heaven greater than he;" and the first mention He makes of baptism as applying to himself, He uses it in the non-physical sense: "I have a baptism to be baptized with," etc., alluding to His approaching sufferings.

Then, when He comes to give the Great Commission, shall we consider the High Priest of the New Covenant as giving it in words that establish a ritual law, or rather in words that are in full harmony with the nature of that New Covenant?

Shall we understand Jesus as saying, Mark xvi. 16: "He that believeth and is (symbolically) *purified*, shall be saved:" or, "He that believeth and *is purified*, shall be saved?" We, without hesitation, cleave to the latter sense. So in Matt. xxviii. 19—why not read it: "Go and teach all nations, *purifying* them in the name" (or *inducting* them into the name) "of the Father, Son and Holy Ghost?" * This makes the baptism required harmonize with the New Dispensation, and the real work of the Church. Also, with the Commission as recorded by the other evangelists. Luke has it (Luke xxiv. 47): "That repentance and *remission of sins* should be preached in his name among all nations, beginning at Jerusalem."

John has it (John xx. 23): "Whose soever sins ye remit they are remitted unto them, and whose soever sins ye retain they are retained." And this last He said, after He had breathed on them, and said, "Receive ye the Holy Ghost."

This gives us the clue to the use of the term *baptism*, so oft found in connection with "remission of sins," or "washing away sins," in other parts of the New Testament. The fulness of meaning of the terms *remission*, *baptism*, etc., in the Commission, precludes the idea of the institution of a ritual law in the case; they are certainly susceptible of the sense we give them: this forbids their being used as proof texts by the ritualists. Paul surely understood the Commission simply in the moral, and not ritual sense, when he says, "Christ sent me not to *baptize*" (alluding to the Judaizing ritualists), "but to preach the Gospel." To abbreviate this New Testament record of the use and meaning of the term *baptism* and its cognates, we will merely cite passages, rendering the word, in each case, in accordance with our previous definitions, as seems in each particular case to be demanded. Of the one hundred times and more that the term *baptism* with its cognates is found in the

---

* *Regenerate* into the name of the Father, etc., would be still more forcible. The Son is *generated* into the name of His Father: we are regenerated into the name of God the Father, etc., and thus become "sons of God," "brethren" to Christ, and in fellowship with the Holy Spirit.

New Testament, over fifty times it refers specifically to John's baptism by name, and the import of this has been elicited. Of the remaining instances of its use, more than one half of them permit the moral or spiritual sense only; and in other cases, the moral sense is at least allowable, as by the use of *baptisma* the moral sense is indicated. Of course, in all the instances where the baptism of the Holy Ghost is alluded to, it must have the moral and not the ritual sense; and the New Testament usage permits the moral sense in many other cases, where ritualists have failed to so apprehend it. Let the reader, then, in harmony with the New Dispensation, give the underlying moral sense when he can, and the ritual only when he must, to the following passages found in the Acts and Epistles.

THE TERM "BAPTIZO" EXEGETICALLY TRANSLATED.

Acts i. 5. "John truly *purified* with water, but ye shall be *purified* with the Holy Ghost."

Acts ii. 38. "Repent and be baptized (or *converted*, see Acts iii. 19) every one of you, (*epi*) upon (the authority of) the name of Jesus Christ, (*eis*) into the remission of sins, and ye shall receive the gift of the Holy Ghost."

Acts ii. 41. "Then they that gladly received the word were *sealed*."

Acts viii. 12. "When they believed Philip preaching the things concerning the kingdom of God, and the name of Jesus Christ, they were *discipled*, both men and women."

Acts ix. 18. "And (Saul) arose and was *purified* (or *cleansed*)."

Acts x. 47, 48. "Who can forbid water, that these should not be *purified?* . . . And he commanded them to *be purified* in the name of the Lord."

Act xvi. 15. "When she (Lydia) *was purified* and her household." . . . . 33d verse. "And (the jailer) was *purified*, he and all his, straightway."

Acts xviii. 8. "Many Corinthians hearing, believed and *were purified*."

Acts xix. 2-5. "He said unto them: Have ye received the Holy Ghost since ye believed?" "Unto what then were ye *converted?* And they said, Unto John's *baptism*. Then said Paul, John verily *purified* with the *purification* of repentance," etc. 5th verse: "When they heard this, they *were baptized into* (*consecrated to*) the name (or cause) of the Lord Jesus."

Acts xxii. 16. "Arise and be *purified*, and wash away thy sins."

Thus far (in Acts) we appear to have but the Judaizing record; save the passage, Acts ii. 38; xix. 2-5, these all probably refer to the persistent Judaizing custom of the apostles, Ananias etc. They all, being Jews, kept up the Jewish baptisms and feasts, to this last date, except Paul when among the Gentiles. Paul (Gal. ii.) rebuked Peter (not for conforming to Jewish customs among the Jews—he did himself, and got into trouble by it), but he rebukes Peter, Barnabas, etc., for compelling the Gentiles to turn Jews. And in the Epistles, Paul and all the other apostles seem to have laid aside their Judaism, and thrown off the yoke of ritual bondage without restriction or disguise. *Baptism* now becomes internal, or spiritual, else it is repressed.

The Epistles all Anti-ritualistic.

Rom. vi. 3. "Know ye not that so many of us as were *merged* into Jesus Christ were *merged* into his death." 4th verse. "Thererefore we are buried with him by (the) *merging* into his death."

1 Cor. i. 13. "Were ye *discipled* into the name of Paul?" 14th and 16th verses. "I thank God that I (ritually) *purified* none of you save Crispus and Gaius and the household of Stephanus; besides I know not whether I *purified* any other." 17th verse. "For Christ sent me not to *purify* (ritually), but to preach the Gospel."

1 Cor. x. 1, 2. "All our fathers were under the cloud, and all passed through the sea; And were all CONSECRATED to Moses in the cloud and in the sea."

1 Cor. xii. 13. "For by one Spirit are we all *merged* into one body."

1 Cor. xv. 29. "Else what shall they do who are *consecrated* for the dead, if the dead rise not? why are they then *consecrated* for the dead?"

Gal. iii. 26, 27. "For ye are all the children of God by faith in Christ Jesus: For as many of you as have been *inducted* into Christ have put on Christ."

Eph. iv. 4, 5. "There is one body and one spirit, even as ye are called in one hope of your calling; one Lord, one faith, one *anointing*" (or *one sanctification*).

Col. ii. 12. "Buried with him (Christ) by *induction*" (or union with Christ), "wherein also ye are risen with him through the faith of the operation of God."

Heb. vi. 1, 2. "Therefore leaving the principles of the doctrine of Christ, let us go on unto perfection, not laying again the foundation of repentance from dead works, and of faith toward God, of the *doctrine of cleansings*," etc.

1 Pet. iii. 21. "The like *antitype* whereunto *purifying* doth also now save us, not the putting away of the filth of the flesh, but the answer of a good conscience toward God."

Thus it will be seen that unless we shrink from giving to

Christ's words in the Great Commission the very sense which that commission requires, viz., the purifying of the nations, and turning man from sin to righteousness, and shrink from making Peter's two forms of address to the listening Jews, "Repent and be *baptized*," and "repent and be *converted*," as found in Acts ii. 38, and iii. 19, synonymous, we have no semblance of a command for any baptismal rite in the New Testament. And let it be noted, that, having passed the book of Acts in the New Testament canon, we do not find a single text favoring ritual baptism, but an invariable disapproval; at the same time, ever bringing into view that true spiritual baptism by which we are inducted into and united with Christ and with all his people. Neither John, nor James, nor Jude, in their epistles, uses the term *baptizo* at all, and Paul and Peter use it in any form than either commanding or commending a ritual baptism. Hear Paul: "God sent me not to baptize, but to preach the Gospel." "One Lord, one faith, one baptism." "Leaving, therefore, . . . the doctrine of baptisms." "Divers baptisms imposed until the time of reformation."

And Peter: "Baptism doth also now save us, not the putting away of the filth of the flesh," etc. Peter had come to comprehend the forerunner John's meaning, and the superior excellence of the internal above the external baptism, when he said, "I have need to be baptized of thee, and comest thou to me?" And what Christ meant when he said, "He that believeth and is baptized shall be saved." And what Paul meant when he said, "By one Spirit are we all baptized into one body." We have cited nearly or quite all the allusions to water-baptism found in the epistles, and they certainly are not very loyal to the Great Commission, if that commission refers to a ritual baptism.

Then note the continual pointing from the letter (the form) to the spirit, *i. e.*, that which is spiritual in all the New Testament, marking as now only to be spiritual that which had been in the "letter," the form, the ritual before. "That is not circumcision which is outward in the flesh. Circumcision is

that of the heart, in the spirit, and not in the letter; whose
praise is not of men, but of God." "Circumcision availeth
nothing, nor uncircumcision, but" [What? the waters of baptism? Nay!] "a new creature." "We are the circumcision
who worship God in the spirit, and *have no confidence in the
flesh.*" "Who hath made us able ministers of the New Testament—not of the letter, but of the spirit; for the letter killeth,
but the spirit giveth life." "How shall not the ministration
of the spirit be rather glorious."

James, the great apostle of the Jews, abiding at Jerusalem,
says: "Cleanse your hands, ye sinners, and purify your hearts,
ye double-minded." And John, the beloved disciple, reiterates: "The blood of Jesus Christ, his Son, cleanseth us from
all unrighteousness;" [not the rite of baptism.] And he adds:
"Love is of God, and *every one that loveth is born of God and
knoweth God.*"

Is any one disposed to inquire why, in the record given by
Luke (in Acts) of the labors of the apostles and early Christian evangelists, ritual baptism appears in several instances?
The answer is, the Jewish garb (the swaddling band of
Christianity) was laid aside slowly—not at all until the pressure of the non-Jewish customs of converted Gentiles began to
bear hard against that which was distinctively Jewish.

If any thing can be proved by historic evidence, it can be
proved that Moses established Jewish baptism, and that,
especially, all proselytes from the heathen were baptized (purified), *with their households*, on reception into the synagogue.
This is the origin of "household baptism," and "infant baptism." Keeping this in mind, we may harmonize those statements of the Fathers, as Augustine, who states that infant
baptism was an "apostolic tradition," and Pelagius, who says
that he had never heard of any that opposed it; with the statement of Neander (oft) that infant baptism was but little
practised in the Christian Church for three or four centuries
after Christ. The *Gentile Churches did not adopt it* for several
centuries; the Jewish (*i. e.* the Judaizers) kept it up through

all this period, and finally carried with them the Roman, and at length the Greek Church.

So, ceremonially, from Moses down to Christ (even until now) the Jews baptized themselves, old and young, to purge from ceremonial uncleannesses. And nothing is clearer than that these purifyings are not only not commanded but repressed in all the Epistles. The Council at Jerusalem, noticed in Acts xv., bound no baptismal ceremony upon the Gentiles, and from that day, as before, Paul specially dissuaded them from it. And if Neander may be accredited, no yoke of bondage to a ritual law would have prevailed, but for the inroads of the Judaizers. The apostles (even Paul himself) when among Jews, kept the ceremonies, the feasts, Passover, Pentecost, etc.: See Acts xvi. 3, xviii. 21, xix. 21, xx. 16, xxi. 26, xxv. 8. But the Gentile Churches were left at liberty touching the whole ceremonial law.

CHAPTER IV.

GLEAMS OF THE CONFLICT BETWEEN RITUALISM AND NON-RITUALISM.

Confusion of the Ritualists—A Hidden Record Revealed.

THUS do we perceive the ritual baptism was continually waning ("decreasing," as John says), and passing out of sight, from the days of John, the ritual purifier, unto the end of the New Testament canon. Paul, in Romans, 1 Corinthians, Galatians, Ephesians, and Colossians, brings to view the spiritual or moral *purifying* and renovation by the *sanctifying* and uniting power of the spiritual baptism almost exclusively. He also, as in 1 Cor. i., and Heb. vi., protests against giving attention to, or going back to queryings about the ritual baptism, saying, he was not "sent to baptize," or to give attention to this matter; and hence urged the churches to "leave" these "rudiments" (principles), and go on unto spiritual perfection. Peter does the same, turning their attention from the baptism that purifies "the flesh," to that which secures the answer of a good conscience toward God, "by the resurrection of Jesus Christ," *i. e.* by Christ working in them in His resurrection power.

Shall we assume that Christ had more "confidence in the flesh," and less in the spiritual baptism, than these apostles, when after His resurrection He gave the Great Commission? And did Paul when he declares he was not sent to baptize (as a Jew), but to preach (as a Christian), and when he affirms there is but "one baptism," fail to apprehend the mind of

126

Christ on the subject? We think not. Who thinks otherwise?

It is no proof that Christ instituted a ritual law, because, forsooth, a ritual law has been assumed by successive generations of Judaizers, even from the days of the Levitical priesthood. Who has fully noted and admitted the "change of the priesthood," and the "change of the law," which Paul announces in Hebrews 7th to 10th chapters?

What is not Proof.

It is no proof that ritual baptism is a seal of the New Covenant, because the doctrine of ritual baptism was pressed to the full extent of the dogma of baptismal regeneration; and was thus accepted by some of the leading "bishops" of the Church in the third and fourth centuries. It is rather against the claim of the ritualists, just as the *sacramentarian* trust of the Coptic, Armenian, Greek, Roman, and Anglican churches is to-day. It is no argument in favor of ritual baptism that the historians of the Church have been ritualists to the extent that they have well-nigh ignored, and kept from our view the anti-ritualists of the early ages, and, as far as practicable, of the succeeding ages.

When they omit to name them, or to write their record, they but do as High Churchmen of our day do toward the Low Church, as we have seen, and as other Dissenters treat the Society of Friends. But let it not be assumed for this cause that all the Church, in all ages, have been ritualists, helping on the feuds that have constantly arisen as to a thousand forms, or aims, or adjuncts of water-baptism. Nay, the more than a thousand differing theories respecting water-baptism that have arisen, and rent the Church into shreds, is no proof of the divine appointment of such baptism; it would impeach the divine wisdom and benevolence to assume it. And the fact that ritualists have doated on calling the anti-ritualists (anti-baptizers) heretics, is no proof that they were heretics—or were not the most holy and exemplary Christians of earth—no more than the book written by the recanting or apostatizing Quaker, Samuel Hanson Cox, entitled "Quakerism not Christianity," is a proof that the church or society thus opposed was not the most spiritual and benevolent church, and the most Christ-like that existed at that day, and equal to any the earth has seen.

We would very cheerfully compare the life of a George Fox or William Penn, early Quakers, with Rev. S. H. Cox, or Macaulay, their vilifiers. Weighed in the balances, the critic and judge, and many of their compeers, would illy stand the test with said Fox and Penn, and many of their compeers.

And so we may trace back the record to early ages. Our record cannot be complete, because of the unfaithfulness of historians (through theological prejudice), as we said ; but we can present a record never yet grouped, that we are not ashamed to compare with the High Church Ritualistic record, —and which, if it could be made complete, we doubt not, would present before us the brightest phase of the Church's piety in the ages long since past—as the Society of Friends presented by far the brightest phase of the Church's piety in the seventeenth century.

Record of Anti-ritualism.

We have found Christ foretelling, and Paul and Peter proclaiming the passing away of the Judaic ritual law—Paul especially in numerous and varied phrases. And the question arises, was this testimony against an exotic ritualism kept up in the churches ? Especially during the great backsliding, when a ritualistic trust became the idolatry and bane of the Church. Neander has most fully and frankly given us the record on this subject. We will quote from this author freely, and from others as we may.

But keep in mind the difficulties that are to throng our path. It has not been popular to give the history of *dissent* from the most prevalent faith, as the history of the true

Church, yet oft has the history of such dissent been the only correct history of the true Church. But popular church history has full oft been only a history of organizations and rituals, of baptisms and Judaisms perpetuated, of tilts and bulls of bishops and popes against schismatics and heretics, which schismatics and heretics were simply endeavoring faithfully to serve God and their generation without leave or instruction from said bishops and popes, and without owning any allegiance to them. The history of *protest* and *dissent* has usually been the true history of Christianity from the days of our Lord's dissent from the Pharisees and Scribes, to the Dissenters and Protestants of England and America.

A Vacuum in Ritualistic History.

Leaving the New Testament record with the filling of the canon (where in all the epistles, we find not one word of approval either of water-baptism or any other Jewish ritual), we are ushered into the succeeding history of the Church. And, ah, what a vacuum do we here find, impossible to be filled by the ritualists, with all their assiduity of research and inquiry. Alexander Campbell, the great ritualistic champion of *immersion* and of salvation thereby, affirms that:

"Having closely and repeatedly examined the epistles of Clement, of Polycarp to the Philippians, of Ignatius to the Ephesians, and to the Magnesians, that to the Gratians, the Romans, the Philadelphians, the Smyrnians, and his epistle to Polycarp, and the catholic epistle of Barnabas, and the genuine works of Hermas," he finds only two passages *in all these* that speak of *baptism*, and then only by allusion, in other words, not *one of them* using the term *baptizo* or *baptisma* in a single instance.

This carries us to the year A. D. 140. Justin Martyr, in the year 140, in an apology addressed to Antoninus Pius, is represented as saying of the Christian teachers and their converts: "We also pray and fast together with them; then we bring them to some place where there is water, and they are *regenerated* in the same way by which we were regenerated, for they *are washed with water*," etc. This, perhaps, is the first

9

allusion to ritual baptism after the canon of Scripture (the *Acts of the Apostles*) ; and here the term *baptize* is not used for wash, but the Greek word *loutron*, meaning *to lave*, or *purify*.* So Mr. Campbell cannot find *immersion*, nor scarce an allusion to baptism, in any of the earliest Christian Fathers.† And Neander cannot find *infant baptism* for about three centuries after Christ.‡ Well, between the two arch-champions of the historical evidences, is it not probable that water-baptism itself was very little thought of, and, heeding Paul's instructions, very little practised ? They had been *brought out* from the Judaic wilderness, and were not yet ready for any cause to plunge into it again. Their version of the GREAT COMMISSION must have essentially differed from the current modern one.

Let NEANDER explain this matter. He says (vol. i. p. 194):

"Christianity having sprung to freedom out of the envelop of Judaism, *had stripped off the forms in which it was first concealed.* . . . This evolution belonged more particularly to the Pauline position, from which proceeded the form of the Church in the Pagan world. This principle had *triumphantly pushed its way through* in the conflict with the Jewish elements, which opposed themselves to the practical development of Christianity. In the communities of Pagan Christians the new creation stood forth *completely unfolded ;* but the Jewish principle *which had been vanquished,* pressed in once more from another quarter. Humanity was as yet incapable of maintaining itself *at that lofty position of pure spiritual religion.* The Jewish position descended nearer to the mass, who needed first to be trained" (*i. e.* in rituals), "in order to the apprehension of a pure Christianity ! Out of Christianity, now become independent, a principle once more sprang forth akin to the Old Testament

---

* As JUSTIN MARTYR was altogether a non-ritualist (see " Chronicles of Non-Ritualists "), it is somewhat doubtful whether he penned the above. The words " regenerate " and " wash," used in a seemingly ritualistic sense, is wholly Jewish in style, and this passage may have been foisted into Justin's writings by some Judaizer, as many other things were.

† *For a period of seventy years from the death of all the apostles, save John, and of about forty years from the death of the Apostle John.* This silence of the Fathers is as significant a rebuke of the ritual baptizers, as any words could possibly be.

‡ *i. e.,* it was not common, he avers.

position—*a new making outward of the kingdom of God*—a new *law discipline*—a new *tutorship* of the spirit of humanity" (*i. e.* putting new wine in old bottles again), "until it should arrive at the maturity of a manly age in Christ. *This retrogression* of the Christian spirit to a form nearly related to the Old Testament position, could not fail, after the fruitful principle had once made its appearance, *to unfold itself more and more.*"

Thus Neander proceeds to trace the introduction of church forms modelled after the Jewish ritual and priesthood, with high priests and bishops graded in accordance with the Mosaic economy, introducing, of course, the same *purifications*, and adding other rites, until we have the full-orbed development of Popery, with all its forms and mummeries.

Hear NEANDER again, same volume and page :

"While the great principle of the New Testament is the unfolding of the kingdom of God from within, from the union with Christ brought about after the like immediate manner in all, by faith, the readmission of the Old Testament position in making the kingdom of God outward, went on the assumption that *an outward mediation was necessary* in order to spread this kingdom in the world. Such a mediation was to form for the Christian Church a priesthood fashioned after the model of that of the Old Testament.

"*The universal priestly character of all saints grounded in the common and immediate relation of all to Christ* as the source of the divine life was repressed, the idea interposing itself of a *particular mediatory priesthood, attached to a distinct order.* This recasting the Christian spirit in the Old Testament form did not take place, it is true, everywhere uniformly alike ! Where some Jewish element chiefly predominated, it might very easily grow up out of this, where the Pauline element among the Pagan Christians had unfolded itself in opposition to the Jewish, still the Christian spirit, grown up to independence, but not being able to maintain itself *at this lofty position*, by virtue of a *relationship springing up in itself with the Jewish position, passed over to the Jewish.* Of such a change which had now taken place in the Christian mode of thinking, *we have a witness as early as Tertullian*, when he, *in a work concerning baptism*, calls the bishop the *summus sacerdos* (chief priest), a title certainly not invented by him, but which had been adopted from a prevailing mode both of speaking and thinking, in a certain portion at least, of the Church.[*] This title presupposes that men had begun already to compare the presbyters with the priests, and the deacons, or the spiritual class generally, with the Levites. . . . . In general, the more men *fall back from the evangelical to the Jewish point of view*, the more must the original, free constitution of the communities,

---

[*] TERTULLIAN wrote A. D. 200, hence the custom of calling leading ministers "chief priests" could come from no other than a Jewish source at that early day.

grounded in those original Christian views become changed. We find Cyprian (A. D. 250) already completely imbued with the notions which sprang out of this confounding together of the different points of view of the Old and New Testaments.

"*This notion of a peculiar people of God*, applied distinctively to a particular *order* of men among the Christians, is something wholly foreign to the original Christian consciousness, for all Christians should be a people *consecrated to God*" (*i. e.* having God's ordination), "and all the employments of their earthly calling should, in like manner, be sanctified by the temper in which they are discharged. Their *whole life and doing* should become a consecrated thank-offering and *a spiritual worship*. This was the original evangelical idea. . . . But although the idea of the priesthood in the purely evangelical sense grew continually more obscure, and was thrust into the background in proportion as the *unevangelical* point of view became predominant, yet it was too deeply rooted in the very essence of Christianity to be wholly suppressed. *In the boundary epoch of Tertullian* we still find many significant proofs *that there was a reaction* of the primitive Christian consciousness of the universal priesthood and the common rights grounded therein against the arrogated power of a particular priesthood, *which had recently* begun to form itself *on the model of the Old Testament. Tertullian, in his work on baptism*, written before he went over to Montanism, distinguishes, with reference to this matter, *divine right*, and *human order*. 'In itself considered,' he says, 'the laity also have the right to administer the sacraments, and to teach in the community. The word of God, and *the sacraments* were by the grace of God communicated to all' [What sacraments were communicated by the grace of God?], 'and may therefore be communicated by all Christians *as instruments of the divine grace*. 'But,' continues Tertullian, 'we may use the words of Paul, "All things are lawful for me, but all things are not expedient." If we look at the order necessary to be maintained in the Church, the laity are therefore to exercise their priestly right of administering the sacraments only when the time and circumstances require it.'"

Now, who does not see by the above extracts from Neander and from Alexander Campbell, that the "Pauline doctrine," as Neander calls it, of making Christianity a system "wholly spiritual," prevailed almost exclusively in the Gentile churches for seventy-five or one hundred years after the death of Paul, so that baptisms and other adjuncts of Judaism were scarcely named or known? But, if we take Neander's philosophy on the subject, "the Christian Church could not maintain itself in this lofty position," but must needs go back to Moses and become "perfected by the flesh"—by a ritual law—which Paul in his letter to the Galatians so stoutly reprimands, and oft denounces in other epistles. Paul, it seems, had started them out on a lofty Christian position, but they must conquer the world by going back to Moses, the Levitical priesthood, the law, and *the ritual*, and, as Neander fitly calls it, "a new law discipline." And it is easy to be inferred also that the ritual came in to add to, and augment the power of the priesthood, for they soon made salvation in this world, and that which is to come, dependent on the rituals (the baptisms and sacraments) as administered by their hands. This is notorious. About Cyprian's time we see a great part of the priesthood, *i. e.* the clergy in Rome and Africa, laid hold of this arm of power to govern the churches at their will.

Baptismal regeneration became the key of the kingdom, which *they held*, and "opened and no man might shut, and shut, and no man might open." These assumptions drew on, as Neander says, gradually—commencing with the "boundary epoch" of Tertullian, about A. D. 175, and culminating by carrying the Western Church into the vortex of the Papacy—manifesting itself more and more from the third century forward.

So the non-ritualistic pyramid we build rests on the broad base, as given by Neander, viz., the Pauline Church was "*wholly spiritual*," and on this side was the *universal Christian consciousness*, and, as far as Church history testifies, *the universal practice of the Gentile churches*, in the age immediately succeeding the apostles. And Neander himself specifies the return to the graded priesthood, after the Mosaic pattern, and the assumption and use of the prerogative of *baptism* as the earliest tokens of an apostasy from Christianity.

We shall know then, hereafter, where to find the true Church, and where the apostate or heretical church. Mark that !

But we have not concluded the evidence on this point,—we have only commenced it.

See NEANDER, vol. i. p. 341 :

"As Christ himself had faithfully observed the Mosaic law, so the faithful observance of it was adhered to at first *by all believers*, and was held to be a necessary condition of participating in the Messiah's kingdom." *

The reader will perceive that this will cover that portion of the apostolic epoch, up to the time when the Apostle Paul became the great apostle of the Gentiles, and commenced protesting against imposing on the Gentiles the yoke of bondage to the Mosaic ritual; which *protest* fills a large share of several of his epistles. In that epoch, then, the "following of Christ" in ritual observances, in *baptisms*, and *sacred feasts*, was but following Moses.† It was in this condition of bondage to Moses that Paul found the whole Church, and it is probable that he had more than one grapple with Peter and James on the subject, before he obtained their full consent to his rejecting "Moses" and the ritual law among the Gentiles. The most remarkable contest of this kind is recorded in the second chapter of Galatians, in which Paul declares that he "withstood Peter to the face," protesting against Peter's requiring the Gentiles to conform to the ritual of the Jews. It was after this event, mark, that Peter wrote to the "elect," scattered abroad, over all the earth, that they were saved by another *baptism* than that which "put away the filth of the flesh." And Paul declares that Peter, James, and John, though themselves had been ministers of the "circumcision," gave to him the "right hand of fellowship" in his non-ritual work among the Gentiles (Gal. ii. 9).

Now hear NEANDER again as to the process of transition from the *Petrine* or Mosaic, to the *Pauline* or Christian dispensation of the Church (vol. i. p. 341):

---

* It ought not to be necessary to stop here and show that Paul's conflict with "the circumcision," as he termed the Jewish Christians, was a conflict with all the ceremonials they conjoined with the circumcision—*baptism, sacrifices*, and the *observance of "days and times."* It was all one economy—a trusting totally in externalized worship and ceremonials, without the heart-renewal. Christ came to preach the way whereby not only Jews but all others could be saved.

† This explains the baptisms recorded in the book of Acts.

"After the preparatory labors of Stephen, the martyr, and other men of Hellenistic origin, and of Peter, that which Christ intended when He said He was not come to destroy the law, but to fulfil it; and when He called himself the Lord of the Sabbath, that which Christ meant by the worship of God confined no longer to particular times or places, but in spirit and in truth; the essence of the *new spiritual creation*, which is grounded in the resurrection of Christ, was clearly conceived and expressed by the Apostle Paul, and *a self-subsisting Christian Church*" (*i. e.* a church not depending upon the canonical interposition of a priesthood), "wholly independent of Judaism formed among the Pagans."

This reasserts the truth of the non-ritualistic position of all the Gentile churches at first. But Neander continues:

"Already a schism threatened to break out between the two elements of which the Christian Church was composed" (viz.), "*The prevailing notion of Christianity in Palestine* which was characterized by a *decided leaning to the Old Testament*, and which suffered the new spirit to *remain enveloped in the old forms of Judaism*, and the independent Pauline development of Christianity among the Pagans. By the compromise entered into between the two parties at Jerusalem, this opposition was harmoniously reconciled, and it was the *triumph of the idea of a Catholic Church*, whose unity, grounded in the faith in Jesus as the one Saviour and Lord of all, was to outweigh all subordinate differences of Jewish or Hellenistic forms of culture. Yet the deep-seated opposition was not wholly overcome, but *continued among some* who opposed Paul's catholicity. About the middle of the second century we find the two parties recognized in the dialogue of Justin Martyr with Trypho. Two classes are there mentioned, that which in their own practice united with the faith in Christ *the observance of the Mosaic law* (some of these not requiring converted Pagans to observe it), and some, *not content with observing the Mosaic law themselves, were for forcing the Pagan believers universally to the same observance*, proceeding on the assumption that the believing Pagans, like all others, *were unclean*,* and that without the observance of the *Mosaic law, no man could be just before God.*"

---

* Up to this point, and even here, Neander studiously avoids specifying *baptism* as a part of the Jewish ritual law that Paul had laid aside in building the Gentile Church upon a "purely spiritual" basis. But here, incidentally, the whole truth comes into view—the Judaizers from Palestine assumed that the "*believing Pagans, like all others,* WERE UNCLEAN—and that without the observance of the Mosaic law," (why don't he say "without *baptism*," for that was the way they washed away their "uncleanness," as also the baptizing Christians taught, and none knew this better than Neander?), "no man could be just before God." Here we may see how Churchly customs could warp even the candor of a Neander.

There, reader, you have an effort for the introduction of baptismal *purifyings* among these newly converted Pagans—about the middle of the second century, and their increase in the popular church from this time onward to the tenth century, when Popery was at its zenith.

Thus are we verifying our position that water-baptism among the Gentiles was not of apostolic origin, but rather the outgrowth of an apostasy from the spirituality of the Christian system, through the influence of Christian teachers from Palestine. We had long been persuaded that there was more opposition to rituals, both in the early and later ages of the Church, than ritualistic historians were willing to record—and like the astronomer who notices the veering of a planet in its orbit, suspecting the cause, he sets his telescope and discovers a new planet—so we having noted the hints that some opposed water-baptisms and sacraments in early ages, set our telescopic glass, and find the age succeeding the apostles almost without any observance of a ritual law—the evidence of which ritualistic historians had carefully concealed—and only by indirect hints does the truth of it come palpably into view. So that our conception is more than corroborated with circumstantial proof, as abundant as could be desired. Both Baptists and Pedo-Baptists freely admit that there were those that rejected baptism all along the ages —the historians call them heretics—but, at the same time, admit that many of *them were the most spiritual and exemplary part of the Christian Church.* We have learned how to weigh their estimate of heresy, and in what rank to place the accuser and the accused. The accused we count as the purest of Christ's chosen flock, and the accusers as versed and educated ritualists, oft wholly unsound in the faith.* And, who does

---

* The Hellenistic Christians of Palestine—converted from among the Jews— retained the Jewish rituals, and were Socinian in faith—and Judaizing teachers of Christianity from Palestine, extended their influence into Northern Africa, thence to Rome, Spain and Britain, until, in the second and third centuries, the doctrine of baptismal regeneration (not very " sound doctrine ") became the doctrine of the popular church, and this apostasy towards sacramentarianism con-

not know that all this talk about *sacraments* has no warrant in the New Testament? Is there any word in the New Testament that answers to the word *sacraments*, or declares who shall administer them? Is not the *idea* wholly Popish and priestly? *Ordinances* are named in the New Testament, but ever as Jewish, and to be disregarded and renounced. And, when reassumed in after centuries, the appeal is not to Christ's, or apostolic *authority*, but to *tradition*. Of this we have abundant proof. It might be assumed in advance that a new dispensation (for all the world) would not be ritualistic like the old (the Jewish), and that Christ would not give a law to make bigots and sectarists, or to befool the unconverted with a vain hope of a ritual regeneration. Can any one assent to the proposition that the commission to convert the world was given a baptismal sheath? or that Christ's spirit can be circumscribed by a ritual? There can be no sacrament but spiritually feeding on Christ. No sacred shrines or fonts, or forms—souls sanctified only are sacred. The heavenly life is not run in the narrow mould of a creed, or guarded and guided and bounded by a rite. Christ has not put salvation at the mercy of human frailty and shortsightedness, or in the power of priestly arrogance thus. No man's spiritual good is at the disposal of any administrator of rites. Likeness to Christ requires no ceremonial or bodily imitation of Christ. If this were implied in following Christ there would be no end of seeking an outward, apish imitation, forgetting the necessity of a moral resemblance. It requires all the powers of

---

tinued to prevail and extend, until the Roman Church was very extensively corrupted, and the number of sacraments was multiplied by the priesthood from nought to one, two, three, five, seven, and even by some to twelve: (See the teaching of Damiani on the subject) ; and every form of superstition soon became connected with their observance, for what began with human caprice, and priestly love of power, could be augmented and diversified by the same caprice, and it would require a huge volume to record but briefly the development and variations and extremes of sacramentarianism from the second century through all the ages of the Papacy. But the true Church continued to be, to a great extent, outside of this Judaized and ritualized Roman Church!

Protestantism, and all their vehemence of logic and protest to keep serious souls from a legal bondage, or a vain trust in the form or shell of religion.

THE SPIRITUAL BAPTISM EXCHANGED FOR BAPTISMAL REGENERATION.

That was simply a fearful apostasy that led the Church so extensively, in the third century, to embrace the doctrine of baptismal regeneration, or that in any age teaches that sacraments can sanctify or save. The arch-deceiver is pleased with the illusive dream. Christ found the Jews in that delusion, and He did not continue two sacraments, to continue the delusion. Rev. J. T. HENDRICK, in his work on Baptism, says:

" No one pretends that these Fathers (Cyprian, Tertullian, Chrysostom, etc.) speak of baptism in any such language as Peter and Paul, and John and Christ did. The difference is as great as that between day and night. But what caused the difference? Their notions of SIN being in MATTER, or in the BODY, and that purity was obtained by the sacraments alone. But we never hear anything of all this from Christ, Peter, or Paul. The religion of Christ was a religion of principles. . . . . The religion of the Fathers, even in the second century, became a religion of sacraments or ceremonies, as the Catholic religion now is. The first symptom of decay in religion, at that time, was, as it ever has been, a revival of the ritual or ceremonial part. . . . . Principles and sacraments in religion never can be kept abreast of each other, they will not remain in a state of equipoise, the spiritual part will be thrown back, and retire, and the merest formalities and grossest superstitions will follow. . . . . No sooner than Christ had died, even before His immediate disciples died, this leaven of Judaism . . . began to work itself into the Church, and did leaven the whole lump, and continued down to the Reformation."

Hear the Fathers talk; first hear CHRYSOSTOM:

" Although a man should be foul with every vice, the blackest that can be named, yet should he fall into the baptismal pool, he ascends from the divine waters purer than the beams of noon; he is made just in a moment."

Again:

" They who approach the baptismal font, although fornicators, etc., are not only made clean, but holy also, and just. As a spark thrown into the ocean is instantly extinguished, so is sin (be it what it may) extinguished when the man is thrown into the laver of regeneration."

So NEANDER says:

"In maintaining against the Cainites the necessity of outward baptism, Tertullian ascribes to water a supernatural sanctifying power."

So we see the earliest trace of the doctrine of baptismal regeneration (for Tertullian wrote in the second century) is found in turning away from the doctrine of a spiritual baptism only, to sustain and enforce the ritual baptism with water. So testifies Neander, vol. i. p. 311:

"But when . . . . from want of duly distinguishing between what is outward and what is inward in baptism, the baptism by water and the baptism by the Spirit, the error became more firmly established that without external baptism no one could be delivered from the inherent guilt, or saved from the everlasting punishment, or raised ,to eternal life; and a notion of the magical influence and charm connected with the sacraments gained ground; the theory was finally evolved of the unconditional necessity of *infant baptism*."

Then note the superstitions of every conceivable form in the earliest ages connected with the introduction of baptism among the Pagan Christians, and deemed by those who practised them *just as sacred as the baptisms themselves*, and, if we mistake not, Tertullian himself declaring them to be of the same origin, viz., TRADITION.

HOW THEY BAPTIZED.

WALL says; part ii. p. 417:

"The ancient Christians when they were baptized by immersion were all baptized naked, whether men, women, or children. They thought it better represented the putting off the old man, and also the nakedness of the cross of Christ. Moreover, as baptism is a washing, they judged it should be the washing of the *body*, not of the clothes."

Also it was repeated *three times*, and called *trine immersion*.

CHRYSOSTOM says:

"Our Lord delivered us one baptism by three immersions."

And TERTULLIAN says:

"We are three times plunged into the water, and when we are taken up, we taste a mixture of milk and honey. When we go to meat, when we lie down, sit down, and whatever business we have, we make on our foreheads the sign of the cross. *If you search the Scriptures,*" he continues, *"for any command for these and such like usages, you shall find none.* TRADITION will be urged to you as the ground of them—custom as the confirmation of them—and our religion teaches us to observe them."

Besides the above connected mummeries, there was also, usually, the holy kiss, unction, confirmation, exorcism, and putting on white robes for so many days. Now, who shall say that the one of these (the baptism for example) is not just as scriptural and apostolical as the others, and no more so? Why did they resort to any of these rites? We shall soon see.

ORIGIN OF INFANT BAPTISM—SYNCHRONICAL WITH ADULT BAPTISM.

The purifyings prescribed by the Mosaic law had no respect to age or sex, but were to be alike incumbent on all that had become in any manner ceremonially defiled. They had no respect to individual character, but *whoever* had contracted ceremonial defilement, must either himself use the prescribed baptisms of purification, or the priest, parent, or ward, must apply them. None that understands the genius of *Judaism* will doubt this—being assured that it was *one law* for *all the people*—in order to continue in the national fellowship. The purifications were to be as universal as the circumcision. When Moses first baptized Israel, he " sprinkled both the book and *all the people.*" This, of course, included those *of all ages.*

It is a singular querying that has arisen in later ages, as to the *origin* of infant baptism. Jewish writers all agree that it was practised near the commencement of the Christian era, and that it had been the practice through their whole national history. *They* certainly did not derive infant baptism, nor adult baptism, from *Christ,* or his forerunner, John. They crucified Christ and beheaded John; surely they did not borrow their baptisms. They reviled Christians and their Messiah with language unfit to be uttered—they did not learn their *liturgy* nor their *ritual.* The proofs of Jewish infant baptism is as complete as the proof of Jewish adult baptism; and inspiration gives abundant proof of the latter. When Paul speaks of the "divers baptisms" under the law, and other New Testament writers of the "household baptisms," we have allusion simply to the Jewish baptisms of purification. When, therefore, the baptism of the infant *is suspended* it is very likely that the baptism of the adult will be suspended, and for the same reason. That both had been immemorially practised, not only, as we said, every Jewish writer testifies, but every non-Jewish writer of Jewish history, who has the least show of fitness for his work.

We will here cite a few of

THE WITNESSES,

leaving a large portion of them to find their place in the *analysis* or *review* of the ritualistic writers.

WOOD, on Baptism, p. 48, states:

"The Rabbis unanimously assert that the baptism of proselytes has been practised by the Jews in all ages, from Moses down to the time when they wrote."

PRIDEAUX (Con., vol. ii. p. 203) says:

"When any were proselyted to the Jewish religion, they were initiated to it by baptism, sacrifice, and circumcision."

DR. LIGHTFOOT, one of the most learned men of any age, says:

"The practice of *baptizing infants* was a thing as well known in the church of the Jews as ever it has been in the Christian Church."

CALMET quotes *Abram Booth*, a father of the Baptist Church in England, as admitting that:

"The children of proselytes were baptized with their parents, among the Jews."

MAIMONIDES, a learned Jewish writer of the twelfth century, who concentred in himself all prior Jewish learning, and great knowledge of both Jewish and Gentile history, affirms that:

"In all ages when a Gentile is willing to enter into covenant with Israel, and take upon himself the yoke of the law, he must be circumcised and baptized, and bring a sacrifice."

Again he says:

"An Israelite *that takes a little heathen child* (in war), or that finds *an heathen infant*, and baptizes him for a proselyte, behold he is a proselyte."

The making of proselytes thus was a very common thing in the process of the Jewish successful wars. And such are the facts of Jewish history which Wall cites as the clew to the interpretation of Christ's commission, Matt. xxviii. 19. We have room here for but one more witness;—the Babylonian Talmud, composed near the close of the second century, by Jewish religious teachers, says:

"When a proselyte is received he must be circumcised, and . . . they baptize (*i. e.* purify) him. The proselytes enter not into covenant but by circumcision, baptism, and sprinkling of blood."

Again:

"He is no proselyte unless he be circumcised and baptized. *If he be not* baptized (purified) he remains a Gentile."

WALL also quotes Selden as affirming that the saying of Paul, 1 Cor. x. 1, 2:

"'All our fathers were baptized unto Moses,'" would not have been understood, "had it not been a custom to enter into covenant by baptism."

On p. 14, Wall adds:

"If any proselyte who came over to the Jewish religion, and was baptized in it, had any infant children, they also, at their father's request, were circumcised and baptized, and admitted as proselytes. Thus they were covenanted to the God of Israel. Thus was it done to proselytes as to Abraham at his first admission to the covenant of circumcision. The proselyte was (necessarily) baptized to cleanse him from heathen pollutions (and the blood of circumcision). The Jews argued respecting this, that there was no more reason for waiting for the child of a proselyte to be grown, or to come to riper years, than for the child born of Jewish parents. And the *Gemara* explains thus: 'If with a proselyte, his sons and his daughters be made proselytes, that which is done by their father redounds to their good.' Thus also, the *Mishna* declares. The *Gemara* proceeds further to explain why and how the infants were baptized: 'Because none is made a proselyte without circumcision and baptism,—and if the father be dead, at the request of the council, which consists of three men, that have care of this baptism, according to the law, and the baptism of proselytes.' These were the godfathers of the candidates, for, as Selden observes, 'If a proselyte be a minor, this court *did profess in his name,' i. e.* in the name of the minor, the 'things required.' Under age, or a minor, was, if a son, under the age of thirteen years and a day; if a daughter, under the age of twelve years and a day."

This preciseness of statement shows that the writer knew whereof he affirmed. But Wall continues:

" The comparative infrequency of proselyte baptism was on the ground that, like the children of natural Jews, the children of proselyted Gentiles, if born after the baptism of their parents, were counted clean without baptism."

Selden, Tayler, Walker, Tombes, Lightfoot, Wall, etc., quote the Jews as teaching this:

" The sons of proselytes in following generations were circumcised indeed, but not baptized (*i. e.* as proselytes), as being already Israelites."

So the Talmud says:

" The unborn child is baptized with the baptism of the (pregnant) mother."

The teaching of Moses is that there should be "*one law,*" both for the Israelites and the stranger that joins them. The Israelites, under Moses, entered into covenant by baptism and sacrifice—(after circumcision) so must every stranger—and then observe all other purifications (baptisms) of the law.

Cherithoth and Rabbi Solomon testify to this.

So CYPRIAN says:

" The case of the Jews who were to be baptized by the apostles, was different from the case of the Gentiles, *for the Jews had already, and* A LONG TIME AGO, THE BAPTISM OF THE LAW, AND OF MOSES."

And corroborating Robinson, WALL says (quoting Tertullian):

" The heathens have used of old a certain rite of baptism, which they said was for the forgiveness of sins."

And GREGORY NAZIANZEN, a Christian Father, all his life conversant with the Jews, says:

" Moses gave a baptism, but that was with water only; before that they were baptized 'in the cloud, and in the sea,' but these were but a *type* or *frame* of ours, as Paul understands it."

WALL hence argues that Jesus Christ, in the Great Commission, designed to require the keeping up of the Jewish purifications, and he interprets the commission only by these, utterly unworthily, as we think. Nevertheless, we admit that he used a word before used in reference to these, but, as both John and himself testify, in the sense of the moral or spiritual *purifying*. We have cited the above authorities and witnesses thus extensively, because baptizers in the Christian Church have remained so extensively unapprised of the Jewish ritual law, and Jewish customs growing out of them, and that all may see where and when their baptismal custom originated, and, therefore, where they belong. Showing, also, what customs John, and Jesus, our Lord, found existing in their day, and what it was that they declared should give place to the " ministration of the Spirit." Nothing is more capable of demonstration than that water-baptism originated with Moses or the Patriarchs, and that numerous Christian sects are seeking to keep themselves in a ritual bondage to Judaism.

Be it noted that the Talmud, the Jewish liturgy, and Church directory, written in the second century, did not borrow baptism (as we said) from the Christian Church, nor from John, who honored Christ ever; nor did it impose a new ritual (ordinance) upon the Jews—no more than " circumcision " and " sacrifice " conjoined with "purification " were new ordinances. None doubt that their circumcision points back to Abraham, and their sacrifices to Moses, or even earlier; why not their baptisms ? If not, when did they originate? Let him that readeth, answer.

But mark, full many have puzzled and confused themselves in searching after a *sacramental baptism* among the Jews, as a purely and distinctly independent rite, having no respect to previously contracted defilement, but established as an initiatory ordinance in taking the covenant of Moses. None of these baptisms we have cited were of that kind, nor was there any such baptism ever established in the Jewish history, nor in the early centuries of the Christian Church. The idea of *purification, regeneration, a new birth* into a purer faith, was in the early Christian Church the same as in the Jewish.

It is true that circumcision was but once in the life (save when Joshua re-circumcised Israel with *knives of stone* for a great occasion), while baptism was repeatable on every new occasion of defilement. It was assumed that all Gentiles came to the covenant with ceremonial defilement, either from " eating blood," "touching a dead body," or from contact with the uncircumcised; hence they could not be at first received into the congregation until baptized—*i. e. purified*—and their purification, as with native Israelites, must be repeated on every new occasion of defilement. And the blood of circumcision itself, as Dr. Gale tells us, was one new occasion of defilement requiring baptism. Baptisms are not always recorded, since *lawful customs* did not need to be recorded in every instance of their observance; specially when the custom is of long standing, the observance of the custom is to be assumed. Yet Mark (a Jew), chap. vii., and Paul (a Hebrew), Heb. ix., bear ample witness to these customs.

Nor is there any doubt that the children of families once proselyted, born after the covenant of Moses had been taken by the father and his household, ceased to be regarded as needing *purification* because of contact with Gentiles, and, therefore, were not baptized only for such causes as were the native Jews. This explains the reason of the decrease of proselyte baptism, which Dr. Wall alludes to in treating upon the latter period of Jewish history. Moreover, a declining and apostatizing nation would not receive many proselytes to its religion. Nor would the (Sadducee) skeptics and infidels pay very much attention to the rites of religion. True, the Pharisees carried their ritualism to the extreme of idolatry of the ritual, but few were attracted to their standard at this time.

Why a Decline of Infant Baptism?

But the great cause of the decline of infant baptism in the early Christian age, was the fervency, pungency, and point of

10

John's preaching, with its result; and afterwards that of Christ and the apostles. John laid the "axe" at the "root of the tree," and required heart-repentance of every individual; that "every tree" for itself should "bring forth good fruit," and not trust in ceremonial purifications, nor a pretence of repentance, or obedience by proxy. He insisted that every one should give evidence of being personally penitent, else he forbade them even the ritual cleansing. The "generation of vipers" must first prove themselves the "children of Abraham," by timely repentance, and bearing its "fruits." The same was true of the preaching of Christ and the apostles. When (being Jews) they observed rites, they sought to make them servants to the truth, and not to hold themselves in servile subjection to the rite. Thus, with or without the outward circumcision, or baptism, or Passover, they preached the circumcision of the heart, and the baptism of the soul, and the "Paschal Lamb" that was "slain" on Calvary, whose blood alone is efficacious to purify and atone.

This would turn even the Jewish mind from Pharisee formalities, and from so much thought about ceremonial defilements, to those defilements that were real and soul-destroying. Hence they would oftener forget the ritual *purifying* of the non-conscious infant, being more entirely absorbed in concern for their own personal regeneration, and eternal salvation. And in behalf of their "households" also, these "weightier matters" would necessarily become their great concern. True, the mould in which their religious ideas had been formed would not be rejected at once; hence, those most churchly in their sentiments and views, would pay the most attention to the circumcisions, the baptisms, and the feasts, in the observance of which they had been educated.

But the dominion of the whole Jewish ceremonial law could not long be retained in the growing life of the Christian Church. It must burst these cerements. The land is too narrow; the shell too contracted to hold a life that knows no boundaries of nation, creed, or ceremony.

A Greater Cause of its Decline.

But a greater cause of the decline of infant baptism (and of adult baptism also) was the slowly developing conviction in the Christian Church that ceremonial defilements were mythical and unreal; that neither Gentiles nor Jews were unclean before God on account of any bodily accident or exposure; that Moses had made use of these regulations respecting purifying to impress the need of a moral purifying,—and hence, when the moral purity was gained, the great work of the law, and the great work of Christ had been gained, and that in the beginning and ending of this work, the Gentile and Jew stood on the same foundation in the sight of a holy God, irrespective of any rites or ceremonies.

This was, in the first place, the outgrowth of John's teaching, that God required heart-repentance of each and all alike; hence even the ceremonially *un*-defiled Jews came to his baptism by thousands; it was, in the second place, a result of Christ's teaching, that not that which " goeth into a man " physically, defileth him, but that which was begotten in and came forth from the heart, and that God sought not worshippers after the form, but worshippers after the spirit.

Christ and Paul saw that to blot out Judaism was indispensable to the resurrection and perpetuity of a genuine Church.

But the non-existence of the supposed ceremonial defilement requiring baptism, was still more clearly shown in the vision of Peter, in the case of Cornelius, to whom the angel said, " What God hath cleansed, that call not thou common or unclean." And yet Peter could not then look further than to see that he might preach to, and eat with *the uncircumcised ;* and seeing the *uncircumcised* purified of the Holy Ghost, he judged they were deserving of entrance into the Jewish (Mosaic) covenant by baptism, without the heretofore indispensable circumcision. But Peter did not even yet give up circumcision and queryings about "meats," and the right to eat with Gentiles when among the Jews (see book of Galatians).

He was doubtless as much inspired in this as in baptizing Cornelius, and no more. And so with Paul, who, after this event, oft observed the Passover and Pentecostal feasts of the Jews. But Paul would allow no such yoke of ritualism to be imposed on the Gentiles. And he (1 Cor. vii. 14) gives them a very good reason why their children *needed no baptism:* they are already "holy" (undefiled), in consequence of their relation to a believing parent, or parents. Although not purified by their own faith, they need no ceremonial purifying, notwithstanding they are born of Gentile parentage. This, though so often overlooked, is to our mind most evidently the interpretation of this passage. And it harmonizes with all Paul's letters to the Gentile churches, in which he tells them that by the spiritual baptism into Christ they are made "one with Christ," and "heirs" through the spirit of adoption, and not by any ceremonial observance.

A DECLINE OF INFANT BAPTISM IS A DECLINE OF BAPTISM ITSELF.

It surely lessens the number of persons to be baptized. And the same view of the radical and saving nature of the true baptism, which would lay little stress upon the application of a mere symbol to a child, would lead the same mind to lay little stress upon the application of the symbol to an impenitent adult. Although he baptized many, because many gave evidence of repentance, yet not as before, when the priests ritually purified all the *ceremonially* defiled, whether penitent or impenitent, John manifestly refused all but the penitent. Nor is there one word of proof that any apostle or Christian father, for, at least, one hundred and fifty years after John, baptized a single infant, or any one not professing repentance. John commenced the change, then, from the Jewish custom to the "REFORMATION" custom. "Households," in a few instances, were baptized, and we object not to conceding that they contained children (if so, they were blessed by the *purifying* as much as Jewish children had been before, and no more); but it is wholly gratuitous to assume that there is one iota of *proof* of the apostolic baptism of infants.

The history of the baptism of infants in Christian and Jewish history is like an hour-glass—the largest at either terminus, with that period near the Christian era left nearly invisible and non-connective. This, if we may trust the most reliable historians, is the unquestionable truth.

OLSHAUSEN says:

"Of infant baptism the New Testament knows nothing."

HAHN says that

"There is no proof of a single infant baptism in the Christian Church for one hundred and fifty years after Christ."

We think that a few Judaizers in Palestine, and in a westward line therefrom, did baptize infants in "households" occasionally; hence Pelagius' (a Briton's) "impressions" on the subject, and Augustine's (rumor of) "apostolic tradition" to that effect. But none of them do say or dare say that the apostles and Gentile churches continuously baptized infants. (Reserving Neander's ample testimony to another page), do not our later Church historians see the gap in the history of infant baptism to be simply *a gap in the history of baptism itself?* This gap, according to Neander, is found in the history of all the Gentile churches.

JUDAIZERS HAVE EVER CONFOUNDED THE JEWISH AND GENTILE CHURCHES.

The Judaizers continued to practise adult and infant baptism, thus transferring the Mosaic purifications to the Christian Church, even as our modern Pedo-Baptist writers claim to build their churches after the Old Testament model—asserting that the Christian Church is but a continuance of the Jewish, with the slight change of the substitution of baptism in the Christian Church for circumcision in the Jewish Church. Conkling's "Text-book on Baptism" is wholly devoted to this effort to identify the two Churches as one and the same, affirming the Jewish Church to be identical with the Christian, even after the ritual law of Moses had been added to Abraham's church of simple faith in the " promise."

Hear him, p. 108, and on:

"To understand the laws and usages of the Church of God the searcher goes to her organization, and consults her constitution . . . . .and asks what does that teach? Who were received into covenant relation then? What were the rites and duties, the privileges, promises, and responsibilities then? He consults the history of the Church to see 'if her constitution has been revised or repealed.' . . . The examination of the *Old Testament Scriptures* with reference to this subject has led us to the following conclusions; nor do we see how our opponents can possibly avoid these same conclusions with *even a plausible argument:* First: we have shown that the Old Testament Church, organized under the covenant of circumcision, was the true visible Church of God; and that infants were divinely constituted members of the Church by the same religious rite that constituted adults members.

"Secondly: We have shown *that the Old and New Testament Church is one and the same Church,* under different dispensations, but *based upon the same covenant, viz., the covenant of circumcision.*"

There, reader, if there be not Judaism in full bloom we know not where you will find it. This writer's make-shift of putting baptism in place of circumcision, afterward, does not change the fact that he makes the Christian Church, in substance, but Judaism, continued. And his proof of the change of the rites reminds us of the sage and astute reasoning of Dr. HOPKINS, in his "Christian Instructor," before cited, wherein he says:

"Baptism and circumcision were for many years practised synchronically in the Christian Church; *therefore* baptism takes the place of circumcision, and was divinely appointed to take its place!"

A Sciolist might inquire, "Where does the Divine Teacher instruct the primitive Christians as to the precise moment when they should drop circumcision and put baptism in its place so as not to be bestrode with and in bondage to both?"

The logic is, like the cob-web, weaker than weakness itself, because it lacks the divine instruction altogether; yet as good as any argument to prove that any ceremonial of Moses belongs to the Christian Church.

HENDRICK'S work on "Baptism" proceeds on the same hypothesis. Hear him, p. 36:

> "Baptism and circumcision, then, are but two forms of the same seal. . . . Circumcision was the seal of initiation into the Jewish Church, and all admit baptism is the same in the Christian Church. . . . Circumcision was a sign of sanctification in the Jewish Church, . . . so baptism is a *sign and means* of sanctification in the Christian Church. . . . *The identity of the Christian and Jewish Church is manifest to all who will carefully examine the Bible!*"

Thus we have in nearly all Pedo-Baptist writers an attempt to weld the Christian Church to the Jewish, not only *spiritually*, but *ritually*. Not content with going back to Abraham, and the first covenant made with him, which is correct, for that was the covenant of promise, made twenty-four years before circumcision was given, they cannot stop short of lugging into that covenant, not only circumcision, which was *never designed for the whole world*—although the covenant of promise was—but also all the ritual of Moses which was established four hundred and thirty years after, and never a part of the promised covenant.

We say "all the ritual of Moses," for when they take but *baptism*, wide as they may differ from the Mosaic design of it, they, nevertheless, must needs have a human priesthood, and all the forms and *orders* of canonical administration, as the advancing papacy established them, both for baptism and other borrowed Jewish rites which they call *sacraments*.

Thus, reader, behold what positions and logic an exigency will force men to occupy and use! These writers are seeking to establish from Scripture the practice of infant baptism. They cannot do it without Moses and the law, thus engrafting Judaism upon Christianity; hence their logic. The New Testament never has been a stronghold for them; hence their resort to the Old. And the book of Hebrews (by Paul) was written in vain for such men,[*] who cannot see a change of the law and "*disannulling of the commandment going before, for the weakness and unprofitableness thereof*," that a *better covenant*

---

[*] So 2 Cor. iii. and Paul's letter to the Galatians.

and a law, not encumbered with sacrifices and a ritual, might take their place, and be fitted to universal acceptance, and not merely for the Jewish nation.

They forgot, also, what Paul says (Gal. v. 6): "For in Christ Jesus neither circumcision availeth anything, nor uncircumcision, but faith which worketh by love."

We now proceed to show that outside of Palestine and the Hellenistic church of that region, infant baptism was not practised from the Apostolic age, and for centuries afterward.

Says NEANDER, vol. ii. p. 319 (bear in mind this volume of Neander's presents the history of the Church from A. D. 312 to 500):

"Infant baptism was very slow in coming into the Greek Church. It was rarely practised during the first half of this period."

He also recites the manner of its inception and advance, vol. i. p. 210. He says:

"Cyprian's idea was, that Christ communicated to the apostles, and the apostles to the bishops, by ordination, the power of the Holy Ghost, whence, alone, all religious acts can derive their efficacy. By the succession of bishops this power of the Holy Ghost is extended to all time.* None can derive this life from Christ alone."

NEANDER pronounces such a theory as "*outwardism that needs stripping*." On p. 313, Neander says:

"When now, on the one hand, the doctrine of corruption and guilt cleaving to human nature in consequence of the first transgression was reduced to a more precise form; and from want of duly distinguishing between what is outward and what is inward in baptism, the baptism by water and the baptism by the Spirit, the error became more firmly established, that without external baptism no one could be delivered from the inherent guilt—could be saved from the everlasting punishment threatened, . . . the theory was finally evolved of the *unconditional necessity of infant baptism*."

To FIDUS, who urged that baptism should be postponed until the child was eight days old, CYPRIAN replies:

"As to what you say, that the child in the first days of its birth is not *clean to the touch*, and that each of us would shrink from kissing such an object:

---

* *Why not call this* THE *baptism then, and the real Apostolic succession?*

even this, in our opinion, ought to present no obstacle to the *bestowment of the heavenly grace ;* for it is written, ' To the pure all things are pure,' and none of us ought to revolt at that which God has condescended to create. Although the child be but just born, yet it is no such object that any one ought to demur at kissing it to *impart the divine grace,* and the salutation of peace (*i. e.*), as a sign of fellowship in the Lord."

Here the "*imparting the divine grace*" is divided between the act of baptism and the act of *kissing.* Which did Cyprian understand to be the *real ordinance* in this case? Thus see to what puerilities ritualism had led some *wise* men at this era of the Church. This Cyprian was a noted bishop in northern Africa, about A. D. 250.

IRENÆUS, who wrote A. D. 200, and who seems to be about the first Gentile Christian teacher (Judaizer) who was willing to adopt infant baptism from his Jewish neighbors, says:

"Infant baptism appears as the medium through which Christ imparts sanctification to infants. Thus the divine grace is imparted to them that they might be sanctified from their earliest development."

And Neander remarks that Irenæus evidently means *baptism* by the term *regeneration* when applied to infants. This was manifestly true, since infant baptism in the Gentile Church was a sprout from the doctrine of baptismal regeneration—and its necessity for all prior to death—leading some, like Cyprian, to haste its application to the instant of birth, lest they die unbaptized and lose heaven—leading others to teach that baptism would be administered in *hades* to those not baptized before death—and others to teach even that *baptism might be administered before birth* (see Robinson, p. 385). There seemed to be no end to the crude conceits of ritualists in the dawn of ritualism in the Gentile Church.

But TERTULLIAN opposed the views of Cyprian and Irenæus, saying that he

"Could not conceive of any efficacy whatever residing in baptism, without the conscious participation and individual faith of the person baptized, nor could he see any danger accruing to the *age of innocence* from delaying it."

Yet even Tertullian, who recommended for prudential reasons the delaying of baptism till just before death, on the ground that otherwise the sins committed after baptism could not be washed away, admits that infants, *being as unclean as any, needed baptism as much as any* (see Kendrick on "Baptism, p. 44). His sentiments were quite divergent from our Baptist brethren both ways.

Says NEANDER, respecting these opposite teachings of ritualists of that day, vol. i. p. 314:

"Infants were baptized to save them from original sin; others delayed baptism to riot in lusts till just before death, and then be cleansed from actual sins. All these rites had reference to one principal thing, without which no one could be a Christian, the forgiveness of sin, the cleansing from sin, the baptism of the Spirit, the birth to a new life, which was mediated by baptism in the name of the Father, Son, and Holy Spirit, and the impartation of the Holy Spirit following thereupon, the individual now being restored to the original state of innocence."

Thus we see that when infant baptism comes (or adult baptism), they bring with them the doctrine of baptismal regeneration in full, showing that this ritualistic view was the common view of all who practised water-baptism from its genesis in the Christian Church and on. Water-baptism in all these early ages was held to be the *saving ordinance* (as Alexander Campbell, in our day, has taught it). The doctrine resulted in the papacy, and is fully incorporated in that system to-day.

THE TWO OPPOSING SCHOOLS.

There were but two opposing ideas relating thereto in the Church in the early centuries, *viz.*, the Judaic, or ritualistic idea, opposed to which was the non-baptizing and anti-ritualistic idea. These contesting views continued rife, in the Eastern Church especially, down to the time of the Reformation under Luther. And Luther himself reformed more in other respects, retaining, in creed at least, the ritualistic idea of baptism as an ordinance that cleanses the soul. The muddle of varying conceits respecting baptism and its adjuncts in the early ages, as at present, it is impossible fully to unfold.

The baptizers baptized in every mode that can be conjectured, and added other rites, *ad nauseam*. *We* now inquire chiefly as to how we should baptize? *They* chiefly contended as to whether they should be baptized or not, and why and when? An ambitious priesthood, finding a ritual necessary to their official rule, piled on the ritual to the extent of their caprices; and persuaded themselves and others that heaven had appointed and sanctioned it all.

See how the human mind can infatuate itself!

Says NEANDER:

"It was by confounding regeneration with baptism, and thus looking upon regeneration as a sort of charm completed at a stroke, by supposing a certain magical purification and removal of all sin in the act of baptism, that men were led to refer the forgiveness of sins, obtained through Christ only, to the particular sins which had been committed previously to baptism. Afterward they looked to penance and supererogation for cleansing—then to purgatory and to baptism there."

Showing the constant tendency to look to things outward for salvation.

Their ritualism also led to the same narrow views as in later ages. Says Neander, vol. i. p. 655:

"The outward materialistic view of regeneration which arose out of the habit of confounding it with baptism, afterward, through narrowness of mind thus induced, issued in the notion of the absolute predestination of those baptized."

For if there was no other evidence of the prospective final salvation of those baptized in their sanctified or changed lives, it could be assumed to rest on the basis of their predestination, thus leaving man to determine by a ritual the number of the elect.

Truly, as Neander says of Cyprian, that

"Embarrassed by his habit of confounding the inward with the outward by his materialism, he thus mingled it *with much that is erroneous.*"

Predestination, we must infer, was to complete the work of salvation where the baptism had left it incomplete.

NEANDER adds:

"Even in the spiritual Clement of Alexandria (A. D. 200) we may discern the influence of the outward and materialistic conception of spiritual matters, when he agrees with Hermas that the apostles performed in hades the rite of baptism on the pious souls of the Old Testament."

But there is no end to the conceits of ritualists respecting baptism, its modes,* its effects, the proper administrators, the time of its administration, etc., etc.

And, so far as history tells us, nearly all these variations have existed since A. D. 150. We may, therefore, well ask, if there be a Christian law requiring ritual baptism, why so soon forgotten, or such utter confusion respecting it? Which one of all this Babel of voices will correctly tell us what it is? its form? import? proper antecedents? sequences? etc., etc.

We have a right to demand a categorical and definitive answer—one that shall satisfy and render of one mind on the subject all those that have uttered these jarring notes. Thus did the law of Moses! and shall the Christian teachers be more ambiguous than Moses? No man may attempt to impose an undefined law upon the Church—no more than a human legislature may attempt to impose such a law upon human society. Levites did not debate the ceremonial laws of Moses; hence see how irreconcilable with himself is Neander, in speaking so oft of the "lofty position of Paul in introducing to the Gentiles a purely spiritual dispensation," one which the Judaizers opposed for this reason, and because of its unrestricted catholicity; and then making such statements as the following:

"Baptism and the Lord's Supper belong to the unchangeable economy of the Christian system."

This is purely dogmatic, and a sop to Cerberus.

Does he give us the law, and show us the "unchangeable priesthood," and the blessed fruits of giving such a law? Nay, but the "unchangeable" fruits have ever been manifest. All

---

* Modes of baptizing as a religious observance were almost as varied as the modes of secular washings and ablutions; for these were all oft called baptisms.

know that in no age or nation has water-baptism or the *Supper*
tended either to catholicity or union among saints, but ever
and forever to the reverse.

The Baptismal Babel.

Every student of history knows that strifes about who shall
administer baptism, how they shall administer baptism, and
when they shall administer baptism, and what adjuncts shall
attend it, have been rife for 1700 years. He knows that baptism has been administered in sanctuaries and out of sanctuaries; by bishops, priests, and deacons; to persons sick and
well, living and dying; infants and adults; by affusion, by
immersion, by sprinkling, by putting bodies into water, and
applying water to bodies; by trine immersion, and by single
immersion; by immersing with the face downward, and immersing with the face upwards; immersing persons naked, and
immersing persons clothed; sprinkling with blood, with sand,
and with tears; following baptism with chrism, sign of the
cross, white robes, confirmation, holy kiss, honey and milk,
and other mummeries too numerous to mention; and that in
all these ages disputes about all these modes and adjuncts
have been rife. Is this ritual then (and the Supper, about
which as many conceits and as many disputes have arisen)
found woven into Paul's "lofty catholic position," to secure
the unity and purity of the Church?—to educate and "train"
the Church to that *higher spiritual life* which she could not
maintain, without going back to these carnal elements?

Where, we again ask, does the New Testament thus teach,
or establish and define a law of sacraments? The evidence
simply is, that Judaizers have interpolated them, and that the
doctrine of baptism as a Christian ordinance, and of baptismal
regeneration, was resorted to by the priesthood to gain power
—to increase converts to their flocks and creeds—seizing even
infants from their birth and before, to write their mark upon
them, with most disgusting details of ceremonial adjuncts.

Tradition the Authority Claimed.

NEANDER offers no word of Scripture proof of a ritual law as he states it—he does not represent the ritualistic fathers as proving their rituals from Scriptures, or even from Christ's teaching or example—he descants upon the need of signs and emblems as helps to faith (the everlasting fallacy of all ritualistic reasonings), and then, through the fathers, turns us over to *tradition* as the foundation for their practice.

Hear NEANDER, vol. i. p. 314 :

"Origen, in whose system *infant baptism could readily find its place*, in this age when the inclination was so strong to trace every institution which was considered of special importance to the apostles, declares it to be "an apostolic tradition."

NEANDER adds :

"Many walls of separation hindering the freedom of prospect *had already been set up between this and the apostolic age.*"

As much as to say that there was no foundation for any such claim of apostolic tradition. So Tertullian had told them, in respect to baptism and its adjuncts, especially its adjuncts :

"You shall find no other ground for them than *tradition !*"

Even AUGUSTINE, in introducing infant baptism into his diocese, can cite no other authority than to claim that it was "*an apostolic tradition.*"

Now it would seem that even weak brethren like ourselves might see the utter fallacy of any such claim. Why not say it was an *apostolic practice*, if it really was? Living, as they did, so near the apostolic age (Tertullian, A. D. 200, and Augustine, A. D. 400), the evidence could not have all faded out in their day—no universal change of custom, and even the record thereof, obliterated. The evidence appears to bear to the point that, at the behest of the Judaizing portion of the Church, Augustine (in the wake of Rome) was endeavoring to introduce infant baptism, as a method of inducting youth and children into the Church, after the Jewish model, and as

Cyprian had done one hundred and fifty years before. His quoting "apostolic tradition" could only refer to the fact that the apostles, when among Jews, did not war against the Jewish customs, either of circumcision or baptism, while there is not a shade of evidence that they required, or even approved of them—*i. e.*, as a law for the Christian Church.

Augustine's referring to it as a "tradition" shows that he did not regard it as a law, nor as a well-known and common custom, and Neander's testimony amply attests the same. James (the apostle) might have practised it among the Jews at Jerusalem (and hence the *tradition*), for he was the "apostle of the circumcision," but there is not the slightest evidence that Paul, or Peter, or John, carried it among the Gentiles.

Remember that Christ did not interfere with the Jewish ceremonial law, for he labored wholly among Jews whose prejudices would not have permitted it; and the New Testament epistles were not written, giving the anti-ritual protests of Paul, until twenty or thirty years after Christ's day. All the confusion arising in the minds of both Baptists and Pedo-Baptists respecting the origin of infant baptism (or of adult baptism) comes from assuming that baptism has a source different from the real Jewish origin, as though somewhere in the early Christian age it had been re-enacted as a *Christian* rite, and that to supplant a Jewish rite (circumcision), albeit all Pedo-Baptists know that it was itself a long-standing Jewish rite. Yet the fallacy pervades the Christian Church that it is a something (ay, a sacrament) starting with Christ and the apostles; and thus with the Christian dispensation, which is a demonstrated error. Is this denied? Then let the reader tell at what precise date, just before or after Christ's crucifixion, *Christian baptism* did originate?

WALL, the great Pedo-Baptist historian, is equally in a muddle on this subject—he cannot fix the point himself; GILL, the great Baptist annotator, is in the same muddle; and ROBINSON (Baptist) has not attempted to make the case any better.

The ritual law of the Baptists, the Pedo-Baptists, and the Episcopacy is, therefore, as great a fallacy as was ever imposed upon the Christian Church. Irenæus, and others, simply revived baptism (infant and adult) in the Gentile churches when they revived *Judaism*.

THE HIDDEN ANTI-RITUALISTIC RECORD REVEALED.

Having traced the tortuous, apostatizing, anti-Scriptural path of the ritualists, in departing from the "simplicity there is in Christ," let us bring out that other record, which those who only search after the canonical robes of *churchianity* and self-proclaimed orthodoxy have failed to see. Keep it in mind that God looks not on things after the outward appearance—the shell that first comes in sight to those who take short and unreflecting views—and that the true Church of Christ has as oft been the unrecognized, the unchronicled, and the *heretical*, so called, as that which has worn the canonical robes. Tracing the record of the ritualists, we shall find their sphere much more limited than modern writers and pulpit orators have conceived. For the first four centuries they seem to have extended their influence from Palestine, and the Judaizers there, only to Northern Africa, Rome, and the regions west, immediately contiguous to Rome. Greece, Macedonia, Syria, Armenia, Persia, and all central Asia, seem scarcely to have felt their influence. As to the Jewish baptisms and customs, they were very slow in reaching this region. In fact, prior to A. D. 250, few of the Christian fathers seem to have been enamored of water-baptism in any part of the Church. Clement and Cyprian had begun to seek a swifter process of converting people to their creeds, and preparing them for their church and their heaven, than by the slow and radical process of true spiritual regeneration. Hence they introduced from the Jews the doctrine of baptismal regeneration. Cyprian, especially (A. D. 250), in the bishopric of Northern Africa, caught the idea, and carried it beyond all precedent or bounds of moderation—even for that superstitious age. From that period, we have the testimony of Optatus, Gregory Nazianzen, Ambrose, Chrysostom, Augustine, Pelagius, and Celestius, that ritualism was the order of the day in the metropolitan churches of Rome and Africa. Infant baptism and adult baptism, with all their antecedents and subsequents, and pretended results, led the Church toward Popery as fast as mind could march and time could move.

But they did not carry the whole Church with them: God reserved many a *seven thousand* that were not bewildered nor carried away with the superstitions of the ritualists. We find hints of this all along.

THE BAPTISMAL VACUUM.

We have seen how Alexander Campbell, the champion of immersion, failed to find any evidence of water-baptism for at least two generations succeeding the apostles, thus presenting to our view the somewhat ludicrous attitude of Baptists and Pedo-Baptists contending with each other about the form and substance of a vacuum. We have also found Neander repeatedly asserting that infant baptism was not practised in the Gentile churches to any appreciable extent for more than three centuries after Christ. Yet infant baptism was a general custom where baptism was practised at all, from the fourth to the sixteenth century! And it is demonstrated that infant baptism of proselytes was as common as adult baptism in all the Jewish history. Also, that from a revived Judaism, the whole scheme and apostasy of the Papacy, with all its ritual idolatry, arose.

Yet Nonconformists, Protestants, and heretics abounded. CONKLING, in his work on "Baptism," says (p. 230):

"Irenæus, Epiphanius, Philastrius, Austen, and Theodoret, each wrote catalogues of all the sects and heresies that had arisen in the Church, *but there are none found who reject infant baptism*, UNLESS SUCH AS REJECT WATER-BAPTISM ALTOGETHER."

Now here is a sword given us, like the Scottish broadsword, that cuts two ways at the same time. Neander affirming that

11

infant baptism was *almost unknown* in the Greek and Eastern
churches for about four centuries after Christ, which being
granted, we have the proof that water-baptism was almost unknown among the same churches during this period.   Thus
we may extend Alexander Campbell's search after *immersion*
to the Pedo-Baptist's search after infant baptism, reaching
ages beyond where even Mr. Campbell could find no baptism
at all and meet the same result.

We find it making but slow advance at most; Theodoret
announces that several of these sects he named rejected
water-baptism; nor does he say that he did not himself
reject it!

And as to the heresies found, we presume that any writer
in either of these "sects" would have found the same number
of "heresies," and would have ranked Theodoret and the other
heresy-hunters named among the heretics.   "Orthodoxy" in
all ages has been "*my doxy*," while "heterodoxy" has *been*
found wherever "your doxy" differs from mine!   But the
assumption has not always been recorded thus on the tab-
lets of heaven; a more impartial record has been kept
there.

By a slip of the pen, undoubtedly, Tertullian recognized
the presence of these non-baptizers (A. D. 200).   Robinson,
the Baptist historian, on p. 72, writes thus : " Says Tertullian
to some *who denied water-baptism :*

"You act naturally, for you are serpents, and serpents love deserts and avoid
water; but we, like fishes, *are born in the water,* and are *safe by continuing
in it.*'"

Tertullian, no doubt, thought this was shrewd, but it simply
reveals his trust in the waters of baptism.   His opponent
might as fairly have chosen his simile, and compared his
water-loving opponent to the eel that loves the mire at the bottom of the stagnant lake, and himself to the dove that delights
to skim the heavenly vault and bask in the sunlight of
God.

TERTULLIAN'S opposition to infant baptism greatly disturbed the Judaizing clergy. ROBINSON notes it by saying:

"The delay of baptism (until near death) greatly distressed the clergy; they perpetually harped upon it," p. 229.

Of course these clergy, in due time, *Cyprianized* those they taught respecting early baptism.*

And NEANDER deals rather roughly with the "apostolic tradition" plea for infant baptism, as we are disposed to do with the apostolic *example* plea for water-baptism in any form. In his "Planting and Training of the Church" (p. 102), he says:

"If we wish to ascertain from whom such an institution was originated, we should say, certainly not immediately from Christ himself. . . . Was it from an injunction given by the earlier apostles? But among the Jewish Christians circumcision was held as the seal of the covenant, hence they had *much less occasion to make use of baptism!* This would agree least of all with the peculiar Christian characteristics of the Apostle Paul, he who says of himself that Christ 'sent him not to baptize, but to preach the gospel;' he who always kept his eye fixed on one thing, justification by faith, and so carefully avoided everything that could give a handle or support to the notion of justification by outward things—how could he set up infant baptism against the circumcision that continued to be practised by the Jewish Christians?"

But how does Neander not see that his reasoning bears as strongly against the supposition that Paul in any manner "set up" adult as infant baptism, in lieu of circumcision? If circumcision was *the* "*seal*" of the covenant, why need baptism at all? especially as this was as "outward" as circumcision, and could "justify" no more than could circumcision. Did not Paul ever tell both Jew and Gentile that *the* "seal" was the "Holy Spirit of promise?"

---

* Says NEANDER: "Tertullian's opposition to infant baptism is proof that it was not then usually considered an apostolic ordinance, for in that case he would hardly have ventured to speak so strongly against it." Yet we may add, he speaks as strongly *against the baptism of young and unmarried persons*, lest they commit some sin after baptism, and it be *too late for baptism to wash it away.* Is this evidence that he considered baptism, at any age, apostolic, or a divine command?

But TERTULLIAN himself contends for baptism, and laments the Gnostic rejection of it.   He says:

"Some affecting superior sanctity among the Gnostics wholly omit baptism."

So he complains of the Caianites of Egypt, and Quintillianists of Greece, that they claimed to be so holy as not to need the healing waters of baptism.   So WALL, vol. i. p. 397, alludes to "some wicked people who were *opponents of baptism*."   Now this was, doubtless, decisive proof of their "wickedness" according to the Judaic standard; yet on the next page he declares that the prophets of the Old Testament did not baptize—but we presume they were justified since the Jewish priests did!

Dr. Robinson's Vision once Retroverted.

And ROBINSON, the Baptist historian (p. 46), caught a glimpse so far back, for once, as to speak of baptism as "a rite instituted of God for the Jews!" and then hear him compliment its working among that people:

"The best use that can be made of a knowledge of the Jewish baptisms is to pity their apostasy, and to set them an example of renouncing the *fatal error* from which all their ills originally proceeded—*i. e.*, the traditions of enthusiasts who issued laws to bind the conscience, and who, like some Etruscan statues, have not one thing to recommend them to attention except their antiquity."

Now it may be assumed that the above anathema upon the devoted heads of Jewish baptizers comes from the fact that these dear apostate Jews have not followed (have never adopted) Dr. Robinson's theory of baptism; hence they are in "fatal error" and follow blind guides.

But he forgets that their following their *Bath Col.* and their traditions is both a consequence and a cause of their apostasy from God, even while most punctiliously following their ritual laws, and practising their baptisms, as they in their original simplicity understood them.   *Their baptisms did not save them.*

And the sprinklers and immersers of the Christian Church have never found the evidence of the truth of the following citation Dr. Robinson has attributed to a bishop of the third or fourth century :

"Jesus took away the sin of the world by being baptized in the river Jordan. . . . When David said, 'Wash me, and I shall be whiter than snow,' it was as much as to say, 'Lord, thou hast cleansed me from the sin of my father, Adam, by taking his flesh on thyself, dipping it in the font, and washing it in the river.' To an objector, who asks, 'What is there in baptism except water, chrism, and a white garment?' he replies, 'Christ, by being dipped in Jordan, sanctified those waters. Baptismal water is water of remission. At the font you receive not *a Jewish* but an evangelical sign. That day, that hour, when you come out of the laver you have within yourself a perpetually running water, and daily remission. Art thou defiled after baptism? Is thy heart vitiated? thy heart contaminated? Dip thyself in abundance of tears —let it be a living water overflowing every fibre.'"

Reader, you have in this extract a complete illustration of the teachers of the second and third centuries, among the ritualists, that taught water-baptism for any cause. Our Saviour, who was baptized by John, a Jewish priest, is here adduced as thereby sanctifying the waters of baptism forever, so that we also, who are baptized, obtain a "daily remission," for "baptismal water is water of remission." This is still the creed doctrine of all the Oriental churches, the Papacy, the Lutheran and the Episcopal churches.

But mark, it is a most singular fact that neither in the above citation nor scarcely in any extant teaching of the fathers is there a reference to any command of Christ or the apostles as enjoining water-baptism; thus evincing that these fathers, at least, laid little stress upon the "Great Commission" as enjoining water-baptism, and that it was not unwittingly resumed as an element of Judaism.

Particularly is this fact noticeable touching infant baptism, since, in respect to that, the greatest of the fathers, as Augustine and Tertullian, but refer to tradition as the basis on which it is to be commended. When Christ said, "Go, teach all nations, baptizing them," surely this would include all classes, infants and adults, the sick and the healthy, if it referred to water-baptism at all.

But not only were the Eastern churches very slow in adopting the Jewish ritual law, but from that section, according to Neander, were continually arising dissenters and protestants, who sought to roll back the incoming wave of ritualism that threatened to engulf and sink all that was spiritual and saving in the Christian Church.

Thus the living Church was full oft forced to become protestants and dissenters.

CHAPTER V.

CHRONICLES OF THE NON-BAPTIZERS — THE TRUE CHURCH FOUND.

JUSTIN MARTYR, A. D. 140.*

IT is a notable fact that the first to break the long silence respecting baptism, that succeeded the apostolic era, was *Justin Martyr,* and that in doing so he has in full corroborated all that we have claimed respecting the post-apostolic rejection of water-baptism, and the sentiment of the church generally, as adverse to it.

In his dialogue with Trypho, the Jew (a document of undoubted authenticity), he attributes the baptism of water to the Jews, as their baptism, and claims for the Church of Christ an infinitely superior baptism, by which we are really purified. He declares water-baptism and circumcision "useless," marks clearly the transition from the legal Jewish Sabbath to the "Lord's Day" rest, and tells Trypho that the whole ceremonial law was given to the Jews as a token for good if they were obedient, but as marking them for destruction if they were disobedient and violators of their national charter. We quote from "Dialogue," Oxford ed., p. 85, etc.:

"You (Trypho) need a second circumcision, and yet you think much of that of the flesh. The new law (the Christian) commands you to keep a perpetual Sabbath, and you rest in one day and think that you are religious, not thinking *why* the commandment was given you. . . . If any be an adulterer, let him repent, and then he will have kept a true and pleasant Sabbath of God. If any has unclean hands, let him *wash,* and he will be pure. For it was not, surely,

---

* N. B.—The date given in connection with the nomenclature of the non-ritualists is designed to mark the period when they were most active and influential.

to the bath that Isaiah sent you to wash away murder and those other sins from which all the waters of the sea cannot cleanse you, but, as one would think, there was of old the very *washing of salvation* which he spoke of, viz.: that which is for those who repent, and who are *no longer purified by the blood of goats and sheep,* or by the *ashes of a heifer,* or by the offerings of fine flour, *but by faith* through the blood and death of Christ, *who died for this very purpose.*"

JUSTIN here quotes, in proof, Isaiah, 52d and 53d chapters, and expatiates upon what they teach. On p. 87 he says:

"Through the *baptism of repentance* and knowledge of God, therefore, which was instituted for the sins of the people, as Isaiah says, we have believed, and we know the same baptism which he preached, and *which alone is able to cleanse those who repent, is the water of life.*

But the cisterns which you have digged for yourselves are broken cisterns, and *unable to be of any use to you,* FOR WHAT PROFIT IS THERE IN THE BAPTISM WHICH CLEANSES THE FLESH AND THE BODY ALONE? LET YOUR SOULS BE WASHED FROM ANGER AND FROM COVETOUSNESS, FROM ENVY AND HATRED, AND THE WHOLE BODY WILL BE PURE.

"And this is the signification of the unleavened bread, viz.: that you should abstain from the old works of evil leaven. You, however, receive everything in a *carnal sense,* and think it to be serving God if you do such works, while your souls are filled with deceitfulness and every kind of evil. Hence God commends you to the practice of new works."

JUSTIN here quotes Isaiah lv. 3 and to the end of the chapter. Also, in the same connection, quotes Deut. x. 12 to the end of the chapter, for the true circumcision—the " circumcision of the heart." Then quotes Lev. xxvi. 40, 41, to show the judgments denounced on the disobedient, and then declares that the fleshly circumcision was given the Jews as a mark to distinguish them from other nations, and from Christians, that they alone might suffer the inflictions God brought upon them for rejecting Christ. He tells Trypho, in this connection, that others, besides Jews, dishonor Christ because of the blasphemies of the Jews against Christ.

He then quotes Isaiah i. 16, " Wash you, make you clean, put away the evil of your doings," and adds:

"God thus commands you *to wash in this laver,* and to be circumcised with *the true circumcision ;* " and adds, " For we should practise your circumcision of the flesh, and should keep the Jewish Sabbaths, and all the feasts, did we not know for what they were enjoined you, viz.: *for your sins and the hardness of your hearts.*   For if we endure all that is inflicted on us by wicked men, and evil spirits, and yet, *in the midst of our indescribable modes of death and torture,* pray that those who so torment may find mercy, *why, Trypho, should we refuse to observe such rites as would do* US *no injury?* such as fleshly circumcision and keeping of the Sabbaths and festivals?   It is because circumcision is not necessary for all, but *only for the Jews,* that, as I said before, you might undergo your present *justly merited sufferings.*

NOR DO WE RECEIVE YOUR USELESS BAPTISM OF CISTERNS, FOR SUCH BEARS NO RELATION TO THE BAPTISM OF LIFE. . . . You who are circumcised in the flesh require OUR circumcision, while *we who possess this* HAVE NO NEED OF YOURS."

Nothing can be clearer than that Justin here contemplates circumcision and baptism as joint and collateral partners in the fleshly ritual—in the economy of Moses ever united; and both equally, and for the same reason, *to be laid aside.*   Can any *Christian* teacher deny this?   Hear him further: to justify his rejection of all these Jewish rites, he proceeds to enumerate the WORTHIES who were saved prior to the giving of the ritual law.   He specifies the case of "Adam (created without circumcision, thus proving it not necessary), then of Abel, Enoch, Noah, Lot, Melchisedek, etc., *saved* without circumcision, the latter having received tithes from Abraham, *the father of circumcision.*"   He then quotes from the prophet Hosea, to show that the Jews alone needed circumcision, "that they should not be a people of God, and not a nation," and that others not thus marked by this mark of the curse should take their places in God's favor.

He thus keenly suggests that all High Church ritualists are, by their very badges of ceremonialism and trust in the external, *thereby* known as "*not* the people of God."   On p. 134, Justin asserts that Christ ended John's baptism, and elsewhere gives an account of the Jewish baptism *in the name of one God,* the "ineffable" name, at the "laver," and says this was called the "*illumination,*" because they who receive it, and know the meaning, are "enlightened in their minds."

But Justin adds, referring to this very baptism of the Jews (and quoting Isaiah i. 16):

"*Our baptism is not of the flesh;* but the devil, hearing of this baptism taught by the prophet Isaiah, *instigated those who enter into their temples*, and who were about to come to them, to sprinkle themselves, and to wash their whole persons, imitating Moses and the prophet I have mentioned."

This after-reasoning implies that thus Satan deceives them by turning their attention from the inward to the outward baptism.

On p. 105, Justin adds:

"He (God) has shown his good-will toward the Gentiles also, and receives sacrifices from us more readily than from you (Jews). What need have I, then, *of circumcision*, who have the testimony of God in my favor? *How can I require that baptism* (of water), *who have been already baptized with the Holy Ghost?* . . And *so many righteous men who kept* NONE OF THESE LEGAL OBSERVANCES have still obtained the express approval of God himself."

Thus we see that if any one would obliviate the fact that baptism was really a concomitant of circumcision in the Jewish ritual, and would therefore urge that baptism has now supplanted circumcision, Justin sanctions no such plea, for he repeatedly groups both together, and folding them in the same Jewish shroud lays them in the grave together.

One other paragraph from this giant witness against the Judaisms that afterward so inundated the Roman Church, and we must pass. On p. 122, Justin says:

"So, I continued, if I were to sum *all the ordinances* which were commanded by Moses, I should prove them to be types, and symbols, and presignifications of what was afterwards to happen to Christ and those who were foreknown as believers in him; but since the things which I have already enumerated seem to me sufficient, I omit them and pass on to the next point in order, viz.: 'As circumcision began from Abraham, and the Sabbath, sacrifices and feasts from Moses, and I have proved that these were commanded on account of the hardness of your hearts (and ascribe it to your own wickedness that God can be thus falsely accused of not having always taught the same righteous (gospel) doctrines to all); so it was requisite that they (these sacrifices, feasts, etc.) should cease in Him who was born of the race of Abraham, of the tribe of Judah, and of the family of David—Christ, the Son of God, who, it was preached, should come as *the everlasting law* and new covenant *for the whole world.* . . . . We, too, who through him have come to God, *receive not this* FLESHLY *circumcision, but the* spiritual one, which Enoch and those like him observed. This, since *we* had been sinners, we received *by means of* BAPTISM (not the fleshly, which he has oft told us is '*useless*,' but the 'spiritual') through the mercy of God; and it would be good for *all to receive it likewise.*"

Having before enumerated those who were saved without circumcision, he concludes this ejection of the Mosaic ritual with a list of the *worthies* saved in the absence of it—*i. e.*, before it was needed or given. He quotes Abraham, Isaac, Jacob, Noah, Job, Sarah, Rebekah, Rachel, Leah, etc., down to Moses, who himself also was worthy to be the mediator of the old covenant, with all its ritual, before that ritual had been appointed.

JUSTIN MARTYR, whose teachings concerning rituals we have thus quoted, was born at Sychem, in Palestine, and preached there, also in Egypt, Asia Minor, and at Rome, and doubtless reflected the sentiments of the non-Jewish Christians of his age in all those lands. He was a man of extensive learning and influence, and a writer of two apologies for the Christians, addressed to the Roman emperors.* A work on external baptism, attributed to him, is undoubtedly spurious, as might well be judged from what is here cited, and as has also been proved and admitted by the best scholars. See *Tombes'* debate with *Marshall*, in a work entitled *Religious Thought in England*, pp. 217–227.†

It may be added that TATIAN, an Assyrian by birth, and an eminent scholar, having read a portion of the Scriptures, became convinced of the truth of their teachings, and embraced Christianity. He proceeded to Rome, and put himself under the teachings of *Justin Martyr*, and like him became eminent for piety and temperance in all things; like him rejected the Jewish rituals, dissuaded from the baptism of water and all use of wine. After the martyrdom of JUSTIN, he became a teacher in Rome for some years, and afterwards returned as a missionary of Christ to his own country. Mosheim says of him:

"His severe . . . system of discipline procured for his followers, of whom Tatian had soon to boast of great numbers in Syria, the people of which country

---

* Nevertheless, he was beheaded at Rome in 165, by the command of one of those emperors.

† But none question the authenticity of Justin Martyr's *"Dialogue with Trypho."*

naturally lean to an austerity of manners, and subsequently in other regions, the denomination of *Encratites*, or '*The Continent;*' *Hydroparastates*, or '*Water-drinkers;*' '*Apotactites*,' or *Renunciants*, *i. e.*, of this world's goods and sometimes *Tatianites*, referring to the author of the sect. This sect continued until the fourth century, and here, and among the *Gnostics*, *the Manichees*, and the *Euchites*, we find the true *temperance reformers* of the early centuries and all rejecting the baptism of water."

IGNATIUS, who wrote even earlier than Justin Martyr, and during his earlier life was cotemporary with the Apostle John, thus writes to the Magnesians. Speaking of Judaism, he says:

"Lay aside, therefore, the evil, the old, the sour leaven, and be ye changed to *the new leaven, which is Jesus Christ.* Be ye settled in him, lest any one among you should be corrupted, since by your savor you shall be convicted. *It is absurd to profess Jesus Christ and to Judaize.* For Christianity did not embrace Judaism, but Judaism Christianity."

IRENÆUS, three-fourths of a century later, writes:

"The Mosaic law was not established for righteous men. Abraham, without circumcision, and Lot, receiving salvation from God; *they* had the meaning of the law written in their hearts; but when righteousness and love to God became extinct in Egypt, God did necessarily reveal himself, that thou mightst know that man *doth not live by bread alone,* but by every word that proceedeth out of the mouth of God. God, standing in no need of anything from man, speaks thus by Moses, 'And what doth the Lord require of thee but to do justly,'" etc.

TERTULLIAN, also, cotemporary with Irenæus, says:

"Christ's disciples could only baptize with John's baptism—Christ's was not established. Hence Christ did not baptize."

GNOSTIC PROTEST AGAINST THE INCOMING PAPACY, A. D. 240.

THE GREAT DISSENT of early ages against a reinstatement of Judaism was found among the Gnostics. Says Neander (vol. i. p. 367):

"It cannot be denied that faith, taken according to the outward view of it, often placed itself in direct opposition to the strivings after knowledge, by holding fast on everything *as positive* as given from without, as an aggregate of separate positive doctrines and precepts. In Gnosticism the opposition between an esoteric sacerdotal doctrine and an exoteric religion of the people, between a philosophic religion and a popular faith, has its necessary ground in the fact that antiquity (*i. e.,* the old dispensation) was destitute of any independent means adapted alike to all the stages of human culture, or satisfying the religious want. The emancipation of religion *from all dependence on the elements of the world,* as well as from all dependence on the wisdom of the world, which knew not God, made Gnosticism a precursor of Protestantism. MARCION," he adds, in this connection, "*may be styled a precursor of Protestantism.*" Protestantism sprang out of the Pauline conception of faith once more restored and reinstated in its rights. At the basis of this whole theory lies the truth that Gnosticism, in so far as it was a reaction against the Jewish element that had become mixed in with Christianity, was a precursor of Protestantism."

The purport of the above seems to be that the Judaizing bishops and clergy dogmatized their own interpretation of revelation in behalf of "*positive doctrines*" and externals in religion. The Gnostics looked away from these dogmas and externals, looked within (esoterically) for a rational religion. *They* were willing to believe in the supernatural (in manifested faith), but they wanted other authority than the dogmatism of Judaizers for their faith. They asked a reason. They would neither trust to *worldly wisdom* nor to an exhibition of rites as the basis of their faith!

As examples of these Gnostic philosophers, who were also Christian teachers, Neander gives an extended account of Valentine, Basilides, and Marcion, whom he pronounces very holy men, and highly commends their philosophical anti-Jewish view of religion. Of Marcion he says, vol. i. p. 461:

"In Marcion we behold a reaction of that Pauline type of doctrine, reclaiming its rightful authority against the strong leaning of the Church to the side of James and Peter—a reaction of the Christian consciousness reasserting the independence acquired for it by the labors of Paul against a new combination of the *Jewish and Christian elements;* a reaction of the Protestant spirit against the Catholic element now swelling in the bud. He (Marcion) appropriated Christianity in a way somewhat *independent of tradition.* So, in the after development of his Christian views, he ever pursued this independent direction, and was unwilling to subject himself to any human traditions. Perhaps," says Neander, "it was the majesty of Christ beaming upon him from the survey of his life, and the contemplation of his words, *whereby he was drawn to Christianity.* . . . Hence the striving might have arisen in him to *purify Christianity from the foreign Jewish elements* with which it had been mixed, and to restore it once more to its primitive form."

Extent of Marcion's Protest.

The reform that Marcion sought may not have taken into view all the elements of Judaism that should have been dishevelled from the Christian Church. He may not, at first, at least, have seen that it would require the rejection of the Jewish purifyings,* as Paul himself was not so careful at first to reject them, and Luther, even, left the Papal creed unchanged in this respect, with the doctrine of baptismal regeneration still glaring upon us.

But it is certain that most of the Gnostics that followed, making practical the teachings of Marcion, did reject water-baptism. Of those who did thus reject this element of Judaism, we may specify the Prodicians, the Carpocratians, the Antitactites, the Valentinians, the Quintillianists, and the Caianites. This Gnostic philosophy, with its different phases, and the different teachers, continued for centuries, and in Greece and Northern Africa constituted a large portion of the Christian Church.

Mosheim, it is true, says some hard things about the Gnostics, as he does of all sects that veer from the *regular ritualistic line of succession.* Nor will we assert that some of the Gnostic sects were not wanting in respect to a full conformity to the moral law. Their aim at Christian perfectibility might have been marred, in certain cases, by a *letting down* of the standard of moral perfection, as in the case of the Valentinians and Caianites. But their ostensible aim at the standard of moral perfection rendered large numbers of them ascetics, to the degree of mortifying the body and its appetites to the extreme of totally crucifying many of the fleshly appetites.† Monasticism (in its earliest and purest stages) was rife among them;

---

* He seems to have initiated priests or the *perfects* with the ceremonial purifying.

† The *Religious Encyclopedia* says: "The greatest part of this sect adopted very austere rules of life; recommended rigorous abstinence, and prescribed severe bodily mortifications, with a view of purifying and exalting the mind."

none that aspired to the estate of the *perfects* was permitted to marry, or heap up earthly riches. Marcion did permit a sort of conventional baptism to the *perfects* as a mark of peculiar sanctity; but this was permitted to none that married, nor ever required of catechumens or infants. Of course, he based it on no divine or human law, but used it as a fit conventional custom in such cases as required the expression of special sanctity. Neander, better versed in Gnostic history than Mosheim, affirms that they manifested the highest extant type of the Christian life in their day. He also asserts that from these sprung the original germ of the mystic form of piety, and the Protestantism of the twelfth to the sixteenth century, that shed such a halo of light, and was almost the only embodiment of Christianity of those centuries. Neander affirms that the impeachment of the morals of those early dissenting sects was generally traceable to their enemies, *and without foundation.*

The Gnostics did not teach heretically respecting Christ, as Mosheim intimates. They undoubtedly carried their philosophy too far, and undertook to explain how and when the divine and human nature of Christ came into union; some fixing it at the period of his baptism, others at his death; but they all received *Christ* as the Divine Saviour, and were unquestionably the most devout and spiritual, intelligent and exemplary of Christ's professed people in their generation. If history be true, their piety and self-denial should have put to the shame the Judaizers, and those apostatizing to the pagan ritualisms of that era.

PREVALENCE AND CHARACTER OF THE GNOSTICS.

"The Greeks seek after wisdom," says Paul; and let it be remembered that the term "Gnostic" simply means "*the knowing ones,*" and indicates that in the Christian Church (*i. e.*, after their conversion to Christianity) the Greeks did not cease to seek after wisdom. The Gnostic Christians comprised nearly all the Greek Christians and those who spoke that language, who were so numerous in the second century that the term *Gnostic* was oft used only as another name for the Gentile Christian Church. And as it is admitted by all that the Gnostics generally rejected water-baptism, it follows that the Greek churches in their day generally rejected water-baptism. And let it be noted (and we learn it from Mosheim, p. 107 *Read's Mosheim*) that Gnosticism waned as night wanes by the rising day.

The Gnostics were from the first the protestants against the transplanting of Judaism, and they continued so to be. They were of an indefinitely broader mind, and took a more philosophic view of Christianity than did the Judaizers. The narrowing boundaries of creeds, and rituals, and dogmatic statements of speculative doctrines, like all enlarged and philosophic minds, they overleaped almost infinitely, aiming as far as their finite apprehension would permit to look upon all these rites, and schools, and systems, as God himself looks down upon them with complacency toward all, of every name, that in true faith and holiness derived their spiritual life from him. So, with the protesting witnesses for Christ all along, they rose above the sultry and murky atmosphere of rituals and dogmatic theology, into the serener, purer, more expansive atmosphere of heavenly life and love; and as it was ever of old, "he that was born after the flesh (the creed and ritual only) persecuted him that was born after the spirit," so it was in all these ages.

Origen, Eusebius, and Dyonisius of Alexandria, examined and more lucidly confuted the Jewish notions, protesting against which was the only occasion of the Gnostic existence as a school of theology. Thus, their opponents "approximating the Gnostic doctrines," the two schools were merged into one, save in respect to ritualism, touching which the Gnostic non-ritual conception appeared in other forms about to be named.

MOSHEIM'S CHURCH HISTORY CRITICISED.

In passing, we cannot well refrain from expressing our utter reprehension of the matter and manner of Mosheim's history, so far as it may be used as an authority in an honest search for the TRUE CHURCH OF CHRIST. It is rather a history of dogmas. Mosheim appears to have placed himself in a certain attitude of assumed technical orthodoxy; cuts and chisels every sect and system by the measuring line of his own creed, without reference (decisively) to the manifested *life of God* in those he criticises. He gives to an almost interminable extent the history of speculative opinions, and ever finds the true Church where the theology was sound *a la Mosheim,* while all else is heresy. He forgets that "sound doctrine," according to Paul, is the "doctrine which is according to godliness (Godlikeness)," and that which secures obedience to the *moral law,* and not to a certain ceremonial law. Neander differs almost infinitely from Mosheim in this respect, since, while he too gives the history of dogmas and speculative opinion with much more seeming charity and fairness than does Mosheim, he dwells the most extensively upon the fruits each system bears in the lives of its adherents.

A CLUE TO THE TRUE LIVING CHURCH.

Thus we have a clue to the true living Church of Christ, where a history of dogmas leaves us altogether in a quandary. If later investigations be correct in their results, Mosheim has oft garbled history to the prejudice of his declared heretics; since Neander's record of the same classes and teachers oft differs from Mosheim's as heaven differs from earth. Casually Mosheim rises above those narrow prejudices, and gives the schismatics from his popular church the reputation of the noble and the praiseworthy. But this is rare.

Dr. WALL charges both Papists and Protestants with garbling history and falsifying records respecting baptism, quoting the ancient writers only partially; which he calls "a great wickedness," as it prolongs the controversy on the subject, and renders it impossible for those whose reading is more limited to know the truth on the subject; but he does not tell us how much *himself omits* of the early history of the question, thus

12

causing many to misread the part he does record. Mosheim, from a manifest bias toward "Church order" and "Church ordinances," seems incapable of reading the early records on this subject with candor. Neander, being a Jew as well as a Christian, saw and more fully admitted the facts and bearings of the question.

Even Dr. READ, the editor of the latest revised edition of Mosheim, laments, as do we, his remissness in giving the history of the true spiritual Church, in the following manner:

"It is much to be regretted, that in reviewing the history of religion in each century, Mosheim had not given a sketch of the vicissitudes of spiritual Christianity, and of the influence of real piety and godliness upon the habits, both of thought and life, of professing adherents of the gospel. *He never leads us to the true interior of the Church of Christ,* to exhibit the mode in which evangelic truth was appreciated by Christian minds at different periods. The historian, indeed, surveys the pulpit, but he never descends to the congregation, or depicts its operation in remodelling individual character. He draws *no sufficiently distinct line of demarcation between real religion and a mere nominal Christianity,* too prevalent in each age, between *spiritual worship* and the *cumbrous ritual* which was GENERALLY SO POPULAR, AND SO RIGIDLY ENFORCED AND PRACTISED. . . . The Christian reader longs to know, not merely whether the technical teaching of the Christian Church was *sound and Scriptural,* but whether its value was duly appreciated by the people; whether they "received the truth in the love of it," delighted in the exercises of spiritual worship, and sought to adorn their faith by *lives of true self-denial and beneficence!* For information upon these points we must look beyond the pages of Mosheim."

MOSHEIM ON THE INFLUX OF RITUALISM.

Yet even Mosheim gives us a picture (dark enough) of the inflowing tide of ritualism, as it, by degrees, prevailed to the perversion of the Gentile churches; and as he traces the *Church genealogy* through these perverted churches, perhaps there is no cause for wonder that he does not oftener treat upon the spiritual life of the Christian Church, for he found very little manifestation of such life in the line of history he pursued. Of course, heretics, be they ever so holy, must not be mistaken for the true Church!

But hear him descant upon the perverting influence of

ritualism in the (true!) Church in the early centuries. We quote from Part ii. chap. 4, paragraph 1 :

"It is certain that to religious worship, both public and private, many rites were added, *without necessity*, and to the great offence of sober and good men. The principal cause of this I readily look for in the *perverseness of mankind*, who are more delighted with the pomp and splendor of external forms than with the true devotion of the heart ; and who despise whatever does not gratify their eyes and ears. Also, there is good reason to suppose that the Christian bishops *multiplied sacred rites* for the sake of rendering the *Jews* and the *Pagans* more friendly to them, for both had been accustomed to numerous and splendid ceremonies from their infancy, and had *no doubt that they constituted* AN ESSENTIAL PART OF RELIGION. Hence, when they saw the new religion TO BE *destitute of such ceremonies* they thought it too simple, and therefore despised it. The simplicity of the worship which Christians offered to the Deity had given occasion to certain calumnies, spread abroad both by the Jews and Pagan priests. The Christians were pronounced *atheists*, because they were destitute of temples, altars, victims, *priests*, and all the pomp in which the vulgar suppose the essence of religion to consist. *To silence this accusation the Christian doctors thought they must introduce* SOME EXTERNAL RITES, *which would strike the senses of the people*, so that they could maintain that they really had all those things of which Christians were charged with being destitute, though under different forms. Also, it was well known that in the books of the New Testament, *various parts of the Christian religion are expressed by terms borrowed from the Jewish laws*, and are in some measure *compared with the Jewish rites*. In process of time, either from ignorance or motives of policy, *the majority maintained* that such phraseology *was not figurative*, but accordant with the nature of things, and to be understood in its proper sense. The bishops were at first called *high priests*, and the presbyters, priests, and deacons, *Levites*. In a *little time*, those to whom these titles were given maintained that they had the *same rank and dignity*, and possessed the same rights and privileges with those *who bore these titles under the Mosaic dispensation*. Also, from the *Greek Mysteries* the Christians were led to claim *similar mysteries*, and they began to apply the *terms used* in the Pagan mysteries to Christian institutions, *particularly baptism and the Lord's Supper !* They also introduced the other rites designated in those terms, *and a large part of the Christian observances of this* (second) *century had the appearance of the Pagan mysteries !*"

This is Dr. Mosheim's indorsed and *valid* Church of the second century ; and if he had said, as he fully implies in the above, that the Greeks and Asiatics, who had been Pagans, took the *orders* of their *priests*, the forms of their *temples*, and their *baptisms* from the Pagan temples and mysteries, he would have told us the truth in plain words ; what, though covertly seeking to hide, he has actually asserted in the above paragraph.

When they were without " priests " and " temples," and worshiped in their spiritual "simplicity," of course they were without " *sacraments* " and other conjoined ceremonies— even this very term, *sacrament*, they borrowed about this time from the Pagan mysteries.

We prefer to trace *the Church* in a line that more completely maintained the " *simplicity there is in Christ !* "

MANES OR (MANI) AND THE ORIENTAL SCHOOL, A. D. 300.

Of the school or system of theology and philosophy founded by MANES, we are not about to assert or claim its orthodoxy, if tested by modern standards, but only to present to the reader a very numerous class of early Christians who rejected a ritual or sacramental law. Modern missionaries to Nestoria in (Persia) found there a body of *Protestant Christians*, direct descendants from the ancient Christian churches of that region (like those of Armenia), yet, it is affirmed, exhibiting more of the genuine spirit of Christianity than those of Armenia, where John found his seven churches of Asia. The term *Nestorian*, it is true, came from the bishop Nestorius (of Constantinople), in whose see was Nestoria in the fifth century. But this became a part of his diocese only because MANES and his successors planted the gospel there in the third and fourth centuries.

As the Jews brought Judaism with them into the Christian Church, and as the Greeks brought much of the Grecian (Platonic) philosophy with them, so MANES unquestionably brought much of the philosophy of the Magi and the sages of the East into his philosophic-theologic system. We are not aware that the philosophic basis and adjuncts of the Christianity of either of these classes of Christians nullified or very seriously modified their practical application of the precepts and rules of Christianity. The Greek Christians were as exemplary as the Jewish Christians, and the Persian and Chaldean Christians as exemplary (if we trust the record) as either. MANES was first eminent as a scholar, a mathematician, astronomer and geographer; he excelled also in medicine, music, and painting In astronomy he was a thousand years in advance of his generation; for he alone in all those years taught the spherical form of the earth. After embracing Christianity he subsidized all his former attainments to the work of converting the world to the new religion.

The new faith and zeal, of course, shone through a glass colored with some of his retained philosophic ideas—as must, in the nature of the human mind, be the case—but that faith and zeal shone brightly. He was ordained a presbyter, and as a self-sacrificing witness against a corrupting ritual idolatry (in the form of Judaism and also of Paganism) he has scarcely been excelled.

By traducing ritualists and heresy-hunters he was much maligned, but his real character shone all the more brightly because of the dark background in which his enemies sought to place him.

Notwithstanding all this traduction he became the acknowledged head of a long line of self-denying and non-ritualistic followers, among whom were included a great number of witnesses for a holy life and conversation, for "temp'rance in all things," and chastity, and death to earthly ambitions and pleasures, above most of the present or any past age. The "pallor" of their countenances and "leanness" of their frames showed most conclusively that they were not to be counted among those who had "lived in pleasure on the earth and had been wanton!" This charge, which venomed enemies so delighted to allege (insinuate) against the Christians, had no background in obvious facts to stand upon in relation to this abstemious and ascetic people.

As a testimonial to the greatness of their numbers and influence, it is sufficient to say that Murdock's edition of Mosheim (1851) gives over one hundred and fifty pages to this

branch of the Christian Church. If they were not fully
Christian, why does Mosheim give them so much space in his
"Institutes of (Christian) *Church History?*" True, nearly
all these pages (150) are occupied with discussions of their
tenets, but it gleams out all along that they were altogether
self-denying and zealous in propagating the faith, and spread
their faith far and wide over western Asia (Persia, Syria,
Arabia), and into Africa; and Mosheim adds, into "*almost
all countries of the civilized world.*" MANES contended with
Jews, Pagans, and Magians for the faith of Christ as expounded by himself. He assailed publicly the religion of
Zoroaster. *Supor*, the king, offended at this, and prompted
by the Magi and priests, determined to put him to death.
"MANES being informed of the design, fled into Turkestan.
There he drew many to his party. . . . In the meantime the
King of Persia died, and his son *Hormisdas* succeeded.
Manes returned to Persia, the new king received him kindly,
professed to embrace his religion, and built for him a tower
wherein he might find protection from his numerous enemies.
But his tranquillity was short, for Hormisdas died at the end
of two years, and Varanes, taking the throne, treated Manes
kindly for a short season, but soon his feelings changed, and
he determined to destroy him. He allured Manes from the
fortress in which he was concealed, under pretence of holding
a discussion with the Magi, when he was seized as a corrupter
of religion, and some say he was cleaved asunder, but the
Greeks affirm that he was flayed alive (A. D. 277)."

He (Manes), as after him did the *Manicheans* generally, held
to one God, in Trinity, Father, Son, and Holy Ghost, manifestly as do the Trinitarians of to-day.* He did not allow
the books of the Old Testament to be the prescriptive law for
the *Christian Church*, and hence rejected all its rituals.

---

* He styled himself the *Paraclete*, by which Mosheim admits that he did not
mean to claim to be the Holy Ghost, but a great apostle, "*sent*" of Christ, for
he elsewhere fully admits the divine nature and work of the Holy Spirit.

NEANDER affirms that Manes and the *Manicheans* rejected Moses (affirming that his economy had passed away), and rejected *baptism.** It is unquestionably true that they rejected both sacraments, *baptism* and the *Supper*, choosing rather to regard the created heavens and earth as God's "ordinances" to be revered, than to "adore" the bread and wine of the sacrament, as Augustine (a former disciple of Manes, but a later opposer of the scheme) admits was the custom of the Sacramentarians of his day. They used lustrations, as do all Eastern nations, whether Christian or not. Like all other people, also, they had feasts of fellowship and charity, if they listed, and sometimes those received into the class of the *elect* or *perfects*, which was the *sacerdotal class*, were permitted to receive a lustration, or washing, as significant of the sanctity they were about to assume.

But both Mosheim and Neander agree that nothing of this kind was required of them as a sacrament or Church ordinance, for both virtually affirm that they admitted no such obligation. The *elect* were supposed to be initiated, as the higher class, into all the *mysteries* of the *order*, and had a right to all their social feasts and immunities, from which the *auditors* or *non-elect*, common class, were excluded. In this we trace a borrowed element of Paganism, for there were no such special immunities even in Judaism. Yet such a "class" division of believers was universal among the Gentile Christians at this period. But the rigorous discipline and ascetic habits of the *perfects* among the Manicheans prevented any approach of envy on the part of the *auditors*, for comparatively few were willing to forego the greater liberties they enjoyed for the seclusion, celibacy, and austerity required of the *elect*.

---

* SCHAFF, in his "Church History," says of the Manicheans, "They repudiated baptism, considering it useless. The perfects sometimes partook of the Supper (he might have said *a* Supper), yet without wine." Such a festival which they observed twice a week does not mark the Christian's *sacrament*, but rather that "*feast of charity*," common in ancient times, and common for a century among our Methodist brethren of later years.

As their influence spread and rebuked the laxness of a corrupt society, rigorous laws were enacted against them, especially at Rome. *Dioclesian* (A. D. 276) issued a law against them, condemning their leaders to the stake, and the common people among them to decapitation and the confiscation of their property (Neander, vol. i. p. 506). But this only concealed the doctrine for a time, for soon many eminent men were enlisted under their banners, and for their own defence they were sometimes in array against the authorities of the East; whose emperors, also, oft sought to crush them by the sword. *Theodosius* framed a law against heresy, A. D. 382, and this was executed against the Manicheans, the first ever enacted or executed for such a purpose.*

But they continued through many centuries as the main body of Oriental Christians, and were at length merged in the noble band of the *Paulicians*.

Yet previously for centuries from among these and the Gnostics came forth anti-ritualistic teachers, leaders of schism from the popular Romanizing Church continually. Of those that thus withdrew and protested, and those that continued to protest without ever having given adherence to the ritualists, Neander gives frequent and, at times, full accounts. The *Novations*, *Donatists*, and *Eutuchians* retained water-baptism the two former being immersionists in the main—the latter (the Eutuchians) retaining baptism only for the sake of retaining their place in the Church, as themselves freely avowed.

THE EARLY GENTILE CHURCH OF THE REGULAR LINE AND ORDER NON-RITUAL—ITS LATER APOSTASY.

Its Early Remission of Baptism.

But if the foregoing record be counted in any manner a record of schisms from the recognized Church of those days

---

* But the palm is given to the *Priscillianists* (also non-ritualists) for having been the *first* to suffer persecution from *Christian* rulers for heresy of doctrine.

(and yet can that be a schism which comprises the main body as to numbers?), we will now call attention to that recognized central column, in which Mosheim finds the TRUE CHURCH! We shall scarcely find less of the non-ritualistic element here than we have found in the aforenamed portions of the Gentile churches.

THOMAS EMLYN, formerly (for many years) of the Church of England, became convinced that baptism with water was no part of the "law of Christ's house," and having extensively searched the Patristic record, stated his full conviction that baptism in the early centuries of the Christian Church came from the Jewish proselyte baptism, and assures us that "*the baptism of Gentile Christians ceased, as it regarded those descended from Christian parents.*"

And GALE (a Baptist writer of the eighteenth century) quotes RABBI ISAAC, a Jewish writer of the early Christian era, as remonstrating with the Christian teachers, because, in their zeal against Judaism, they had "*abolished all the Jewish rites, baptism not excepted.*"

And Dr. DALE has assured us that the form of "laying the hand upon the head (and offering prayer), with no water present, was practised in *innumerable cases* as the form of consecration, in lieu of baptism in the early centuries.

And WALL asserts that the delay of baptism till just before death (to wash away the sins of a life-time) occasioned *many to die without baptism!*"

But still the Church remained, and the non-baptizing churches were long in the ascendency. Tertullian's effort among the Judaizers to have baptism delayed till just before death had its due effect, and numbers of the most influential leaders of the Church were not baptized until they were about thirty years of age, and some much older. Gregory the elder, and his wife Nouna, both eminently pious—he being called to the pastorate of Nazianzen (early in the fourth century)— was baptized at maturity; and his son, Gregory, always a catechumen, having been pious from his youth—*the son of a bishop*—was not baptized till thirty years of age: thus imitating the Jewish baptisms into the priesthood—for he also became a noted minister and writer. Chrysostom, a Syrian, born at Antioch, A. D. 347, father and mother both pious—his father dying when he was in his cradle, his mother provided for his education, and he became learned, eloquent and accomplished, and was baptized at twenty-eight. Basil, descended from two opulent families of Pontus in Cappadocia—his ancestors had suffered immense persecutions and losses for being Christians, some of them martyred—was baptized at twenty-eight. Theodosius, the emperor, born of Christian parents, was baptized at maturity. Five emperors (of the Eastern realm, at Constantinople) were not baptized until of man's age, or *old age*. These were Theodosius II., as mentioned; Constantine, not till the age of sixty-two (the year of his death); Constantius, Gratium, and Valentinian II.; and *Theodosius I., not at all!* And not until middle life—not only Basil and the two Gregories—but Nectarius, Ambrose, Hierome, Augustine, Alypius, and Adevdatus. Of course, these preachers did not preach early baptism—save Augustine when he came to prescribe a new method of church replenishment and salvation by water; nor did they, in their congregations, practise early baptism, nor deem that the method of entering the visible Church, and there is no evidence that they proposed baptism only for those who would occupy some sphere requiring uncommon sanctity, as was the case with the Gnostics and Oriental Church. And Wall admits that owing to the postponement of baptism, many children were instructed from their youth in the Christian religion, BUT NOT BAPTIZED AT ALL. And all this evinces that baptism crept into the Christian Church (the Gentile) from the Jewish custom of purifying from sin, or baptizing into the priesthood, at the time of entering that office. It also suggests the inquiry whether those not about to assume a special office of responsibility in the Church would deem it incumbent on them to give attention to the subject of baptism at all. Tertullian wrote a book on baptism against the doctrine of Quintilla, a female minister, who had been at Carthage a little time before, and taught that water-baptism was needless, and that faith alone was sufficient; to whom, he intimates, many adhered. And this same Tertullian plead earnestly against baptizing infants and unmarried persons, and against haste in administering baptism, urging that "true faith, whenever present, is sure of salvation," and that the soul is "not consecrated by water, but by the truth professed." * Under the influence of such teachings, Theodosius and many other eminent persons did not receive baptism until they had become aged. (See *State Churches*, p. 462.)

Hence when we find Gentile Christians of that day (second century) who taught or practised baptism, we need not infer that they deemed it *an ordinance of Christ*, or that they inculcated it as a duty devolving upon all Christians upon profession of faith. They conceived it rather as a proper method of introduction to the sacerdotal office and to places of special sanctity and dignity in the Church, or a preparation for death, while, like the Gnostics and Orientals, they imposed no such ritual upon the mass of believers as a mode of publicly

---

* Tertullian's inconsistency and vacillating is seen in that occasionally he is found zealously defending water-baptism, if applied to persons just before death, to wash away sins (the sins of a lifetime), and he is much ruffled "Because a woman of the Caianite sect *has carried a great number* with her most venomous doctrine, making it her first aim to destroy baptism." He also complains as bitterly of a certain woman (*Thecla*) who claimed authority to administer baptism; himself deeming it an overstepping of the province of her sex.

But let the reader say whether (baptizing their candidates naked, as was customary in those days) it was not as well omitted, or at least as fit that women should baptize their own sex, if they must be baptized, as that it should be done by canonical administrators of the male sex? Thecla's example was, doubtless, highly commendable in view of the circumstances. And Quintilla's course, in wholly rejecting baptism, still more commendable— banishing, as it did, the numerous superstitious adjuncts and indecencies which were connected with the rite of baptism at that epoch among the Gentile Christians.

avowing their faith in Christ. This is evident also from th
fact that catechumens, as we have seen, remained generall
unbaptized, and many that assumed the ministerial offic
received baptism only when about entering upon their work
thus, like Israel in Aaron's day, setting apart the priests b
special baptisms and anointings (irrespective of prior cere
monial uncleanness), which baptisms were not thus require
of the common people. This is evinced also from the fact tha
infant baptism, when first introduced to the Gentile churches
was considered as equivalent to setting apart its recipients t
the priestly function. Thus Gregory Nazianzen says: "Bap
tism is a seal—*i. e., a means of securing human nature agains
all moral corruption,* by the higher principle of life communi
cated." "Hence," says the historian, "he looks upon infan
baptism as a consecration to the priestly dignity from th
beginning"—*i. e.,* from the period of this consecration by bap
tism. (*Neander,* vol. iii. p. 665.)

When, however, Augustine (later) commenced teaching the
doctrine of *original sin,* he pointed to baptism as the *purifier*
of "human nature," and necessary for all! And the doctrine
of baptismal regeneration, and by consequence of infant bap
tism, increased with the increase of the doctrine of origina
sin, and (in the rising Papacy) with the devising of this
method (viz., infant baptism), as the most successful in multi
plying candidates for the Church.*

---

* All this is concurrent with Neander's general testimony as to the non-
prevalence of infant baptism in the Gentile churches, and also with the testimony of Dr. Miller of Princeton, who asserts that "*During the threescore years
after the ascension of Christ, we have no hint of the baptism of infants born of
Christian parents.*"

Indeed, the opposition to infant baptism generally was so great for one hundred and fifty years after Tertullian, that the Council of Neo-Cesarea, in A. D.
315, discussed the question, and decided that *a pregnant woman might be baptized, because the baptism* DID NOT REACH THE CHILD. Hence Zonaras and
Balsamon infer that it was contrary to Greek custom at this period to baptize
infants.

TOMBES, of England, in public discussion with Marshall, inquires why

When and why "Orthodoxy" first became a "Pervert."

And when baptism came to be applied to infants, it radiated from those centres of ecclesiastical domination, Rome, Alexandria and Antioch, where the metropolitan churches were, and was used to increase the revenues and influence of these bishops. None of them pretended to appeal to Christ for their commission to baptize infants or adults! We learn from Mosheim that it was not customary to baptize any in those regions, and at the era of which we now speak (third and fourth centuries), without previous catechetical instruction, and many *preferred* to omit baptism till just before death; and if any had been baptized in infancy, it was repeated just before death, in the case of some!

Baptism, on the faith of parents or sponsors, says Mosheim, is scarcely mentioned in the third century. And Eusebius, who wrote in the fourth century, says that baptism on the faith of others sets aside the holy baptism, and sets aside the faith and confession that should precede it. Basil became anxious that catechumens should not wholly omit baptism, and late in the third century reasons with catechumens thus:

"Why do you deliberate? What do you wait for? Instructed in the doctrine of Christ from your infancy, are you not acquainted with it? *When will you be a Christian?* When shall we acknowledge you for our own? Last year you deferred baptism to this! do you now intend to put it off till the next?" (Rob., p. 77.)

Ignatius, Clemens, Epiphanius, Athanasius, and Eusebius said nothing of infant baptism, if such a practice was common in the Christian Church?

Even Augustine does not say that the baptism of infants was common—his own case was an example to the contrary—but taking his cue from Cyprian and his council of sixty-six bishops, he, with them, commenced urging baptism as the *only way of escape from original sin.* Hence, it appears that infant baptism among Greeks commenced with baptizing proselytes—*i. e.,* children of Pagans only! and not, as now, children of believers only, and advanced until assuming that *all* children were born sinners (unclean), all must be purified, or regenerated by baptism!

Invalid Claims of the Baptists.

Now we are not unaware that from such exhortations of Basil and the reasonings of Tertullian respecting delay of baptism, the Baptists claim that the primitive churches *were Baptist churches;* but how exceedingly far from being such as Baptist churches now are, will be seen by the fact that Baptists *baptize into the Church* or into the profession of faith. Whereas, from the day that Paul declared that he "was not sent to baptize but to preach the gospel," the primitive Christians among the Gentiles have practised the very reverse, or very *diversely* from the Baptist ideal. The primitive Christians baptized into the priesthood, or for the purifying of sin, just as the Jews had done, and not because they had been purified, and without any reference to their relation to the visible Church; for certainly those who were exhorted to postpone *baptism until just before death* (and for a century or two, that was continually the exhortation), were not thereby exhorted to continue *out of the Church.* And when Basil asks: "When shall we claim you for our own?" he refers evidently to their coming into the ranks of the "*perfects*" from being mere "auditors" and catechumens. They should enter the ranks of those matured in Christian doctrine, discipline and instruction. This was somewhat analogous to the modern Methodist transition from "probationers" into "full connection" of those who had been recognized as "seekers" and as Christians also before. And multitudes of these "catechumens" and "auditors" thus exhorted, both Wall and Mosheim testify never were baptized at all. None of the Manichean or Marcionite "auditors" were required to be baptized either in infancy or at any other age, nor was the neglect of baptism censured by any others at that period, as we see, but rather commended. No *paramount obligation* of baptism was urged in the Gentile churches, in these centuries, but by an exceptional few that were Judaizers, that is certain. Yet Baptists have the boldness to claim the practice of those ages as a sample of the Baptist Church! The churches were all independent, to be sure, as Neander and Mosheim both fully declare, but were generally non-ritualists, as the dissenters from Rome were in all later ages, much resembling the Independent Churches of England and America, only they rejected ritual baptism as a law, while the Independents of our day, laying less stress upon it than many others, do not reject it.

Baptism in those early days was never made a condition of fellowship, never made a door into the Church, never proclaimed as a New Testament law. Yet infant baptism was never wholly laid aside among the Judaizing portion of the Church. The idea (*a la Jews*) was to use baptism to purify from sin as we said, and in case of danger of death, baptism was administered in infancy by some. Augustine was sick in infancy, or youth, and his mother wished him baptized; but having some remaining hope of recovery it was omitted, lest he should relapse, and the effects of the baptism be lost. He did recover, and did relapse into fearful sin, and was not baptized until just about entering on the ministry.

"Many others," says Neander, "looking upon baptism as the purifier, deferred baptism by their own choice, to give themselves up to vices, expecting their future baptism [just before death] would purify them, *magically annihilating* their sins."

"Neither your Church nor mine!"

Let any one scan the records of the Church in the early ages, and he will repronounce with emphasis the words of PRESSENCE, of France, who, in order to enlarge his acquaintance with those ages, visited Rome and explored the archives and records there. A Papal bishop of Paris, after his return, asked him what he found there? "NEITHER YOUR CHURCH NOR MINE!" was the prompt response. So he might have replied to an inquiry from any of the extant churches of Christendom: if all their present tenets, customs, modes, and ceremonies are taken into the account. And it is for a marvel to note, in the *Religious Encyclopedia*, the Baptists claiming not only the Novations and Donatists as their proto-types, but also the *Paulicians* and *Catharists*, both of the latter rejecting baptism altogether, through their whole history, and the *Novations* teaching that sins after baptism were unpardon-able; and, therefore, baptism (by immersion to be sure) should be delayed till just before death. The *Donatists* held that no baptism but theirs was of any account, and in this they resembled the Baptists of our day—whether it be to the praise of their charity or not—but they also baptized infants, and were never sticklers on that point.

And hence, is it uncharitable to say that superstition and a blind credulity prompted all the baptisms (of water) of those days, as a manifestly blind allegiance to baptism governs the sects of to-day?

Modern Pedo-Baptist Churches not found there.

That the Pedo-Baptist churches of to-day were not found in those early ages, is manifest from these facts, viz.: In the early days when infant baptism had been introduced, children were not baptized on the faith and church-standing of parents, but to regenerate the children, to constitute them catechumens and auditors—to constitute choirs and candidates for church orders and church supporters of the children themselves as they advanced in years. And none were rejected for lack of faith, or of church-standing of parents, but all that were offered were received gladly and baptized. Neither were these baptized children withheld from the *eucharist*, and disgusting details of its being administered to them were rife in those days. Witness Cyprian's telling of an infant child that ate of the bread offered to an idol, and when the eucharist was administered, note the result:

"When the deacon offered her the cup, the girl by a divine instinct turned her head away. The deacon persisted, and put in her mouth some of the sacrament of the cup. Then followed *retchings and vomitings*—the eucharist could not stay in her polluted mouth and body."

Probably exorcism or baptism must precede; then the child

could retain the bread and the wine of the sacrament. Mosheim also witnesses: "It appears by many and undoubted testimonies, that the Lord's Supper was looked upon as essential to salvation, and therefore was administered to infants." Also "the remission of sins was deemed the immediate and happy fruit of baptism; while the bishop, by prayer and the imposition of hands, was supposed to confer those sanctifying gifts of the Holy Spirit which are necessary to a life of virtue." This is, perhaps, the only instance we have noted in those early days where the three rites, *baptism*, the *eucharist*, and *confirmation* (consolumentum) were practised by the same persons—*i. e.*, among the Gentiles.

Touching infant communion, Neander also says:

"In the North African Church, the practice proves that a belief of a supernatural sanctifying power in the outward tokens of the holy supper prevailed, hence came the *daily communion;* hence also, with infant baptism, *infant communion.* While John vi. 53 was improperly understood of the outward participation of the holy supper, it was concluded that no one could attain to salvation without the participation in it, just as it had been concluded from a misapprehension of John iii. 5 that no one could be saved without baptism."

INFANT BAPTISM ADVANCES SLOWLY—CONFUSION OF TONGUES.

Yet Neander adds, on this point:

"But although in theory the necessity of infant baptism was allowed, yet it was far from being generally prevalent in practice, but, as we suggested, *only in certain parts of the Church.*"

Augustine judged that denying original sin was *to abolish infant baptism.* Query: Has Christ, by giving an indefinite law of baptism, laid a just foundation for such conceits, superstitions, and unending vagaries? *Who,* at that day, was so oracular that he could tell just what Christ's *ritual law* did require? Listen, reader, to the tenfold babel of confusion that has ever floated over the earth from many times ten thousand voices, "of every age and nation, of every tongue and tribe," that speak upon this subject.

Though Christ did not declare that those dying without baptism were lost, yet the ritualistic fathers "hazarded nothing" (says Robinson, p. 234) "by affirming that infants dying without baptism were not saved, for they could not be contradicted. And they gained much by the early baptism of such as grew up to manhood, for premature prejudices govern mankind more than deliberate disinterested reasoning. The gradation, or rather degradation, is curious: the belief of the primitive Christians was reason yielding to evidence (this was succeeded by *orthodox* faith). Faith is supplanted by credulity; credulity by prepossession; prepossession by *a charm;* and *on this* they built a church against which, they flattered themselves, the gates of hell should not prevail . . . . Monks got hold of children to baptize and educate, all the rest of Popery followed of course."

Robinson, p. 406, thus continues:

"The reduction of the Christian religion to the size of children has been the ruin of the credit of Christianity; and the *institutes* have shared the fate of the doctrine—they have been dismounted from their original pedestals, frittered to puerile playthings; and at length despised and broken, thrown away. The river becomes a bath; the bath a font; the font a basin; the basin a cup; the cup a cruet, a sponge, or a syringe (for ante-natal baptism); and hence, in disgust, many threw the whole away (*i. e.,* Judaism was cast out)."

This was true of those who could not see the magic power of rituals; on the part of these it waned, on the Papal side it waxed, as Robinson has shown, till "faith yielded to credulity, credulity to prepossession; till superstition more and more found a '*charm*' in sacraments."

Robinson continues:

"It hath happened the same with the Lord's Supper. Remembrance of Christ was essential to this as belief was to baptism; but when the sacrament was administered to infants, the doctrine being lost, the utensils were reduced. Infant communion began with the cup given to boys at Alexandria; it went on with a spoon in which a few crumbs of bread were soaked in wine, and put into the mouths of the little ones [and that was salvation too]. When little infants became communicants, the spoon fell into disuse, and the bread—for they sometimes would not swallow it. Then the priest dipped his finger in the wine, *and moistened the lips of the babe.* At length it was wholly omitted."

So the Reforming Episcopalians (in certain cases) propose to omit the water in the consecration of children to-day, and may God speed them in their work!

On p. 307 Robinson says:

"Those who embraced the doctrine of the necessity of infant baptism to salvation did not foresee where it would end; for, first affirming that baptized infants dying in infancy will be saved, and those not baptized neither saved nor condemned—neither glorified nor punished, they went on to say that infants dying unbaptized were inevitably punished with the torments of ever-lasting fire."

Some of these ritualists held that Old Testament saints and the New Testament saints, dying unbaptized, might receive a baptism of fire in hades, and afterwards be saved; hence arose the Papal doctrine of purgatory, and the later doctrine of an intermediate state between death and the full and final heaven.

CONTENTION ABOUT THE BAPTISTERIES.

To return to the original object aimed at in baptizing infants (see Robinson, p. 320):

"The Arians and Catholics contended for ages about the baptisteries; finally the Catholics gained them—this was taking them from the *people-men*, and giving them to the *priest-men*. When Christianity spread into the country the people met for worship where they could, but all came to the baptismal church in the city for baptism. Thus the city bishop became *the* bishop and father of all. [Thus the episcopacy of Popery arose.] The bishop who declaimed and published books did very well; but he who intrigued, and bribed, and taught, *and got possession of a baptistery*, was the life of the cause! *These baptisteries multiplied believers.*"

D'Aubigne attests all this a thousand years later. Hear him (vol. i. p. 382):

"Indulgences were more or less an extraordinary branch of Roman commerce; the sacraments were *a staple commodity.** The revenue they produced was of no small account. To assert that faith was necessary before the sacraments could confer a real benefit on the soul of the catechumen took away all their charm in the eyes of the people. For it is not the Pope that gives faith —it is beyond his province—it proceeds from God alone. (The Pope could baptize with water.) *To declare faith necessary was to deprive Rome both of the speculation and the profit.*"

Thus substituting the external baptism for that which is from God would enable an apostate Church to perpetuate and even enlarge itself as long as men are willing to be led to their own ruin blindfold, and to accept of a false religion in place of the true—thus preparing to eat the fruit of a fatal

---

* Luther fought hard against the former, but defended the latter.

delusion.   In another place, and for later years, Dr. Robinson shows how converts were more swiftly made by baptism,
a specimen of the labors of Papal missionaries in those days.
No wonder these Pagan converts to the Papacy were not reformed by their conversion.   He says:

"In the beginning of the seventeenth century, a Jesuit, Lobo, baptized converts (in Abyssinia), standing in ranks—for there were many.   He cried
aloud: 'Those in this rank are named Anthony; those in that rank are
named Peter.'   And so with the women, 'those in such a rank are named
Martha.'"

Thus have hundreds of thousands of Pagans and Mohammedans been pretendedly baptized unto Christ, after the Papal
order, who have given no more evidence of conversion to the
truth, or to the love of God and man and the moral law,
than they exhibited before baptism or before they had heard
of Christ.   And such are nearly all their converts in Asia
and Africa.   But their *object* is secured, viz., *a nominal adherence to the Catholic faith.*   In further allusion to the objects
to be attained by thus baptizing the non-regenerate and non-
conscious, Robinson (p. 408) thus replies to Wall's claim that
all national churches practise infant baptism:

"Very true, infant baptism, as was intended (not commanded), *created
national churches*, and gives them continuance as it gave them being.   It was
for this cause that Dr. Gill called infant baptism the main ground and pillar
of Popery, and a great number of Baptists are of the same opinion."

My brother, *water-baptism* is the ground and pillar of
Popery.

WHAT SAVES RESPECT FOR THE BIBLE AMONG NON-RELIGIONISTS.

Scanning thus the unending conceits and superstitions of
sacramentarians, the reader will see clearly that were it not
for the self-evident and eternal principles of the *moral law*, contained in both Old and New Testaments, the superstitions and
absurdities in which many churches are intrenched, upon
which also many church dynasties are built, with their mani-

fest bigoted attachment to these superstitions, to the extent, oft, of persecuting to the death all that reject and oppose them, reflecting and philosophic minds would utterly reject as offensive and disgusting not only the sacred records but all else that sectarists and sacramentarians hold and teach. Religious systems, as they have stood for ages, colonnaded with *orders*, liturgies, formularies, and sacraments, minus the moral law with its heavenly precepts and promises, would have become long since an unendurable "body of death," or at least their shadow would have been so utterly dark that no gleam of heavenly light could have been seen through the dark shrouding curtains of their superstitions and ritual idolatry.

From the day that Cyprian (A. D. 250) commenced his strenuous efforts to open heaven's gates to infants by baptism instantly after their birth into the world, and from Augustine's persecuting the Donatists to death (see Rob., p. 192) because of their departure from his church customs—respecting baptism especially—the subject has been rendered utterly reproachful and anti-Christian—if aught of human teaching respecting the way of salvation and the assumed canonical church could be anti-Christian.

COMPLICATIONS OF BAPTISMAL HISTORY.

Even Robinson is compelled to admit (p. 249) that "baptism is one of the most curious and complicated subjects of ecclesiastical history;" and he well adds, "among men who have stepped off the ground of Scripture and laid *another foundation.*" He continues his record thus:

"It was variable as the wind, and in every province *practised for a different reason*. At Alexandria, inserted in rules of academic education; at Jerusalem, administered to promiscuous catechumens [see where the catechumen process started]; in the deserts of Egypt, united to monastical tuition; in Cappadocia, applied as an amulet to entitle the dying to heaven; at Constantinople, accommodated to the intrigues of the court; *in all* places given to children extraordinarily inspired, and in the end, by an African genius (Augustine), affixed to the supposed universal depravity of human nature, and so reduced to an ordinary universal practice. . . . .

Baptism the Source and Arm of Ecclesiastical Power.

"Children were so absolutely necessary to ecclesiastics that they were obliged to have them at all adventures. With an imperial child, ecclesiastics subdued cities; with noble children, monks built and endowed monasteries; with poor children, as Basil observes, the clergy formed choirs; and in fine, *of children necessity compelled them to form the whole Catholic Church.* . . . How essential, then, to their schemes, to fill the world with exclamations of 'Suffer little children to come unto me' (to us)! The first European rule of infant baptism was made at an irregular meeting of seven obscure men (of a province in Spain), without a knowledge of neighboring bishops, in the year 517. *They were a low, illiterate,* mongrel sort of African Jewish Christians. Their Judaism appears in the above council by its canons, in which they regulated the feasts of the *Passover and Pentecost,* and the keeping of the (Jewish) Sabbath, and called the bishop of Carthage pope [*i. e.,* high priest]." So, on p. 311, Robinson speaks of "a class of people at Rome, who were *of the synagogue,* but not in the Church, who had a general knowledge of Christianity mixed with inveterate customs of Judaism; the true parents of the modern Church of Rome, who established their own theology by law, persecuted dissenters, and denominated themselves *the Church of Rome.* . . . By such," he adds, "the Aaronical system of religion *was lifted into a throne,* and erected on the ruins of the New Testament, and of the reason and rights of mankind." Now, reader, note what follows: "*Unconnected as baptism may seem to be with all this, it was, however, the chief instrument of acquiring power and producing a revolution in favor of pontifical dominion.* By this the hierarchy was formed, and by this, *and not by argument,* was chiefly supported."

How can we avoid emphasizing Robinson's testimony? But hear him again (p. 312):

"One of the strongest prejudices of unbelievers against Christianity is that the monstrous system of Popery grew out of it. This is, however, a fallacy. Had the Church of Rome proceeded from the house of Aquila (see Acts xviii. 2, 18, 26, etc.) the argument might have had some force, but if it proceeded from the unembodied Jews, before mentioned, the prejudice falls to the ground."

Here, surely, is a fearful break in the canonical lineage of the Christian (Roman) Church! It came from non-canonically baptized Judaizers, outside the genuine Church! But to quote Robinson:

"The hierarchy was formed long before Constantine established it; and the forty-four city congregations, described by Cyprian sixty years before, were all in union with one high-priest. There were *real Christian churches* in the city with whom they held no communion, and these they persecuted as far as they could. Constantine only brought the great faction into public places and suppressed the rest. Pope Sylvester dedicated the first edifice to the Romanizing (Judaizing) party, November 9. It was named after Solomon's temple, *to distinguish it from idol temples.* Also, for the same reason, a painting or statue of Jesus was placed there !—probably the true origin of pictures, images, and all ecclesiastical idolatry."

It seems there was no other way to distinguish the temples of Christ from the Pagan temples, but by the pictures and images of Jesus which they venerated !

"A wooden table there was called an altar, and they denominated those who officiated there *Levites. . . .* The same effects which the baptistery had produced at Rome followed in all other cities, as Venice, Naples, Florence, Pisa, Milan, Boulogne, Viterba, Modena, Verona, Ravenna, Aquileia, and many other cities. The priest of the congregation that claimed the baptisteries became a prelate; the other priests in the city his clergy; some of them were called his ' cardinal ' priests and deacons, chiefly because they assisted him to administer baptism. From these sprang suffragans, prebendaries, *canons !* chapters, conclaves and councils. . . . Cardinals derived their titles from baptismal churches. The city fashion of building baptisteries was, *as all fashions are,* soon imitated by country towns, . . . and the bishop of the city baptismal church inspected and regulated the affairs of the town churches, and provided them with teachers and administrators of ordinances, and generally supplied them with oils and ointments from the metropolitan baptistery. The fetching of this chrism at Easter ! from the city baptistery, *became* in time an evidence to prove the dependence of these baptisteries on that in the city. The bishop who supplied the baptisteries acquired the most parishes. *It was the baptistery, precisely,* and neither the parsonage house nor the church, which constituted the title to the whole. For this reason baptismal churches are called *titular churches. All these baptisteries were dedicated to John the Baptist* (an ante-Christian, Jewish priest) and not to Christ."

Thus we see how Judaic baptism for proselytism and power came to prevail in the Christian Church, and like a tidal wave in due time flowed over the Roman Church, and that baptism, and naught else, became the *key,* soul, and basis of the hierarchy, and the real basework of the Papacy. Is it any wonder that there should continue to this day a priestly and ministerial jealousy for the alleged divine authority of water-baptism ?

THE PRISCILLIANISTS, A. D. 400.

The non-ritualists continued their testimony in Asia, eastern Europe and northern Africa, until, in the fourth century, an extra effort was made to possess the religious mind in Spain. It is probable that ritualizers from northern Africa (Cyprian's diocese), or from Rome, had prepossessed the ground, hence here arose the first conflict between these rival systems, that ended in the persecution unto death of the leading non-ritualists, by a professedly Christian government. The Marcionites and followers of Manes had been put to death (for heresy or schism), their accusers, evidently, being in part Christian, but the ruling powers were Pagan or infidel. But this persecution took place after the "cross" had taken the throne of the Cæsars, which dominated in Spain.

The record, in brief, is this: One MARK, a native of Memphis, in Egypt, opposed to the ritualistic tendencies of portions of the Church in northern Africa and in Rome, proceeded to Spain to preach the faith of Christ in that region. The work had proceeded to some lengths, and embraced persons of reputation for learning and piety, when PRISCILLIAN, bishop of Avila, a man of honorable birth, and possessed of eminent abilities and fortune, and renowned for his eloquence, became a convert to the doctrine. He was soon accused of heresy, and with several other bishops, also accused in the same manner, tried for heresy. He was banished from Spain, but soon returning, he was again tried, and with the others acquitted, and they were restored to their sees.

But, afterward, Priscillian was again brought to trial with other of his associates; *testimony against himself was extorted by the rack*, and on such testimony Priscillian, with some of his adherents, was put to death. He was executed at Treves, A. D. 385. This is stated to have been the first execution for heresy by any Christian government.

Respecting the charges against Priscillian, Dr. WILLIAMS is candid enough to say:

" Whether they were true or not (*i. e.*) respecting his doctrine, *it is more certain that he was cruelly persecuted even* unto death *for his opinions.*"

And Dr. WILLIAMS adds, alluding to these martyred bishops:

" Their principal accuser, Ithacius, seems to have been *capable of everything he charged on them ;* he was audacious, talkative, impudent, luxurious, and a slave to his belly."

Such an accuser, pretending to guard the safety and honor of the Church by persecuting Christ's self-denying ministers to get rid of competition with their self-denying labors, is an illustrative example of what many *Christian* persecutors have been in all succeeding ages.

MARTIN, the bishop of Tours, nobly stood up against the persecution of these men, saying, " it was enough that they had been expelled from the churches " (as though this were not persecution !) and Martin protested that " it was a new and unheard-of evil for *a secular judge* to interfere in matters purely ecclesiastical." These were Christian sentiments, and deserve mention as having been uttered by a bishop in the case of the trial of his brother bishops before a civil court on charge of heresy. It was an unsuccessful resistance to the first attempt among Christians to punish heresy (so named) with death.

And let the reader remember that this is one of the earliest cases where *Protestantism* was persecuted by *Popery*. It is nothing more nor less than this. Even Mosheim is forced to state that the rules of life of these Priscillianists were very severe ! And he adds that what their enemies state about their flagitious practices " rests on no credible testimony." What sort of character would the Papists of any age have given to those Protestants whom they have persecuted ? Which testimony is to be received, that of the persecutors, or that of the persecuted ? Presumptively we mean. They were accused of dissimulation, and it is apparent to any candid thinker that this accusation had for its foundation simply the fact that they chose to explain their own doctrines rather than to accept the allegations of others. The charge is refuted also by the fact that they did acknowledge their objections to the priesthood and to the growing structure of the Papacy, until they paid the forfeit with their lives.

It was not for rejecting *baptism* only (which they did reject), but a priesthood also, and a Church they considered not according to Christ, that they suffered martyrdom!

GLANCE AT THE CHARACTER OF THE PRISCILLIANISTS.

Again we ask the reader to pass judgment touching this matter; here was a people, devout, pious, earnest, professing faith in Christ as a Saviour, preaching repentance and right-eousness, preaching the divine unity of Father, Son, and Holy Spirit, and trusting to, and seeking the Holy Ghost as a sanctifier. Yet a people that did not receive the *orders* and *sacraments* of the Papal Church. On the other hand, was this same Papal hierarchy, growing in power and influence, jealous and eagle-eyed against all rivalry and defection from its despotic pretensions, orthodox in doctrinal outline, save that it had utterly rejected Christ as Saviour, trusting rather in *sacraments* and *church benedictions* for this; and rejecting Christ as Head of the Church, placing its own behests, laws and impositions in the place of Christ, and abjuring free indi-vidual inquiry as *the* law for every servant of Christ, and ready to persecute to the death all dissent. Now, which is the HERETIC, the persecutor or the persecuted? Which has de-nied Christ, and substituted its own works for salvation through him?

Yet turning away from Christ's own test, "Whosoever doeth the will of my Father in heaven, the same is my brother, and sister, and mother;" these heresy-hunters, to cover their real motives, when they persecute (or perhaps modern heresiolo-gists do it for them), make such speculative charges as these: Denying the incarnation of God in Christ at his birth; teaching the pre-existence of souls; teaching the doctrine of emanations from God, and the co-existence of *Eons;* asserting the eternity of matter, or that the material world did not originate from God; declaring the human body a prison of the soul until the time of death, and denying the resurrection of the flesh; asserting that the soul of man is a particle of the Divine Nature; denying the triune personality of the Godhead, etc.

How many of these charges were made by their cotemporary Christian persecutors, perhaps Irenæus, Tertullian, Clement, and Augustine, will inform the reader; while the evidence is ample that modern Papal historians (and perhaps some Protestant) are fond of rehearsing the same. Yet if any one will adduce any evidence that the Papal writers upon polemic or dogmatic theology of those days, or upon the earth's cosmogony, or upon the divine nature, were any more advanced or more "sound" in faith, or clear in statement, or made any better use of that portion of theology which they did understand, we are ready to receive it.

We will only suggest that many Jewish conceits were as crude and unfounded as those of the Greeks—their superstition and love of marvels and "signs" no less a stumbling-block to faith—their ritualism and exclusiveness were not only annoying, but nauseating to all around them. Nothing of this proves them any *better* or *worse* Christians, when truly converted to Christ. Perhaps the Sadducee became as faithful a servant of Christ as the Pharisee, after grace had wrought its work in his heart. So with the Gnostic and Manichean. The only question is, How much did grace renovate their hearts? not how soon did it correct all their philosophical and speculative notions.

Mosheim forgets all this; but Neander does not! Mosheim's heretics are, therefore, oft Neander's purest saints—the manifest tokens of a still existing true Church of Christ. Like the followers of Simon Magus and Carpocrates,* some of the

---

* All know that *Simon Magus* (a Gnostic) was never converted, and who can assume that *Carpocrates* had ever truly renounced his Paganism?

Gnostics were, doubtless, antinomians, having blotted from their minds the moral as well as a ceremonial law. What then? There was a Judas among the apostles, and there have been too many "Pharisees" as well as "Sadducees" in the Papal Church! The true test must be applied to each and to all! "Every tree is known by its fruits." "Figs are not gathered from thorns," nor fruits of righteousness from heretics. But the lack of the fruits of righteousness proves heresy even in the dominant, persecuting Church.

Recurring to those charges of speculative error, urged against the non-Catholics, we may be permitted to say that we have heard men that would not be willing to be called either "Pagan" or "infidel," querying respecting the origin of matter, whether creation meant formation, or a real induction into being; yet was not their love to God and man questioned, nor their consistency as Christians impeached for this reason! So theologians of our day write volumes respecting the origin of evil; the pre-existence of man; the birthplace of Satan; the eternal procession of the Son of God; the tri-personal nature of Deity; the parties to, and purport of, the covenant of grace—some taking one view of these questions, and some another. Yet who thinks of either party being disowned as heretics for what they write on these subjects? Who thinks that either party is the better or the worse for their want of knowledge on these questions? As to there being good and evil, light and darkness, and a dominion or kingdom of each in God's moral universe, and a Ruler, a God, or Satan in each, what Pagan, Jew, or Christian ever doubted? Why, then, allude to the crude explanations or outlines of these views, found in the ancient writers? Their philosophy or conception of the origin or nature of things, especially in the spirit world, was not perfect. And are the philosophies or conceits of theologians of to-day all perfect, rational and harmonious? Let those who sneer at the darkness of past ages remember that the darkness is not all past yet, and ere they excommunicate all unwisdom, heed well the inquiry, "Thou that teachest another, teachest thou not thyself?" Want of knowledge, simply, is the source of these multifarious speculations. If ignorance be sin, then probably they are all sinners that write on such subjects; or, if it be deemed sin that all do not coincide with *Mosheim*, we presume the dissentients will be willing to refer the matter to another tribunal than his. Yet upon such abstruse, impenetrable, and impracticable matters are the philippics of Tertullian, Irenæus, and Clement against heretics largely composed. So caustic is their language oft, ("*basilisks*," "*serpents*," "*vipers*," are not unusual terms applied by Tertullian to those he is criticising,) and so obscure their points, that the critical reader is justly at a loss to know which is the heretic —the one arraigned, or the one sitting as judge!

WHICH WILL THE READER CHOOSE?

As to embodied and enduring heresy, which will the Christian reader choose, Augustine's Papal retinue (a fatal retinue) of 1400 years of the reign of the doctrine of *baptismal regeneration*, as witnessed in the Papacy in all these centuries, only compensated by certain abstract doctrines of eternal decrees and a limited atonement, and but a few marked saints among them in all these ages; or will he choose the Protestant dissenters from Rome, in all these centuries, with all their mental freedom and spiritual illumination, and enthronement of Christ as Saviour, without a ritual law, and with persecutions to the death? Which will he choose to deem Christ's peculiar people? Which have so partaken of Christ's "baptism," that he "is not ashamed to call them brethren"?

Again, the statement so oft and so wantonly made by Mosheim, that dissenting sects reject the *Old Testament*, thus evincing their heresy, calls for a faithful rebuke of the historian for its general lack of candor and unquestionable exaggeration. Neander seldom makes such a charge, or attempts to sustain such historians as Mosheim, who have evidently drawn too largely from Catholic sources in their inquiries.

As to the charge itself, be it said that Church historians can point to sects, too numerous to mention, that recognize the Mosaic dispensation as having passed away, and, with Paul believe that "the law was our schoolmaster (footman) to lead us to Christ, but after that faith is come we are no longer under a schoolmaster."

The whole Baptist Church so believes to-day. And the Pedo-Baptist Church, in a very undefined and inconsistent form, professes so to believe. And so does every Protestant sect, in terms, teach the same doctrine. Yet neither did those ancient nor do these modern sects doubt that the prophecies of the Old Testament point to Christ—likewise its sacrifices and oblations, and, in general, its ritual and its laws. Save a few, these all (the ancient and the modern) have believed that God was the Teacher and Supreme Lawgiver of the Jews; the Inspirer of their prophets; their Guide to the land of promise; their great Deliverer from peril oft; and the High God was their Saviour. But all Christians have been supposed to hold that we live under the covenant of faith, and not under the law. Why, then, this undiscriminating impeachment of so many millions, most truly Christian, for accepting of Christ rather than Moses as their Teacher and Saviour?

OUR PROTEST AGAINST ANATHEMATIZING THE RIGHTEOUS.

We protest, in behalf of our common heritage in the Word of Inspiration, and in behalf of the freedom of the Church of Christ from bondage to a collapsed *economy,* and its "carnal ordinances" and ritual law—those "beggarly elements" which only bound the Jews to a temporary and fleeting heritage—against imputing heresy to men who have believed that dispensations may change, or pass away; leaving still "the foundation of God standing sure, having this seal, The Lord knoweth them that are his," and those "naming Christ's name carefully departing from iniquity."

We think it becoming Church historians, who wear churchly

robes fitted very closely, to beware how they defame the "martyrs of Jesus" all along the ages, who, without any external baptism, were first baptized with the Holy Ghost, and then took angels' wings at their "baptism of blood," and were conveyed home to heaven, as being any less Christian, or any less Christ's chosen witnesses than those who have not "drank of Christ's cup, and have not been baptized with the baptism that he was baptized with." These martyrs have worshipped at a holier fane, and sought and found a purer shrine than any that Moses or the Jewish priests ever built.

> "The Temple once which brightly shone
>   On proud Moriah's rocky brow,
>   Not there doth God erect his throne,
>   And build his shrine for worship now.
>
> "The sunbeam of the orient day
>   Saw naught on earth more bright and fair;
>   But desolation swept away,
>   And left no form of glory there.
>
> "But God who reared that chisel'd stone
>   *Now* builds upon a higher plan,
>   And rears the columns of his throne—
>   *His temple in the heart of man.*
>
> "O man! O woman! know it well,
>   Nor seek elsewhere his place to find;
>   That God doth in his temple dwell—
>   *The temple of the holy mind.*"—UPHAM.

THE EUCHITES, OR PRAYING ONES, A. D. 400–600.

To the latter part of the third century, and early part of the fourth, is attributed the rise of this most interesting class of pietists and non-ritualists, albeit Mosheim asserts that they were known (by other names, perhaps) in Syria, Egypt, and other Eastern countries, even before the Christian era. In this statement he evidently refers to Philo, the Essenes, and other pious Jews, and converts to the same mystic form of piety. Be it so or not, their trace is dim or lost in the main, after the advent of Christ, until we reach the period named at the head of this record, when the *Euchites* come into full view as an earnest, consecrated, self-denying Christian people.

MILNER'S "History of all Denominations" and Mosheim speak of their continuing, under different titles, as *Messalians* and *Bogomiles,* until the twelfth century. It is certain that these latter were also non-ritualists, and manifested the same spirit and zeal for Christ as did the early *Euchites.*

The *Euchites* held that deliverance from sin could not be brought about by anything outward; hence they treated with contempt the sacraments, and the special means of grace which they proposed, as that by which all spiritual good was obtained, was *prayer!* hence they gained the appellation of the PRAYING ONES.

Milner asserts that the name *Euchite* "became a common name for persons of eminent piety and zeal for genuine Christianity as opposed to the vicious practices and insolent tyrannies of the priesthood!" And it is notable that such was the state of the popular Church and society, the priesthood, and the laity, that those in the early centuries, among the Gentiles, who would live "godly in Christ Jesus," oft resorted to the monastic life, as the most favorable to their aim, both as it respected communion with God and freedom from the persecutions of men! Conceding the rights of conscience and tolerating diversities of religious sentiment, has been a plant of very slow growth in our poor sin-cursed and bigotry-cursed world. If any would censure the monastic and ascetic tendencies of those ages, they should first consider the temptations and trials to which they were exposed from without (practically unknown now); also how potent the influences of the customs of a dissolute society, and the spirit thereby engendered, requiring a mighty internal struggle oft, to break away and stand for life, clear of their fascinating and corrupting influence. These ascetics were manifestly determined to stand clear of all these, and preach Christ until death, looking for their reward in the glory to which Christ, their head, had gone, and not here, and they were willing to count all on earth as loss to win that crown, and share in that reward which Christ had gained, and which he, through the same life of self-denial and suffering, was inviting them. We who enjoy the Christian freedom of to-day do not approve their course because of its ultimate result upon monastic society as a whole, and its constant reflex influence on those thus secluded from contact with the varying phases of human society, which society they should live to *re*-form and mould after the "mind of Christ;" but little do we realize the obstacles in their way, when even a corrupt popular Church was their foe and their greatest persecutor. Seldom did even the prophets among the Jews have such opposition, to such an extent and so constantly, at least. There is *some* apology for Christians taking the wings of a "great eagle and flying into the wilderness" of retirement from the "face of the dragon," and choosing solitude rather than domestic responsibilities, when espionage, proscription, imprisonment, in such prisons as were common in those days, banishment, confiscation, and often death, was the penalty of diverging from *the Church*, which united "Church and State" held the keys of life and death, to woo or awe into fealty all religionists by the usurped authority they conjointly exercised.

The Apostle Paul, even, dissuaded from family responsibilities in the then "present distress," for it was neither prudent nor seemly for a Christian to talk of feasts when the enemy was devouring his substance; nor to count himself at home when his house was on fire, or when (about to be) banished to a strange land, or to seek to provide for, and bless a family, when his own life was in "jeopardy every hour." And this "jeopardy" was as great under the pressure of Papal persecutions, as before under those of infidel Jerusalem or Pagan Greece or Rome. And the "present distress" of Paul continued as to the dissenters from the ritualistic (Roman) Church through all those ages until within a century of this date (1874). Not only the Catharists, Waldenses, and Albigenses, of Continental Europe, have known the

14

power of this "dragon" of persecution at the hands of the Papacy, but the dissenters from the "State Church" of England, two hundred and fifty years since, felt the weight of the motive, either to be "hermits" (*eremites*), and silent at their own homes, or to "take wings and flee into the wilderness," which latter thousands of them did; while thousands of others, bishops, *i. e.*, ministers, and people, "had trial of cruel imprisonment," ministers (two thousand of them) driven from their parishes, and Christian worshippers in their chosen assemblies arrested, branded, fined, imprisoned, or banished, and some even punished with death. But this is a diversion. We only allude to these facts of history to show that we are not competent to say, at this late day, how many of those who chose the life of the anchoret, or followed Christ and Paul in celibacy and the chastening of the flesh, had reasons for it that would, in the circumstances, satisfy our own minds of its propriety.

Not that we would be understood as asserting that the *Euchites* were all anchorets: far from it, they were for ages and centuries a flourishing society, sustaining among themselves all the relations and vocations of life. But there was a strong tendency in the most fervent and pious among them to this mode of life, as, indeed, was true *of all Christendom* at this era. And be it known that even BASIL, *the Great*, as all our modern writers and Church historians call him now, and for 1500 years counted the great pillar and light of the Church of that age, was the special organizer and champion of the monastic and recluse life. For once, we will quote in full from the *Religious Encyclopedia* the article referring to this man:

"BASIL, called the *Great*, to distinguish him from other Greek patriarchs of the same name, was born in 329, at Cæsarea, in Cappadocia, and after having studied at Athens, he for a while taught rhetoric and practised at the bar. In 370 he was made bishop of Cæsarea, where he died in 379. He was the most distinguished ecclesiastic among the Greek patriarchs. His efforts for the regulation of clerical discipline of the divine service, and of the standing of the clergy; the number of his sermons; the success of his mild treatment of the Arians; and, above all, his endeavors for the promotion of the monastic life, for which he prepared vows and rules, observed by himself, and still remaining in force, prove the extent of his influence. The Greek Church honors him as one of its most illustrious patron saints, and celebrates his festival, January 1. His followers are widely extended; there are even some in America. *They lead an austere life.* The vows of obedience, chastity, and poverty, framed by Basil, are the rules of all the orders of Christendom, although he is particularly the father of the Eastern, as Benedict is the father of the Western order. In point of genius, controversial skill, and a rich and flowing eloquence, Basil was surpassed by very few of the fourth century."*

Of one thing we may be sure: they did not refrain from preaching Christ; they went among men so far as to preach Christ to them; they did it faithfully; seconded by their own example of self-denial, they loved and endured all things, even for those who hunted and hated them. They had naught else to live for, and for Christ and his cause they did live, and for that cause they laid down their lives!

The *Euchites* lived secluded from a lucre-loving world, and, as we said, derived their name from their *incessant prayers*, with song, "for they believed," says the historian, "that the evil spirit in man can only be expelled by continual praying and singing, . . . and that this demon being once expelled, the soul will return to God pure."

---

* HENDERSON says that "Basil, having retired into a desert, founded a monastery, and having drawn up several hundred rules, his society spread *all over the East*, and soon into the West. Some say that Basil saw himself the spiritual father of more than ninety thousand monks in the East only. The historians of this order say that it has produced 14 popes, 1805 bishops, 3010 abbots, and 11,085 martyrs, besides an infinite number of confessors and virgins. It also boasts of several emperors, kings, and princes who have embraced its rule. Thus we see that monasticism was early honored in the highest places of the popular Church. Nevertheless it has foll oft furnished the only safe retreat, the *nest* in the covert where has been hatched the earliest and the latest *protests* of Christian freedom and righteousness against priestcraft and a perverted Church authority, from the days of BASIL and the *Euchites* to the days of MARTIN LUTHER. It corrupted the *canonical* Roman Church far more than either the Greek or the dissenters. It resulted in binding the yoke of celibacy on the Roman priesthood to this day, which was never only in part true of the Greek Church, or among any of the protesting sects. At length the Roman Church became wholly the pervert on this subject, while the dissenters wholly threw out the evil leaven."

" This sect," Mosheim says, " drew over many to its ranks by its show of
piety, and the Greeks waged war with it through all the subsequent centuries."
He adds in another place, " It should be remembered that the terms *Euchites*
and *Messalians* were used with great latitude among the Greeks and the Orientals, and were applied to all who endeavored to raise the soul to God by re-
calling it from all influence of the senses, though these persons oft differed
very materially in their religious opinions." The chief charge against them,
at a later day, was, " that they resisted the outrageous domination of the
priesthood, and derided the monstrous mass of superstition which was sanctioned by public authority." And all who did this the Greeks (the potentates)
" were accustomed to designate by the odious names of *Messalians !* or *Euchites !*
just as the Latins at a later day denominated all the opposers of the Roman
pontiffs as *Waldenses* or *Albigenses*."

Among this class of praying pietists, the *Bogomiles* originated at a later day, whose founder, one BASIL, a monk, was
burned alive at Constantinople.

"So many instances of men of this description occur," says
the historian, " both in ancient and later times, that it is not
strange that such men (of such sentiments) are found in the
East [see " Spiritual Christians of Russia "] at this era. The
name of the sect, *Bogomiles*, was derived from the divine
mercy which they are said to have incessantly implored, thus
showing that they were only a branch of the *Euchites* or
praying ones."

The testimony of Mosheim, that these praying peoples
"endeavored to raise the soul to God, by calling it from the
influence of the senses," is good testimony as to their moral
and spiritual elevation, and the purity and sanctity of their
lives, since Mosheim is so unwilling to bear such testimony to
the character of the non-ritualistic dissenters. Yet even
Mosheim will find very few of the dissenters of any of the
ages that were not non-ritualists (a fact that historians have
culpably ignored), since few that rejected the priesthood of
Rome established a priestly caste among themselves, and,
therefore, had none to consecrate the elements of a sacrament.
An attempt at such consecration with "common" or unpriestly
hands would soon render the ceremony contemptible in the
eyes of all sedate, reflecting, and spiritual-minded persons.

And no true Christian philosopher, recognizing the great central truth that love to God and man is alone the true religion, and the ultimate test of all theology, will fail to recognize the claims of every society, sect, school and brotherhood, that affords the decisive evidence of being God's accepted and elect ones, in that they bring forth the fruits of the Spirit. Nor can such sustain the claims, or write in honor of the popular forms of Christianity as embodied in the huge ritualistic dynasties and stale corporations of the past. Nor do they trace the true spirit of Christianity in the narrow grooves of any current ritualism, or mere scholastic and sectarian creed. HALLAM's "Middle Ages" and MILMAN's "Latin Christianity," for example, deal damaging blows against the churchly claims of those ages, and they do not set in any enviable light either the scholastic teachings or the cringing servitude to narrow dogmas which they found so common even in the higher ranks of the clergy.

Reading their keen analysis, and bold exposure of the systems (or nutshells!) of these scholastic divines, one is led to ask himself, Can there not be true fealty to Christ and jealous regard for sanctifying truth, without crucifying charity within ourselves and narrowing our horizon to some little parish circuit or denominational fold, and dwarfing our souls to take in only the interests of a party no worthier nor more sacred in God's sight than a thousand others that have been and *are to-day?* Was it so with Christ and Paul? These Christian philosophers (*Hallam* and *Milman*), underneath all these rituals and systems, find an interior basis, or a *spiritual church*—crossing all surface distinctions and superficial boundary lines, in a manifestly received love of God, common to them all. And they have found God dishonored most by those who have exhibited the most marked churchly tendencies and who most strenuously observed the ritualistic lines. No reader of the religious history of these ages can deny this.

THE PAULICIANS, A. D. 600–900.

We now reach the era of the PAULICIANS, a protesting and non-ritualistic sect that arose in Armenia, western Asia, in the time of Constans, and were most prevalent and active in the seventh and eighth centuries; some affirm that they arose through the instrumental labors of two eminent religious teachers named *Paul* and *John*. Others, with more reason, perhaps, affirm that they were so called from their constant aim to copy the spirit and teachings of the Apostle Paul. Neander, vol. iii. p. 263, thus introduces them:

"They were for restoring the life and manners of the Church to apostolic simplicity; they maintained that by the multiplication of external rites and ceremonies in the dominant Church *the true life of* RELIGION *had declined*. They combated an inclination to rely on the magic effects of external forms, particularly the sacraments. Indeed they went so far on this side as to wholly reject the outward celebration of the sacraments; they maintained that it was by no means Christ's intention to institute the *baptism by water* as a perpetual ordinance, but that by baptism he meant only the baptism of the Spirit, for by his teachings he communicated himself as the Living Water for the thorough cleansing of the entire human nature. So in respect to the supper: They held that the eating of the flesh and drinking of the blood of Christ consisted simply in the coming into vital union with him through his doctrines, his word, which were his true flesh and blood. It was not sensible bread and sensible wine, but his words, which were to be *the same for the soul that bread and wine are for the body*, which he designated as his flesh and his blood."

The Paulicians flourished from the year A. D. 600 to 900. How they were treated by the Judaizing and Romanizing popular Church may be seen by taking some illustrative examples. Neander, vol. iii. p. 588:

"It may be conjectured," says Neander, "that Bishop Jacob was one of those men who, by the study of the sacred Scriptures and of the older church teachers (he himself living in Armenia, where Christianity was exceedingly corrupted by superstition and a host of ceremonial observances growing out of the mixture of Christian and Jewish elements), had caught the spirit of reform,—a conjecture corroborated by the fact that two synods were unable to convict him of any heresy. If he was actually connected with the Paulicians, it was assuredly with those of the better stamp; with those who, in their efforts to bring about a restoration of apostolic simplicity, and in their opposition to the intermixture of Judaism and Christianity, *represented the spirit of Marcion.* His opponents themselves acknowledge that he was distinguished for his austerity of life; and his priests, who travelled through the land as preachers of repentance, were men of the same simple and abstemious habits. 'His own act alone,' said they, 'can help the individual who has sinned,' *i. e.,* without intervention of priests. He (Jacob) met with great success among the clergy, the people and the nobles, until finally the Catholicus, or spiritual chief of the Armenian Church, craftily succeeded in getting possession of his person. He first *caused him to be branded with the heretical mark,* and then to be carried from place to place with a common crier, *to proclaim him a heretic* and expose him to public scorn. After this he was thrown into a dungeon, from which he managed to effect his escape, but was finally killed by his enemies."

SYLVANUS CONSTANTINE, to whom some attribute the honor of founding the sect of the *Paulicians,* but who more properly may be said to have given new vitality and energy to it—by himself and the younger ministers he sent out— founded many churches of the Paulicians in the seventh century. He gained his religious views by reading attentively the New Testament (which was very rare in those days), and especially the writings of the Apostle Paul. He sought to reach the very spirit and teachings of primitive Christianity. Says Gibbon: "Whatever might be *the success,* a Protestant reader will admire *the spirit* of the inquiry." "Christianity in its primitive simplicity and power," says Jones (" History of Christian Church."), "was by such teachers widely diffused through Armenia, Pontus and Cappadocia. . . . Constantine was, however, seized at Colonia by the arm of persecution. By a refinement of cruelty he was placed before a line of his disciples, who were commanded, as the price of their own pardon and the proof of their repentance, to massacre their spiritual father. They turned aside from the impious office, the stones dropped from their filial hands, and of the whole number only one man, named Justus, could be found base enough to become his executioner. Thus after twenty-seven years of evangelical labor this venerable leader of the Paulician churches fell a martyr to the truth of the gospel."

" Thus the Paulicians and other kindred sects," says Neander, " though occasionally suppressed, continually sprung up anew in Armenia, till the middle of the eleventh century, and from this point they spread abroad to other regions, particularly the adjacent provinces of the Roman empire, partly to escape the violence of persecution and partly from the desire to multiply converts to their doctrines."

"Their first migration was to Italy, whence, in process of time, they sent colonies into almost all the other provinces of Europe and formed a considerable number of religious assemblies, who adhered to their doctrine and who were afterwards persecuted with the utmost vehemence by the Roman pontiffs. In Italy they were called *Paterini,* or *Gazari,* from Gazaria, in Lesser Tartary, where their predecessors had been supposed to originate. In France they were called *Albigenses.*" (See "*Religious Encyclopedia.*") Even Mosheim has treated the Paulicians with great candor. He says:

"The Paulicians recommended to the people the most ardent zeal and constant and assiduous perusal of the Scriptures, and expressed the utmost indignation against the Greeks, who allowed to priests alone access to these sacred fountains of divine knowledge; and they refused baptism and the supper, affirming, of the supper, that Christ's last supper was only 'those divine discourses and exhortations which are spiritual food and nourishment to the soul, and fill it with repose, satisfaction and delight.' They refused to venerate the wood of the cross, or to worship the Virgin Mary, or to admit the sanctity of churches more than of private houses; disapproved of incense and a consecrated oil for absolution; denied that there were ranks and orders in the ministry; rejected the Papal burial service, with fees attached, also the sacraments of *penance, the mass,* the doctrine of purgatory, and the adoration of saints and images."

Now will the Christian reader judge which were the heretics in God's sight—these pure and noble people, suffering all manner of persecution, or those who persecuted them? In all these ages, the dissenters from the Papacy who rejected water baptism were more numerous by far than dissenters who retained it. And in later ages, nearly all the Mystics and other dissenters, who believed in Christian holiness and a true spiritual life, like these Paulicians, were anti-baptizers; they had no priesthood, or canonical administrators, or church to baptize them.

THE ORLEANISTS (IN FRANCE).

We next reach the period of the *Orleanists*, who arose about the year A. D. 1000, undoubtedly a continuation of the Paulicians in their Western field. Neander, vol. iii. p. 595, says of these:

" They rejected also the sacrament of baptism with water, probably explaining it as the baptism of John. . . . But they substituted in its place a baptism of the Holy Spirit, which was to be connected with the imposition of hands (as in the apostolic days), as the symbol of initiation to their sect. And this again *evidences their relationship to Oriental sects* and to the later Catharists. This rite (imposition of hands) was certainly the same thing with what was designated among these sects by the term *consolamentum* (form of communication of the *Comforter*, the *Paraclete*). By virtue of this imposition of hands, whoever submitted to it in a suitable frame of mind would be filled with the gifts of the Holy Spirit and purified from all sin. . . . With a spiritual baptism they held also to a spiritual eucharist, by which those who received this baptism would be refreshed and find all their spiritual needs completely satisfied. Whoever had ever once tasted of this heavenly food, said they, would abide steadfastly in the truth and resist all temptations to apostasy."

Here, then, we find a spiritual-minded people closely resembling the most spiritual and Christlike of the Protestant denominations of to-day—specially those that inculcate the doctrine of personal sanctification and Christian holiness upon their members, as George Fox, John Wesley, C. G. Finney, etc. But "those that will live godly in Christ Jesus shall suffer persecution." And these exemplary Orleanists by no means escaped it. Says Neander, p. 596:

"In the year 1022 the king himself (Robert of France) came to Orleans, where a numerous synod had assembled, to try and pass sentence upon the sect. Fallen upon during one of their secret meetings, of which information had been given by Arefast, all who were found present were arrested, together with Arefast himself, and conveyed in chains before the spiritual tribunal, where also the king and queen assisted. When Arefast presented before them the doctrines they had taught him, they no longer hesitated to avow openly their adherence of them, but declared:

" 'Think not that this sect, because ye have so lately come to the knowledge of it, has sprung up within a short period. For a long time we have professed these doctrines, and we expected that these doctrines would one day be admitted by you and by all others; this we believe still. We have a higher law, one written by the Holy Spirit in the inner man: we can believe nothing but that which God, the Creator of all things, has revealed to us! Do with us as you please. Already we behold our King reigning in heaven, whose right hand shall exalt us to an eternal triumph, and crown us with celestial joys.' "

All except one ecclesiastic and one man who recanted were condemned to the stake and died there!

BARCLAY, in his treatise on Sacraments, quotes from several authors, as Alanus, Pitticus, and Floracensis, corroborating the record of the martyrdom of these Orleanists, who denied water-baptism. Alames also speaks of these that were burnt for denying it, for they said, "That baptism had no efficacy either in respect to children or adult persons; and therefore men were not obliged to take baptism;" and ten canonics (ministers) were burnt for that crime.

Floracensis, a Papal monk, has given this record:

"I will give you to understand concerning the heresy that was in the city of Orleans, for it was true that King Robert caused to be burnt alive near fourteen of that city, of the chief of their clergy, and the more noble of their laics, who were hateful to God, and abominable to heaven and earth; for they did stiffly deny the grace of holy baptism, and also the consecration of the Lord's body and blood."

Thus their whole heresy consisted in denying the validity of sacraments.

Neander infers that the influence of this sect was widely felt among the monks and ecclesiastics from a letter of Filbert, a bishop, to the abbot Adeodat, where he "inveighs against the corrupt tendency of those carnally-minded men, who represented the sacraments as toys, holding it to be impossible *that outward and earthly ordinances could produce any such effects as are ascribed to them.*"

Thus those who refused to trust in rituals were, by the church bishops, pronounced "carnally-minded" as well as heretics!

They surely had the mark of God's people in suffering calumny and various kinds of persecution and bodily torture.

THE ARRANIANS, A. D. 1100.

On p. 597, vol. iii., Neander gives us the following account of another "peculiar people:"

"Some years later, a people were found in Arras and Liege called *Arranians*, who were for removing out of the way everything which could serve as a substitute for one's own moral efforts, or as an excuse for moral inactivity. 'Each man,' said they, 'must be holy by his own act, and within himself—by *that alone*, and not by any magical operation of sacraments can man become pure. Outward baptism and the outward eucharist are nothing.' To show the inefficiency of baptism they pointed to the immoral lives of the persons baptized, and to the fact that in the children on whom baptism was performed, not one of the conditions was to be found upon which such efficacy must depend; no consciousness, no will, no faith, no confession. The doctrines which they received agreed in all respects, as they affirmed, with the doctrines of Christ and of the apostles. It consisted in this, to forsake the world, to overcome the flesh, to support one's self by the labor of one's own hands, to injure no one, to show love to all the brethren; and 'Whosoever practised these *needed no baptism*—where it failed, baptism would not supply its place.' They were opposed, like the Paulicians, to the worship of the cross and of images; they spoke against the priestly consecration, the value of the consecrated altar, and of a consecrated church. 'The church,' said they, 'is nothing but a pile of stones heaped together;' the church has no advantages whatever, over any place where the Divine Being is worshipped."

They were simply true Christian Protestants. But Neander adds:

"They were accused of heresy; a synod was convened at Arras to try them— the archbishop addressed to them a discourse in refutation of their tenets, [how refute them?] and in defence of the Catholic faith. But they explained, and were not convicted, but preached their tenets more cautiously thereafter.

"But Ramihed, probably of a similar faith, was also brought before the archbishop—but he testified his orthodoxy on every point, so that no advantage was gained over him. A synod was afterward convened to try him, and here again testifying his orthodoxy on every point, the archbishop simply required of him that he should receive the holy eucharist in testimony of his innocence. To this, however, he refused to consent, declaring that he could not take the eucharist, neither from the hand of abbot, of priest, nor of the archbishop himself, because they were all guilty of simony and of covetousness, under some form or other. This sufficed to arouse against him the indignation of the clergy, who *at once declared him a heretic.*"

Now what does the reader think of Neander's remarking
upon this judgment of that synod:

"It is clear that a process of this kind furnishes no ground for a certai
judgment respecting the doctrines of this person."

Does it not furnish ground for a judgment that the cour
that tried him was itself guilty of heresy and apostasy from
Christ? But with rather cool charity, where it should be
warm, Neander adds:

"Perhaps we may find in this case the indication of a spontaneous move
ment of the Christian consciousness, and of a pure interest for Christian piety
against the corruption of the clergy."

We may add, do we not see in these events as clear a need
of purifying the clergy, as when Luther attempted that work
400 years later? However,

"This man was hunted down as a heretic by the fanatical vengeance of the
populace; when seized, he followed his pursuers without fear. He was con
fined in a cabin, and while prostrated on the ground in prayer a torch was ap
plied to the building, and he was consumed in the flames."

Thus another martyr gained the crown, and the signet of
the Almighty upon his blameless and consecrated life. Neander adds:

"But as he had gained many followers by the purity of his life, so the enthusiasm of his followers was only increased by the mode of his death. His
followers continued to multiply in the towns of this district until the twelfth
century; especially among the weavers, which, from its peculiar character,
has ever been the favorite resort of the mystical sects."

So we discover that the Mystics also were anti-ritualists, the
flower and glory of the true Church in the days of the dark
eclipse of the faith in the Papal Church. Neander's seemingly tacit admission that the Arranians, and Ramihed, a
spiritual prince among them, really held errors of doctrine
(albeit he does not name one that was evolved on trial, yet
the trial was for life or death for that very purpose), and
Ramihed was persecuted to death, only because he refused to
accept a sacrament at the hands of a simoniacal and ritualistic
clergy, is not ingenuous. It shows that he himself was still

possessed of a false idea of ritualistic sanctity and *church* authority! He fully attests the purity of life of the Arranians and their zeal for a purer church; in other words, that they were the genuine reformers of that period; and that in defence of such principles of reform and in active obedience to the desire for reform they were hunted to the death! By such only casual manifestations of the obscurity of his own perceptions, does Neander evince his ritualistic bias after the Lutheran type.

THE GERHARDITES, A. D. 1040.

But to continue our anti-ritualistic record:

"From the year A. D. 1027 to 1046," says Neander, "there appeared in Turin a sect, with GERHARD at their head, who discoursed thus: 'We have a priest, not that Roman one, but another, who daily visits our brethren, scattered through the world; and when God bestowed him on them, they received from him, with great devoutness, the forgiveness of sins. Besides this priest, who is without the tonsure, they know of no other, nor did they acknowledge any other sacrament than his absolution.' Thus," says Neander, "we find in this sect, as in that at Orleans, the consciousness of a fellowship extending through different countries. By their priest, they doubtless meant the Holy Spirit, which formed the invisible bond of fellowship, and bestowed on them the inward clearing from remaining sin, and the inward consecration of the divine life. *This inward working of the Divine Spirit stood to them in the place of all sacraments.* The sufferings to which they were exposed on account of their doctrines they encountered cheerfully, considering them the means of expiating sins, before and in the present life, and thus preparing them to return purified to the society of the higher world of spirits. Those, therefore, who were deprived of the privilege of dying as martyrs, died cheerfully under self-inflicted tortures."

Here was a tincture of ancient Jewish and our modern Edward Beecher doctrine of pre-existence, with a not uncommon Christian hungering for martyrdom; but nothing that stains the spotlessness of their character, unless it be their self-martyrdom in certain cases.

"The archbishop of Milan sent soldiers and arrested a number of these; they were led to the stake, and the choice given them either to bow before a cross erected on the spot, and confess the Catholic faith, or to die. Some chose to do the former, but the majority, placing their hands upon their faces, plunged into the flames."

Another proof of their heresy, is it not?

On p. 604, Neander gives an account of the part Bishop Gebuin acted in the destruction of *Gerhardt*. He hints that Gebuin, in order to cover his own deed, intimated that GERHARDT became a maniac and leaped into a well and perished there.

"There are many things in this story," says Neander, "calculated to excite doubt. . . . It is possible that in this case we have a perverted, spiteful representation of facts, and that his death was really brought about by the fanatical hatred of heretics, and was represented by his enemies as *an act of suicide.*"

Alluding to such reformers, Neander aptly remarks, vol. iii. p. 602:

"Not only was there an anti-ritualistic impulse felt in Europe, through sects originating in the East at this era, but we find such (heretical) tendencies traceable to other quarters. The revived study of the ancient Latin authors in the ninth to eleventh century called forth in many an antagonism of the cultivated understanding to the dominant Church doctrine, and engendered many opinions which were regarded as heretical."

Some of these taught that the moral among the heathen were predestinated to salvation if they had never heard the gospel; and that they were saved without the intervention of the Papal Church priesthood. "And Glaberius Rudolph testifies that the predilection for Paganism (for the salvation of men outside the Church we presume) had given birth at the same time to similar heretical tendencies throughout Italy and in Sardinia; and he informs us that the individuals accused of these tendencies were, some of them, beheaded, while others died at the stake."

"It is quite possible," continues Neander, "that this writer had not clearly discriminated the heretical appearances, and that we must suppose such to be here meant as had proceeded from the Oriental (*i. e.*, the anti-ritualistic) influence. When he says that persons from Sardinia spread these false doctrines in Spain, we must assuredly believe that *Oriental* rather than *Pagan* doctrines were meant; for how is it possible to suppose that Pagan doctrines could (from Sardinia) get admittance to Spain more than elsewhere?"

From the apostolic age, Spain had been a marked field of

Christian labor, and the people there were doubtless ripe for an anti-ritualistic movement.

THE LEUTHARDITES—ARNOLDITES, A. D. 1150.

But the record of non-ritualists may still be unrolled, thereby unfolding the record of the true spiritual Church of Christ, kept alive amid the surrounding darkness and apostasy of ritualism in the Papal Church; having this insignia of its genuineness, viz., "The blood of the martyrs is the seed of the Church;" thus marking where the "little flock," to whom the kingdom is given, may be found. Neander says:

"According to DOLCINO, a reformer of the twelfth century, 'The last period that might be called the time of the Holy Ghost (has come), inasmuch as the distinguishing characteristic of this period was to be the free inspiration by the Holy Spirit in the apostolical benediction, and righteousness of a life no longer depending, as before, on outward means and ordinances, but purely producing itself from within outwards.'"

Neander then gives an account (vol. iii. p. 603) of one LEUTHARD, who appeared among the country people of France, and claiming to have a vision from God calling him to preach, he went into a church to pray, and finding there a cross and an image of Christ, he demolished them both.

"Not certainly," says Neander, "out of spite to Christianity, for he himself appealed to the Sacred Scriptures; but, most probably, because he imagined he saw in them something that savored of idolatry. . . . In support of all he said he quoted the testimony of the Scriptures."

ARNOLD (of Brescia), a disciple of Abelard, an eminent reformer of the twelfth century, by his bold and lofty spirit, his knowledge of Christian antiquities, and the vehement eloquence of his public harangues, roused Italy, France, and Switzerland against the abuses of the Roman Church and clergy, and even converted the Pope's legate to his opinions. He was charged with heresy, and, together with his adherents, called *Arnoldites*, was excommunicated by Innocent II. "But it is probable," says Davenport, "his real crime was his having taught that the Church ought to be divested of its worldly possessions and reduced to its primitive simplicity."

Dr. Wall allows that he was condemned along with Peter de Bruys, for rejecting *infant baptism*.

In 1144, he appeared at Rome, and there elevated the standard of civil and clerical reform, with such success as to gain even the Roman senate; and for ten years possessed the chief power in the Eternal City. Adrian IV. succeeded, however, in expelling him, in 1155, by laying an interdict on the city. The reformer retired to Tuscany, but was there seized and taken back to Rome, where he died by the hands of the executioner, being excommunicated, crucified, and burned.

"It is to be remembered," Neander says, "that it was by means of these reformers and Oriental sects that the Scriptures were diffused among laymen. Touching the mode of procedure against false teachers, it is to be observed that it was Byzantine despotism which set the example of enforcing conviction by the fagot and the sword. The Western Church had originally declared itself opposed to such a procedure (yet not always with self-consistency), but the fanaticism of this age found no punishment too severe for those who were regarded as godless outcasts; and the clergy followed the general current of the times. From common practice grew up the theory of ecclesiastical law, which was supported by the grand mistake of confounding together the different positions of the Old and New Testaments. The fanatical fury of the people, having been once roused against the heretics, and an abstemious life having come to be regarded as a characteristic mark of heretics, sprung from the Oriental sects in Greece, Mesopotamia, Armenia, etc. These men who distinguished themselves by the rigid severity of their lives were constantly liable to incur the opprobrium of heresy; aye, and even to be falsely accused of secret immoralities," as Neander admits, "insomuch," as he says, "that a writer of this period could say that a pallid face was looked upon by the people as a sure sign of heresy; and good Catholics have fallen victims, together with heretics, to the blind fury of the mob."

Thus it seems that the blind fury of persecutors became so impetuous as not to stop to discern friend from foe, and many a poor Papist of a cadaverous countenance had to pay the forfeit of his appearance (as Peter almost—for his bewraying speech) with his life. Such is the madness the blood-thirsty spirit of persecution begets. "Being exceedingly mad against the saints," says Paul, "I persecuted them even unto strange cities."

But the most extensive anti-ritualistic protest since the immediate post-apostolic age occurred during the latter period of what are termed *the middle ages*, in the twelfth and thirteenth centuries, though commencing a century or two earlier. Here was developed a great revolt from the Papacy and its usages, extending throughout Italy and large portions of Europe, under the banner of a people calling themselves

THE CATHARISTS, A. D. 1200.

This name, from the Greek word *Katharos, pure* or *perfect*, was adopted to designate the fact that they assayed to purify themselves from the corruptions of the dominant Church, and to witness against all sin everywhere! These embraced nearly all the Protestants of the period named, and were far more numerous than any other class of Protestants prior to the Lutheran reformation.

Neander, vol. iv. p. 574, thus speaks of them:

"They sought to point out the opposition between the Old Testament and the New, and appealed to the opposition between the Sermon on the Mount and the Mosaic law. . . . They said of the members of the dominant Church that they had sunk back on the foundation of the Mosaic law. . . . They contended not only against infant baptism, *with arguments always readily presenting themselves against the institution as apostolical,* but *also against water-baptism generally.* . . . When it was objected that Christ had suffered himself to be baptized by John, they replied it had been done on the part of Christ by way of accommodation to a prevailing custom, and to avoid giving offence.

"The Church, moreover, had for a time used water-baptism, because men were accustomed to the rite, or because it would invite them by this symbol to the baptism of the Spirit. They affirmed that in the Sacred Scriptures baptism was a term *often employed to express repentance,* or the *preaching of the divine word.* The baptism of the Spirit—the true baptism—should be performed by the imposition of hands, in connection with prayer, which they designated by the term *consolamentum.* In evidence of the power and significance of this act, they referred to the Apostles Peter and John, who were sent to Samaria for the purpose of communicating, by the imposition of hands, the Holy Ghost to those who had received water-baptism.

"In regard to the Lord's Supper, they explained the words of the institution in a symbolic sense: 'This is,' they made equivalent to—'this signifies my body.' They referred in proof to those paragraphs in the New Testament, where the thing itself is mentioned in place of that which it may serve to represent, as for example, 1 Cor. x. 4: 'And did all drink the same spiritual drink,' etc. They referred to the fact that Christ himself says, 'My *flesh* profiteth nothing—my *words* are spirit and life'—*i. e.*, are to be spiritually understood! Christ's *words* by which he communicates himself are his true body. They combated the doctrine of the sacrament of penance, . . . contending against the externalization of religion in the dominant Church. They said, 'God dwells not in houses made with hands.' The Catharists were zealous in disseminating their principles everywhere. According to the testimony of their first opponents themselves, *it was their blameless and strict mode of life* that distinguished the Catharists generally; for they abstained from cursing and swearing, and a simple yea or nay was a substitute with them for the strongest attestations.

"The most absurd reports of unnatural excesses and other abominations said to be committed in the secret assemblies of the sect were spread among the multitude—accusations similar to those brought against the primitive Christians by the Jews, *and such as are ever wont to be repeated against all opponents of a dominant religion.* The fanatical multitude exercised a speedy justice, *hurrying away much people at once to the stake!*"

Yet their zeal resulted in a wide spread of their principles. Says Neander:

"According to the testimony of Sacchoni, who had been for seventeen years one of them, but who afterward wrote against them, there were countless numbers who belonged to the second class of Catharists"—*i. e.*, who were not of the ascetic class, but only four thousand belonging to the class of the "*perfects.*"

This was written in the early part of the thirteenth century. Neander is forced to admit (p. 590) that these non-ritualistic sects exerted an advantageous influence; just as he affirms of Paul, in the planting of the Church, that he "effected more without Judaism than all the other apostles with their Judaism."

"They, the Catharists, Arranians, Paulicians, etc.," says Neander, "awaked in the ignorant and uninstructed people, who had been misled by incompetent priests to place the essence of religion in a round of ceremonies, a more lively interest in spiritual concerns. They called up in them the idea of a divine life, presented religion to them more as a matter of inward experience, and, perhaps, as this was the particular bent of the Paulicians, made them better acquainted with the Scriptures; for there can be little doubt that by means of the Paulicians translations of particular portions of the Scriptures were already circulated among the laity."

Here, then, was the true Protestantism of that era.

"When the laity, thus awaked, spoke from their own experience, when, in the attitude of polemics, and combating the additions foreign to Bible Christianity in the doctrine of the Church, they were able to bring forward their arguments from the teachings of Christ and the apostles, it is easy to see how superior they would prove in disputation to the ignorant and incompetent clergy."

Where is the record of any other Protestants like unto these in moral power and influence in all these centuries?

But we have not finished the record of the true Church, known by the infallible sign of purity-seeking, and the endurance of persecution inflicted by a false church, and ever specially instigated by the priests of that false church, as it has been from the beginning (see Gal. iv. 29), "He that is born after the flesh (only) persecutes him that is born after the Spirit." Thus also the *true Church* may be distinguished from the false—for *the true Church never persecutes.*

CHAPTER VI.

CHRONICLES OF THE NON-BAPTIZERS (*Continued*)—A HIDDEN RECORD REVEALED.

THE MYSTICS, A. D. 1250–1500.

THE term *Mystic* by Papists, and some Protestants, whose conception of religion and the Christian life is that they are mainly the observance of the externals of the Church, their rubrics and ceremonials, has been used as a term of reproach applied to all those sects and portions of the Church which teach rather that the Christian faith in its manifestation reveals an *inner life*, a moral transformation and regeneration of man's spiritual nature, resulting in the death of sin, and an internal consciousness of soul-communion with God.

Vagarists, like a *Cocceius* or a *Swedenborg*, have been styled *Mystics* by both Papists and Protestants, for a very different reason it is true, viz., for giving loose rein to conceit and fancy, both in their interpretation of Scripture and their general religious theorizing; but those that Papal and some Protestant historians have usually called *The Mystics* have been, in the ages in which they lived, the very elect of God, the salt and life of the Church of Christ, the savor of whom was almost the only evidence that there was still extant a living Church of the Lord Jesus among men. Yet all these have been to a great extent non-ritualists and non-sacramentarians, both in spirit and practice. They were protestants against the sacramentizing tendencies of the Church of Rome from the outset.

The *Mystics* of the twelfth and thirteenth centuries, according to Neander, were but the shelving out of the Protestantism of the second, third, and fourth centuries; and of which Justin Martyr, Tatian, Marcion, Ambrose, and Origen were noted examples. JUSTIN dwells much upon the true baptism (of the Spirit), and ORIGEN, much upon the indwelling Christ. Formalists and ceremonialists, in all ages, have been prone to call all this *Mysticism*. Nicodemus, a ruler of the Jews, was very much stumbled by just such *Mysticism* taught by Jesus. Paul everywhere preached this great *mystery*, "Christ in you the hope of glory," which the unregenerate "princes of this world knew not." Yet this "knowledge" is the elemental and fundamental distinction of the true "sons of God." Christ's kingdom is spiritual. To speak of it, or what appertains thereto, correctly, is not to speak *figuratively* or *metaphorically*, but to speak *didactically* and *veritably* of *spiritual* things. Spiritual entities are as veritable and *literal* as are material or physical entities. Christ's teachings are *spiritual*, *i. e.*, of spiritual things—they need not be spiritualized—they set forth technically, and intrinsically, the things of a spiritual kingdom, not in allegory, but in plain, didactic teaching. Christ's baptism is literally a spiritual baptism. Christ's Supper is literally a spiritual Supper. The water of life is literally and truly spiritual. The rest to which Christ invites the weary is spiritual. The tabernacle which "God pitches and not man" is literally a spiritual tabernacle. The Jerusalem from above is spiritual. The true circumcision is spiritual. The Christian's sacrifices and offerings are not ritual but *literally spiritual*.

The *Mystics* well understood this matter. Let us turn to the thrilling record.

BRETHREN AND SISTERS OF THE FREE SPIRIT.

Turning to "Milman's History of Latin Christianity," we find a most striking record that overlaps, in part, the record of the *Catharists*, presenting a phase of Christianity under the name of *Mysticism* which furnishes the proof that there has never been a period in which our Lord had not his witnessing people, a true Church known of him, while all around, especially in the popular Church, was darkness in its densest form. The record of these will fill up the whole period from the subsidence of the prevailing influence of the *Catharists* to the days of the Reformation under Luther; so that no void is found since Christ was glorified in which his true spiritual Church is not revealed, witnessing against ritualism and spiritual wickedness in high places and low. It is true that during the period covered by the testimony of the *Mystics* the Waldenses, Albigenses, and others, witnessed against the Popish hierarchy, but there was no light so clear, glorious, and extensive as this. In vol. viii. of the above work, on pp. 396 and on, we find the following record:

"From 1247 to 1272 the Franciscan Bertholdt, of Winterthur, preached with amazing success through Bavaria, Austria, Moravia, and Thuringen. The dissidents under their various names were everywhere. At the beginning of the fourteenth century Alsace was almost in possession of the

"BRETHREN AND SISTERS OF THE FREE SPIRIT.

"They were driven out and scattered; but expulsion and dispersion, if it does not multiply the numbers, usually increases the force and power of such communities. *Mysticism* within the Church strove to fill the void caused by their expulsion. Of these Mystics the most famous names are Rysbroeck of Cologne, Master Eckhart, John Tauler, and Nicolas of Basle. The life of Tauler will show us the times and the personal influence of these men.

"It occupies all the early part of the fourteenth century. . . . No wonder that religious men sought that religion in themselves which they found not in the Church and in the cloister. They took refuge in the sanctuary of their own thoughts from the religion which was contesting the world.

"In all the great cities rose a secret organized brotherhood, bound together by silent, infelt sympathies, and self-named

"THE FRIENDS OF GOD.

"This appellation marked a secession, a tacit revolt, an assumption of superiority. 'God was not to be worshipped,' they said, 'in the Church alone, with the clergy alone, with the monk alone, in the ritual, or even in the sacraments. He was within, in the heart, and in the life. This and kindred brotherhoods embraced all orders, priests, monks, friars, nobles, burghers, and peasants. They had their prophets and prophetesses, above all, their preachers. Some convents were entirely in their power. They sided with the town councils in denouncing the unlawful-ness and wickedness of closing the churches against the poor. Christian love,' they claimed, 'was higher and holier than bishop or Pope.' They were Mystics to the height of Mysticism—each believer was in direct union with God—with the Trinity, not the Holy Ghost alone! They denied all special prerogative to the clergy, the laymen had equal sanctity, equal communion with the Deity, saw visions and uttered prophecies. Their only sympathy with the Waldensians was their anti-sacerdotalism. . . . They honored, loved the Bible, but sought and obtained revelations beyond. . . . Temptations were a mark of God's favor, not to be deprecated. But though suffering was a sign of the divine love, it was not to be self-inflicted suffering. They disclaimed asceticism, self-maceration, and self-torture. All things to the beloved were of God, all therefore indifferent—seclusion, poverty, death. . . .

"Nicolas of Basle, as specially inspired, held boundless influence and authority over all, whether 'Friends of God,' or not, over Tauler, Ruhlman, Mersevin, and others. . . . As the days of the Church grew darker, under the later Popes, visions multiplied. Nicolas visited Gregory XI. at Rome to reprove the Pope's inertness, his sins. Gregory, at first indignant, was soon overawed and won by the commanding holiness of Nicolas."

TAULER THE PREACHER OF THE HIGHER CHRISTIAN LIFE.

"John Tauler was an earnest disciple and powerful apostle of this lofty Mysticism. He preached with wonderful success in Strasburg, in some of the neighboring convents, in towns, and villages, and cities. He journeyed even to Cologne, the seat of this high Mysticism, where the famous Rysbroeck taught with the utmost power and popularity. . . . Tauler threw aside all scholastic subtleties; he strove to be plain, simple, comprehensible to the humblest understanding. He preached in German, with deferential citations in Latin. Tauler sought no Papal license—it was his mission, it was his imperative duty, as a priest, to preach the gospel. . . .

"But Tauler was to undergo a sterner trial—to be trained in another school. In Basle he had been marked by men of a different caste, the gauge of his mind had been taken, the depths of his heart sounded, his religion weighed and found wanting. In Strasburg appeared a stranger, who five times sat at the feet of Tauler and listened to his preaching with serious, searching earnestness. He was a layman; he sought an interview with Tauler, confessed to him, received the sacrament at his hands. He then expressed the wish that Tauler would preach how man may attain perfection, that perfection which he might aspire to on earth. Tauler preached his loftiest Mysticism. The stern stranger now spoke with authority, the authority of a more determinate will, a more firm conviction, 'Thou art yet in slavery to the letter; thou knowest not the life-giving Spirit; thou art but a Pharisee; thou trustest in thine own power, in thine own learning; thou thinkest that thou seekest God's honor, and seekest thine own.' Tauler shuddered, 'Never man before reproved me for my sins.' He felt the spell of a master. 'Twelve years,' said the layman that was rebuking the self-righteousness of Tauler, 'I have been toiling to the height of spiritual perfection, which I have now attained,

. . . . by self-mortification and chastisement, which have now ceased to be necessary.'

"He gave Tauler simple moral rules, counselled him to preach no more, to hear no more confession, to deny himself, and to meditate on the life and death of Christ, till he had obtained humility and regeneration. . . . . Tauler, for about two years, despite the wonder of his friends, and the taunts of his enemies, was silent.

"The first time, at the end of this period, when he attempted to preach he broke down in a flood of tears.

"The stranger who thus reproved and won him was the famous Nicolas of Basle. The secret influence of these teachers, unsuppressed by years of persecution, may appear by the work thus wrought in the mind of Tauler, and from the fact that long after Tauler's death, that Nicolas of Basle, venturing into France, was seized and burned as a heretic at Vienne, in Dauphiny.

"Tauler adhered to the Church; many of the Waldenses did so, to escape persecution, and to infuse their own zeal. From that time the German preaching of Tauler (now unmingled with Latin) in churches, in private assemblies, in the houses of Beguines, in nunneries, was more plain, earnest, and as usual flowed from his own heart to the hearts of others. He taught estrangement from the world, self-denial, poverty of spirit; not merely passive surrender of the soul to God, but with this, love also, to the brethren, and the discharge of the duties of life. Men were to seek peace during these turbulent times, within their own souls. He not only preached in German (not in the unknown Latin tongue), he published in German, '*on following the lowly life of Christ.*'

"The black plague fell on the city of Strasburg, which was still under the ban of the Pope.* In Strasburg died 16,000; in Basle, 14,000 victims. Amid these terrible times of wild visions, wild processions of self-scourged penitents, of crowded cloisters, and *massacred Jews*, the calm voice of Tauler, and of some who spoke and wrote in the spirit of Tauler, rose against the unpitying Church, and remonstrance was addressed to the clergy, that the poor, innocent, blameless people were left to die untended . . . refused the last consolations of the gospel. 'Christ died for all men,' said they; 'the Pope cannot by his interdict close heaven against those who die innocent.' In another paper the broad maxim was laid down, that he who confesses the true faith of Christ, and sins only against the person of the Pope, is no heretic. The people took comfort, and died in peace, though under the Papal interdict.

---

* In the fourteenth century, the citizens of Frankfort-on-the-Oder resisted their ecclesiastical superiors, were excommunicated, and remained for twenty-eight years without baptism or other rites. The return of the priests to perform their accustomed ceremonies seems to have been regarded as a farce.

The author of the "Ploughman's Complaint," speaking the secret anti-papal sentiments of the masses of the people of England, about the same time calls out for the spiritual baptism, thus, "Ah, Lord, *thou badst* thy disciples go and *fullen* (purify) all the folk in the name of the Father, Son and Holy Ghost," which was tantamount to claiming that they did not need the water-baptism administered by the priests.

"It was for these unforgiven opinions that Tauler and his friends, Thomas of Strasburg and Ludolph of Saxony, fell under the suspicion of the new Bishop Bertholdt and the clergy. [Note, in all the history of the Church, few, if any, have ever suffered persecution but at the prompting of the corrupt clergy.]

"Tauler had been called to render an account of his faith before Charles IV., the priest's emperor, when at Strasburg. The Mystics were commanded to recant, to withdraw from their writings these obnoxious tenets.

"Tauler disappeared from Strasburg, he was now heard in Cologne. He returned to Strasburg only to die, A. D. 1361. His last hours were passed in the garden of the convent in which his only sister had long dwelt, a holy and blameless nun. He sought her gentle aid and consolation. One hard Mystic reproached his weakness in yielding to this last earthly affection. He was buried in the cloisters, amid the respectful sorrow of the whole city.

"Tauler had been dead nearly a century before the close of our history (1450), but his sermons lived in the memory of men; they were transcribed with pious solicitude and disseminated among all who sought something beyond what was taught in the Church, and that which the ritual, performed, perhaps, by a careless, proud and profligate priest, did not suggest, and which was not heard in the cold and formal confessional which man might learn for himself, teach to himself; which brought the soul in direct relation with God—trained it to perfection—to communion, to assimilation, to unity with God."

Tauler's Religion Unselfish and Unceremonial.

"Tauler's Mysticism was far beyond the sublime selfishness of á Kempis' 'Imitation of Christ'—it embraced fully, explicitly, the love of others. But it resembled á Kempis in that it was *absolutely and entirely personal religion*, self-wrought out, self-disciplined, self-matured, with *nothing necessarily intermediate between the grace of God and the soul of man.* The man might be perfect in spirit and in truth, within himself, spiritualized only by the Holy Ghost! Tauler's perfect man was a social being, not a hermit; his goodness spread on earth: it was not all drawn up to heaven. Though the perfect man might not rise above duties, he *might rise above observances;* though never free from the law of love to his fellow-men, he claimed a dangerous freedom as regarded the laws and usages of the Church and dependence on the ministers of the Church. Those who were *content with ritual observances,* however obedient, were still imperfect; outward rites, fastings, were good as means, but the soul *must liberate itself from all these outward means:* ... must still await something higher, something to which all this is but secondary, inferior; *having attained perfection it may cast away all these things as unnecessary.* The whole vital real work in man is within.

"Penance is naught without contrition. Mortify not the poor flesh, but mortify sin. Man must confess to God. Unless man forsakes sin the absolution of Popes and Cardinals is of no effect! the confessor has no power over sin. His own works make not a man holy: how can those of others? Will God regard the rich man who buys for a pitiful sum the prayers of the poor? Not the intercession of the Virgin, nor of all the saints, can profit the unrepentant sinner.

"All this, if not rebellion, was sowing the seeds of rebellion against the SACERDOTAL DOMINATION; . . . Tauler lived not only in his writings. The cherished treasure of Mysticism was handed down by minds of kindred spirit for nearly two centuries. They were afterward appealed to by Luther as the harbinger of his own more profound and powerful religiousness: the 'FRIENDS OF GOD' persisted, if not organized, to maintain visibly, if not publicly, their *succession of apostolic holiness!* "

Here was the true "*apostolic succession.*" And mark, if we lose sight of these anti-ritualistic "dissidents," as Milman terms them, and the long prior array of protesting non-ritualists, before cited, we have no continuous Church of Christ— there would be found long periods without any of the semi-ritualistic sects, such as the Donatists, Waldenses, Arnoldists, and the Baptists and Pedo-Baptists of our day. That the Papal, Lutheran, and Episcopal Churches are still ritualistic, who will deny? With the record of these protesting anti-ritualists we have one continuous "succession" of the Church in the apostolic spirit, work and sufferings. But to conclude our narrative of the anti-ritualistic "Friends of God:"

"Ten years after the death of Tauler, Nicolas of Basle, not yet having ventured on his fatal mission into France, is addressing a long and pious monition to the '*Brethren of St. John*' in Strasburg. Near the close of the century, Martin, a monk, was arraigned at Cologne, as an infatuated disciple of Nicolas of Basle. From this process it appears that many 'Friends of God' had been recently burned at Heidelberg. As says Anhang, p. 238, 'Who were judged and convicted by the Church in Heidelberg, as impenitent heretics, and were burned together, if they were *amici Dei, the friends of God.*'"

It was at an age when (as Milman records on p. 395, "Latin Christianity") men could do such things.

"As the Dominican Conrad, one of the holy Papal orders—who had been forced at times to leave the overcrowded church for the open air, on account of the multitudes which gathered round the fierce Inquisitor to hear his sermons, and to witness, at the conclusion of his sermons, *the burning of a holocaust of heretics.*"

"Tauler was, therefore, one of the voices, if not the most powerful and influential, which appealed directly to God, from the Pope and the hierarchy; which asserted a higher religion than that of the Church; which made salvation dependent on personal belief and holiness, not on obedience to the priest;

which endeavored to renew the long-dissolved wedlock between Christian faith and Christian morality; and tacitly admitted the great Wycliffite doctrine, that the bad Pope, the bad Bishop, the bad Priest, was neither Pope, Bishop nor Priest. It was an appeal to God, and also to the moral sense of man, and throughout this period of nearly two centuries succeeding, before the appearance of Luther, this inextinguishable torch passed from hand to hand, from generation to generation."

We have presented to the reader these extended extracts from Milman, that the reader may see where the Reformation commenced, or, rather, how its spirit was maintained in these more recent pre-Reformation ages, as in all the former—a record with which our modern churches are not familiar, because many of them are only half-reformed from ritualism themselves, and their historians have ignored the true history of the Church of Christ in the vain effort to trace a ritualistic and *canonical* descent of Christianity through the dark ages. No such *canonical* descent can be traced; but the *true spiritual Church*, the persecuted bride of Christ, with all her beautiful garments of salvation, which the ritualistic churches have called the marks of heresy, *can be traced*. Deem them heretics whoever will, for their anti-ritualism, they have been God's ' peculiar people," God's chosen witnesses during all the ages of Church apostasy. As conceded by Milman (vol. vii. p. 408):

"Their influence was seen in the earnest demand for reformation by the councils; the sullen estrangement notwithstanding the reunion under the sacerdotal yoke during the Hussite wars; the disdainful neutrality when reformation by the councils seemed hopeless; it is seen in the remarkable book, the ' *German Theology*,' attributed by Luther to Tauler himself—of which two translations have recently appeared in England, yet of which the real character and importance cannot be appreciated without a full knowledge of the time at which it originated. Its value," says Milman, " was not so much what it taught as 'German theology,' *but what it threw aside as no part of* GENUINE *Christian faith.*"

Thus was the German impatience of ecclesiastical dominion manifested, foreshadowing that when the impending Revolution should come it would be altogether irresistible.

RESULT OF THE REVIVAL OF LETTERS.

The revival of letters also, compelling the priests to reason and prove or yield their pretensions, was a great preparatory step to the Reformation. They were not permitted to decide all questions *by authority*, and thus hold honest and thinking minds in bonds of superstition. And if the semi-ritualists of our day would forget the dictum of their church creeds and church authorities, and come down to the merits of the question, and reason concerning their rituals and sacraments, there would be some prospect of an open door from the wilderness or labyrinth in which their ritualism still holds them.

The ritualists of the Christian era must needs traverse the wilderness of rites without any compass, and build their superstructure without any plan or pattern. In taking leave of Milman, we may well cite his words as on p. 503, vol. viii.:

"The Latin, or more objective faith (in forms), tends to materialism, to servility, to blind obedience or blind guidance, to the tacit abrogation, if not repudiation, of moral influence by the undue elevation of the dogmatic or ritual part. It is prone to become Paganism with Christian images, symbols and terms; it sets itself, in its consummate state, altogether above and apart from Christian and universal morality, and makes what are called works of faith (*i. e.*, in church forms) the whole of religion: as the murderer who, while he sheathes his dagger in the heart of his victim, if he meantime does homage to the image of the Virgin, he is still religious; or the tyrant, if he retires in Lent in sackcloth and ashes, may live the rest of the year in promiscuous concubinage, and slaughter his subjects (for conscience' sake) by thousands, and still be religious!"

Thus it is the ritualist that becomes the antinomian, and not he who worships God only *in spirit and in truth.*[*]

In Rysbroeck of Cologne we find but the counterpart of the teachings of Tauler throughout.

---

[*] THE CEREMONIAL.—Surely the coming of Christ was the great epoch and central fact of time. Types and ceremonies had their place before it, pointing forward to it. They are now but as finger-boards beyond the goal, pointing the wrong way—pointing to the law that made nothing perfect. Looking at the shadowy past, we behold them as shadowing of good things *to come.* S.

THE PETRO-BRUSSIANS, SCOURGERS, ETC.

Collateral as to time with the *Friends of God* were the Petro-russians and other non-ritualistic sects. Indeed, a branch of the Waldensian Church, following the lead of Nicolas of Basle, who was originally one of them, came into general agreement with the Friends of God.

Says Neander, vol. v. p. 390:

"The predominating spirit of mysticism communicated itself also to them, and there grew up a section of Waldensian *Friends of God* which, paying less homage than did the others to the church spirit, developed itself with greater freedom of doctrine in opposition to the dominant Church."

Yet these, perhaps, did not reach farther in their anti-ritualism than Tauler's preparatory stage to the highest spiritual life.

Says Neander, vol. v. p. 408:

"We have seen how Tauler regarded the pious observance of all outward rites prescribed by the Church as a preparatory school for the highest stage of spirituality. . . . The casting aside of these ordinances should not be a purposed thing: it should be a natural falling off of them, as if the internal development of the religious life had progressed to such a point that the outward rites, no longer needed as supports, should fall away of themselves."

Yet Tauler adds:

"We gladly strip away the leaves to let the sun pour its rays without hindrance upon the young grapes! So all helps that become hindrances fall away from the Christian."

This was the sentiment also of the "Beghards" and of the Brethren of the Free Spirit." The "SCOURGERS" announced that all the sacraments in the Church were profaned by her pollutions and had lost their validity; that but one sacrament remained, which was to copy after their manner

---

or as they are allowed to stretch into the Christian era, they are but shadows of shadows—nothing more. John's baptism was the fulfilling, the dying effort of the CEREMONIAL. It prepared the way for the true baptism, and as the spent surges of ocean prostrate themselves at the base of some mighty rock, so the CEREMONIAL reverently laid itself down at the feet of Christ, and the eternal MORAL LAW stands thereby revealed and upheld.—*Friend's Review.*

(of self-scourging) the sufferings of Christ. This was sel
applying the *baptism* which Christ said he must be " baptize
with."   Many of these died at the stake.   In truth, nearly a
the dissidents from Rome, from the days of the Catharists t
Luther, were permeated with the non-sacramentarian spiri

As says Neander, vol. iv. p. 592:

" Of the Catharists we afterward meet with no farther traces; but that re
action of the Christian consciousness was continually exhibiting itself in othe
forms. . . . We saw how the reforming bent of the Hildebrandian epoc
invited the laity to rise against the corrupt clergy. . . . Thus arose sepa
ratist tendencies—the laity would have nothing to do with the clergy.   Suc
people, they thought, were unfitted to perform any sacramental act.   Fro
these beginnings it was easy to proceed farther, to declare the sacraments of th
corrupt Church generally *null and void!*"

Thus a sect arose in the territory of Cologne, under the lead
of PETER OF BRUIS, which drew upon themselves the atten
tion of their common opponent.

Neander, vol. iv. p. 593, says of them:

" The worldly and corrupt Church, they taught, had lost the power of ad
ministering the sacraments!   The successors of Peter (the apostle) had los
their authority, because they had not followed him in a life of consecration t
God!   Baptism in the Church was the only rite they would acknowledge, an
they acknowledged this because, whoever might administer the rite, it wa
still CHRIST that baptized.   As, then, they did not substitute the consolamen
tum in the place of baptism, they were, by this circumstance, distinguishe
from the Catharists."

He, with the *Pietists* and many others in the south of
France, rejected infant baptism as non-apostolical, and in
rejecting the mass repudiated the Lord's Supper altogether
saying that CHRIST alone could administer it—and this he
had done but once—and that was to be the end thereof for
all time.

THE WALDENSES AND ALBIGENSES,
A. D. 1100–1500.

The history of these Protestants of the mountains and valleys of Italy and France affords another illustration of the
warping effects of going to the records of mediæval dissent to

find our Church. The full, unbiased history of these Christian reformers has seldom, if ever, been given by any one church historian. Jones has given the Baptist version, and Conkling and Hendrick the Pedo-Baptist version. But when all the records are collated, not only of these men, but all others that are accessible, the reader will not require an extended period of time to deduce the evidence that he can find among the Waldenses "*neither your Church nor mine.*" True, they were Protestants from Rome, and in this generic sense they were homogeneous with all Protestant sects. But when you inquire after the particulars of their faith and customs, no church of the present day fully answers to the pattern.

Their immediate predecessors, furnishing the first outlines of their faith, were undoubtedly the *Catharists;* these were scattered among those valleys of Piedmont and elsewhere, in fleeing from persecution, and formed the germ of the Waldensian Church. This is admitted by every historian we have scanned; each traces the record of the Waldenses through the Catharists and Paulicians to the primitive protesting sects, the Donatists, Novatians, Erians, etc., *i. e.*, in tracing the accredited Protestant Church.

DURING 600 YEARS ALL PROTESTANTS REJECTED WATER-BAPTISM.

And if a continuous record of dissent from Rome and the continuous light of a pure Church be asserted, this is the only method of sustaining the assertion; for it is a veritable historical fact that *for six hundred years, i. e.*, from A. D. 500 to A. D. 1100, no such Church can be found but among the non-ritualistic (non-baptizing) Euchites, Paulicians and Catharists. True, *Claude* and *Paulinus* in the seventh century did preach against some of the corruptions of Rome, still remaining, however, in the Roman Church; there was no protest and schism, save as we have named, that would be claimed as the record of the true Protestant Church.

The Waldenses and Albigenses being but a continuation of

the Catharists, we should look to find their principles to a greater or less extent preserved among them, and this we do find in every respect save that of the practice of baptism and the supper, and it is difficult now to tell how far they departed from the non-ritualists before them in respect to these. It is certain that *Peter Waldo* found the same division of the congregations into *auditors* and *perfects*, or *catechumens*, and *accepted*, as had been maintained in all the non-ritualistic as well as Catholic Churches. Whether he found baptism only permitted, or really required of those who entered upon the estate of the *perfects*, history leaves a doubt. There is no doubt that they rejected the (infant) baptism of the Catholics; and also, rejecting the other mummeries which the Papal Church mingled with their baptism, they (Waldo at least) prescribed *immersion* for adults, catechumens or infants, that the impression of the *one act of baptism* might be thereby enhanced in order to atone for the lack of other ceremonies. Some assert that they rejected infant baptism altogether; others, that they did not. The probability is, that, like all their baptizing predecessors, Catholic or Protestant, they baptized the infants of proselytes when received, but usually required their own members to train their households as catechumens to a certain age—as did their prototypes, and also the Mennonites that came after—ere they were baptized. But this baptism was not a "sacrament" with them, for there were no canonical priests to consecrate the water and administer it. But why does this catechumen baptism differ from infant baptism, for what catechumen at the age of sixteen or eighteen is either self-responsible or self-judging respecting his baptism? As well look for the children of Jews to grow up Christians, or Pagans to turn Jews *en masse*, as for the *catechized* child to be or do otherwise than as instructed. Any other result would be a prodigy.

So far as historic record teaches, Peter Waldo was the first to place baptism and the supper in the Protestant creed as a requisite, and this he did in a seeming protest against the perversions of Rome, by rejecting their baptisms and giving the *cup* as well as the *bread* to the laity—a great step towards reform in his day.

The evidence appears to sustain the record, thus: Peter Waldo had a penchant *for* baptism, as he also had against the order of the *perfects* in the Church, and rejected the latter, but *conditionally* imposed the former upon the Waldensian churches. We say conditionally, for it was required, unless "inconvenient," and its saving efficacy was denied; salvation was of God, and not of sacraments and rites in their teaching. And as all the Romish adjuncts and sequences of baptism were repudiated, and all consecrations, and ordinations, and canonical administrations were rejected, we may assume that the obligations of baptism hung loosely upon them; for it is doubtful whether lay baptism or self-baptism ever reached the dignity of a sacrament either among the Jews or Christians.*

Says the *Encyclopedia:*

"They rejected images, crosses, relics, legends, traditions, auricular confessions, indulgences, absolution, clerical celibacy, *orders, titles,* tithes, vestments, monkery, masses and prayers for the dead, purgatory, invocation of saints and of the Virgin Mary, holy water, festival processions, pilgrimages, vigils, lent, pretended miracles, exorcisms, consecrations, confirmation, extreme unction, canonization and the like. They condemned the use of liturgies, and, most of all, the wicked lives of both people and clergy in the worldly communion of Rome."

---

* Denying, as they did, the hierarchy, and claiming the universal priesthood of all saints, and therefore admitting the right (but not imposing the obligation) of any of the laity to administer the ceremonies of induction, or fellowship, and to preach—of course this would soon remove the charm and the sanctity of the "sacrament" from any ritual. Thus would the priestly rule, like a magician's wand, which had been based on the sacraments in the Papal Church, soon cease, as priests would thus cease to be the sole dispensers of heaven's favors through these; rituals deprived of the canonical charm would be no more sacraments than the layman's prayers or exhortations, and being intrinsically of no value, would soon dwindle into unmeaning forms or disgusting mummeries. No Protestant sect has ever maintained the sacraments without establishing a *ministerial order* to consecrate the elements and perform the functions of their office canonically.

All this shows that no ceremonial or ritual of the Church had any special fascinations for the Waldenses. They clung to the Scriptures (valuing most highly the New Testament) and to salvation by faith in Christ and a holy life. But the effort of any sect of the present time to secure their daguerreotype as a mirror for themselves is fitly rebuked by the editor of the *Encyclopedia* thus. Having alluded to their principles and the light that shone out upon the darkness from this body, the editor continues:

"Hence it is hardly to be wondered at that the Waldenses, like the Scriptures, have been resorted to by all parties of Protestants in defence of their peculiar sentiments! . . . Each party sought to find a predecessor, and to trace a line of succession up to the apostles through these. . . . The natural consequence has been, that all have been tempted to mould the character of the Waldenses to the support of their own particular views, instead of collecting into one point all the light of history, and calmly abiding the issue. For, after all, an uninterrupted succession, however gratifying it may be to be able to trace it, is necessary only to a church which regulates its practice *by tradition*, and not by the pure word of God."

This is well spoken, and the more pertinent will it appear when we keep in mind the fact that the exact photograph of any mediæval or earlier sect is not now extant, and never can be, for forms may not be ever-enduring, while the life from God may be; and he that seeks the true Church from the forms or ceremonials that have been observed by any, is more bewildered and is doomed to a more grievous disappointment than he that seeks the substance by putting forth his hand to touch the shadow! The divine fiat, in writing "change" on all things external, has rendered even a divinely appointed formula or ceremonial impossible of perpetual continuance.

But to return to the Protestantism of the Waldenses, we will admit that, aside from Peter Waldo's attachment to baptism and the eucharist, it was complete, and a pattern for all. Now the only point we would consider further, touching these witnesses for a pure faith and a primitive Christianity, is this: How far did this retention of ordinances prevail among that people? Neander asserts that many of the Waldenses rejected baptism as a part of Popery and a means of priestly rule, at least, as sustaining the sacerdotalism of the priesthood.   And it is not denied that the *Albigenses* were non-ritualists to the full extent of rejecting all ordinances and sacraments.   For this reason, and for no other, they are sometimes stigmatized with the (designed to be) reproachful title of Manicheans by certain historic champions of ritual law.   We will, however, allow the editor of the *Encyclopedia* to speak in their defence, and not our own pen.   He says:

" *Sismondi*, in his late 'History of the Crusades against the Albigenses,' writes thus : ' Those very persons who punished the sectaries with frightful torments have alone taken it upon themselves to make us acquainted with their opinions, allowing at the same time that they had been transmitted in Gaul from generation to generation, almost from the origin of Christianity. We cannot be astonished,' he adds, 'if they have represented them to us as with all those churches which might render them the most monstrous, mingled with all the fables which would serve to irritate the minds of the people against those who professed them.   Nevertheless, amidst many puerile and calumnious tales, it is still easy to recognize the principles of the Reformation of the sixteenth century among the heretics who are designated by the name of *Vaudois* or *Albigenses*.' "

Dr. ALLIX, a very learned Protestant writer of France, in the latter part of the seventeenth century, wrote a very able work—" History of the Ancient Churches of the Albigenses," in which he completely exculpates them from the false charges of heresy preferred against them by the monks of those days, and gives a record of their spread into Spain and into England.

And in proof of the extensive retention and prevalence of the non-baptizing doctrines of the Catharists among the Waldenses and Albigenses, we will cite the testimony of Drs. WALL and HIBBARD, which, because of their hostility (as here manifested) to all non-ritualists, is all the better for establishing the fact.

Hibbard, the Methodist writer on Baptism, thus speaks of the *Waldenses*, p. 318 :

" The word Waldenses simply signifies *valleys*, or 'inhabitants of valleys,' and was applied to all the sects which inhabited those valleys.   Of the sects that arose in these regions some were *Manicheans,* and with many impious and absurd tenets *denied all water-baptism,* retaining only a 'baptism of fire,' as they called it, which they administered only to adults."

Mr. Wall, alluding to these and contiguous sects, says :

" Though the authors do not well distinguish the names, yet most generally these sects that *denied all baptism* and held other vile opinions are denoted by these names, Cathari, Apostolicii, Luciferians, Runcarians, Popelicans, *alias* Publicans, Paulicians," etc.

So all these Protestants against the Papal sacramentarianism held " vile," " impious " and " absurd " opinions—the only one specified being this—they " denied all water-baptism." What impiety ! They did not allow sacerdotal hands stained with every Papal abomination to *regenerate* them in baptism, or bear consecrated bread to their lips, and thus feed Christ to their souls, nor " confirm " them in the Papal faith ! Climax of impiety ! They rejected the validity and saving efficacy of water-baptism and the mass, and preferred to trust in Christ, and preach practical holiness and a spiritual regeneration as the doorway into the redeemed Church, whose names are written in heaven. Is not their impiety most manifest? and is it not equally manifest that the apostate Papacy that held the (seven) sacraments as the keys of the kingdom, was *the* true Church of this day ? Judge ye !

That the foregoing testimony as to their prevalence of anti-Baptist sentiments in the days and in the ranks of the Waldenses, listen, further in proof, to the record of those that claim to be offshoots or branches from this parent stock. We quote from the *Religious Encyclopedia.*

THE PUBLICANI OR ENGLISH WALDENSES, A. D. 1166.

Of the " PUBLICANI "—a party of English Waldenses— Rapin gives the following account of these people on the authority of Archbishop Usher :

" Henry (the king) ordered a council to convene at Oxford, in 1166, to examine the tenets of certain heretics called *Publicani*—very probably the disciples of the Waldenses who began then to appear. When they were asked in the council who they were, they answered, they were Christians and followers of the apostles. After that, being questioned upon the creed, their replies were very orthodox as to the Trinity and incarnation. But (says Rapin) *if the historian is to be depended on, they rejected baptism and the eucharist,* marriage and the communion of saints. They showed a deal of modesty and meekness in their whole behavior. *When they were threatened with death in order to oblige them to renounce their tenets,* they only said, ' Blessed are they that suffer for righteousness sake.' "

The Baptist historian, in order to subsidize the above record to his own cause, suggests that it was only infant baptism that they rejected—forgetting that up to the period here named, infant and adult baptism had *ever* run parallel with each other—unless forsooth, as in the case of State Churches, *all* were required to be baptized in infancy.

To reject infant baptism among the Papists for many centuries would be to reject baptism itself. So among the adherents of the Church of England at a later day. He also interpolates the record of the historian, who does not say they rejected early baptism and practised *believers' baptism,* but that they "*rejected baptism and the eucharist.*" * Probably they did also reject "marriage" as "solemnized" into a "sacrament" by the Papal Church, and (as among the Friends of our day) the parties to the marriage union made their own vows and plighted the troth for themselves. Their "communion of saints" was undoubtedly in the love and worship of Christ and *fellowship of spirit* one with another, which is the only true communion of saints!

---

* This would make their sentiments harmonize with the Catharists, of which the Waldenses were undoubtedly the successors.

John Allen (a Friend), author of "*State Churches,*" says (p. 474): "William, of Newbury, mentions thirty religious persons who came into England from Germany in 1170, and denied baptism and the eucharist. The chief of them were Gerard and Dulcimus. They were probably some of the early Waldenses." He adds: "The Waldenses became generally known about the same period. *They* laid little stress on the outward baptism and supper, finding fault with the Papists for relying too much on these things." REYNER, their historian, says: "Some of them hold that baptism of material water and other sacraments profit nothing to salvation."

THE LOLLARDS, A. D. 1350.

But the teachings of one other branch of the Waldenses, or, as Dr. Allix claims, and doubtless more correctly claims, a branch of the Albigenses (for the names were oft interchanged and intermingled), we will cite in proof of the general non-ritualistic character of those Piedmontese Protestants and all the early Reformers, and that will suffice in respect to these.

We quote again from the *Religious Encyclopedia:*

"LOLLARDS, a religious sect, differing in many points from the Church of Rome, arose in Germany, about the beginning of the fourteenth century, . . . and were so called from *Walter Lollard,* a German preacher (as Perrin, in his history of the Waldenses, calls him), a man of great renown, who came to England in the reign of Edward III. (about A. D. 1315), and who was so eminent in England that, *as in France,* they were called Berengarians, from Berengarius, and Petro-Brussians, from Peter Bruis, and in Italy and Flanders Arnoldists, from the famous Arnold of Brescia; so did the Waldensian Christians for many generations after bear the name of this worthy man, being called LOLLARDS. Bishop Newton, having mentioned the Lollards, says: 'There was a man more worthy to have given name to the sect, the deservedly famous *John Wickliffe,* the honor of his own and the admiration of succeeding times.' In England the followers of Wickliffe *were* called Lollards, by way of reproach, though the first English Lollards came from Germany. Lollard and his followers rejected the sacrifice of the mass, extreme unction, and penance for sin, arguing that *Christ's sufferings were sufficient.* He is likewise *said to have set aside baptism as a thing of no effect.* . . . Among the articles required by law, guiding the inquisitors in their examination of the Lollards, one was: 'Whether an infant dying unbaptized can be saved?' This the Lollards constantly asserted in opposition to the Church of Rome, which decreed that no infant could be saved without it. *Fox* says, that among the errors they were charged with were these: 'That they spoke against the opinion of such as think that children are damned who depart before baptism, and said that Christian people are sufficiently baptized in the blood of Christ, AND NEED NO WATER.'"

The reader will perceive that here the historian gives a flat denial to the glosses and assumptions of the Baptists, that the Lollards rejected only infant baptism, for he asserts that they held respecting *all Christians* that they are "*sufficiently baptized in the blood of Christ;*" and, therefore, "*need no water-baptism.*" Of course "infant baptism," as well as adult baptism, were swept away by their teachings. There might have been an occasional ritualistic baptizer among them, as a Peter Waldo among the Piedmontese, but the baptism of the "blood of Christ" was the only baptism that, as a people, they recognized. They set aside the Romish priesthood and the *sacraments* that are connected only with a priesthood.

And Fox says:

"It was upon these charges that, in the space of four years, one hundred and twenty Lollards were apprehended and suffered greatly, a number of them being burned at the stake. . . . From this period to the Reformation, their sufferings were very great. More than one hundred are recorded by name who were burned to death. The Lollards' tower still stands as a monument of their miseries, and of the cruelty of their implacable enemies. *This tower was fitted up for this purpose* (viz., their persecution) *by Chicheby, Archbishop of Canterbury.* It is said that he expended two hundred and eighty pounds to make this prison for the Lollards. The vast staples and rings to which they were fastened before they were brought out to the stake are said to be seen in a large lumber-room *at the top of the palace,* and ought to make Protestants look back with gratitude upon the hour that terminated so bloody a period."

Hence we see that the Waldenses and Albigenses, with their branches in England, met with the same visitation of fire and fagot, and the wasting sword of martyrdom (until many a ten thousand of those in Piedmont and France met with death in every conceivable form of torture, as is well known), as had been the common retribution upon all former non-ritualists and dissidents from the Papal Church.

And let it be noted that up to this period in our record we have found *no debates* respecting *modes of baptism,* although it is undeniable that a *variety* of modes has been all along practised, nor has there been any recognized *order of a priesthood,* with its adjunct of *sacraments—i. e.,* among the Protestants— from the beginning until this time. True, Tauler maintained his position in the Church for influence sake, and his office of priest until he fell in his armor, but surely would not have taught that Christians may outgrow the need of sacraments (so called) and rituals, if he had recognized them as a standing appointment of the Great Head of the Church.

Martin Luther, therefore, in binding a yoke of bondage to *sacraments* on so many Protestant sects, turned the Church backward toward Judaism or the Papacy, rather instead of leading it forward in the freedom of Christ, and the unending and disgraceful discussions respecting "ordinances" (modes of baptism and *the Supper*) have been the baleful fruits.

THE OXFORD REFORMERS: ERASMUS, COLET, THOMAS MORE, ETC., A. D. 1520.

While the anti-sacramentarian opposition to the Papacy was spreading on the continent, a collateral movement was inaugurated in that great centre of theologic and philosophic advance—Oxford, England—not taking the form of rejecting all rites, at first, as so oft on the continent; but depreciating their sanctity and value, and pleading for a Catholic tolerance of differences, and an outward union of all in the one Church (centring at Rome, to be sure); but allowing any degree of non-conformity or divergence in the ceremonials of the Church. True, this effort to maintain such unity in such diversity as was manifest on the part of those of the Catholic faith on the one hand, and of the Protestant faith on the other hand, like Wesley's attempt to maintain an external fellowship with the apostatizing Church of England, was chimerical. Yet the specific object, the enlarging of an organic fold to such a breadth as to receive all that would work for Christ and righteousness, was noble and praiseworthy in its conception, though not practical in its unfoldings, especially in the then state of advance respecting the spirit and terms of true Christian fellowship. Yet the attempt led to the announcement by ERASMUS, COLET, MORE, etc., of nobly true and worthy principles of church organization; and of what constitutes the true Christian life, and the basis of Christian union.

Their Anti-Sacramentarianism.

In a work of T. Seebohm, entitled *The Oxford Reformers,* on p. 378, etc., we find the following record:

"Erasmus sought to bring out the facts of Christ's life as the true foundation of the Christian faith, instead of the dogmas of the scholastic theology. After thoughtfully dwelling upon the facts of the life of Christ, he proceeds to examine his teachings, and concludes that there were two things which he peculiarly and perpetually inculcated—faith and love; and after describing them more at length, he writes, 'Read the New Testament through, you will not find in it any precept which pertains to ceremonies. Where is there a single word of meats or vestments? Where is there any mention of fasts and the like? *Love* alone he calls *his* precept. *Ceremonies give rise to differences; from love flows peace.* . . . And yet we burden those who have been made free by the blood of Christ, with all those almost senseless, and more than Jewish constitutions.'"

Seebohm, alluding to Colet, p. 386, says:

"No sooner do most reformers clear away a little ground, and discover what they take to be truths, than they attempt, by organizing a sect, founding endowments, and framing articles and trust-deeds, to secure the permanent tradition of their own views to posterity in the form in which they are apprehended by themselves. Hence, in the very act of striking off the fetters of the past, they are forging the fetters of the future. Even the Protestant Reformers whilst on the one hand bravely breaking the yoke under which their ancestors had lived in bondage, found themselves, as the result of the Reformation, bound still tighter under Tridentine decrees; whilst those who had joined the exodus and entered the promised land of the reformers, found it to be *a land of almost narrower boundaries than the one they had left.* . . . If Colet did not do this, he resisted with a singular wisdom and success a temptation which besets every one under his circumstances. . . . But Erasmus expressed the view of Colet as well as his own when he said, 'Why should we try to narrow what Christ intended to be broad?'"

So Colet, in bestowing a large endowment upon a college, did not bind its faculty to his already conceived ideas, but left that faculty open to the progressive light of truth, thus: he refused to put his school under the charge of ecclesiastics and clergymen; but committing it to benevolent Christian men, in whom it should be manifest that the love of God dwelt, he ordains thus:

"And notwithstanding these statutes and ordinances before written, in which I have declared my mind and will; yet because in time to come many things may and shall survive and grow by many occasions and causes, which at the making of this book was not possible to come to mind. . . . Both all this that is said, and all that is not said which shall hereafter come into my mind while I live. . . . I leave wholly to the discretion of the wardens and assistants, with such other counsel as they shall call to them, good, lettered and learned men, trusting in their fidelity and the love they have to God and man and to the school—they to add and diminish of this book, and to supply it in every default."

Reader, is not this a matchless rebuke of the denominational endowments, and title-deeds of trust to sectarian bodies— whether of colleges, churches, lands, or *creeds !* in our day far too common ? The language of the above sounds very much like that of the large-hearted David Brewster to the Pilgrims departing for their bleak wilderness home in New England :

"I am persuaded that much light of truth is yet to break forth from God's word which we have not reached."

Compare with this the bigotry of Luther, who once could make the declaration that all the Greek and other Christians who did not acknowledge the primacy of the Pope were heretics and lost, and yet was compelled to admit to Prof. Eck that among the articles on which the Council of Constance grounded its condemnation of John Huss (for which he was burned) were some fundamentally Christian and evangelical ! A few months later, after the divine light had reached his mind more fully, he was obliged to exclaim :

"I taught Huss's opinions without knowing them, and so did Staupitz; we are all of us Hussites without knowing it ! Paul and Augustine are Hussites ! I do not know what to think for amazement !"

Bigots and persecutors are all destined to the same amazement, either in this life or the next, when they come to see how little of the truth they have seen, and how little of the love of Christ they have exercised, when they have been ready to pour anathemas or the fiery wrath upon those who have differed from them in theory, yet were poorer in God's sight, perhaps, than they.

THOMAS MORE, having heard COLET speak with much warmth and energy of that living sacrifice of men's hearts, which rites and ceremonies were only meant to typify, remembered the lesson well. Hence we find him in later years replying with great vigor to a monk who had written an anonymous letter to Erasmus, complaining that Erasmus had denied the infallibility of the holy doctors and fathers of the Church! MORE inquires:

"Do you deny that they ever made mistakes? .... When Augustine, in support of his view, adduced the story of the wonderful agreement of (so-claimed) inspired translators of the Septuagint, writing in separate cells, and Jerome laughed at the story as absurd, was not one of the two mistaken? When Jerome translated the Epistle to the Galatians, and made it read (as now) that Paul censured Peter for dissembling, and Augustine denied that the translation was correct in this respect, was not one of them mistaken? .... Augustine asserts that demons and angels have material and substantial bodies. I doubt not that even you deny this. He asserts that infants dying without baptism are consigned to physical torments in eternal punishment. How many are there who believe this now? unless it be that Luther, clinging by 'tooth and nail' to the doctrine of Augustine, should be induced to revive this antiquated notion."

So, calling the attention of the same monk to his own order, he exclaims:

"Into what factions, into how many sects, is the order cut up! Then what tumults, what tragedies arise about little differences in the color or mode of girding the monastic habit, or some matter of ceremony, which, if not altogether despicable, is, at all events, not so important as to warrant the banishment of all charity. How many too there are (and this is the worst of all) who, relying on the assurances of their monastic profession, inwardly raise their crests so high that they seem to themselves to move in the heavens, and reclining among the solar rays, to look down from on high upon the people creeping on the ground like ants; looking down thus, not only on the ungodly, but also upon all who are without the circle of the enclosure of their order, so that for the most part nothing is holy but what they do themselves. ... They make more of those things which appertain to their religious order than of those very humble things which are in no way peculiar to them, but entirely common to all Christian people, such as the vulgar virtues, faith, hope, charity, the fear of God, humility, and others of the kind. Nor, indeed, is this a new thing. Nay, it is what Christ long ago denounced to his chosen people. 'Ye make the word of God of none effect by your traditions.' ... There are multitudes enough who would be afraid that the devil would come and take them alive to hell, if, forsooth, they were to set aside their usual garb, whom nothing can move when they are grasping at money!"

"Are there only a few, think you, who would deem it a crime to be expiated with many tears, if they were to omit a line in their hourly prayers, yet have no scruple at all when they profane themselves by the worst and most infamous lie . . . I once knew a man devoted to the religious life, one of that class who would now be thought 'most religious,' but, nevertheless, more careless of the precepts of God than of monastic rites, slid down from one crime to another, till at length he went so far as to meditate the most atrocious of all crimes, a crime execrable beyond belief, and one pregnant with *manifold* guilt, for he purposed to add sacrilege to murders and parricide. He associated with himself ruffians and cutpurses, and they committed the most horrible crimes that I ever heard of. Just prior to this career of crime, these assassins, 'when they came to the private chapel of *this religious man*, they appeased the sacred virgin by a salutation on their bent knees, and then rose purely and piously to perpetrate their crime! . . . . I relate this not to defame all monks with such crimes, . . . but because people trust so much to such things (forms of worship), that under the very security which they thus feel they give themselves up to crime.'

"Reflecting upon these things, you may learn not to grow too proud of your own sect; nothing could be more fatal. Nor trust in private observances, but that you should place your hope rather in the Christian faith, than in your (sect) faith, and not trust in those outward things that you can do for yourself, but in those which you cannot do without God's help."

The True Christian Life needs no Ceremonial or Sacramental Mediators.

"You can fast by yourself, you can keep vigils by yourself, you can say prayers by yourself—you can do these things by the devil! But, verily, Christian faith, which Christ Jesus truly said to be in spirit; Christian hope, which, despairing of its own merits, confides only in the mercy of God; Christian charity, which is not puffed up, is not made angry, does not seek its own glory—none, indeed, can attain these except by the grace and gracious help of God alone.

"By how much the more you place your trust in those virtues which are common to Christendom, by so much the less will you have faith in private ceremonies."

Well does Seebohm remark, after quoting some passages from More where the Papal ritualism was not altogether rejected:

"That these passages prove that More and his friends had not set aside monasticism, or even Mariolatry, as altogether wrong, cannot be too clearly recognized. In an age of transition, it is the direction of the thoughts and aims of men which constitutes the radical difference or agreement between them, rather than the exact distance that each may have travelled on the same road. Luther himself had not yet, in his hatred of ceremonies, travelled as far as the Oxford Reformers, though in after years he went farther. . . . They seemed to meet in their common hatred of the formalism of the monks, and in their common attempt to grasp at the spirit—the reality of religion through its forms and shadows. And much as Luther's friends might differ from some of his statements, and the tone he sometimes adopted, their respect for his moral earnestness, and their perception of the amount of exasperation to which his hot nature was exposed, made them readily pardon what they could not approve."

THE "UNITED BRETHREN," A. D. 1530.

Before Luther had come to the conclusion that himself was a *Hussite*, Erasmus had been in correspondence with Schlechta, a Bohemian, on the religious dissensions in Bohemia and Moravia, with special reference to the Hussite sect of the *United Brethren*. Schlechta had informed Erasmus that

"Setting aside Jews and unbelieving philosophers, who denied the immortality of the soul, the people were divided into three sects: First, the Papal party, which included most of the magistrates and nobility (like the Church of England of a later day); Secondly, a party which acknowledged the Papacy but differed from other good Catholics in dispensing the sacrament in both kinds to the laity, and in chanting in the vulgar (known) tongue; Thirdly, the sect of the 'Pyghards,' or 'United Brethren,' who, since the time of John Zisca, had maintained their ground through much bloodshed and violence. These regarded the Pope and clergy as manifest 'Anti-Christ,' the Pope himself, sometimes as the 'Beast,' and sometimes as the harlot of the Apocalypse. They chose ignorant and even married laymen as their priests and bishops. They called each other 'brothers and sisters.' They acknowledged no writings as of authority but the Old and New Testaments. Fathers and schoolmen they counted nothing by. They thought lightly of the sacraments, used no salt or holy water in baptism, and rejected extreme unction. They saw only simple bread and wine, no divinity, in the sacrament of the altar, and regarded these only as signs representing and commemorative of the death of Christ, who they said was in heaven. The suffrages of the saints, and prayers for the dead, they held to be vain and absurd, also auricular confession and penance. Vigils and fasts they looked upon as hypocritical. Their priests used no vestments, and no forms of prayer but the 'Lord's Prayer.' The festivals of the Virgin, apostles, and saints, they said were invented by the idle. Other pernicious! dogmas of theirs, Schlechta thought were not worthy of mention to Erasmus! If, however, he added, the first two of these three sects could be united, then, perhaps, this vicious sect, now on the increase, owing to recent ecclesiastical scandals, might, by the aid of the king, be either exterminated! or *forced* into a better form of creed and religion."

Erasmus' reply to Schlechta showed how much of the spirit of compromise and of churchly conservatism yet remained in his mind :

"You point out [said he to Schlechta] the three sects of Bohemia and Moravia; I wish that some pious hand could unite the three into one!"

The second party, Erasmus thought, " erred more in scornfully rejecting the judgment and custom of the Roman Church than in thinking it right to take the eucharist in both kinds, which was not an unreasonable practice in itself, (when did the Papacy ever pretend to quote the Bible to substantiate their ritualism ?) though *it might be better to avoid singularity on such a point.*" So *conformity* is the sole reason for following the Popish priests.

"As to the 'United Brethren,' he did not see why they should assume that the Pope was antichrist because there had been some bad Popes, or that the Roman Church was a 'harlot' because she had often had wicked cardinals and bishops. Still, however bad the 'United Brethren' might be, he would not advise or resort to violence."

Thus we see that Erasmus had simply reached the point where he could tolerate dissent.

He could see no blame to be attached to their calling one another "brothers and sisters!" He wished the practice could obtain among all Christians, if only the fact were consistent with the words! He says:

"In thinking less highly of the doctors than of the Scriptures they were in the right—that is, preferring God to man; but *altogether* to reject them (*i. e.*, the doctors of divinity) was as bad as altogether to accept them. . . . It is impious to condemn what was instituted, not without good reason, by the fathers!"

Here we have the sickly reasoning of Church conformity and compromise in every age glaring out against all attempts to break the yoke of a ritual bondage from the days of the apostolic contest with Judaism to the era of dissent from the Papacy and Prelacy in England.

WHAT ERASMUS ADMITTED.

Erasmus admitted that Christ and the apostles officiated in their every-day dress, but thought it well to *follow the fathers*, in the wearing of vestments, in his day; and in regard to observances of days, he admitted that the number of festivals had become so enormous that the laborer was robbed of his needful earnings, and that on no days were crimes so frequent as on these festival days.

Erasmus thought that

"Even many of these might be reconciled to the Church of Rome if, instead of *everything being defined*, we were content with what is evidently set forth in the Scriptures as necessary to salvation! And these things are *few* in number, and the *fewer the easier* for many to accept! 'Nowadays,' he says, 'out of one article we make six hundred, *some of which are such that men might be ignorant of them or doubt them without injury to piety.* It is in human nature to cling by 'tooth and nail' to what has once been defined!'"

Erasmus proceeds to define what he deems the essentials of faith, thus:

"The sum of the philosophy of Christ lies in this, that we should know that all our hope is placed in God, who freely gives us all things through his Son Jesus; that by his death we are redeemed; that we are united to his body in baptism [Erasmus doubtless misconceives the baptism that unites to Christ]; ... that if adversity comes, we should bear it in the hope of the future reward which is in store for all good men ... thus we should always be progressing from virtue to virtue, and, whilst assuming nothing to ourselves, *ascribe what is good to God*. That if there be any one who would inquire into the Divine nature, or the nature of Christ, or *abstruse points about the sacraments*, let him do so; only *don't let him try to force his views upon others.*

"In the same way as very verbose instruments lead to controversies, so too many definitions lead to differences.... Let me therefore examine myself, whether there be anything in me inconsistent with Christ—*whether there be any difference between me and my neighbor.*

"As to the rest, *how* the same body (of Christ) can exist in so many places at once ... and with what body we rise again, though I do not disapprove of these things being inquired into in moderation, yet it conduces very little to piety to spend too much labor upon them. Men's minds are diverted by these and other innumerable subtleties, from things of vital importance. I know that the pure blood of Christ and his body are to be taken purely *by the pure* as a most sacred sign and pledge both of his love to us *and of the fellowship of Christians amongst themselves.*"

Here Erasmus admits that those who partake worthily of a sacrament must *first be pure*, which on its very face annuls the doctrine that the sacrament itself makes the partaker of it pure. And his teaching, that it should be taken in the exercise, and as a proof of brotherly love, establishes the principle that that brotherly love (the essence of religion) should pre-exist in each individual, thus perpetuating the sign after the substance has come; like keeping the promissory note after the debt is cancelled, or the photograph of an individual already and all the while present. It should be borne in mind that this discussion respecting the non-ritualism of the "United Brethren" elicits the fact that Erasmus yet clung to all the sacraments of the Papal Church (yet wishing full liberty to all that dissented), holding himself, as do both the Church of Rome and of England hold, *the Church* has a right to ordain and establish rituals and bind them upon succeeding generations simply by *Church authority.* This doctrine alone can reconcile even the Papists to the unending mummeries they connect with the administration of baptism, the eucharist and all their other sacraments. They do not pretend to be following Jesus Christ nor his apostles in these concomitant innovations and contrivances of priestly craft and superstition.

Erasmus argued well for tolerance of different views, and blamed Schlechta, in the letter we quote from, not for holding the views he does respecting sacraments, but for making them a ground of separation from fellow-Christians; and also blames him (Schlechta, who was also a dissident from Rome) for his disposition to persecute and "exterminate" the "United Brethren." He also blames *the Church* for narrowing her boundaries so as to shut out these ultra-dissenters from her communion; and hints that

"It would tend greatly to the establishment of concord, if secular princes, especially the Roman pontiff, would abstain from all tyranny and avarice. 'For,' said he, 'men easily revolt when they see preparations for enslaving them, when they see that they are not to be invited to piety, but caught for plunder.

If they saw that we were innocent, and desirous to do them *good*, they would verily easily accept our faith.'"

This is very well put. A standard reared whence benevolence shines forth, with however much of superstition and cumbersomeness of ritual even, will draw many earnest and inquiring minds, who seek that element of the soul's life, good-will, to its lifted banner. Erasmus saw and admitted that the scholastic subtleties of theology as taught in the Augustinian system could not, by any ecclesiastical authority, be settled and established as the creed of the Christian, notwithstanding it endured 1400 years. Yet its definitions, after the lapse of these years, remained as unsettled as ever, and consisted of hypotheses that never could be settled by the human reason unless they were utterly rejected.

But Luther and the Hussites practically assumed that *somewhere* in the Church was an authority capable of establishing any hypothesis as a dogma of the Church. In this respect the Reformers Luther, Wickliffe, and Huss were behind the Oxford Reformers, who denied any such Church authority (though even they sought conformity in rituals), yet contended for freedom of doctrine and worship. And this stand taken for freedom of conscience, three hundred and fifty years ago, is the germ of the Reformation there and of the Protestantism which we now enjoy.

Its abettors have all along been accused of "free-thinking tendencies," and have endured the sneers of the "Orthodox," self-styled such, whose only influence was toward conservatism and the icy chilliness of a spiritual death, yet endured because in the Church, while the energy of an earnest piety and a true spiritual life has ever been with the Reformers.

This record of the Oxford Reformers should not close without stating the fact that Colet was still so blinded by his relations to the Papacy that he wrote a work, "De Sacramentis Ecclesiæ"—*i. e.*, concerning the sacraments of the Church, in which he argues that the Church, mysteriously and mystically, comes into *marriage* or union with Christ in the sacraments

17

(the seven sacraments of Rome) as the bride comes int
union with the husband in actual marriage on earth. H
bases his argument on Eph. v. 32. Here is a *real mysticism,* a
the reader will see—mysticism upon a groundless concei
respecting the appointment and virtue of sacraments; whil
those who rejected sacraments, and taught the need instea
of a vital union with Christ, through the Holy Spirit, were i
no proper sense *mystics,* only as all spiritual knowledge o
God and of Christ within is a mystery to the unbelieving an
carnal mind. The *power,* as distinguished from the *form* o
godliness, has ever been with those who have exalted th
spiritual union above the formal, and even oft to the exclusio
of the letter of the sacrament or any other rite.

THE REFORMERS—LUTHER, CARLSTADT, ZWIN GLE, ETC., A. D. 1525-1575.

Our record has now reached the period of the Reformatio
under the lead of Luther, Zwingle, Melancthon, Carlstad
and others. And, while noting the vast strides of the Re
formers from the wilderness of Popery, who is not struck wit
the palpable evidence that very few of the mightiest mind
even, can attain and grasp all truth, and press forward al
needed reform in their first effort? The light of truth shine
as men can bear the light and receive it. Luther did, in
deed, by one fell swoop dash away four of the seven sacra
ments of the Papal Church at the outset. But his deter
mination *to adhere* to the Church of Rome for the purpose o
reforming her made all further progress in the line of anti
sacramentarianism very difficult.

LUTHER CONFESSES TO HAVING LEARNED MUCH OF THE MYSTICS.

Luther read the Mystics, and confesses to having receive
great spiritual profit from their teachings. They confirme
him in his disgust for the dry teachings of the schoolmen, i
his contempt for the works and observances so much trump

eted by the Church, and in the conviction of man's need of
divine help, and in his attachment to the Bible. "I prefer,"
he wrote to Staupitz, "the Mystics and the Bible to all the
schoolmen."

Says D'Aubigne, vol. i. p. 213:

> "Perhaps also the *German Theology* (a work of the Mystics) aided him in
> forming a sounder idea on the sacraments, and, above all, on the mass.
> Luther republished this work (*German Theology*), and in the preface declared
> that next to the Bible and St. Augustine, he had never met with a book in
> which he had learned more of God, Christ, man, and of all things!"

This, he says, mark of the great work of the Mystics.

> "One would say," continues Luther, "that there had never lived men be-
> fore us who taught as we teach. Yet, in truth, there have been many. But
> the anger of God, which our sins have deserved, *has prevented us from seeing
> and hearing them!*"

Luther avowed in full the anti-Church doctrine of the Waldenses and the Catharists, and it is amazing that when he
preached justification and salvation by faith only, that he did
not see the utter contradiction there is between salvation by
faith and salvation by sacraments. But he did not. With
the Waldenses and others he boldly declared that every
Christian is a priest—all are "kings and priests to God"—and
"*all have the right to administer the sacraments!*" And still
making baptism and regeneration synonymous, or at least
coincident, as had been the great folly of the Papacy, he thus
makes each human member of this universal priesthood the
saviour of another, or others, through baptism. True, he
dwelt largely and glowingly on salvation by faith, but that
he understood them as coincident may be inferred from his
insisting, as he does, that all baptized infants are believers,
and that their faith is born with their baptism. See
D'Aubigne, vol. ii. p. 123:

> "Perhaps to what I have said on the necessity of faith, the baptism of
> little children may be objected. But as the word of God is mighty to change
> the heart of a wicked man, who is not less deaf nor less helpless than an in-
> fant, *so the prayers of the Church*, to which all things are possible, change

the little child by the faith it pleases God to place in his heart, and *thus puri-fies and renews.*"

Again, he says:

"That children themselves believe in baptism, that they have a faith peculiar to them—*what has reason to do with faith and with the word of God?* Does it not, on the contrary, resist them? No man can attain to faith unless he becomes a fool, *without reason,* without intelligence, and like a little child!"

Thus it will be seen that Luther's sacramentarian illusion, still retained, requires the doctrine that the soul-humiliation, which is the real antecedent of faith, should take the monstrous form of absolute dementation, in order that a baptized child may be called a true believer. Luther's three sacraments, Baptism, Penance, and the Lord's Supper, are sustained by similar logic. Alluding to baptism, he says: "God has preserved this sacrament alone free from human traditions." When the reader calls to mind the fact that then, for 1200 years, the words of Robinson, the great Baptist historian, had been true: "Baptism rose pure in the East, it rolled westward, diminishing in lustre; often beclouded by mists, and sometimes under a total eclipse, at length it escaped the eye, and was lost amid attenuated particles, shades, nonentities, and monsters"—he will know how to appreciate Luther's effort thus to save the Church idol and arm of strength—*water-baptism!*

There was but needed the development and triumph of the anti-Jewish moral sense of the Greek word *baptizo*, in the mind of Luther and all former ritualizers, to have saved them from such incongruous teachings about the way of salvation. Then they would have seen, that like as Christ had meat to eat his carnal disciples "knew not of," so his great commission referred to a baptism that too many in all ages have "known not of."

But Luther's most palpable and pertinacious sacramentarianism was in relation to the Mass or Eucharistic Supper! This created and perpetuated an almost lifelong contest between Luther and his co-reformers. Many of these co-reformers seemed to cut loose from the Papacy so far as to see the intrinsic worthlessness of all ritual observances; for they taught that faith could be exercised and salvation received without a previous or coincident ritual observance. And if so, then surely the ritual had nothing to do with the attainment of salvation.

True, the other Reformers generally deemed the eucharist useful as a symbol or memorial (but who could tell how?)— yet some, it seems, like the Mystics and most of the previous Reformers, were for understanding them only in the spiritual sense. This alarmed Luther very much. D'Aubigne, vol. iii. p. 159, says, speaking of these spiritualizers:

"They were not content with undervaluing the external word—*i. e.*, the Bible (a false insinuation probably), they went so far as to despise the sacrament of the Lord's Supper, as something outward, and to speak of *an inward communion as the only true communion*. From that time, in every attempt to explain the doctrine of the Lord's Supper in a symbolical manner, Luther saw only the danger of weakening the authority of the Holy Scriptures, of substituting arbitrary allegories for their real meaning (just as ritualists and adventists of our day tremble when their outwardism is assaulted), of spiritualizing everything in religion, . . . of substituting, by this means, for the true Christianity a mysticism, a theosophy, a fanaticism, that would infallibly become its grave."

Thus has every ritualist trembled for the ark when their ritualism was assaulted, while history has never verified the charge of theosophy or fanaticism against those who have regarded the Christian dispensation as a spiritual dispensation wholly, while it has ever verified the charge of a fiery, persecuting, theosophic fanaticism against the ritualists!

The *Mystics* were "God's friends," while the Papal ritualists were God's enemies and the enemies of the Church. How gratuitous, then, D'Aubigne's after concession:

"We must acknowledge that, had it not been for Luther's violent opposition, the mystical, enthusiastic, and subjective tendency *would then perhaps have made* rapid progress, and would have turned back the tide of blessings that the Reformation was to spread over the world."

Was the "tide of blessings" turned back by the anti-ritualism of the Mystics three hundred years earlier, or the anti-ritualism of the Catharists six hundred years earlier, or that of the "Friends" a hundred years after Luther? This conceit, that a half-way reformation from the Papacy was better than a whole reformation would have been, is a conceit that has neither philosophy nor Christianity for its basis. The bondage of Protestant sects to rituals and opinions to this day is witness, rather, of the baleful fruits of this superstition, bigotry, and remaining Papal ritualism of Luther.

CARLSTADT'S OPPOSITION TO LUTHER'S SACRAMENTARIANISM.

Carlstadt opposed Luther's ritualism most persistently, and warred also upon the images of the saints, which the Papists had placed in every church and cathedral, which Luther was also willing to save, as he wished to diverge from the Papal Church as little as possible. Hence, Luther persecuted Carlstadt, and drove him out of the diocese of his jurisdiction, and greatly crippled his ministerial influence. Carlstadt maintained that nothing could be more injurious to real piety than confidence in outward ceremonies, and in a certain magical influence of the sacraments. Well asks D'Aubigne, vol. iii. p. 157:

"Did Carlstadt arrive at this opinion unaided? No; ... the historic filiation of the reformed doctrine, so long overlooked, now appears clearly established; unquestionably we cannot fail to see in this doctrine the sentiments of several of the fathers."

And by D'Aubigne's showing it appears that Luther was at first inclined to favor this view, for he writes, in a treatise on the mass which appeared in 1520:

"I can every day partake of the sacraments, if I only call to mind the words and promises of Christ, and if I nourish and strengthen my faith in them.

"D'Aubigne adds, 'It would even appear that the idea frequently occurred to him at this period that a symbolical explanation of the Lord's Supper would be the most powerful weapon to overturn the Papal system from top to bottom.'"

The spiritualizing view of Carlstadt was received by the Swiss Reformers, Zwingle, Œcolampadius, Bucer, Hedio, and others; while the German Reformers (Wittembergers, as they were called), Melancthon, Jonas, Osiandar, Brenz, etc., adhered to Luther. Zwingle said:

"The bread and wine are in the eucharist what the water is in baptism. It would be in vain to plunge a man a thousand times in water, if he does not believe. Faith is the one thing needful."

Luther, on the other hand, contended that

" ' Christ had determined to give believers a full assurance of their salvation,' and had, therefore, 'added his real body to the bread and wine. Just as iron and fire, which are, nevertheless, two distinct substances, are confounded together in the heated mass of iron, so that in each of its parts there are at once iron and fire, in like manner the glorified body of Christ is found in all the parts of the bread.' "

Luther even went so far as to say, "he would rather receive the blood only with the Pope, than the wine only with Zwingle." So intensely did Luther revolt from the Protestant view of Zwingle.

"The reforming tendency, however, predominated in Zwingle; this was directed to two great objects—simplicity of worship and sanctification of life. To harmonize the worship with the necessities of the mind that seeks not external pomp but invisible things—this was Zwingle's first aim. The idea of the corporeal presence, in the Lord's Supper, the origin of so many ceremonies and superstitions of the Church, must therefore be abolished. He found the Roman doctrine of the eucharist, and even that of Luther, presupposed a magical influence prejudicial to sanctification; he feared lest Christians, imagining they received Jesus Christ in the consecrated bread, should thenceforward less earnestly seek to be united to him by faith in the heart. Faith, he said, leads to a real union with Divine things. Thus, it was not a leaning to rationalism, *but a profoundly religious view*, that led him to his peculiar doctrines."

This statement of Zwingle's spiritual view of sacraments is precisely similar to that of the anti-ritualists, who find the *only supper* of our Lord in John vi.—in eating by faith "that bread that came down from heaven and gives life to the world!" They fear that by a ceremonial eating of outward bread they may lose sight of the true spiritual bread, as the Jews, by a fleshly circumcision, lost sight of the circumcision of the heart. The common arguments used as defences or

reasons for these outward observances they conceive to be as
groundless as if we should ask a promissory bond or parch-
ment will or sign of a patrimony already received, or should
ask a tent or booth to dwell in, after the "mansion" is finished.
They ask, would not a continual concern for the sign or parch-
ment, now worthless, turn their attention from the inheritance,
and cause their really losing sight of the kingdom won?
Sticklers for rituals do thus lose sight of the things those rites
ostensibly represent. The *signs* of redemption are valued at
the cost of *love* to those redeemed. See the Protestant world
marred by an inheritance of ritualism, unknown to the Protestants before the time of Luther. If they ostensibly use
rites merely as memorials of the Author and Finisher of our
salvation, they are continually in a contest as to the manner
and the persons fit to use these memorials. And everywhere,
in the evangelical churches, those are found the most spiritual
who value them least! We think a candid investigation will
show this.

Take the different modern views of the eucharist—that it is
a pledge of Divine love—that it is an "outward sign of an
inward grace"—that it is a memorial of the redemptive work
and sufferings—and these views differ from each other; or the
view of Zwingle and John Calvin, the fathers of Presbyterian-
ism: that in it Christ is spiritually or essentially present,
though not in body—and does not the idea of being obedient
to God, by observing an outward rite, or of seeing Christ in
an emblem, turn faith's eye and duty's eye away from the real
point of concern respecting moral responsibility and Christian
duties, and tend to induce a self-satisfied frame of mind in
those who give no other evidence of piety than in the observance of such ceremonies? True, it may be replied, that if
proper instruction is connected with the observance of the
ceremony, it will be a help in impressing moral duty. I
reply, there is no superstition or ceremonial observance of
Jew, Greek, Roman, or Protestant, even to the "*Ave* Maria,"
or the counting of beads, or turning toward Mecca or Jerusa-

lem to pray, but : .ay be made use of by a spiritual mind, to impress moral duty. But that spiritual mind must needs continually warn the worshipper, in the use of the rites, not to trust in the rites, and even to guard himself from unduly trusting in them. And cannot these moral duties be as fully and impressively inculcated without this constant temptation to a ritual trust? which ritual trust has been the death-knell of piety in all ages. Thus it is proven that the external emblem tends to weaken faith in things unseen and spiritual, to sectarize the mind, and freeze charity. Did not circumcision and Judaism generally have this effect? God "found fault" with that scheme, "disannulled the commandment going before, for the weakness and unprofitableness thereof," and now writes his law in our hearts, and works there by his Spirit's power—without emblems—by the direct and mighty energies of the Holy Ghost.

And as to a memorial, we need more a memorial of those dead and departed from us than of those forever with us: "Ye do show forth the Lord's death till he come," says Paul; and Christ explains by saying, "I will no more drink of the fruit of the vine, till the kingdom of God be come." To those who do not recognize the kingdom of Christ and of God as having begun in power in that generation of Jewish believers, and to all who receive Christ in full by faith, according to Christ's words of promise, we have naught to say, only to quote Christ's words, "We will come and make our abode with you!" and John's, "We know that the Son of God has come, and has given us an understanding, and we are in him, that is true, even in his Son Jesus Christ. This is the true God and eternal life." Do we need the outward emblem when we have "the witness" and the "eternal life" within? or can *emblems* convert or bring to Christ those that have not the witness? If so, then the doctrine of regeneration and salvation by baptism and the sacraments is true. Let this matter be well pondered.

ZWINGLE STRENUOUSLY OPPOSES LUTHER'S SACRAMENTARIANISM.

Zwingle oft reasons with great force, and in an unanswerable manner, for the spiritual view, as opposed to sacramentarianism. Luther having published his " *Treatise against the Celestial Prophets*"—i. e., against the spiritualizers—Zwingle no longer hesitated to oppose Luther's teachings boldly. In his " *Commentary on True and False Religion*," he says:

"Since Christ, in the 6th chapter of St. John, ascribes to *faith* the power of imparting eternal life, and of uniting the believer to him in the closest union, *what need have we of more?* Why should he afterwards have ascribed this virtue to his flesh, whilst he himself declares that his flesh profiteth nothing? The flesh of Christ, so far as it suffered death for us, is of incalculable utility, for it saves us from perdition; so far as it is eaten by us, it is of no use whatever."—D'Aubigne, vol. iii. p. 302.

But the ritualists reasoned thus: Brenz, assuming the task of defending Luther, frames this apology:

"If an emperor give a wand to a judge, saying: 'Take; this is the power of judging;' the wand, no doubt, is a mere sign; but the words being added, the judge has not only the symbol, *but the power itself.*"

This reasoning was received in Germany with acclamation; but its utter fallacy is seen by considering the case, thus: that though an emperor might give a wand at the very moment he gave authority to a judge, and the wand was ever to be the symbol thereof, yet Christ does not give spiritual life and power in connection with sacraments, or at least has made no such promise; therefore the analogy falls to the ground.

Zwingle also attacked the sentiment that what one person, consecrate or unconsecrate, could do for another, could be of any saving efficacy. Speaking of the mass, Zwingle says, p. 234:

"My brethren in Christ . . . our only aim is to show that the mass is not a sacrifice that one man may offer to God for another, unless any one should maintain also that a man can eat and drink for his friend. Another adds, in Zwingle's behalf, 'Let us teach Christians to receive Christ in their hearts.'

* Thus,' says D'Aubigne, 'was the reform carried on in Zurich ' (where Zwingle dwelt) and in all Switzerland. The words of Jesus Christ were once more spirit and life."

And mark what follows, p. 256:

"While the different orders and parties in the Church of Rome were incessantly disputing among themselves, the first effect of the gospel was to restore charity among the brethren. The love of the first ages was then revived in Christendom. 'Peace dwells in our city,' exclaimed Zwingle; 'among us there is no fraud, no dissension, no envying, no strife. Whence can proceed such harmony, except from the Lord, and that the doctrine we preach inclines us to innocence and peace?'"

Thus it appears that in connection with Zwingle's spiritual preaching there was a great revival of God's work in Switzerland, resulting also in great harmony and fellowship among the saints, and doubtless in the conversion to God of many before unconverted. And while the Spirit of God was with them, they maintained that unity of spirit; for D'Aubigne adds, "Charity and unity prevailed, although there was no uniformity." And then, also, free discussion was tolerated, for Zwingle called in question the Augustinian doctrine of original sin, which had ruled the Papal Church for ages, and had been the basis of their teaching respecting baptismal regeneration. Zwingle gave the name simply of *disease* to original corruption, and reserved the term sin for the actual transgression of the law. These teachings caused discussions, but "not a cessation of brotherly love," says D'Aubigne. So Zwingle continued the observance of what he termed "the Lord's Supper," but having divested it of its chief Papal features, and claiming to observe it simply as a memorial of Christ, it did not, while the life of Christ was in them, mar their fellowship, or blind their spiritual eye.

Nor could Zwingle escape wholly from the Judaistic observance of infant baptism.

In a public discussion upon the subject at Zurich, Zwingle and his friends maintained the following theses:

Zwingle's False Theses Publicly Maintained.

" 1. *Children born of believing parents are children of God, like those born under the Old Testament, and consequently may receive baptism.*

" 2. Baptism under the New Testament is what circumcision was under the Old; consequently, baptism ought now to be administered to children, as circumcision was formerly.

" 3. We cannot prove the custom of rebaptizing, either by examples, texts, or arguments drawn from Scripture; and those who are rebaptized crucify Jesus Christ afresh."

Now the marvellous assumptions of the foregoing theses, since Zwingle claimed to be neither a Jew nor a Papist, were these :

1. That the children born of Jewish parents were, therefore, children of God, in accordance with the Jewish delusion that sonship to God was attained by natural generation—*i. e.,* in being the children of Abraham after the flesh—the great error that Paul and all the apostles continually refuted.

2. That Christ had placed baptism in the Christian Church in the place of circumcision in the Jewish Church, when no word of that import is found in the New Testament, and baptism and circumcision both were retained by the Judaizers in the Christian Church for not less than two centuries after Christ.

3. While it is true that *re*-baptizing as a mark of conversion or proselytism was not provable from Scripture, nor was baptism itself of those born of believing parents, yet *re*-baptizing was no more " crucifying Christ afresh " than was the first baptism ; either was but at the behest of a Jewish law, a seeking to " begin " wholly " in the flesh," or, " having begun in the spirit," a seeking to be " made perfect by the flesh."

And the two former theses, it will be seen, were based upon or traced to Jewish custom or law, and not upon any New Testament law. Nor was the third thesis traceable to any law ! Thus we see how easy it is even for reformers to teach for doctrines the commandments of men !

And thus are we also introduced to Zwingle's inconsistencies of doctrinal teaching: at one time making faith in Christ all in all for salvation, and the way of escape from the Papacy, and then turning toward a legal perpetuation of a ritual observance where no law can be found.

LUTHER EQUALLY INCONSISTENT.

Luther is equally inconsistent with himself. In his doctrine of justification by faith, he seems to have renounced the Papal doctrine of salvation through the sacraments. But in words only did he renounce it. In words only did he renounce the Papal doctrine of transubstantiation; he changed it simply for the equally absurd doctrine of the immanence of Christ's glorified body. To get rid of the theory of a repeated miracle every time a priest or administrator should say the words of consecration over the bread and wine in the eucharist, by which, as Rome taught, they were instantly converted into the body and blood of Jesus Christ, for that time only, " he substituted the universal miracle . . . . of the ubiquity and omnipresence of the body of Christ. Christ is present in the bread and wine," said Luther, " because he is present everywhere, and, above all, wherever he wills to be." Yet, in his contest with Zwingle on the subject, he asserts in self-contradiction, " He is present, *not as in a place!*" Yet the elements, he insisted, were the real body and blood of Christ, and by eating and drinking we are really made partakers of Christ.

Thus it is seen, not as a new discovery, that it is more than human for any man to be entirely self-consistent. Yet even Luther's partial reform, in denying the supremacy of the Pope, and the exclusive sacerdotal authority of Romish priests, in giving the cup as well as the bread to the laity, and in teaching that faith was also necessary in order that the sacraments might be of saving efficacy, greatly alarmed the priests and minions of the Papacy. " God is blasphemed," they said; " the sacraments, the mother of God, and the saints are despised." And this because the Reformers continually appealed to the Scriptures and not to the Pope for " instruction in the way of life." "Convince us by the Holy Scrip tures," demanded the Reformers everywhere.

Thus was laid the foundation for all future advance in th light of truth, until not only sacramentarian errors but al other errors should be dishevelled from the Church in thei turn. But Luther's obstinacy was a continual check t Zwingle's radicalism in reform. Zwingle continually sough to prove that the Lord's Supper was only emblematical of tha spiritual eating of Christ's body which is by faith, and whicl alone is saving. Zwingle dreaded a conflict with Luther or these subjects lest it might produce a rupture (for it is in con flicts respecting the shell and not the kernel that ruptures ar most likely to come), and Zwingle's fears were not groundless, for not only did that noted council called by Philip, prince of Hesse, recorded in D'Aubigne, vol. iv. pp. 76–100, end in coldness and almost a rupture between the Swiss and German reformers, but it has resulted in the permanency of a High Church Lutheranism, with its sacramentarian creed differing little from Popery, to this day, while the Protestant successors of Zwingle have branched off in a hundred sects, built upon ritualism in its more or less palpable or disguised features.

The Reformers of the fifteenth century could not rid them selves of the superstitious conception of the real presence of Christ in sacraments; they only contested whether the "union of Christ with the sacraments was effected by the faith of the communicant, or by the *opus operatum* of the priest!"

Hence from the moment that Luther rejected the mystic spiritual interpretation of these things they were only *on the way* out of the sacramentarian wilderness of Popery, and by no means in true spiritual freedom and light. They were in the bondage of the letter in many respects, and not in the "liberty" of Christ. Like the Jewish Levitically educated dis ciples of Christ, who, when Christ warned them to "beware of the *leaven* of the Pharisees," could only see the carnal bread for man's dying body in the warning, so these reformers, and many in our day, only see outward bread, and fonts or pools of water, in the eating of Christ and the baptism he enjoins.

Luther's extreme conservatism on these subjects has left a grievous legacy of ritualism to his succeeding co-religionists, filling those nations where *Lutheranism* still reigns with *Rationalism*, Ritualism, and cold formalism, based on a speculative philosophy and the Church creed, to a very lamentable extent. Luther's purpose, "never to depart from the doctrines and customs of the Church (of Rome), except when the language of Scripture rendered it necessary," was tantamount to elevating every ceremony of a Jewish or apostate Romish Church, with all its mummeries, into a law, if not *expressly* forbidden by Scripture. Carlstadt inquires of Luther, "Where has Christ commanded us to *elevate the host?*" alluding to the Romish custom of elevating the wafer ere its distribution. "And where has Christ forbidden it?" was Luther's reply. Who does not see that such a plea leaves the Church a prey to every puerile ritualistic innovation that Christless and dramatic priests might see fit to introduce?

And in concluding this presentation of the conflicts of the ritualistic and anti-ritualistic tendencies in the Reformation of the fifteenth century, we cannot but trace the result of Luther's committal to his conservative and semi-ritual position on his own heart and mind. As usual, it created the same uncharitableness in him as in others, thus evidently grieving the Spirit of God to his own hurt. With uncharitable haste he would ascribe the opinions of others that differed from him to "the wickedness of their hearts, or the wiles of the devil." "One or the other of us must be ministers of Satan, the Swiss or ourselves," said he of Zwingle and his coadjutors in Switzerland. "Opposition roused a sort of frenzy in Luther's mind," says D'Aubigne, "and these frenzies were followed by exhaustion." His health was affected by them; one day he fainted in the arms of his wife and friends, and was a whole week *as if in death and hell.* "He had lost Jesus Christ," he said, "and was tossed to and fro by the tempests of despair!" This was just at the close of one of his fierce debates with the

Swiss Reformers respecting the Lord's Supper. Was it the
fruit of the spirit of life and love from God, through the Holy
Ghost, that affected the mind of Luther? Let the Eternal
Judge decide.

We must haste to the last great anti-ritualistic movement
in the Church of Christ, which has extended even to our day,
and which commenced in a great revival of God's work in the
seventeenth century, through a people calling themselves the

SOCIETY OF FRIENDS, A. D. 1625–1875.

This society, generally known by the term *Quakers*, is a
protest in the midst of a protest, "a wheel within a wheel," a
reformation of a reformation—*i. e.*, to complete a reformation.
It embodies the last great protest against ritualism that the
Church of Christ has witnessed, having commenced a little
over a century later than the Reformation under Martin
Luther (*i. e.*, about A. D. 1625), and continued to the present
time. It has done a great work, looking toward purifying the
Christian Church of exotics, and a ritual and formal type of
religion, but not all that needs to be done in that direction.
Its mission is, therefore, not yet ended. George Fox, the
leader in this work, found even the *Protesting* Churches of
England with a "form of godliness" merely, to an alarming
extent, while the spirit of the Reformation, as seen in Luther's
time, had too extensively passed away. This was especially
true respecting the Church of England, which was merely a
national Church, dissevered from the Papal by the spleen and
rivalry of the lascivious King Henry VIII., in revenge for
the Pope's withstanding his purposes of divorce and re-
marriage. True many of the early Reformers that adhered
to that Church, as Latimer, Ridley, Cranmer, and others,
were devout and truly pious men; and many dissenting
bodies had maintained to a large extent the spirit of the
Reformation; which Reformation itself, however, as we have
seen, did not cast off the ritualistic element, but mainly
through Luther's churchly tendencies, and obstinate sacra-

mentarian ideas, was turned into a channel where the ritual-istic element was circumscribed, to be sure, but still retained to a very dangerous extent.   The Puritan dissenters who had preceded the era of George Fox, or were cotemporary with him, had eliminated some of the incumbent ritualism of the Church of England, and had rejected the principle that the State could be the proper head and lawgiver of the Church, but they were not prepared to plant themselves on the princi-ple that the Church of Christ was wholly spiritual, without the adjunct or deformity of a ritual law, nor were they pre-pared to suffer for their opposition to the worldly spirit, and worldly customs, and State authority over the Church, as the Society of Friends appeared to be.   True, great numbers of them suffered, not imprisonment perhaps, as a general fact, like the Friends, but thousands of their ministers suffered ejectment from their parishes and churches, and ministers and people fled from the country, first to Holland, and then to America, to find an asylum where they might enjoy religious freedom, and not be compelled to sustain a Church to which they could not in conscience conform.*   But the Society of Friends went to the full extent of refusing to pay tithes, or to conform to popular customs, even in the presence of kings and nobles, and rebuked priestcraft and the claims of a false hier-archy everywhere.   In the language of an epistle read before a theological class (at Oberlin) more than a quarter of a cen-tury ago, we may without detraction of any say, " The martyr spirit was passing away.   The apostolical zeal of the first re-formers was declining.   The moral sunlight that in the fifteenth and sixteenth centuries broke forth upon the earth, so long shrouded in midnight, was become dim.   The form of godliness was being substituted for its power.   The spirit of God moved upon the hearts of a few.   They saw the apostasy

---

* This was true especially of the *Brownists* and *Independents*, who, in many respects, resembled the Society of Friends respecting the true ministry and the true Church, and are the pioneers of the Congregational Church of the present day.

of Zion. They saw the tide of desolation coming. They were willing to be led by the Spirit of the Most Holy. They were willing to stand in the breach at such an awful hour. But of whom do I speak? *Quakerism* (with but little qualification) may be said to have been but another name for the pure light of *Christianity* in the seventeenth century. . . . It is not in man to gain all truth by one advance step—from frozen climes to reach the equator by a single stride! Nor does noonday burst upon the earth from deep midnight by one gleam of sunlight."

Moreover, in human progress, sometimes reactions occur. The Protestants from Romanism retained much of the lumber and superstition of Popery, and seem at length (in the Established Church) to be relapsing into Popish formality and impurity. And even the Puritans having, for a short season, shared the disaster of being an *established* Church, were elated, became bigoted also—persecuted all dissent (except under Cromwell) till vital godliness seemed expiring, and a bold, defiant infidelity about to deluge the land. Power is not wisdom, but oft beguiles those, that before its possession appeared wise, far away from all that is wise or amiable.

About this time the Spirit of God moved upon the mind of George Fox, and a few kindred spirits, who, witnessing the fearful declension of the Church, the fearful licentiousness of the Court and officers of government, the desecration of the Sabbath by every species of gaming, sporting, and profanity, and that sanctioned by the royal authority, and the manifest disposition of bishop, priest, and king to tolerate anything but godliness in the Church and in society, were constrained to cry out in language of stern rebuke and remonstrance, and in their practice to witness against the general demoralization.

Cotemporary Demoralization of Society.

Indeed, so great was the general demoralization in the reigns of James I. and Charles I., that the writers we have oft quoted—William and Thomas Evans—in introduction to "Friends' Library," say: "Many of the clergy of the Established Church had become corrupt and licentious; they seldom preached; neglected their congregations and places of worship; and were engaged in practices, not only unbecoming the sacred character, but in some cases even scandalously immoral. They encouraged rather than repressed the licentiousness of the times; and seemed much more addicted to mirth and amusements than to the duties of the ministerial office. King James drew up a royal declaration, stating that 'for the people's recreation, his majesty's pleasure was, that after the end of divine service they should not be disturbed, hindered, or discouraged from any lawful recreations, such as dancing of men or women, archery, leaping, vaulting; nor from having May games, whitsonales, morrisdances, setting up May-poles, etc. As might have been expected from such royal permission, the sports degenerated into noisy and tumultuous revels, with tippling, quarrels, and sometimes even murder." *.

In the reigns of Charles I. and II. the case was no better. In 1640, a hundred of the clergy of the Established Church were tried by order of Parliament, for scandalous offences charged against them, and eighty of them were convicted. When the disorders that grew out of the royal indulgences, and from the vicious example of the ministers of the Established Church, became so great that they seemed unendurable, the justices in some of the counties petitioned the judges to suppress these disorders, which they did. But Archbishop Laud, then Primate of England, summoned the judges before the king and council, and a sharp reprimand, and an order to revoke the prohibition, was the result. The archbishop was informed by the bishop of Bath and Wells, where the prohibition had been enforced, that the restoration of the wakes and revels would be very acceptable to the gentry, *clergy*, and common people; in proof of which he had procured the signatures of seventy-two clergymen, and believed if he had sent for a hundred more he could have had the consent of them all. Such was the state of morals in the court and Church and the nation when the Puritans and Friends arose to rebuke it.

Perhaps more than any others George Fox and William Penn reached the ears of king and government; and being in no case political partisans they exhorted to a reform of the laws in this wise: George

---

* In the reign of Charles II. the court was devoted to licentious pleasures, while religion and religious things were made a mere laughing-stock. The restoration opened the very flood-gates of vice and wickedness. Says Bishop Burnet, "A spirit of extravagant joy spread over the nation that brought in with it the throwing off the very profession of virtue and piety; all ended in entertainments and drunkenness which overrun the three kingdoms to such a degree that it very much corrupted all their morals. . . . The Friends reminded the king of the fate of Sodom and Gomorrah, and so contrary were their example and precept to the prevailing corruptions, and so plain and fearless the rebukes they administered, that they were subjected to much abuse, yet were they oft instrumental in turning sinners from the evil of their ways. Friends went to the courts of justice and exhorted the officers to the discharge of their duties, and preached against the prevailing licentiousness in the markets and places of public entertainment."

Fox, being deeply affected with these immoralities, said: 'Let all the laws of England be brought into a known tongue!'

"'Let no swearer, nor curser, nor drunkard bear any office whatever, nor be put in any place of trust.'

"'Let none keep ale-houses or taverns but those who fear God—that will not let the creatures of God be destroyed by drunkenness.'

"'Let no man keep an ale-house or tavern that keeps bowls, shuffle-boards, or fiddlers, or dice, or cards.'

"'Let neither beggar, nor blind people, nor fatherless, nor widows, nor cripples, go begging up and down the streets; but a house be provided for them all, and also meat, that there may be never a beggar among you.'

"'Let all the wearing of gold lace and costly attire be ended, and clothe the naked, and feed the hungry, with the superfluity; and turn not your ear away from the cry of the poor.'

"George Fox adds: 'I was under great suffering of spirit because of the sanguinary character of the penal code of Great Britain, specially concerning their putting to death for small matters, and reminding the rulers that it was contrary to the law of God in old time, as well as to the benign spirit of the gospel.' He urges to amend the laws, thus: 'Let no one be put to death for stealing cattle, or money, or any outward thing; but let them restore, and mind the law of God—which is equity and measureable to the offence.'

"'Let none be jailors that are drunkards, swearers, or oppressors of the people, but such as may be good examples to the prisoners.'

"'Let none lie long in jail, for that is the way to spoil the people, and to make more thieves, for there they learn wickedness together.'

"'Let all jails be in wholesome places, that the prisoners may not lie in the filth and straw, like chaff, etc.'

"Respecting certain nuisances, he said:

"'Let these things be mended.'

"He enjoined masters to train their negroes in the fear of God, and after certain years of servitude to *set them free.* And all Friends he exhorted to instruct and teach the Indians and negroes that Christ, by the grace of God, tasted death for every man.*

Thus he showed the benevolence of his spirit, his love of 'peace on earth,' his 'good-will to men,' and in times of persecution his good-will even to enemies. Thus the Friends earned their chosen appellation, and their known character as peacemakers. What George Fox thus inculcated by precept, William Penn, in America, illustrated in practice,

---

* This concern for the welfare of the African slaves was ever retained by the Friends, and induced their universal coöperation with Wilberforce and Clarkson, in the suppression of the slave-trade. Also, in their overleaping the boundary lines of the denomination, in the case of an appeal made to them in behalf of the Oberlin College (Congregational), in 1838. This university in Ohio, having opened its doors to rich and poor of all nations and colors, and both sexes, became embarrassed in its finances, in consequence of popular prejudices and commercial revulsions in America; hence, an embassy, consisting of Rev. John Keep and William Dawes, Trustees of Oberlin, was sent to England, who raised about $30,000 in aid of the institution, in a few months, chiefly contributed by the Society of Friends.

in his colony in Pennsylvania. They have ever opposed war and oppression, and have exerted a mighty influence in more than one nation in promoting peace, securing the amelioration of the condition of prisoners and the oppressed, and the exercise of the spirit of philanthropy and Christian love everywhere.

Thus have they shown, moreover, that in rejecting a *ceremonial law* they have the more effectually established the *moral law*. They have shown that their peculiar mode of preaching holiness, or the *higher Christian life*, has been justified by their practice thereof, in the face of all Christendom, and of a frowning world.

And Richard Baxter, no great friend of the Quakers, testifies that what they suffered at the hands of wicked rulers had a great tendency, through their constancy, patience, and offering themselves as substitutes, in suffering, one for another, in changing the mind of the government toward them and others. He says, 'The Quakers did greatly relieve the sober people for a time, for they were so resolute and so gloried in their constancy and sufferings, as they were dragged daily to the common jail, yet desisted not—but the rest came the next day—abundance of them died in prison, and yet they continue their assemblies still.'

Orme, the biographer of Baxter, also remarks: 'Had there been more of the same determined spirit among others, which the Friends displayed, the sufferings of all parties would sooner have come to an end. . . . The conduct of the Quakers was infinitely to their honor. In withstanding the interferences of government with the rights of conscience, by which they finally secured those privileges they so richly deserved to enjoy, their heroic and persevering conduct entitles them to the veneration of all the friends of civil and religious freedom.'"

These sufferings *for your enfranchisement*, Christian reader, they endured through a period of thirty years.

They aimed ever to manifest their consistency by a rigidly consistent example. Indeed, such must have been the firmness and enthusiasm of these devoted and persecuted witnesses to the self-denying principles of the gospel, that it were not to be wondered at if, at times, their zeal was not according to the highest wisdom, and lead them into certain extremes of action which a less lax state of society respecting morals would not have required. That long perversion of the gospel and its institutions, and grievous abuses of sacred functions, may require bold and unaccustomed forms of rebuke, is undeniable, and also a total disuse of what otherwise might have been admissible. Nevertheless, that the real principles and practices of the primitive Quakers did approach exceedingly near the gospel standard, perhaps nearer than any cotemporary religious reformers, there seems to be no room to question.

God was truly with them in mighty power, and this mighty power of truth and of life, from God working within them, as the power working within the earth causes the earth to *quake* and *tremble*, and as they called on the obdurately wicked at times to *tremble* before God, they at length gained the appellation of *Quakers* or *Tremblers*—a name given them in derision, but really indicative of the highest honor conferred on them by God himself.

God set his seal upon their labors in a most marked manner, so that not only were numbers brought to confess to the truth in the face of great obloquy and reproach, but also to the enabling of them to endure the loss, oft, of all that earth calls dear; and in stripes, in imprisonments, in confiscation of goods, in barbarous treatment at the hands of petty officers of government, and a surrounding host of petty spies and informers, watching to detect them in some act of violation of the infamous conformity laws, that they might pounce upon and make a prey of them, they stood firm, and endured with meekness all this; and triumphed ultimately over the foes of God and man by longsuffering and patience.

Yes, they gained the Christian signet through suffering and martyrdom, enduring with such fortitude and meekness their afflictions, that in due time the civil powers became ashamed of their conduct in persecuting the inoffensive, who were ready to suffer for conscience sake, and were ready to relax the rigor of those laws requiring such persecution, and were ready to annul them long before the clergy and bishops would consent. Thus was the Protestant cause in England (and also in America) dishonored by a spirit of bigotry and persecution, on the part of Protestants, which what themselves had suffered at the hands of the Papacy should long before have cured. But their longsuffering triumphed even over church prejudices, and the bigotry of sectarians; for they were found ever as ready to plead for tolerance and lenity toward others who were suffering for conscience sake as for themselves. William Penn, one of their number, gained great influence at court, and through his intercessions very many were set at liberty from long imprisonment, both of Quakers and the Puritans. And to their influence, as much as to any other cause, is to be attributed the ultimate decline of the spirit of persecution for conscience sake.

THEIR VIEWS OF THE CHRISTIAN LIFE.

As we said in the former part of this record of anti-ritualism, nearly or quite all the anti-ritualists have held to the moral standard of completeness in the Christian life—that Christian perfection, or entire sanctification of body, soul and spirit, commenced by entire consecration to Christ, and his work of purity, love, and mercy, was the proper work of the true Christian. This has been emphatically true of all the preceding ages, and is no less exemplified in the history of the Society of Friends. Its origin was not so much in a contention respecting theological tenets, as in an effort to promote spiritual holiness, to be made manifest in heart and life. Hence those doctrines and usages which they saw were working practical mischief they discarded as anti-Christian, and taking the practical precepts of Christianity, and the law of love, as their creed, they based their scheme upon these. Indeed, while reading their writings, especially the accounts of the religious life and teachings of their members, we have been most forcibly impressed with the evidence that herein was manifest a great revival of God's work in the century in which they arose, and have been as forcibly struck with the likeness to the great work in the days of Tauler, four hundred years earlier, and also its likeness to the great work of God in the days of Wesley and Whitefield, a hundred years later, and also its likeness to the work of God as promoted by the revivalists, Edwards, Finney, and others, two hundred years after the rise of the Quakers. Wesley and Finney taught the same doctrine of full salvation, or the perfectibility of the Christian character through Christ, and were likewise instrumental in the promotion of a general revival of spiritual holiness in the churches of Christ. They differed from George Fox and his coadjutors in that they did not so fully eschew the ritualisms of the churches. Yet these (Wesley and Finney), of course, could not accomplish their work without turning the attention of all they addressed away from the form to the substance of the life in Christ, and they succeeded only as they weaned sectarists and formalists from their trust in the shadow, and induced them to seek the true spiritual life of faith and obedience to the moral rather than the ceremonial law. That the Friends may truly be compared to Tauler, Wesley, and Finney, in inculcating this inward life of fellowship with God, and a moral likeness to Christ, we will quote from "Introductory Remarks" to a memoir of George Fox (a work published in England), to show. On page 54 the writer says:

"Many of them (*i. e.*, the Friends) were persons who had been highly esteemed for their piety in the societies with which they had formerly been connected, and several of them had been preachers. In the progress of their religious experience they were convinced that they had been resting too much on a bare belief of what Christ had done and suffered for them when personally on earth, and also in the ceremonies of religion, without pressing after the knowledge of 'Christ, in them the hope of glory,' to feel his righteous government set up in their hearts, and the power of the Holy Spirit giving them the victory over sin in all its motions, and qualifying them to serve God in 'newness of life.' They saw that the Holy Scriptures held up to the view of Christians a state of religious advancement and stability far beyond that which most of the professors of their day appeared to aim at or admit; a state in which sin was to have no more dominion over them, because the law of the spirit of life in Christ Jesus had set them free from the law of sin and death. That this was an inward work, not effected by the bare assent of the understanding to the blessed truths contained in the Bible, hearing sermons, sprinkling or dipping in water, or partaking of bread and wine, but a real change of the heart and affections by the power of the Holy Ghost inwardly revealed, regenerating the soul, creating it new in Christ Jesus, and *making all things pertaining to it of God.*"

Here we have a reply, in verity, to those bigoted and superstitious ritualists who cry out, *antinomianism*, or *broad church*, against those who set aside a ritual law, and thus are ready to embrace in their fold all who truly love God, and really *intend* to obey the *moral law*, let ceremonies go where they will! for what is the avail of an excellent moral law, highly eulogized, to be sure, and looked at with admiration, but never kept, nor expected to be? Is not that the real essence of antinomianism? And will God accept your ritual obedience in place of the moral? That is the very essential delusion of both Judaism and Popery! And "if the uncircumcision" (the non-ritualists) keep the righteousness of the moral law, is not that *all that God requires?* To what purpose was a ritual ever appointed but to that end? And if the ritual itself became the end, in man's eye, shall not the ritual be "blotted out," that the true end of all dispensations, and all worship, and all seeking unto God, may be seen, viz., to secure obedience to the moral law, even love to God and our neighbor?

But let me quote again, and this time from the memoir of George Fox, as found in the "Friends' Library" (vol. i. p. 30): speaking of Fox, the writer says:

"The success accompanying his ministry was great, and the report of his piety and zeal having spread far, many came from different parts of the country to see and converse with him on religious subjects. . . . Others were exasperated at the reception which his doctrine met with. They could not endure to hear of perfection, and living a holy and sinless life; and began to plead for sin and imperfection, by which the tender convictions and attractions the spirit of grace are quenched! 'Of all the sects in Christendom,' says George Fox, at this time, 'I found none who could bear to be told that any should come to Adam's perfection; into that image of God, that righteousness and holiness that Adam was in before he fell; to be pure and clean, without sin, as he was.' Therefore, how should they bear to be told that any should grow up to the measure of the stature of the fulness of Christ, when they cannot bear to hear that any should come, while on earth, into the same power and spirit that the prophets and apostles were in?"

If this testimony of George Fox be correct, we see where the true testimony for Christ and against sin was found in that age; consequently where the true and living Church was. God's witnesses and hidden ones have never been wholly banished from the earth since the day of our Lord's ascension to glory, and "receiving gifts for men!" Again, George Fox, in describing his commission as a minister, says:

"He was sent to turn people from darkness to light, to the grace of God, and to the truth in the heart which came by Jesus, that all might come to know their salvation nigh! I saw that Christ died for all men; was a propitiation for all, and that the manifestation of the Spirit of God was given to every man to profit withal. These things I did not see by the help of man, nor by the letter, though they are written in the letter, but I saw them in the light of the Lord Jesus Christ, and by his immediate spirit and power, as did the holy men of God, by whom the Holy Scriptures were written. Yet I had no slight esteem of the Holy Scriptures: they were very precious to me. . . . I could speak much of these things and many volumes might be written, but all would prove too short to set forth the infinite love, wisdom, and power of God, in preparing, fitting, and furnishing me for the service he had appointed me to: letting me see the depths of Satan on the one hand, and opening to me on the other hand the divine mysteries of his own everlasting kingdom."

Thus the reader may see how, through the searchings and teachings of the Divine Spirit, this eminent servant of God was enabled to "comprehend with all saints the length and breadth and depth and height of the love of Christ; and to be led according to the apostle's (Paul's) prayer into all the fulness of God!" But, says the writer we have just cited,

"As the nature of his principles was opposed to the outward and lifeless profession of religion, which too much prevailed in that day, tending to draw the people from a dependence on human teaching and external ceremonies to the work of regeneration by the Holy Spirit in their own hearts, he met with much opposition and cruel usage. His first imprisonment took place in 1648, at Nottingham, where he entered a place of public worship on a First Day morning and spoke to the people on the subject of the Holy Scriptures, showing that the Spirit of Christ, by which the holy men of old wrote the Scriptures, was that by which only they could be rightly understood. As he was speaking the officers arrested him, and took him to a filthy prison, where he was detained until the sheriff, taking compassion on his uncomfortable situation, removed him to his own house. How long he remained there does not appear, but he says it was 'a pretty long time,' and after that, being discharged, he travelled as before in the work of the ministry. At Mansfield, in 1649, he entered the place of public worship, and attempted to speak to the people, but they fell upon him and cruelly beat him with their hands, Bibles, and sticks; then put him into the stocks, where he remained some time, and finally stoned him out of the town. . . . In the year 1650 he visited Derby and preached to the people, for which the officers arrested him and took him before the magistrates, who, after an examination of eight hours' length, committed him and John Fretwell, who was with him, to the house of correction, where they were confined six months. During the examination, Justices Bennet and Barton endeavored to draw from him some expression by which they might prove him guilty of holding blasphemous opinions. They asked him 'If he had no sin?' to which he replied, ' Christ, my Saviour, has taken away my sins, and in him there is no sin.' Then they asked him 'How the Quakers knew that Christ did abide in them?' and were answered, 'By his Spirit that he had given them!' Finding nothing in this whereon to ground a charge, they ensnaringly asked, ' Whether any of them were Christ?' To which George Fox promptly replied, ' *Nay, we are nothing; Christ is all.*' But although he thus cleared himself and his fellow-professors from their imputations, yet they made out a mittimus and sent him and his companion to prison, as persons charged with uttering and broaching divers blasphemous opinions, contrary to the late act of Parliament."

This was three years prior to the period that Cromwell's Parliament acted in favor of religious freedom, and annulled the former tyrannous conformity laws. This same writer, speaking of this matter, says:

" After the dissolution of the monarchy by the death of Charles, and the consequent suppression of the national form of worship, much greater latitude was allowed to the ministers of religion."

CROMWELL AND THE INDEPENDENTS AIDED THE FRIENDS IN MAINTAINING RELIGIOUS FREEDOM.

" During Cromwell's victorious campaign in Scotland the ministers of that nation (Presbyterian) objected against him for opening the pulpit doors to all intruders. To which he replied, ' We look on ministers as helpers of, not lords over, the faith of God's people. I appeal to their consciences, whether any, denying their doctrines, or dissenting from them, will not incur the censure of a sectary? And what is this but to deny Christians their liberty, and assume the infallible chair? Where do you find in Scripture that preaching is included (*i. e.*, limited) within *your* functions? Though an approbation from man may have order in it, and may be well, yet he that hath not a better than that hath none at all! I hope he that ascended up on high may give his gifts to whom he pleases, and if those gifts be the seal of missions, why are you envious though Eldad and Medad prophesy? You know who has bid us covet earnestly the best gifts, but chiefly that we may prophesy, which the apostle explains to be speaking to instruction, edification, and comfort, which the instructed, edified, and comforted can best tell the energy and effect of.'"*

---

* So the " Lord Commissioner, Fiennes, in 1657, warns the Parliament of the rock on which many had split, which was a spirit of imposing upon men's consciences in things wherein God leaves them a latitude, and would have them free. . . . As God is no respecter of persons, so he is no respecter of forms, but in what form soever the spirit of imposition appear he will testify against

Thus did Cromwell and Fiennes sustain in full the position assumed by the Friends to their justification in claiming to exercise the ministerial function in obedience to the call of God, and not of man—a position that all Protestants have in theory, before and since, admitted, though they have not always been ready to sustain it.

We allude to this here, because a false sacerdotalism and ritualism are mutually dependent upon each other, and a priesthood holding the keys of the Church, and the "keys of the kingdom," in its own hands through sacraments, is usually the embodiment of sectarianism and ecclesiastical tyranny.

It was from such convictions of Cromwell, and the Independents and Friends, of the injustice of proscription on account of religious faith, that the following was inserted in the Constitution of a new form of government instituted by the Parliament, under Cromwell, when declared *Protector of England, Scotland, and Ireland:*

"It is ordained, 1. That the Christian religion contained in the Scriptures be held forth and recommended as the public profession of these nations.

"2. That none be compelled to conform to the public religion by penalties, or otherwise; but that endeavors be used to win them by sound doctrine and the example of a good conversation.

"3. That such as profess faith in God by Jesus Christ, though differing in judgment from the doctrine, worship, and discipline publicly held forth, shall not be restrained from, but shall be protected in, the profession of their faith, and the exercise of their religion; so as they abuse not this liberty to the civil injury of others, and to the actual disturbance of the public peace; and provided this liberty be not extended to Popery or prelacy, or to such as, under a profession of Christ, hold forth and practise licentiousness."

---

it. If men, though otherwise good, will turn ceremony into substance, and make the kingdom of Christ consist in circumstances, in discipline, and in forms, . . . in vain do they protest against the persecution of God's people, when they make the definition of God's people so narrow that their persecution is as broad as any other, and usually more fierce, because edged with a sharper spirit. It is good to hold forth a public profession of the truth, but not so as to exclude those that cannot come up to it in all points from the privilege that belongs to them as Christians, much less to the privilege that belongs to them as men."

The reader will discover that the above articles favoring religious liberty, while simply just in form toward all dissenters, were, nevertheless, unjust toward the Papists and Episcopalians, for however much these had persecuted dissenters, now was the time to render good for evil, and teach even to persecutors the more excellent way of impartial religious toleration.

It is to be confessed, moreover, that although Cromwell and the Independents desired such toleration, yet many others of the dissenters even regarded it as unsafe. The Presbyterians of that day would by no means assent (no more than did the Independents in Boston at a later day); hence there was much suffering on the part of the Friends and Baptists (see twelve years imprisonment of John Bunyan). The Presbyterians, having the power of government, or as members of Parliament, insisted as strenuously on *uniformity* as had the Episcopalians. The "divine right" of the prelacy they would simply change for the *divine right of the Presbytery!* They pronounced toleration the "root of gall and bitterness," as "contrary to godliness, opening a door to libertinism and profanity, and that it ought to be rejected as *soul-poison.*" "Liberty of conscience," they said, "is the nourisher of all heresies and schisms!" Strange they did not see that this was full-orbed Popery. But they did not till afterwards their own backs felt the smart, as they had before, and they drank freely of the bitter cup they were so anxious others should drink.

This cup they drank in the reign of Charles II., when conformity to the Episcopal Church was again rigidly enforced. Tithes for the Established Church were exacted of all ; heavy fines for not attending on the worship of the Established Church ; in default of the payment of these, goods and lands were seized and sold, and thus many were despoiled, and finally banishment was enforced on pain of death if these laws were disregarded. Oaths were required of Friends, especially the oath of allegiance, and tithes, and conformity, all which they could not in conscience render, and a confiscation and im-

prisonment, and banishment, or death was the result in many
thousands of cases.

Let it be understood that all the dissenters of England at
this time were for reforming, not only from Popery, but also
from much that was akin to Popery in the Established Church.
As the last quoted writer says:

"It is interesting to observe that the different religious societies which have
arisen since the Reformation all aimed at the attainment of greater degrees of
spirituality, and a more fervent piety, than was generally to be found in the
sect from which they sprung. The idea that forms were too much substituted
for power, and a decent compliance with the externals of religion for its heart-
changing work, seems to have given rise to them all. Each successive advance
lopped off some ceremonial excrescences, with a view of making the system
more conformable to the apostolic pattern. . . . It is no arrogant assumption
to assert that, to whatever point in the Reformation we turn our attention, we
find the germ of those principles which were subsequently developed and
carried out by the founders of the Society of Friends. . . . Opinions very
similar to those held by this society, on the subjects of the indwelling and
guidance of the Holy Spirit, baptism, and other ceremonies, superstitious rites,
war, oaths, and a ministry of human appointment, were extant, antecedent to
the rise of the Friends. During the fifteenth century there were a number of
persons in England who denied the necessity of water-baptism, and held that
'Christian people were sufficiently baptized in the blood of Christ, and *needed
no water*, and that the sacrament of baptism with water, used in the Church,
is but a light matter, and of small effect.' 'Some of these,' says the same historian, 'suffered death by fire, for adherence to their principles; and for a long
time afterwards, those who entertained similar views were the objects of severe
persecution.' "

We are amazed that this writer should state that the distinguishing tenets of the Society of Friends, specially relating to
ceremonials, had not previously been held by any considerable
body of people. He certainly had not read the record of the
past, and was not aware to what extent churchly historians
had falsified history by their omissions in this respect. It is
not only true that such anti-ritualistic bodies have prevailed
in great numbers in all the past ages, embracing nearly all the
dissentients from Popery, but it must also be with candor conceded that in precise proportion as those bodies which admitted
the divinity of our Lord, and taught salvation through his
atonement, have disesteemed the ceremonials of religion, have

they exalted the moral law, having substituted, as if by intuition, or a divine teaching, the moral law for a ceremonial law.

True a revolt from the externals needful to manifest Christian faith may be carried too far, even to a perfect *quietism;* but it is quite a different thing to admit the obligation, and faithfully practise moral duties, from binding a yoke of an undefined ceremonial upon the Christian Church.

Wickliffe, the earliest reformer from the Papacy in England, denied that all sins are abolished in baptism; asserted that children are saved without baptism, and that the baptism of water profiteth not without the baptism of the Holy Spirit. Thus we see that in England, as in Germany and France, the anti-ritualistic leaven was working out its legitimate result of a complete deliverance from the former bondage of a ritual law, through all the period of the Reformation. This complete emancipation crystallized and took form and embodiment in the Society of Friends.

The Highest Type of the Christian Life with the Non-Sacramentarians.—Cotemporary Demoralization of Society.

But let it be remembered that their opposition to a ritual law and to the baptism with water was induced by the general apostasy and corruption of those churches most marked by a ritual trust, while it is the universal admission that the highest manifestation of the Christian life is only attained by the baptism of the Holy Ghost. The aim to attain and exhibit the fruits of such a life has been manifest from their rise, and was a special need of the Church during the first hundred years of their testimony, since during this period they were the only witnesses for full salvation from sin, and the higher life of holiness in all the Christian world. Luther and the Lutherans had rejected the doctrine; Calvin and the Calvinists had done the same; the Papists and the English Church were sunk in corruption; the Methodists had not yet arisen;

the Independents, Presbyterians, and Baptists, who had a little
earlier origin, had rejected the doctrine that the gospel offered
freedom from sin in this life; hence it is true with respect to
the Friends as in all former ages, that a complete history of
the advocates of the higher Christian life, and of full salvation through Christ, must embrace in every age those, and
oft only those, who rejected the baptism of water. Touching
this matter, hear William and Thomas Evans again (Int'n,
p. 17):

FRIENDS SPECIAL WITNESSES FOR THE HIGHER CHRISTIAN LIFE.

"It is not correct to say that Friends spake little on the great doctrines of
justification and remission of sins through Jesus Christ, our propitiation; for
they frequently and earnestly insisted on them. But finding that these were
generally admitted by all Christian professors, while many either entirely
denied or undervalued the work of the Holy Spirit in the heart, they were engaged to call the attention of the people to this as the life of true religion;
without which the Scriptures could not make them wise unto salvation, and
Christ would have died for them in vain. While thus enforcing this important
doctrine of Holy Scripture, they were careful to recognize the whole scope of
the gospel in all its fulness. They declared against that construction of the
doctrine of Christ's satisfaction which taught men to believe they could be
justified from sins while they continued in them impenitent; asserting that
the very design of Christ's coming in the flesh was *to save his people from their
sins*, and to destroy the works of the devil. Yet they fully and gratefully
acknowledged the mercy of God in giving his dear Son a ransom and atonement for mankind, that the penitent sinner might be justified freely by his
grace.

"They ever held the Sacred Scriptures as paramount authority as a guide
to faith and duty, and constantly appealed to them; thence they drew all
moral precepts and instruction in the way of life through Christ, but ever insisted that only by the power of the Holy Ghost those truths were sent home
to the heart and affections, regenerating and making all new in the image of
Christ. Convinced that this great work was in danger of being overlooked
amid a round of ceremonial observances, they zealously preached the doctrine
of the new birth, calling their hearers to come to Jesus Christ, the true light,
that they might experience him to shine in their hearts. But the offices of the
Holy Ghost, or Comforter, as the guide into all truth, as the unction from the
Holy One which teacheth of all things, and is truth and is no lie, was the
great theme of their contemplation and ministry; and it stands forth con-
spicuously in their writings."

The writer adds:

"When we turn to the sacred volume and read there the numerous testimonies borne to the great importance of this doctrine in the gospel plan, we cannot wonder to find it prominently set forth by a people professing eminently the spirituality of religion. . . . In carrying out these views of the spiritual nature of the gospel, and of the great work of the soul, described as the 'washing of regeneration and the renewing of the Holy Ghost,' the primitive Friends were led to the adoption of their peculiar sentiments respecting water-baptism and the use of the bread and wine. They found it stated in the sacred volume that, as there is 'one Lord and one faith,' so there is but 'one baptism,' and that the baptism which now saves is not the putting away the filth of the flesh but the answer of a good conscience toward God, by the resurrection of Jesus Christ. Corresponding with this is the saying of the apostle to the Romans: 'Know ye not that so many of us as were baptized into Jesus Christ were baptized into his death?' and also to the Galatians: 'As many of you as have been baptized into Christ have put on Christ;' and to the Colossians: 'We are buried with him by baptism, wherein also ye are risen with him, through the faith of the operation of God, who hath raised him from the dead.' Sensible that these blessed effects were not the result of dipping or sprinkling the body with water, and apprehensive that many professors of religion were trusting in the outward ceremony, while neglecting the necessary work of 'repentance toward God and faith in the Lord Jesus Christ,' they pressed upon their hearers the necessity of experiencing that one saving baptism. . . . Convinced that the gospel is not a dispensation of shadows but the very substance of heavenly things themselves, they believed that the true communion of saints consisted in the divine intercourse which is maintained between our merciful Saviour and the souls of his faithful disciples, agreeably to his own gracious words: 'Behold I stand at the door and knock; if any man hear my voice and open the door, I will come into him and sup with him, and he with me.'"

"As there is a strong tendency in the human mind to substitute the form of religion for the power, and to satisfy the conscience by a cold compliance with exterior performances while the heart remains unchanged, and inasmuch as the baptism of the Holy Ghost and the communion of the body and blood of Christ, of which water-baptism and the bread and wine are admitted to be only signs, are not dependent on these outward ceremonies nor are necessarily connected with them, and are declared in Holy Scripture to be effectual to the salvation of the soul, which the signs are not, Friends have always believed it their place and duty to hold forth to the world a clear and decided testimony to the living substance—the spiritual work of Christ in the soul, and a blessed communion with him."

We may close this survey of the general character and work of this anti-ritualistic body with the words of the writer we are quoting:

19

"Happily for the society it has nothing to fear from investigation, conducted in the spirit of candor and fairness, concerning the soundness of its faith or its works of faith and love. A long list of worthies have illustrated the power of that gospel they preached, both in life and in death."

The fervor of their piety and the earnestness of their consecration to Christ—exhibiting, of course, the frailties common to fallible men—has never been excelled, we are confident, by any equal number of the household of faith in any age of the Church.

In a succeeding chapter, we purpose to give the testimony of several of their writers (with others) to the non-value of rituals and sacraments, as taught and observed by many of the churches

THE SPIRITUAL CHRISTIANS OF RUSSIA.

The Friends in their ministerial travels in various parts of the Christian world have discovered here and there those who earnestly *protest* against the ritualism into which the Papal, Greek, and Armenian churches have relapsed. STEPHEN GRELLET, himself converted from the Catholic faith directly to the Friends' views (as he says, being awakened by the warning voice of God only, crying " eternity, eternity," in his ear), travelled much in different parts of Europe, especially among the French, who spoke his native tongue, and in Russia, where also, among the higher classes, the French tongue is much spoken. He gives the following account of a theological teacher, and a class of Christians called Malakans, the former found in the Crimea, and the latter extending their societies from the Crimea, the Asiatic border, even to Siberia. He says:

"In the evening we went to the monastery to see Macarius, rector of a seminary for the sons of the clergy, . . . he is a man of great religious tenderness, and he imparted some of the exercises of his mind, and the ways in which the Lord, by his Spirit, is pleased to lead him; paths which very few about him can understand. He has been much tried about the various ceremonies of the Greek Church, the bowing down before images, and also respecting the ministry, baptism, and the Supper. 'His views,' says Grellet, 'are similar to ours.' Also, 'we had a visit from an old man, eighty years of age, one of the people called Malakans, who call themselves *Spiritual Christians.*' This people are a branch (orthodox) of a people called *Duhobertzi*, who, with these, have suffered much persecution from the clergy and the government on account of their religious principles. Macarius, attending with us (Grellet and William Allen) one of their meetings, at the close thus broke out, in a flood of tears, and exclaimed, 'In what a state of darkness and ignorance have I been! I thought I was alone in these parts, endeavoring to walk in the light of the Lord, to wait for, and sensibly feel the influences of his Spirit, so as to be able to worship him in spirit and in truth, and behold, how great has been my darkness, so that I did not discover that blaze of light, here round about me, among a people poor in the world, but rich in faith in the Lord Jesus Christ.' . . . . They were very free to give us every information we asked for, and they did it in few words, accompanied, generally, with some scripture, as their reasons for believing or acting as they did; these were so much to the purpose that any one acquainted with the Friends' writings might conclude they had selected from them the most clear and appropriate passages to support their testimonies. On all the cardinal points of the Christian religion, the fall of man, salvation by Christ through faith, the meritorious death of Christ, his resurrection, ascension, etc., their views are very clear; also respecting the influence of the Holy Spirit, worship, ministry, baptism, the supper, oaths, etc., etc., we might suppose they were thoroughly acquainted with our religious society, but they had never heard of us, nor of any people that profess as they do. William Allen (Friend preacher), who accompanied Grellet, says of them: 'They believe in the Holy Scriptures, and in the divinity of our Lord and Saviour as fully as we do ourselves, and that the influence of the Holy Spirit is not withheld from any. They believe that the only true baptism is that of Christ with the Spirit, and reject water-baptism as unnecessary. They consider that the communion with Christ is wholly spiritual, and make use of no outward ceremony.' The Malakans extend on the east even to the Caucasus mountains, and, counting all their societies, Grellet says they 'number about one hundred thousand.'"

Here then, unknown to western Protestants, is found a numerous class of Protestants, as large as some of our denominations in America, who have, doubtless, continued their testimony against a ritual law from the days of Paul, the apostle, the Paulicians of the eighth century, and the Catharists of the thirteenth century to the present time: a people who, amid the surrounding darkness, have maintained the true spiritual worship, and have known God and have been known of him though earth has known them not.

CHRISTIAN UNIONISTS OF AMERICA.

It is but proper to add in the conclusion of this chapter that some of the advocates of Christian union, such as would be attained by the merging of the different evangelical denominations, have come to the discovery that to attain such union, and at the same time insist on the invariable observance of an external baptism, is a thing utterly impracticable.

Such begin to concede to applicants for church fellowship personal liberty in this matter, to observe rites, or not to observe them, as a branch of the Protestant faith in America, "New Lights," so called, have done for an age or more.

Formerly, affiliation with such religious societies and people as the Friends, or any others that rejected or treated lightly the forms and ceremonies of the churches, was not sought; a larger charity is beginning to swell the heart of Christendom, and the great truth is beginning to be appreciated that, at least, harmony and reciprocity among all churches would be a blessing, and such fellowship and harmonious affiliation is more generally sought. Thus is seen advancing the glorious day when all those " hidden ones," so long known of God only, shall be also known of man as God's " peculiar people," and a canonical investiture with human authority will not be counted on as highly as being " clothed with power from on high" through the energies of the Holy Ghost.

Then shall prejudice give place to universal Christian charity, and schisms shall disappear in a common unity; and there shall be " one Lord, and his name one," o'er all the earth, and Christ's redeemed flock will be content with their " one Lord, one faith, one baptism."

CHAPTER VII.

THE EUCHARIST—AGAPÆ—LORD'S SUPPER—FEAST OF
CHARITY (LOVE FEAST)—PASCHA (PASSOVER)—EAS-
TER—MASS.

Is the Lord's Supper a Sacrament?

WE here touch a theme prolific in titles, either in ancient
or modern times. Our own strictures thereon need be but brief,
since we shall freely cite the testimony of others respecting it,
and if our non-sacramentarian principle be the New Testament principle, the observances that have been called by the
names given at the head of this chapter are no more *sacraments*
than are the twelve sacraments of Damiani, and the seven of
the Papal See. There has been no less confusion and chaos
in the Church respecting a sacramental supper than respecting
a sacramental baptism.

The attempt to rear a sacramental superstructure, called by
the name of the "Lord's Supper," has indeed reared a fabric
"chaotic, vast, and vague," showing the workmanship of a
thousand *diverse*, if not *adverse* and *perverse*, workers in its
rearing, rather than the *oneness* of mind and wisdom of the
"wise Master Builder," the great Head of the Church. None
will claim that this statement is an exaggeration. Of the
nine terms used at the head of this chapter, to designate the
feasts of the early Christian Church and the later Papacy, the
first five given we understand to refer to one and the self-same
thing, viz., the *Love Feasts* of the early Church.

The other terms, *pascha*, etc., simply designate the Jewish
Passover, being the Hebrew word and two English words by
which it is translated, and the word *mass*, which latter word

designates that corruption of the Jewish Passover which has obtained among Papists. That the eucharist was simply a voluntary "feast of charity" in memorial of Christ and his love, and a token of fellowship among saints, especially as between the rich and the poor in earlier days, we have the ample testimony of the best historians of the Church. And that the Jewish Passover, in its annual observance by Judaizers, was sought to be engrafted upon the Christian Church, and by the name of *pascha* or *Easter* continues unto this day in some portions of the Church, we have equivalent ample testimony.

That there were the same collateral elements of Judaism and Gentilism manifested in different observances in the early churches no careful reader of the records of that era will question.

That the Jewish converts kept up the *pascha* (passover) for two or three centuries we have but to refer to Mosheim, and every other church historian, to show. And that (instead of the ten feasts of the Jewish dispensation, required to be observed) the Christians, both Jews and Gentiles, did also keep their "feasts of charity" (alias the *Lord's Supper*), the evidence appears conclusive. That Jude's "feast of charity," Paul's "Lord's Supper," and Luke's "breaking of bread," from "house to house," with "gladness and singleness of heart," refer to one and the same thing our greatest scholars now admit. Prof. John Morgan (of Oberlin), in his "Greek Exegesis," expressed his full assurance that they were one and the same.

If this be admitted, the query arises, did Jesus Christ enjoin a "daily" *sacramental* remembrance of him in "breaking bread from house to house"?

We remember that the Apostle Paul enjoins, "Whatsoever ye do, do it heartily, as to the Lord and not to men," but we are not aware that Christians have therefore assumed that every act is to be counted a *sacrament*. And yet the true Christian ideal is, that whenever we "eat or drink," we should "offer thanks," and with joy offer our *sacrament of gratitude* to God. "In everything we should give thanks," and our hearts be full of praise in remembrance of what Christ has done for us, granting us a deliverance infinitely greater than Israel received when delivered from Egyptian bondage.

Is it an abuse of Christ's words to enlarge their scope, and *literally* "as oft as we eat the bread" God gives, and "drink of the cup" that overflows from his bounty, remember Christ and what his death has purchased, and thus "show forth *the Lord's death* till he comes?" We candidly ask, could not Christ as properly have used these words if he had foreseen that the disciples would never again keep a passover festival, but would "daily" break the bread and drink the cup, especially with the poor and the needy coming into the fold, whom the rich could *and did* thus feed, "with gladness and singleness of heart?" Moreover, would not such a *feast of love*, or "Lord's Supper," be infinitely more honorable to Christ, and beneficent to man, than any mere formula or stated ceremonial imitation of no intrinsic worth to any one, could be? We think so, and here we have precisely *the kind* of Lord's Supper, or *eucharist*, or *agapœ*, or "feast of charity," that was so common in the early Christian Church. And, not only so, but the only kind then extant, save the pascha or Jewish passover, continued by Judaizers. Christ, as a Jew, did keep the Jewish passover, and took occasion at the last one he attended with his disciples to turn their attention away from past temporal deliverances, to the deliverance he would give them from sin and spiritual foes, through his death and resurrection. But even this was in connection with a full (passover) feast, and so all his disciples for ages kept their *love feasts* and their passovers in very nearly the same form.*

---

* *Christ copied the Jewish customs in the passover.*

The Jewish patriarch called together his household, and their immediate attendants, and himself officiated as priest in the celebration of the passover. Christ did the same.

He had no family but his attendant disciples, and these, as their head, he

And in the interval between Christ's resurrection and ascension, in the *New Dispensation* (for Christ's last passover feast was not in the New Dispensation), Christ drew near to his disciples by the Sea of Tiberias; and as they were fishers, and had toiled all night and taken nothing, they might well need food, so Christ asks, "Children, have ye here any meat?" They said "No." Jesus, being in the *resurrection* (as he was), could still realize their bodily wants, and knowing that "mercy" is better than "vain oblations" saith unto them, "*Come and dine!*" Here, then, is an example worthy of all acceptation, in this world where the *form and shadow* is so apt to usurp the place of the *substance*. It is indeed a question well worthy of frequent pondering whether the "*Lord's Dinner*" be not of much more practical importance, and its oft observance would not tend much more to Christ-likeness, than the innumerable church bickerings over the *Lord's Supper*.

Rev. ROBERT PATTERSON, of Chicago, on the occasion of a national thanksgiving, touched this matter discreetly and adroitly in an address to his church (see p. ——), one of the best lectures on the Christian's *real feast of love* (of more account than signs and shadows) ever written. It deserves transcribing in letters of light and placarding on the front of every pulpit and speaking-stand in Christendom. And if the tomes of dry

---

assembled and partook of the passover with them, himself, like the patriarch, distributing the bread and cup after the paschal lamb was eaten. Had he been about to institute a new ordinance for all his followers, he would have, unquestionably, called together *all* such followers, within reach, and set the example of the undivided communion and fellowship of saints in the beginning. But there were "above five hundred of the brethren" in and about Jerusalem at the time he partook of the last passover with the "twelve," yet only these, his regularly attendant "household," were with him at the feast. Moreover, the sisters in the faith are as much a part of Christ's believing household and of his Church as the brotherhood, but not one of these was invited to be present or was present at the final passover.

Did Christ intend to reject all the sisterhood from the communion of saints? In truth the assumption that Christ instituted a new ordinance for *all his* followers, with only a fraction of these present, is the most baseless (*i. e.*, bare of evidence in its favor) of any practice that has gained so long a standing in the Church.

theology and creeds that fill a volume, and the sacraments so punctiliously observed, should all give place to such a sacrament as he sets forth, of which *Christ* is the prime minister, it would be the greatest blessing the Church or the world ever experienced. It matters little when Christ invites us to a feast whether it be a *dinner* or a *supper* (as modern sacramentarians show by their example); the great thing is to spread the feast, and bid the poor and needy draw near, to help the lame to walk there, the deaf to hear, be eyes to the blind, and "bid the weak be strong."

That this is Christ's ideal of the true feast of fellowship, feast of charity, feast of love, rather than a *sacrament* with empty signs and tokens merely, is evident also from the fact that Christ has abundantly told us (John vi.) that his real supper "in his kingdom" is wholly spiritual. "The words that I speak unto you, they are spirit and they are life. The flesh profiteth nothing."

To eat symbolic "bread," or drink the material blood, or the "wine," what does this profit, if Christ be not seen by faith? and if he be seen by faith, of what avail the "flesh," or the external sign?

That Paul had in mind this very distinction between the sacramentarian's ritualistic idea of the acceptable sacrament and offering, and the Christian's idea, seems evident from his monition in 1 Cor. xi. 20, 21 :

"When ye come together therefore into one place, this is not to eat the Lord's Supper. [Why?] For in eating, every one taketh before other his own supper : and one is hungry, and another is drunken."

That is, the rich, who brought abundance to the feast, displayed their wealth by excess and riot in feasting, leaving the poor, who had little or nothing to bring to the supper, hunger and shame!

Paul suggests that if they would spread delicate feasts for *themselves* only, they (the rich) had "their own houses to eat and drink in," and should not come into the *love feast*, the assembly of the saints, where the "rich and the poor meet to-

gether," to make their display. They should rather feed the
poor first, thus "tarrying one for another," as was the case
when the right spirit pervaded the partakers of the feast.

This would render it a feast after the pattern and mind of
Christ, a "supper of the Lamb," and "acceptable and well-
pleasing to God."

Now Paul did not close his reprimand of the Corinthian
Church for their improper way of conducting the "Lord's
Supper" by telling them that it was merely designed to be a
"token" and "memorial" of Christ's death and resurrection,
and therefore they should only use *symbols* or *emblems* of his
body broken and his blood shed (no ancient feast or "sacrament" was thus minified), nor does he in the least inhibit
the feast: he only enjoins that they should see to it that the
rich and the poor all fare alike at this "Supper of the Lord,"
who died for all alike.

This Paul received "of the Lord," or (may we say) "heard
respecting the Lord" (for Paul was not at the last passover
Christ ate with his disciples), that Christ, the same night in
which he was betrayed, "took bread, and when he had given
thanks, he brake it, and said, Take, eat; this is my body which
is broken *for you:* this do in remembrance of me!" and thus
they ate a full feast. No longer were they to remember
Moses, and the bondage their fathers escaped, but henceforth
turn their attention to the Great Deliverer from Satan's yoke
and sin's captivity. Christ had said (not in the form of command but thus), "as oft as ye do it, do it in remembrance of
me."

Did Paul change Christ's "as oft" to a specific command,
"Do this (oft) or at intervals, in remembrance of Christ?"
We beg leave to suggest that Paul was not so prone to establish a ceremonial law (in his inspired writings we mean), but
warns against "ordinances," "days," and "meats," and
"times," and "seasons," from the beginning to the end.
Read his letters to the churches once more and see. The inspiration of 1 Cor. xi. is not different from the inspiration of

Ephesians ii. and iii. and Col. ii. and iii.—*i. e.*, the same Spirit inspired each.

Nor does his inspiration exceed that of Christ the Master. Paul should be understood, then, as simply rehearsing Christ's instruction to eat and drink henceforth in remembrance of Christ and not of Moses, and after the pattern of Christ's dispensing love to his family of disciples. Their "giving of thanks" now (not annually nor casually), but daily and constantly, should be in view of what Christ had done, the Great Redeemer and Purchaser of all blessings temporal and spiritual. Hence the Christian expresses these "thanks" *every time* he comes around a table spread with God's bounty, and thus, if *he* is sanctified in heart, *every meal becomes a sacrament.* So it was with the converts following the Pentecostal effusion of the Holy Spirit. "Daily," from house to house, they "brake bread, one with another, with gladness and singleness of heart."

This was in harmony with the Christian ideal: Christ all in all, in all and through all, and above all; all principalities and powers, and rites and ceremonies, and dispensations and seasons, being now subjected to him, and lost in him.

Moses gave the passover ; it pointed to *Christ, our Passover.* The feast continued until Christ, our Passover, came, and *now* to keep up a *type* or *symbol* after the *real* Passover has come is like a finger-board pointing the wrong way, and, therefore, away from our goal. It is like asking for moonlight after the sunlight has come.

And Paul (1 Cor. x.) no less plainly than Christ (John vi.) assures us that Christ's true Passover, true Supper, and our true "communion" therein, *is spiritual.* Paul says (1 Cor. x. 15, 17), "I speak as to *wise men :* judge ye what I say. The cup of blessing which we bless, is it not the communion of the blood of Christ? The bread which we break, is it not the communion of the body of Christ? For we, being many, *are one bread and one body ; for we are all partakers of that one bread.*" Is not this the spiritual communion of Christ's spiritual household? And this Paul afterwards compares to Israel "after the flesh," all partaking of the altar, so we *spiritually*, and only thus, *all partake of Christ.*

In this sense only are we the "one bread," and the "one body" of Christ.

We have our "*communion*" then within ourselves (with Christ), and not in any heathen temple (of which Paul was speaking), nor at any mere earthly carnal board.

Christ's bread is the "bread that came down from heaven" "to give life unto the world." What Christian needs be told that the communion of the "body of Christ" and of the "blood of Christ" is not physical, *i. e.*, literal in that sense, nor *symbolic*, if real, but "*in the spirit*," and not in the letter?

But recurring to the actual festivals of the early Church we are aware that many have *presumed* that there were two such feasts; the one the early Church designating by the title of the "Lord's Supper," the other by the title of *agapæ* or love feast. And our Methodist brethren within the past century have, in many places, retained the two; the one, the "supper," they deemed a real *sacrament*, the other only a voluntary expression of Christian fellowship, love, and good-will. Many have supposed that the same distinction between the two was known in the early Church, the one being observed as a sacrament, the other merely as a voluntary free-will offering, in token of their love to Christ and to one another.*

---

* If any distinction of feasts did at all exist, as we have before said, it was, on the part of the Judaizers, on the one hand a continuance of the passover, which has now become the Papal mass, and the Church of England Easter (annually observed), for the term Easter, found once only in the New Testament, is rendered direct from the word *Pascha* therein found. These Judaizers did, of course, change the intent of this feast, making it annually a feast unto the Lord, and not to Moses, but to what extent this Judaizing portion of the Church observed also the eucharistic feast of charity, at stated times, for Christian fellowship and the benefit of the poor among them, doth not clearly appear in historic records, since modern church historians have so utterly confounded both the *pascha* and the *eucharist* of the early Church with what they without warrant term *The Lord's Supper* as now observed in the symbol.

But who does not see that the objects, or design of each, are thus made to flow into one, and become precisely homogeneous? and moreover he that will search the record will see that they became in early ages precisely one and the same. Neander, in one instance, confuses himself in trying to find a distinction between these in the early record, but, we believe, in every other instance, permits their identity to stand apparent to all.

Mosheim utterly confounds the *pascha*, the Jewish Passover, long retained among the Jewish converts, with the Lord's Supper, and indeed only here can he find a Lord's Supper, if he insist that there be one separate from the *agapæ*, or early *feast of charity*.

This *pascha*, observed in precisely Jewish style, for seven days, and commencing on the 14th day of the 1st month, the month Nisan or Abib, and only changed to interpolate one day's remembrance of Christ's resurrection by a joyful feast on that day, rather than the "unleavened bread and bitter herbs," was kept up two or three centuries, and soon occasioned bitter controversies respecting the proper day on which to remember the resurrection of Christ, as we shall see when we quote Mosheim's testimony respecting it.

We first quote Neander's testimony respecting the *agapæ* or love feasts, which, if they be not found to be a *real sacrament*, of the Lord's appointment, we shall have to recur to the Jewish pascha, observed only once each year, as the only alternative if such sacrament must be found.

As to the *identity* of the *agapæ* and Lord's Supper, Neander thus speaks (vol. i. p. 327):

"So long as the *agapæ* and the *Lord's Supper* were united together, the celebration formed no part of the divine service!" Mark it was wholly separate from the religious convocation, and was simply the spread board of the after-noon conclave of Christian kindred and friends at their homes! But Neander continues, "This (divine) service was held in the morning, and not until towards evening did the Church reassemble at the common love feast, and for the celebration of the Supper."

The reader will note that here is a partial assuming that

the one feast consisted of two parts, the *love feast* and th
Lord's Supper; as though the Lord's Supper itself were no
a *love feast* and an expression of fellowship and unity of spiri
of which this eating and drinking together was designed to b
the exhibition and proof. This, besides remembering Christ
as in all things else, filled the great design, provided charit
was especially shown to the poor on these occasions.

Hear Tertullian on the *agapæ* in apologizing for the Chris
tian customs:

> "The cause of the supper (*agapæ* is his theme) being a worthy one, esti
> mate the propriety with which it is managed (see Paul, 1 Cor. xi.) as it
> religious end demands. . . . No one approaches the table till prayer has firs
> been offered (the universal custom at all meals in those days); as much is eater
> as suffices to satisfy the demands of hunger—as much is drunk as consists witl
> sobriety."

Was there aught in all this that resembles the modern cus
tom of *communicating* by signs or tokens with bits of bread
and the sip of wine? And does not the difference of custom
betoken a different intent in the customs of that day and
this?

The primitive Christians, Gentiles as well as Jews, con
ducted their feasts very much in the same manner (as well as
their baptisms); hence, when Neander says, without citing
one text as proof, "The celebration of the two symbols of
Christian communion" (it should be of Christian *non-commu-
nion*), "baptism and the Lord's Supper, belonged to the unchangeable plan of the Christian Church, as framed by its
Divine Founder." If he had said they belonged to the unchanged forms of Judaism or Gentile ante-Christian festivals,
transferred to Christianity, he would have much more nearly
hit the point and declared an undeniable truth. Let Neander himself be our witness to this. Hear him ("Planting
and Training of the Church," p. 103):

> "As to the celebration of the Holy Supper, it continued to be connected
> with the common meal, in which *all members of one family joined,* as in the
> *primitive Jewish Church* and agreeably to its first institution."

There, reader, is not that proof of unchanged Judaism engrafted upon Christianity? But hear him again (p. 100, *ibid.*):

"Some have endeavored to find, in 1 Cor. v. 7, a reference to a *Christian Passover*, to be celebrated in a Christian sense, with a decided reference to Christian truth, but we can find a reference only to a Jewish Passover, which was still celebrated by the Jewish Christians. . . . This practice of outward Judaism he (Paul) applies in a spiritualized sense to Christians. '. . . Purify yourselves from the old leaven . . . for Christ has been offered as our Paschal Lamb. Therefore as men purified from sin by Christ, our Paschal Lamb, let us celebrate the feast, *not after the manner of the Jews*, but so celebrate it that we may be a mass purified in heart from the leaven of sin."

Now these words of Neander teach that the Jewish Passover was simply engrafted by transfer into the Christian dispensation with some change of idea and verbiage to suit the Christian rather than the Jewish ages. It shows, also, that the Gentile Christians, by degrees, came to conform more and more to the Jewish mode of conducting religious festivals, for the *agapœ* were of Gentile origin, while the *pascha* was "of the Jews."

Hence mark the reasoning, as drawn from the historic record given by Neander:

(*a*) The passover was still celebrated by Jewish Christians. (*b*) Christians celebrated their *agapœ* at the same meal with the Lord's Supper. (*c*) They celebrated the "Holy Supper" precisely in the same manner as the Jews their passover, *i. e.*, as families; or at most as contiguous parts of the same congregation of believers. What is there in all this to justify modern efforts to enforce a union of *all* Christians around the sacraments? (*d*) The Jewish Passover was *spiritualized* by the Apostle Paul—1 Cor. v. 7. Hence there is no Christianized outward passover or agapæ. (*e*) The *agapœ* was to be temporary, but the Supper ("spiritualized") to be *unchangeable!*

Now if any reader, either from history or from the logic above employed, which is Neander's, to an iota, will unravel the web or solve the mystery, and tell us which is the Lord's Supper, and which the love feast, and which the Jewish

Passover, we will confess the gratitude we owe for kindly assistance in the time of need.

But Mosheim does not hesitate to tell us that the celebration of the "Lord's Supper" and that of the "Jewish Passover" was precisely one and the same thing in a large portion of the Christian Church, especially in the second century. Hear him (vol. i. p. 523):

"There arose toward the close of the second century, between the Christians of Asia Minor and those of other parts, particularly such as were of the Roman Church, a violent contention respecting a matter that related mainly to the form of religion, or divine worship, a thing in itself truly of light moment, but in the opinion of the disputants of very great importance. . . . The Asiatic Christians were accustomed to celebrate their passover—that is, the paschal feast, which it was at this time usual with the Christians to observe in commemoration of the institution of the Lord's Supper—on the 14th day of the first Jewish month—that is to say, *at the same time when the Jews ate their paschal lamb*. This custom they stated, themselves, to have derived from the Apostles Philip and John. . . . But the rest of the Christians, as well in Asia as in Europe and Africa, deemed it irreligious to terminate a feast of the great week (the passover week) before the day devoted to the commemoration of the Saviour's return to life, and therefore deferred the celebration of their passover or paschal feast, until the night immediately preceding the anniversary of Christ's resurrection from the dead. These alleged the authority of Peter and Paul. . . . Hence arose another difference greater still. As the Asiatic Christians always commemorated our Lord's return to life on the third day after their partaking of the paschal supper, it was a circumstance liable to occur (and must occur) that they kept the anniversary of Christ's resurrection, which soon acquired and still retains the denomination of *Pascha* or *Easter*, on a different day from the first day of the week, which is commonly termed *Sunday*—whereas the other Christians, as well those of the East as of the West, made it a rule to hold their annual celebration of our blessed Saviour's triumph over the grave on no other day (*i. e.*, of the week) than that it actually occurred, viz.: the first day of the week."

The reader will see that the one class followed the day of the month—the third after the 14th of Nisan—the other the day of the week; hence the constant collision on this momentous matter.

And let the Christian reader, bewildered by Episcopacy, Popery, Judaism, or any other sacramentarian or ritualistic fantasy, see, in language that cannot be gainsayed—carrying

demonstration at every point—the fact that so far as the
Lord's Supper was observed at all by these Christians, it was
simply observing the Jewish Passover—called by that name
then—observed on the same week, beginning on the same day
of the month, *once each year*, and continuing through the same
period of time, *one day* of that time being set apart to commemorate Christ's resurrection, and about this they differed
and continually quarrelled.   This, moreover, was called
Pascha or *Easter*, and was the *only day* that had any special
reference to Christ *in the whole seven*.   He that cannot see in
this simply the Jewish Passover perpetuated, and thereby
what is termed the *Lord's Supper*, it seems cannot see what is
perfectly palpable in its very face!   Now, why do not all
church historians, like Mosheim, tell us *how* the *Lord's Supper*,
as a *sacrament*, was introduced into the Christian Church?
True, it would amply expose the Judaism of its origin.   And
we presume that even the above frank exposé of the union of
Judaism (the passover and the Lord's Supper) is expunged
from later editions of Mosheim.

Is it not time that the Protestant Reformation had really
escaped from Judaism, at least, since Popery has only made
it indefinitely more a yoke of unparalleled bondage to the
grossest added superstitions—teaching that in eating this
sacrament we eat the "body and blood, and soul and divinity
of Jesus Christ, without which there is no salvation to the
soul?"

And this pretence of making use of the Lord's Supper to
show charity for saints, and all that is said about counting
others worthy to come to the Lord's table *with us*, is both
arrogating a Popish prerogative, and driving a spear to the
very vitals of charity—since more religious feuds and fires of
strife are kindled over it than over aught else pertaining to
the worship and customs of the churches.   All bigotry fastens
first on this (or baptism, its assumed antecedent), and all religious spleen and much personal rancor make use of this as
the dagger to thrust an enemy through.

20

If any one is worthy—*i. e.*, will come to Christ—Christ will receive; that is enough. What are we that we should sit as judges one over another, and make it a law that they must be received by us also! The whited sepulchre is the most apt to set at naught his fellow. He comes forward with superstition solemnized on his very countenance, and seeking to cover his hypocrisy with the saint's garb and atone for his sins with sacraments, would deceive the Almighty as well as contemn his fellow-men (the very elect) if he might.

Are not the great sacramentarian churches simply vessels of corruption, moral rottenness painted in gorgeous colors? Yet the Greek Church has 150 or more *holy days* (more "holy" days than holy bishops, we fear!), and both Greek and Papal Churches more saints' days than the secular days of the year. Is this charity, thus robbing the poor worshipper of his time as well as tithes? Which will God choose, mercy or sacraments? Let us have charity indeed in feeding the poor, and not its lying pretences, while peeling and robbing society!

Then will that which is perfect come! The Sun of Righteousness will shine in splendor upon the earth. When Christ is in you, the shadow pointing forward or backward, like type or tombstone, may pass away. The "Son of God is come," then let the emblem cease, and what the loss? O Lord God, when will thy churches prize that which thou prizest, and cease the thought that thou art enamored of a punctilious (yet superstitious) routine of ceremonies?

To this exposé of the origin and meaning of the *pascha* and *agapæ* of the early Church agree the words of Christ—Luke xxii. 15–18 and 28–30:

"With desire I have desired (*i. e.*, with great longings I have desired) to eat this PASSOVER with you before I suffer. For I say unto you, I will not any more eat thereof until it be fulfilled in the kingdom of God."

Now what is there in these words that sounds like teaching that the passover was then and there fulfilled, in the middle of that feast, and that a new feast was instituted before that feast concluded? Not the shadow of a hint in that direction. We do not forget that Matthew says, "*As they were eating*, Jesus took bread and brake it," etc.; but that is precisely the way a feast is *continued* or prolonged, for the occasion at least, and not the way to end it and establish a new one! Moses, in establishing the passover, was not thus indefinite. Christ says, in the 16th verse, "I will not any more eat thereof (*i. e.*, of the passover) until it be fulfilled in the kingdom of God." As much as to say, I will then drink the new wine of the gospel kingdom with you, and I will give to you the "heavenly manna," and ye shall "sup with me and I with you" in the coming kingdom. To this also agree the 28th to 30th verse, as soon we may see.

That this "kingdom of God" is the kingdom about to appear in glory on the earth, the 18th verse fully establishes. "For I say unto you, I will not drink of the fruit of the vine until the kingdom of God shall come." Now this form of phrase is never used to designate the passing away of all earthly things, and the transplanting of the whole Church in the "upper kingdom"—that is termed Christ's coming to take his saints to himself, that they may see his glory there. But all promises of "supping with Christ," "drinking the wine new with him," etc., refer to the fulness of Christ received by his saints here—else you take away the Christian's militant kingdom. Hence when Christ says, 28th to 30th verse:

"Ye are they which have continued with me in my temptations, and I appoint unto you a kingdom as my Father hath appointed unto me, that ye may eat and drink at my table in my kingdom, and sit on thrones, judging the twelve tribes of Israel."

Now the "table" is to be as literal and external as the "thrones," and no more so, and none interpret the thrones as external, but spiritual.

And the Apocalyptic seer—Rev. vii.—will tell us who these twelve tribes of Israel were (they were *all on earth*); and the twelve apostles, by their teachings and doctrines, ruled men, just as Christ, by the Father's appointment, ruled the Church. He planted and continues to rule it *by his Spirit* to the end. So we see the "eating and drinking" here promised (*at this very passover*), of Christ's disciples with himself and with each other in that new "coming kingdom of God," was to be *altogether* SPIRITUAL. Thus are we to "eat at Christ's table" in Christ's "kingdom," while, by the *power of the Christian life* and the *energy of the Holy Ghost*, we *sit on the thrones judging* the twelve tribes of Israel, and even the "world" and the "angels" of God.

Having thus presented, in brief, our view of the nature of Christ's kingdom and the "supper" therein to be eaten, our brevity may be excused by herewith presenting the amply corroborative testimony of others.

OTHER WITNESSES.

Were not our space limited we would gladly cite the whole of Robert Barclay's unanswerable refutation of the claims and pretensions of sacramentarians, but the history of the inception, and spread, and excessively perverting tendency of the sacramentarian idea, as given by John Allen, an English Friend, in his exceedingly able work entitled *State Churches*, will be still more satisfactory and instructive to the reader.

ORIGIN AND ADVANCE OF PAPAL AND PROTESTANT SACRAMENTARIANISM,

FROM JOHN ALLEN IN "STATE CHURCHES."

"At the feast of the passover, it was customary among the Jews for the master of the house to take unleavened bread, then giving thanks to God, to break it and give to the family; likewise to take the cup, give thanks, and distribute it to the household. This our Lord fulfilled according to the law; but at the last passover supper he also drew their attention from the paschal lamb and the deliverance of their forefathers, the objects originally commemorated by the passover, to the breaking of his own body, and to the deliverance of man from sin, being the great purposes typified by both.

"He therefore directed that 'as often as' they who were Jews observed the rite in future, they should do it 'in remembrance' of him,

who was 'the Lamb of God, that taketh away the sin of the world.'
While the writer would acknowledge his reverent sense of the inestimable benefits which mankind have received by the coming of the Lord Jesus Christ, by his death as a sacrifice for the sins of the world, and by the gift of the Holy Spirit purchased thereby, he would, nevertheless, see the mists of superstition and ignorance dispelled, which have obscured these great doctrines, that the glorious light of truth may be more clearly seen, and that the tenfold husks which have enveloped the living kernel may be removed, and the value of the inward substance more fully accepted, appreciated, and enjoyed.

"The practice of breaking bread and drinking wine together, as a religious ceremony, prevailed extensively in the early periods of Christianity, and was observed in various modes, according to the views of different churches. And this observance has been for ages, touching its nature, effects, and mode of celebration, the cause of more bitter controversy between Roman Catholics and Protestants and of more blood being shed than any other matter of difference.*

---

* Every reader of history is familiar with the so-called *Thirty Years' War*, which raged in the heart of Europe from 1618 to 1648. It was a *religious* war, and involved the great mass of Papists and Protestants,—the former under their *Catholic League*, the latter in their *Evangelical Union*. Schiller, in his history of this war, says, "From the interior of Bohemia to the mouth of the Scheldt, from the banks of the Po to the coasts of the Baltic, it desolated countries, destroyed harvests, and laid towns and villages in ashes; extinguished, during half a century, the rising progress of civilization in Germany; and reduced the improving manners of the people to their ancient barbarism."

In the Electorate of Hesse, seventeen towns, forty-seven castles, and three hundred villages had been burnt to the ground. In the Duchy of Wurtemberg, eight towns, forty-five villages, and thirty-six thousand houses, had been laid in ashes, and seventy thousand hearth-fires completely extinguished. Seven churches, and four hundred and forty-four houses, had been burned at Eichsted. Many towns that had escaped destruction were almost depopulated. Three hundred houses stood empty at Nordheim; and more than two hundred had been pulled down at Gottingen, merely to serve for fuel. The wealthy city of Augsburg, which contained eighty thousand inhabitants before the war, had only eighteen thousand left when it closed; and this town, like many others, has never recovered its former prosperity. No less than *thirty thousand* villages and hamlets are said to have been destroyed; in many others the population had entirely died out; and the unburied corpses of the last victims of violence or disease were left exposed about the streets or fields, to be mangled and torn to pieces by birds and beasts of prey.

Germany is said to have lost *twelve millions* of inhabitants by the contest, and the population, which amounted to sixteen millions when the war broke out, counted hardly more than four millions when the war closed. The Duchy of Wurtemberg was reduced from half a million to forty-eight thousand;

"For the long period of nearly two hundred years from the time of Henry IV., about A. D. 1400, to the reign of James I., it was made the principal test of religious faith, both in England and on the continent of Europe; and the Roman Catholics more especially, but not exclusively, when they possessed the chief secular power, condemned and burnt as heretics, without distinction of age or sex, those who differed from their own views upon it. The grand question was, not whether the rite ought to be retained or not, for in the former opinion most coincided, but as to *the real presence,* that is, whether the words pronounced by the priest, 'This is my body,' are to be taken literally or figuratively; or whether they did or did not convert the bread into the real body of Christ. To prove the sentiments of the accused, the most minute distinctions and the most subtle interrogatories were framed; which often tended to confound both parties, and to involve them in wide contradictions and fearful absurdities. Yet on the issue depended life or death to hundreds if not thousands! In consequence of a difference of opinion on this mysterious question many of the most eminent Christians of

Bohemia from three millions to eight hundred and ninety thousand, and Saxony and Brunswick suffered in the same proportion.

In the last campaign of the war, the French and Swedes burned no less than a hundred villages in Bavaria alone; and the skulls of St. Cosmas and St. Damianus had to be sent from Bremen to Munich, in order to console Maximilian for the ruin he had brought over his beautiful country. But even these pitiable relics failed to allay the fears of the unhappy elector; the share which he had taken in bringing about this desolating contest pressed heavily on the latter years of his life. In vain he prayed and fasted; the dreadful future was constantly before his sight, and the once valiant soldier and ambitious prince died at last a trembling and despairing bigot.

The crimes and cruelties of which the troops were frequently guilty would appear almost incredible, were they not attested in a manner to render doubt altogether impossible. But independent of private accounts, we have various reports from the authorities of towns, villages and provinces, complaining of the atrocities committed by the lawless soldiery. Peaceful peasants were hunted for mere sport, like the beasts of the forest; citizens were nailed up against doors and walls, and fired at like targets; while horsemen and Croats tried their skill at striking off the heads of young children at a blow! Ears and noses were cut off, eyes were scooped out, and the most horrible tortures contrived to extract money from the sufferers, or to make them disclose where property was concealed! Women were exposed to every species of indignity; they were collected in bands, and driven, like slaves, into the camps of the ruffian soldiery, and men had to fly from their homes to escape witnessing the dishonor to which their wives and daughters were subjected!

Houses and villages were burnt out of mere wantonness, and the wretched inhabitants too often forced into the flames, to be consumed along with their dwellings. Amid these scenes of horror, intemperance, dissipation, and profligacy were carried to the highest pitch. Intoxication frequently prevented

Europe were consigned to the stake—a dreadful result, which could not have been accomplished without that unscriptural union or alliance of the secular and ecclesiastical power. . . . Whatever was condemned as heresy was looked on as a sin against God, *and the worst of crimes.* To make it appear the more heinous offence, public burning was judged the most proper punishment, being also a representation of everlasting burning.*

"It was a common practice at the execution of heretics to fasten about their necks scraps of scripture and other evidences of their supposed guilt found in their possession, that the whole might be burnt together. Of all the matters which in England were condemned as heresies, *and punished in this awful manner,* the differences of opinion with respect to the bread and wine have been by far the most prominent and fruitful of victims. Manifold as these differences were, and mysterious as were the points in question, excuses were rarely admitted, at the time of the

---

the Austrian General, Goltz, from giving out the countersign; and General Banner was, on one occasion, so drunk for four days together that he could not receive the French ambassador, Beauregard, who had an important message to deliver. "Such was the state of triumphant crime," says a writer of the period, "that many, driven to despair, denied even the existence of a Deity, declaring that, if there were a God in heaven, he would not fail to destroy with thunder and lightning such a world of sin and wickedness."

The peasants, expelled from their homes, enlisted with the oppressors, in order to inflict upon others the sufferings which they had themselves been made to endure. The fields were allowed to run waste, and the absence of industry on one side, added to destruction on the other, soon produced famine which, as usual, brought infections and pestilential diseases in its train. In 1635 there were not hands enough left at Schweidnitz to bury the dead, and the town of Ohlau had lost its last citizen. Want augmented crime, even where an increase was thought impossible. In many places hunger had overcome all repugnance to human flesh, and the tales of cannibalism handed down to us are of far too horrible a nature to be here repeated.

The cup of human suffering was full even to overflowing, and the very aspect of the land was undergoing a rapid change. Forests sprung up during the contest, and covered entire districts, which had been in full cultivation before the war; and wolves and other beasts of prey took possession of the deserted haunts of men. This was particularly the case in Brunswick, Brandenburg and Pomerania, where heaps of ashes in the midst of wildernesses served long afterwards to mark the spots where peace and civilization had once flourished. In many parts of the country, the ruins of castles and stately edifices still attest the fury with which the war was carried on; and on such spots tradition generally points out the surrounding forests, as occupying the sites of fertile fields, whence the lordly owners of the mansions derived food and subsistence for themselves and their numerous retainers.

* Now which will the reader judge to be the most justly obnoxious to the "everlasting burning," the judges or their victims in these cases?

Reformation, by the combined politico-ecclesiastical authorities, and the bloody statutes 'de hæretico comburendo' were enforced with rigid and dreadful severity.

.   .   .   .

"The earliest Christian writers scarcely allude to this rite. . . . Tertullian speaks of the celebration of the eucharist in connection with the meals of the early Christians; as we read of the 'breaking of bread' in private houses and public assemblies. Irenæus contended, about the year 200, that the eucharist should be regarded as 'a sacrifice;' thus opening a floodgate through which the Church was deluged with error. . . . Public prayers were followed by oblations of bread, wine, and other things; every one offering according to his ability; and partly from hence, all those who were in necessity derived their subsistence. . . . The wine, in many churches, was mingled with water, and the bread was divided into several portions; some being carried to the sick or absent members of the church, as a token of love and fellowship. The ministers, likewise, received from individuals meal or flour, with which a large loaf was made, called *panis dominicus* (the priest's loaf), for use in the communion, and for distribution to the people. Participation in the ceremony was, even then, by many considered essential to salvation, and was by Tertullian first called a 'sacrament.'

"A writer in the *Encyclopedia Britannica* thus describes the celebration of the eucharist by early Christians in some places: 'After the customary oblations had been made, the deacon brought water to the bishops and presbyters standing around the table, to wash their hands, according to the language of the Psalmist, 'I will wash mine hands in innocency, and so will I compass thy altar, O Lord.' Then the deacon cried out, 'Embrace and kiss each other,' which being done, the whole congregation prayed for the peace and welfare of the church, for the tranquillity and repose of the world, for wholesome weather, and for all ranks and degrees of men. After this followed mutual salutations of the ministers and people; and then the bishop or presbyter, having sanctified the elements by a solemn benediction, broke the bread and gave it to the deacon, who delivered it to the communicants, and next handed them the cup. During the time of administration, they sang hymns and psalms; and having concluded with prayer and thanksgiving, the people saluted each other with a kiss of peace, and the assembly broke up. In consequence of abuses which crept in, the parting kiss was discontinued after a time.'

". . . . As the churches in North Africa were the first to bring prominently into notice the necessity of infant baptism, so in connection with it they introduced the communion of infants; for as they neglected to distinguish with sufficient clearness between the sign and the divine thing which it signified, and as they understood all that is said in the sixth chapter of John's gospel concerning eating the flesh and drinking the blood of Christ to refer to the outward participation of the Lord's Supper, they concluded that this, from the earliest age, was absolutely necessary to the attainment of salvation.

". . . . The eucharist was generally received once a week, or oftener, in the second and third centuries, by the diligent and zealous. Ambrose seemed to regard every celebration to be as great a mystery and miracle as the incarnation! The idea being now generally received that this rite was a 'sacrifice,' altars were substituted for tables, and other sacrificial appendages followed. Priestcraft found in this idea a strong support, and grasped it with eagerness.

"The sign of the cross was introduced. Pomp and splendor were displayed, and rich vessels of gold and silver were deemed necessary articles. The word 'mass' was not known in the primitive Church, nor is it found in the works of Augustine, Chrysostom, and other writers of the fourth century. They termed the ceremony 'the supper of the Lord,' 'the mystical supper or table,' 'the eucharist,' 'celebration of the sacrament,' 'the Lord's board,' 'oblation,' 'communion,' 'mystery,' etc. Certain Christians, called *Aquarii*, used water at the eucharist instead of wine. The Ebionites did the same. Others used water mingled with wine, which was said to denote the union of the Church with Christ. This was the general practice. Some substituted milk, honey, or grapes for wine. The Ascondnitæ and Messalians, or Euchites, held that the sacrament of bread and wine did neither good nor harm and rejected its use. They subsisted through several hundred years. . . .

". . . . At a council, held in 506, the laity were ordered to communicate three times in a year under penalty of not being reputed Catholic Christians. A provincial council at Cæsarea Augusta, in 519, pronounced a curse upon those receiving the sacrament who ate it not in the church.

"The eucharist had already been administered to infants; it was now given to dead persons. It formed a part of the divine worship, was used to consecrate every religious act, and was occasionally celebrated at the tombs of martyrs, whence followed *masses for the dead*.

"The bread and wine were held up to the view of the people before distribution, that they might gaze on it with reverence. The bread was usually broken to signify the breaking of the body of Christ. At other times it was pierced with a spear and said to be immolated. With the remains of the eucharist, and with other oblations, it had long been usual to hold occasionally the 'agapæ, or feasts of charity,' being a liberal collation of the rich to feed the poor; but this practice giving rise to various abuses was prohibited in the sixth and seventh centuries.

"THE CANON OF THE MASS, instituted by Pope Gregory the Great about the year 620, for the celebration of the eucharist, occasioned a remarkable change by the 'introduction of a lengthened, pompous, and magnificent ritual.'

"It was still generally performed in the language of each particular country, and the first time it was openly said in Latin appears to have been at the Council of Constance, by the Pope's legate, in 681.

"The administration of the sacrament was now deemed the most solemn and important part of public devotion, and was everywhere embellished with a variety of senseless appendages. The burning of incense received general sanction. Charlemagne made some attempts to stem the torrent of superstition, but with little success.

"To the ceremonies of trying the guilt or innocence of individuals by cold water, by single combat, by the fire ordeal, and by the cross, was added the celebration of the eucharist, and other rites, to give to these barbarisms a religious and imposing aspect.

"During the same period it was degraded and profaned by being introduced occasionally into ridiculous and absurd festivals, *instituted in imi-*

tation of the heathen, with no higher object than to promote sport and di
version at the cost of religion, and even of common decency.*

". . . . The superstitious custom of performing solitary or secre
masses by the priest alone, on behalf of souls said to be detained in pur
gatory, was introduced by degrees, and proved a rich source of emolumen
to the clergy. There was also the dry mass, without the bread and win
or consecration; and the two-fold or three-fold mass, several being
thrown into one service, and all being celebrated with one canon; thi
was apparently a device of the priests to save labor.

"Voluntary oblations of money were sometimes made by those who
received the sacraments; the priests were prohibited from encouraging
this usage, but it became a rule, and was expected as such. In some
countries it still prevails. The Popish priests do not usually require
payment for the sacraments; they do not sell, but they accept gifts, either
for themselves, or for some miraculous image, or for the souls in purgatory, for which masses and other oblations are necessary. . . .

". A canon of one of the provincial councils enjoined that baptized infants should receive communion before they partook of any nourishment.
The priests also were required to administer it *in the morning* before they
tasted other food. The practice of giving the bread and wine to children is said not to have been abrogated in France till the twelfth century; in Germany it was retained later; and in the Eastern churches it
is still continued. And great importance was attached to the kind of
cup used in performing the ceremony. In connection with this, Boni-
face, the martyr, said, about 750, that formerly golden priests made use of
wooden cups; but now, on the contrary, wooden priests used golden
chalices. The Triburentian Council decreed that no priest, by any
means, presume to make the sacred mystery of the body and blood of our
Lord in cups or chalices of wood.

.   .   .   .

"For a very long period the sacrament of the bread and wine was
viewed and employed by the great body of Catholics as a sort of charm
or amulet, to heal bodily diseases in men, or in cattle; to insure success,
and avert calamities, as well as to administer truth to the soul. Voy-
agers carried with them consecrated bread as a pledge for their preservation. It was often administered with absolution to the sick or dying, and
was then termed the *viaticum,* or provision for their journey into the next
world. It was sometimes even buried with the corpse. These notions
were warmly urged by the corrupt and selfish priests.

"It had been common to pronounce the consecration of the eucharist
audibly and intelligibly, that the people might hear, and answer 'Amen,'
but in the tenth century the contrary practice of 'intonation,' or *pronounc-
ing the services in a low voice,* began to be introduced to render them more
mysterious.

"It had been the ancient practice for the people, or laity, to partake
of both the bread and the wine, which was termed 'receiving the sacrament in both kinds,' but about 1100 was introduced a new custom, which
in 1414 was solemnly enjoined by the Council of Constance, that the

---

* So anti-Christian secret societies (as Masonry, in some of its highest degrees) make an equally profane use of sacraments.—AUTHOR.

priests should restrict the wine to themselves, and distribute the bread or wafer alone to the people. This practice has proved another cause of great contention.

"The oblations of common bread by the people for the purpose of the eucharist, having commenced at a very early period, were generally continued until the eleventh or twelfth century, when wafers and unleavened bread were introduced by the priests, under the plea of decency and respect, the people being ordered to bring a penny each, instead of the former contribution. The Eastern churches still used leavened bread, and great disputes followed. In the ancient Church the bread had usually been broken into many parts, that each one of the people might partake. Afterwards, it was broken by the Greeks into four parts, by the Latins into three, and by some other churches into nine parts.

"The large wafer, or thin, small cake now used in the Romish churches, is still broken into three parts, to retain a shadow of the ancient custom, but the people generally do not partake. At one time all who attended divine worship were expected to share in the eucharist; but by degrees this was relaxed, and those who would not partake of it were allowed a sort of consecrated bread, called 'eulogia.' This appears to have been introduced in the ninth century.

"At length arose in the eleventh century the famous controversy respecting the manner in which the body of Christ was believed to be partaken of in the eucharist. Christian professors had long differed on this mysterious subject; but an opinion gained ground that the figurative interpretation ought to be dismissed; and after the consecration the same identical body of Christ, that was born of the Virgin, that suffered upon the cross, and that was raised from the dead, was in reality present.

"Others declared that none but saints and believers received the body of Christ in the sacrament; while a few others held that the bread and wine were merely signs and symbols of Christ's absent flesh and blood, which were partaken of by faith. This controversy, involving a religious and mysterious question of great moment in their view, was carried on very fiercely for some ages between the different parties and their leaders. . . .

"Absolution, or the remission of sins, was generally understood to attend the worthy reception of 'the sacrament;' these being deemed 'the keys' given to Peter and his successors. Salvation was said to be impossible without a participation in these 'tremendous mysteries;' albeit at first the form of absolution was imperative or precative, not indicative and absolute. Thus the *one great offering* was overlooked, and religion made a thing of rote, to be shared equally by the righteous and the wicked!

". . . It was not until the Council of Lateran, in 1215, that the great question was decided, when Innocent III., that bold and unscrupulous pontiff, sanctioned the notion of the 'real presence,' and established the term 'transubstantiation,' asserting it in gross and positive terms, as the authorized doctrine of the Romish Church. This doctrine teaches the duty of paying divine worship to Christ, under the form of the consecrated bread or host (from *hostia*, a victim), and inculcates the idea of a propitiatory sacrifice; Christ being understood to be truly and properly offered up on every occasion of the mass being performed. Who may set bounds to the authority of men that declared that they had power to produce at their own bidding the Deity himself?

"The same Council of Lateran reduced the obligation to receiv
the eucharist to *once in the year*, at Easter, when every man and ever
woman were enjoined to confess all their sins to the priest. This ru
was afterwards made canon law. Private and solitary masses soo
became general, and such continued the state of things till th
Reformation.

"A new train of ceremonies and institutions followed the notion o
transubstantiation, in honor of what was blasphemously called the *deifie
bread*. Hence arose the customs of kneeling and adoring the sacramen
or host, which was elevated for the purpose; and of carrying about thi
'divine bread' in solemn pomp through the public streets, and wit
lighted candles, though at noon. An annual festival of the holy sacra
ment, called '*Corpus Christi*,' was instituted by Urban IV., in 1264, giv
ing a finishing touch to the highest expression of superstition an
absurdity.

"The standing posture was anciently adopted at the reception of th
bread and wine; sometimes, however, the communicants knelt. Th
original practice of receiving it when sitting appears to have become
limited almost to Poland. In the French Reformed Church the com
municants stand singly. The ceremony of kneeling was not introduced
into the Church, say the Puritans, till antichrist was at his full height,
and there is no one action in the whole service that looks so much like
idolatry. The Romish priests admit that they should be guilty of idola
try in kneeling before the elements, if they did not believe them to be
the real body and blood of Christ.

". . . . In consonance with prevailing ideas, Archbishop Peckham en
joined, 'The sacrament of the eucharist shall be carried with due rever
ence to the sick, the priest having on at least a surplice and stole, with a
light carried before him in a lantern, with a bell; and the people, by the
minister's discretion, shall be taught to prostrate themselves, or, at least,
to make humble adoration, wheresoever the King of Glory shall happen
to be carried under the similitude of bread!'

". . . . When the doctrine of the corporeal presence was first received
in the Western Church, the whole loaf was believed to be changed at
each celebration into the entire body of Jesus Christ, so that in the dis
tribution of parts, one had an eye, another an ear, another a finger, etc.,
etc.; *and this was supported by pretended miracles suited to that opinion.*
Such continued to be the doctrine of the Church of Rome for nearly
three hundred years. But when *the Schoolmen* began to sift and form
the tenets of that Church, they adopted a more refined and subtle way
of explaining the mystery, and taught that there was an entire body in
every crumb of bread and in every drop of wine. Wickliffe and others
showed the absurdity of these gross notions by cogent appeals to plain
reason. Afterwards Christ's body was, by some, believed to be present
in the manner of a spirit, which was *only occasionally seen*. The more
superstitious of the people fancied that they must 'see their Maker,'
according to the common phrase, before they could lie down in peace in
their beds at night! Consistently with this coarse, corporeal idea, they
charged the Protestants with giving the people the *creature* instead of the
Creator! From that period, this doctrine, strengthened by the notion
of the infallibility of the Pope and the Church, has continued to be
generally held by the Romanists.

" Enlightened men, however, testified against it from time to time, while infidelity denied it and Christianity for its sake! Various sentiments, contradictory of each other, continued to be entertained by its supporters [and myriads were martyred for not embracing some one or other of these conflicting sentiments].

"The priests freely acknowledged to Luther the impostures which they practised on the vulgar in administering the eucharist—by introducing other words in the pretended consecrations, and mixing impious jests with the proceedings. Yet so almost incredibly low and gross were the notions of even sincere religious people, that Farel, one of the French reformers, confesses, 'The wafer which the priest held in his hands, placed in the box, and shut up there, being eaten and given to others to eat, *was* to me the true God, and *there was no other, either in heaven or on the earth.'* . . . .

"At the Reformation in the sixteenth century, Luther, whose eyes were but partially opened with respect to ceremonies, while he rejected the doctrine of transubstantiation, held the opinion, not less incomprehensible, that the partakers of the Lord's Supper received the real body and blood of Christ *along with* the bread and wine. This was termed *consubstantiation.* Occasionally, however, Luther expressed more spiritual views.

"Calvin believed that the bread and wine were not the actual flesh and blood of Christ, but that these were *sacramentally* received by the faithful in the use of the outward elements.*

"Zwingle and Œcolampadius took much more spiritual views of the subject than Luther. They held that the flesh and blood were not really present, but that the bread and wine were only external, commemorative symbols, designed to excite in the minds of the partakers the remembrance of the sufferings and death of Christ, and of the benefits arising therefrom. . . . .

"By the corporation and test acts, passed in the reign of Charles II., the taking the 'sacrament of the Lord's Supper' was made necessary to the holding of all places of trust in England and Wales—the object being the exclusion of dissenters—an object which was enforced for a century and a half. These acts never extended to Scotland. The effect in England was to make the ceremony, in many cases, a mere passport to office for the unscrupulous and irreligious. . . . .

"The high church notion of self-restricted authority appears in the following, under date of 1820 : 'A person not commissioned from the bishop may break bread and pour out wine, and pretend to give the Lord's Supper; but it can afford no comfort to receive it at his hands, because there is *no warrant* from Christ to lead communicants to suppose that, while *he* does so here on earth, they will be partakers in the Saviour's heavenly body and blood.' Hence all such observances by non-conformist ministers are vain and fruitless. . . . .

"The doctrine of *a real presence,* the mode mysterious and undefined, and beyond all human power of comprehension, is admitted by the formularies of the Anglican Church : and this Church, though restricting the term 'sacrament' to two rites, uses three others—confirmation, absolution, and ordination—by which (they claim) grace is to be con-

---

* What does he mean by Christ being " sacramentally received? "—AUTHOR.

veyed; and, therefore, according to her own definition, she virtually upholds five sacraments.[*]

"Great indeed are the difficulties involved in the idea of a permanent outward institution. Whatever may be the professed principles of the Christian Churches in relation to this rite, it is manifest that it obtains less regard than formerly from the religious community at large, and has lost much of that superstitious reverence with which it was formerly observed. The great majority of the Christian world have long given practical evidence that they do not hold it to be essential. The number of communicants, as they are termed, when compared with the serious and devout worshippers, is in general extremely small. Wide differences on the mode, character, and effects of the ceremony, and the dreadful persecutions following those differences, have led many to believe that, where there is so much of questioning, discordance, and bitterness, the whole matter is open to reasonable doubt. There is too much cause to fear that religion itself has been called in question, and has lost its hold on the minds of many, on this very ground. Yet reflecting persons oft hesitate to express their doubts, from an unwillingness either to shock the conscientious convictions of others, or to bring upon themselves suspicion and obloquy. They, therefore, merely disuse it without undertaking to form a decided opinion, or to judge for others respecting it.[†]

"Many of them evince that they have submitted to the operation of the Holy Spirit on their hearts, and that they fully appreciate the blessings derived from the offering of Jesus Christ, 'once for all,' for the redemption of fallen man. Such doubters are permitted to feed on him by living faith, and to hold spiritual communion with him, thus partaking of true Christian fellowship and redemption, without the medium of the outward ceremony.

"The reformation from Papal forms must surely be carried further,

---

[*] Yet the Protestant churches in general allow of but two sacraments (technically so called), and those of them who observe this sacrament of the supper receive the elements only as bread and wine, symbolical of the flesh and blood of Christ; and many sects are becoming very irregular in their communions, oft omitting it for months and years without compunction, if circumstances are unpropitious to its observance. The Papist, on the other hand, without the "sacrament" is without the Church and without salvation. He receives the elements as transubstantiated into something *divine*, by the consecration of the priest. Hence the necessity that he should be of a separate, sanctified class, that he should observe celibacy; and hence the unlimited veneration and confidence which he enjoys among the people. Thus is one error fruitful in producing and strengthening others.—AUTHOR.

[†] Who is sufficient, with an army of popes, cardinals, bishops, priests, clergy, pastors, etc., against him, to form an enlightened opinion upon such a disputed question; since at every turn, lo here, lo there, lo this, lo that, is shouted in his ear; and he is utterly bewildered, and it requires long and unwearied research, in perfect independence of spirit, to unearth the data from which a correct conclusion may be reached.—AUTHOR.

and be suffered to abrogate the two observances still cherished by many Protestants as sacraments, in the same manner as it has abrogated grosser portions of them, and all the five others formerly acknowledged as such. Those who observe them are earnestly and respectfully requested to give the subject a serious and unprejudiced consideration, with a sincere aspiration to be rightly directed by the Holy Spirit."

In the above extract from John Allen, setting forth the vagaries, meanderings, and absurdities of sacramentarians, who does not recognize the unutterable folly of externalizing the *Supper of our Lord,* and "communion" with Christ? Not less a degradation of Scripture terms is the externalizing of Christ's command and teachings respecting *baptism.* The whole Church needs to be rescued from this sacramentarian delusion and folly, and from stumbling at that stumbling-stone.

ALEXANDER CAMPBELL A WITNESS.

The great Protestant dissenting ritualist and prince of heresiarchs, Alexander Campbell, treating on the theme, "Breaking the Loaf," in his work entitled "Principles . . . and Positions," makes some remarkable concessions, and is forced to admit that no law requiring the *eucharist* is found in the New Testament. One of his concessions is (see p. 331), that early Christians, particularly those claiming the greatest sanctity, seldom partook of the sacrament—never, except occasionally, being present at a *pascha* (*passover*); or, if present on other occasions, contented themselves with being spectators and not partakers. He also, on the same page, quotes John Brown, of Haddington, a Presbyterian professor of theology, as inferring from the words of Christ, "As oft as ye do this, do it in remembrance of me," that there is *no law* on the subject, and therefore the Church cannot be condemned either for a partial or total neglect of the observance. And Mr. Campbell adds, "If the words 'As oft' leave it discretionary with any society how often, they *are* blameless *if they never once,* or more than once, in all their lives, show forth the Saviour's death. This interpretation [he says] makes an observance *without reason*, *without law*, without privilege! and consequently *without obligation.*"

How Mr. Campbell should necessarily infer that it is "without privilege," because without "law" or "obligation," does not readily appear, if "privilege" implies option in its acceptance or rejection—leaving the invited innocently free to either course—to the profit or the loss of either course.

On pp. 324 and 325 Mr. Campbell's own ritualism stares upon us, together with his concession of being "without law" on the subject. He says:

"The congregation in Corinth met every first-day for showing forth the Lord's death.   From Acts ii. we learn that the breaking of the loaf was a stated part and most *prominent object* of their meeting. [Neander tells us that on the first day, near evening, there was a *special* meeting of Christians for a neighborly feast of charity, but not for a sacrament.] . . . We have seen, then, that the saints met every first day in Corinth, and when they assembled in one place it was *to eat the Lord's Supper.* . . . Notice what is said, chap. xi. 20: 'When you come together into one place (and act unworthily), this is not to eat the Lord's Supper.'   When a teacher reproves his pupils for wasting time, he cannot remind them more forcibly of the object of their coming to school, nor reprove them with more point, than to say, 'When you act thus, this is not to assemble to learn.' . . . But it is agreed on all hands, that whatsoever the congregations did with the *approbation* of the apostles, *they did by their authority.*   For the apostles gave them all the Christian institutions.   Now, as the Apostle Paul *approbated* their meeting every week, and their coming together into one place to show forth the Lord's death, and only censured their departure from the meaning of the institution, it is as *high authority as we could require.*   When Acts ii. 42, xx. 7, 1 Cor. xi. 2, and xvi. 1, 2, are compared together, it appears that we act under apostolic teaching and precedent when we assemble every Lord's day for the *breaking of the loaf.*   No example can be adduced from the New Testament of any Christian congregation assembling on the first day of the week unless *for the breaking of the loaf* and to attend to those means of edification and comfort connected with it."

The above argument of Mr. Campbell is correct as to the historic fact that the "first-day" gatherings of the saints, as recorded in the New Testament, were oft, at least, for the "breaking of bread" to the hungry. And so did they "daily" and "from house to house" "break bread," continuing steadfastly in the apostles' doctrine. If the "first-day" breaking of bread was a *sacrament*, "approved" by the apostles because historically registered, so were the "daily" ministrations *sacraments*, for they are also approvingly recorded in the New Testament history, and *deacons* were appointed to attend to this very matter. Can there be no act, example or ritual observed by Christ and the apostles but thereby it is fastened on all succeeding ages as a yoke of bondage, requiring servile physical imitation? Reader, what is the freedom of a spiritual dispensation according to this learned interpreter?

Rev. JONAS KING, missionary of the American board in Greece and southern Europe, since about A. D. 1830, or earlier, thus warns the American churches against form-worship in their churches and religious assemblies. It will be seen by this extract that he also affirms that the feast *called Easter* is naught but the Jewish Passover continued (which Mosheim calls the "*Lord's Supper*"), and which Dr. King here asserts (as do we) *was not* required, or expected to be observed by Christians converted from among the "heathen."

"I am sorry to be obliged to say, I perceive a tendency to that which has been the bane of most of the churches in the eastern world—a tendency to forms and ceremonies in the worship of God, to the observance of fast-days, so-called, and of feast-days, which were never appointed by God, and were not kept by Christians in the first age after Christ—feast-days which have in the Eastern churches been productive of great evil by promoting idleness and other vices, with which it is usually accompanied. Even the *passover*, improperly translated *Easter* in the 12th chapter of the Acts of the Apostles, was not considered as a feast to be kept by Christian churches gathered from among the heathen. An ecclesiastical Greek writer in the fifth century says that it was a love of idleness that led many to keep the passover (*pascha*, the word translated, in the 12th chapter of the Acts of the Apostles, *Easter*, but in every other place in the New Testament *passover*), which was a Jewish feast which no Christian was under any obligation to keep; and St. Chrysostom said that, *every time we partake of the Lord's Supper*, we celebrate the *passover*, now generally called here *Easter*, which latter was a heathen festival celebrated in the month of April by northern pagans. In the Oriental Church it is still called passover.

"Many, I have no doubt, suppose that Christmas has been kept from the time of the apostles, whereas it was not kept in the Eastern Church till the fourth century after Christ, and was then introduced from Rome. Of this

21

I have proof from one of the sermons (homilies) of Chrysostom, delivered at Antioch about three hundred and eighty years after Christ, in which he urged Christians to keep Christmas, and said, 'It is not ten years since this day became known to us.' A Greek writer (a bishop) in the seventh century declared that no one knows the day, nor even the month, in which Christ was born. The twenty-fifth day of December was a heathen feast, from the keeping of which it was found difficult to draw Christians; and so it was *baptized*, if I may so say, *with a Christian name*, and has since been kept by many as a Christian feast, just as the feasts of Bacchus are, in substance, still kept by the Greeks, but under a Christian name.

"Of the various feast-days which many at the present day seem inclined to keep, I only mention these two, Christmas and the *passover* (improperly termed *Easter*), which seem to be the least objectionable of all. As in society etiquette and formal visits abound where there is little love or friendship, so in religion, where love to God and true piety decrease, there is generally a tendency to forms. Having seen the deplorable effect produced by the multiplication of forms and ceremonies and feast-days in the Eastern Church, I have come to the conclusion that religion as taught in the Bible is better than it is as remodelled and taught by men; and that as everything as it comes from the hand of God is very good, we should receive religion as he has given it to us, without any addition or diminution, though under the appearance of piety.

. . . .

"The greater part of the traditions and commandments of men our Puritan fathers rejected; and they were called Puritans because they wished to receive nothing in religion which is not found and clearly taught in the pure word of God. Many of them were men of great talent and learning and of ardent piety. Of the name they bore I am not ashamed, though I wish to take no other name than that of *Christian*, according to the word of God. And to that word we owe, as a nation, all the civil and religious privileges which we now enjoy—all our prosperity and happiness hitherto unexampled in any other part of the world.

"And the mixing of the traditions and commandments of men with the pure word of God by the Jews was the primary cause of all their error, and the consequent misery brought upon them, and all they have suffered in their dispersion among all nations for eighteen hundred years. And the mixing of the traditions and commandments of men with the pure word of God, by the Christians in the east, was the primary cause of their degradation and subjection to the Mussulman power for hundreds of years. And the degradation of morals among multitudes in the Western Church, and the want of civil and religious liberty, may be justly attributed to the same cause. And in so far as we see that same cause operating in any other church, we have reason to fear its consequences in that church, and its influence on society.

"There is no safety for any individual nor for any church, but in keeping close to the pure word of God, and the simplicity of the gospel of Jesus Christ.

"To that simplicity let us all return, if we have in any degree wandered from it. Let us not be allured by pompous ceremonies of any kind, by gorgeous dresses, theatrical performances, or enrapturing strains of music, to leave the simplicity of the gospel of Jesus Christ, who, when he sent out his disciples to preach the gospel, told them not to take two coats, and who himself, when he preached in Judea and Samaria, and till he was led out to be crucified, wore as we have reason to believe simple garments and a seamless vesture on which the Roman soldiers cast their lots.

"*Simplicity in rites and forms, simplicity in religious worship, simplicity in the places where they met for prayer* and religious instruction, characterized Christians everywhere in the time of the apostles, and I may say, during the greater part of the first century after Christ. And never did Christianity appear more lovely, and never was the preaching of the gospel more efficacious in pulling down the strongholds of sin and superstition and paganism, than during that period.

"The vilest of men may be and often are delighted with pompous rites and ceremonies, and frequent the churches where such rites and ceremonies exist as they do the theatre and opera, for mere amusement, without receiving the least apparent spiritual benefit.

"And now, my beloved countrymen, as I am expecting ere long to bid my native land once more farewell, and perhaps for the last time and forever, and return to that land which has been so long the field of my missionary labors, I hope you will receive with kindness what I have said on a subject which seems to me of great importance. My love for my country has never been in the least degree diminished by my distance from it, or by length of absence; on the contrary it has been greatly increased by comparing it with other countries through which I have travelled and in which I have resided. When in foreign lands, I have often felt as the captive Jews did by the rivers of Babylon, and have often said of my country as they did of theirs: If I forget thee, O America, let my right hand forget its cunning. If I do not remember thee let my tongue cleave to the roof of my mouth; if I prefer not America above my chief joy.

"I love my countrymen in the east and in the west, in the north and in the south, and pray that we may all yet be united in love, and that we may all unite in doing good to our fellow-men who do not enjoy the civil and religious privileges which we enjoy; and thus do the work which I believe God has raised us up as a nation to perform.

"With never-failing love, and desire for the peace and prosperity and happiness of this great nation, I remain as I ever have been, your fellow-citizen,"—JONAS KING.

Henry Ward Beecher on the Lord's Supper.

I thought I would say a few words this evening, in answer to several questions that have been propounded to me on the subject of *The Lord's Supper; or, The Communion of the Last Supper.*

"You will remember that this very simple and tender service took place on the night of the betrayal of our Lord. It was almost the last free act of his life. He was on the very edge of the cloud whose bolts were about to descend upon his head. The disciples had made preparation, you will recollect, being sent by the Master, to celebrate the passover—perhaps the most conspicuous and important of the three great festivals which the Jews were accustomed to celebrate every year, marking their great national release from bondage. And we have a very accurate account, derived from authentic Jewish writings, of the whole mode in which the passover was accustomed to be celebrated. The paschal supper, the mode of its preparation, administration and participation, was all very minutely put down in the Jewish books, so that we are not left without a knowledge of the particulars of that gathering when Jesus and his disciples sat eating the paschal supper.

"They were all Jews in feeling as well as in nationality. Our Master was accustomed to enter into all the proper acts of Jewish worship without questioning. He worshipped according to the customs of his own people, in the synagogue, everywhere. And he seemed to have a special fondness for this passover, to which he went up, several times, from Galilee.

"They were in the act of eating the passover—the unleavened bread, the bitter herbs, and the prepared lamb. Then, at the close of this paschal service, the remains being there, the Saviour gave new significance to the bread. Handing a fragment to every one that was present, he said,

"'This is my body, which is broken for you.'"

"They came into the meaning of it afterward.

"And then he took the cup, which had been used already in the Jewish passover of the paschal supper, and again gave it to them, as it were a fourth time, and said it was his blood shed for them.

"It will be perceived, therefore, that our Master did not institute this service—the communion of the Lord's Supper—as a specialty by itself, but that he grafted it upon a service that pre-existed. It is in evidence that the early Christians, long before they were formed into any methodical and really organized Church, were accustomed to repeat this observance every night. It was originally an evening service; *and the earliest Christian families were accustomed to conclude their evening meal in this way: after they had supped, bread was broken, and each took a morsel.* And then the wine cup was passed, and they drank of that, at the same time, reminding each other of the Lord Jesus.

"This very same mode of celebration continued, although not as often as every day. It seems afterward to have become a weekly service—and doubtless for this reason: that the brethren of a neighborhood gathered together on one day for religious enjoyment and instruction, and closed that public service with this simple administration of the Lord's Supper. *There was no command* that it should be observed every day. *There was no command* that it should be observed every week. *There was no command that it should be observed at all.* It carries with it, evidently, the air of expectancy on the part of the Saviour, that his disciples would maintain some such observance; but how, or under what circumstance, was not determined by the Master, and certainly it was not determined in the first years of the existence of the Church. And it was celebrated more or less frequently just according to circumstances. It was probably more than two hundred years before it began to be a sacrament, or a ceremony by which men were supposed to swear themselves into the service of another. It was full three or four hundred years before it ever began to be called an *awful* service, a *solemn* service, a service peculiarly filled with awe. In the beginning it was an affectionate service; and in all the earlier days of its celebration subsequent to Christ's resurrection, that event seems to have thrown such a joy over the minds of his disciples, that even the memory of his death was full of exhilaration and joyfulness. They believed that death was not able to hold him, but that he lived again; and when they participated in these memorials of his death for them, it was, in the earlier historic periods, unquestionably a service of great joyfulness and cheerfulness. They congratulated each other, and often exchanged the holy kiss in their assemblies.

"Afterward it became corrupted. It became a sacrament. Men began to surround it with various ceremonies. And then they began to teach that it was a special channel through which otherwise incommunicable blessings were sent down. And then it began to be divided, and the laity were not permitted to have anything but the bread—not the cup at all. Then it began to be taught that the Lord's body and blood were absolutely in the bread and wine; and that they who participated in the bread took, actually, the Lord Jesus Christ physically, and the whole of him—each one the whole, and other such monstrous teachings.

"In the beginning, then, it was simply a service of love, and a memorial service at that. But the sign, the token, the remembrance, does not itself do anything. And so the bread and the wine symbols. They stand between the soul of Christ's disciple and Christ himself, and point the one up to the other, for the simple sake of keeping alive personal affection— a sense of personal love. The whole of Christianity may be said to be this love between the sinful soul and the ever blessed Saviour.

"'The love of Christ constraineth us; because we thus judge, that if one died for all, then were all dead: and that he died for all, that they which live should not henceforth live unto themselves, but unto him which died for them.'"

"It is this yearning of Christ to be loved, to be remembered in love, that was the occasion of his instituting this simple memorial service. That is what it meant; that is what it still means.

"In the early church, the Lord's Supper was administered by every person himself. Persons sat about the table, and each, himself, took the bread and wine; but when many families began to meet together, that became inconvenient. They could not all sit about a table. It was a service in the congregation; and then it was more convenient that there should be officers appointed to pass the elements. This mode was adopted as being shorter and more facile. But the right to the Lord's Supper is not conferred by the officers of the church, nor by the church itself, on anybody. The right to the Lord's Supper belongs to every soul that loves the Lord Jesus Christ. It is not mine to give to you. I have nothing to give. I am to be your servant in administering it. The church may facilitate the administration of it, and make it an orderly service; but the church does not own the Lord's Supper, and the church does not give anybody the right to it. You have a right to spread your table in your own house, as the primitive Christians did, and to break the bread in the name of the Lord Jesus Christ. The father of a family has a right to do it for his wife and for his children. And he has a right to take the cup and administer the wine to them. Under such circumstances it is the Lord's Supper administered by your own self. You do not need ordination and permission to qualify you to administer it to yourselves or to others. The right is inherent in every one who is a true disciple of the Lord.

"The Roman Church once said that the Bible belonged to the church, and it was administered by the priest; but the Protestants threw off that shackle, and said that the Bible was everybody's. And now each man owns his own Bible. And it is just the same with ordinances as it is with the Bible. There was no church to give them to men; and when the Lord Jesus Christ instituted them, they were given to his followers and to every individual among them."

Who can be wholly consistent? Mr. Beecher can deny at one breath a "command" to observe the "Supper," and at the next, talk about an "institution" and the freedom and sovereignty each individual for himself possesses relative to "ordinances." We presume he uses these terms in this way because it is the customary dialect of the churches. We know that he disowns any bondage to ordinances. See what he says elsewhere respecting baptism.

PRES. E. G. ROBINSON'S (BAPTIST) TESTIMONY RESPECTING THE SUPPER.

It may be here stated as one of the hopeful results of the recent discussion respecting the conditions or terms of Christian fellowship, and especially of the supposed obligations and limits of sacramental communion, that not only so prominent a religious teacher as H. W. Beecher has denied that a veritable sacramental law has been imposed on the Christian Church, but also a widely known teacher, at the head of the leading Baptist theological seminary in the land, Rev. E. G. ROBINSON, D. D., LL. D., President of Brown University, Providence, R. I., has come before the public with a discourse in which he asserts that the communion of saints around what is termed the "Lord's table" is not a command of Christ binding on the Christian Church, but is a purely voluntary memorial of Christ's redeeming work and love, and is to be observed only at the option of each congregation or company of Christian believers; and that the antecedents of such commemoration must also be optional, *i. e.*, decided in the exercise of Christian freedom.

THE "EPISCOPALIAN" TOUCHING THE ORIGIN OF SACRAMENTS.

Wherein does the above teaching differ from that of the Reformed or Evangelical Episcopalians, as set forth in the "*Episcopalian*," commenting upon certain articles found in the "*Reformed Church Monthly*"? Hear it:

"Our Protestant brethren of the Reformed Church are pestered with the same errors of doctrine which have disturbed our church peace, and have led away multitudes of our people after them. A series of articles exposing the Nevinite errors of sacramental grace, which are essential Popery, is passing through the '*Monthly*,' and they contain some startling exposures. The doctrine of baptismal regeneration is clearly stated thus, p. 401: 'It is the doctrine that *the grace of baptism consists in an emanation from the substance of God transmitted to the soul of the child or adult baptized, through baptism as the organic channel*.' We agree with the writer when he says that doctrine 'calls forth our opposition and condemnation. *This doctrine* we pronounce unscriptural, contrary to the established faith of the Reformed Church (and of every Protestant Church), and very hurtful in its tendencies.' He adds, 'to sacramental grace, in the gospel sense, we hold.' But there is no gospel sense of that grace; *there are no sacraments in the gospel*. That word is a military, ecclesiastical, and misleading term, and it cannot be redeemed. They are ordinances of religion of a purely symbolical kind, and they are means of grace, like prayer, praise, and preaching, in no other way, and in no other sense. Baptism and the Lord's Supper are subject to the same laws as are any other means of grace. In regard to importance, an inspired pen puts baptism so far below preaching the truth of Christ that the writer (St. Paul) omitted it, and rarely administered it. Our brethren had better get rid of the unscriptural term, and that will help to banish the false doctrine. Jehovah forbid his people to take the name of heathen gods in their mouths, and so should his enlightened people decline to take the nomenclature of false doctrine in their mouths. Call them what the apostle calls them, *Ordinances*. We would do all we can to encourage the true Protestants and representatives of the Reformed Church to banish all false, patristic, pantheistic, and Popish errors from their Church. But this is the day of 'the great falling away,' and 'many shall be tried, and purified, and made white.' 'When the Son of man cometh, shall he find faith on the earth?' 'Hold fast the truth, that no man take thy crown.'"

JOSEPH JOHN GURNEY (AN EMINENT MINISTER OF THE SOCIETY OF FRIENDS) THUS WRITES RESPECTING CHRIST'S LAST PASSOVER SUPPER:

"I. When the Lord Jesus celebrated his last passover supper with his disciples, 'he took bread, and when he had given thanks, he brake it, and said, Take, eat; this is my body which is broken for you; this do in remembrance of me. After the same manner also he took the cup, when he had supped, saying, This cup is the new testament in my blood: this do ye, as oft as ye drink it, in remembrance of me.'

"II. The words used by our Lord on this solemn occasion afford no more evidence that the bread which he brake was *itself* his body than they do that the cup which he held in his hand was *itself* the new testament in his blood. The bread was distinct and separate from his body, occupying a different part of space, and could not *possibly* be the same with it. But the bread represented his body, which was about to be broken for many; and the wine in the cup was a symbol of his blood which was about to be shed for many, for the remission of sins.

"III. It was at an actual meal, intended for bodily refreshment, that our Saviour thus addressed his disciples; and when, in conformity with his command, the earliest Christians partook of the 'Lord's Supper,' there was no mystery in the observance; much less was any miraculous change wrought upon their food. Convened from time to time, *at their social repasts*, they brake their bread, and handed round their cup of wine, in the sweet fellowship of the gospel of Christ, and in solemn remembrance of his death.

" IV. The Scriptures do not appear to afford us any sufficient proof that the command on which this custom was founded was intended for the whole Church of Christ in all ages, any more than our Lord's injunction to his disciples to wash one another's feet. There is nothing however in the practice itself, as it was thus observed by the primitive believers, inconsistent with the general law, that all mere types and figures in worship are abolished under the gospel. Let Christians, when they eat their meat together ' with gladness and singleness of heart,' still be reminded, *by their very food*, of the Lord who bought them. Let them, more often than the day, gratefully recollect their Divine Master, ' who bare our sins in *his own body*, on the tree,' and whose *precious blood* was shed for all mankind.

" V. But no sooner was this practice changed from its original simple character, employed as a part of the public worship of God, and converted into a purely ceremonial rite, than the state of the case was entirely altered. The great principle that God is to be worshipped in spirit and in truth was infringed; and, as far as relates to this particular, a return took place to the old legal system of *forms* and *shadows*.

" VI. It is probably in consequence of this change—the invention and contrivance of man—that an ordinance, of which the sole purpose was the thankful remembrance of the death of Jesus, has been abused to an astonishing extent. Nothing among professing Christians has been perverted into an occasion of so much superstition; few things have been the means of staining the annals of the Church with so much blood.

" VII. ' *It is the Spirit that quickeneth*,' as our Saviour himself has taught us, ' *the flesh profiteth nothing ;* ' and Christianity is distinguished by a *spiritual* supper, as well as baptism. To partake of *this* supper is essential to our salvation. We can never have a claim on the hopes and joys set before us in the gospel unless we feed, by a living faith, on the bread which came down from heaven, and giveth life to the world—unless we ' eat the flesh of the Son of man, and drink his blood.' Now they who partake of this celestial food are fellow-members of one body; they are joined together by a social compact of the dearest and holiest character, because they all commune with the same glorious Head. They are *one in Christ Jesus ;* and when they meet in solemn worship—Christ himself being present—they are guests, even here, at the table of their Lord, and drink the wine ' new,' with him ' in his kingdom.'

" May this be the happy experience of all who read this volume, whether they use or disuse what is called the sacrament of the supper ! "

Thomas Clarkson, of the Church of England, stating and endorsing the Friends' View of the Lord's Supper.

"There are two suppers of the Lord recorded in the Scriptures; the first enjoined by Moses, and the second by Jesus Christ.

"The first is called the Supper of the Lord, because it was the last supper which Jesus Christ participated with his disciples, or which the Lord and Master celebrated with them in commemoration of the passover. And it may not improperly be called the Supper of the Lord on another account, because it was the supper which the lord and master of every Jewish family celebrated, on the same festival, in his own house.

"This supper was distinguished, at the time alluded to, by the name of the passover supper. The object of the institution of it was to commemorate the event of the Lord passing over the houses of the Israelites in Egypt, when he smote the Egyptians, and delivered the former from their hard and oppressive bondage.

"The directions of Moses concerning this festival were short, but precise.

"On the fourteenth day of the first month, called Nisan, the Jews were to kill a lamb in the evening. It was to be eaten in the same evening, roasted with fire; and the whole of it was to be eaten, or the remains of it to be consumed with fire before morning. They were to eat it with loins girded, with their shoes on their feet, and with their staves in their hands, and to eat it in haste. The bread, which they were to eat, was to be unleavened, all of it, and for seven days. There was to be no leaven in their houses during that time. Bitter herbs also were to be used at this feast. And none, who were uncircumcised, were allowed to partake of it.

"This was the simple manner in which the passover and the feast of unleavened bread (which was included in it) were first celebrated. But as the passover, in the age following its institution, was not to be killed and eaten in any other place than where the Lord chose to fix his name, which was afterwards at Jerusalem, it was suspended for a time. The Jews, however, retained the festival of unleavened bread wherever they dwelt. At this last feast, in process of time they added the use of wine to the use of bread. The introduction of the wine was followed by the introduction of new customs. The lord or master of the feast used to break the bread, and to bless it, saying, 'Blessed be thou, O Lord, who givest us the fruits of the earth!' He used to take the cup, which contained the wine, and bless it also: 'Blessed be thou, O Lord, who givest us of the fruit of the vine!' The bread was twice blessed upon this occasion, and given once to every individual at the feast. But the cup was handed round three times to the guests. During the intervals between the blessing and taking of the bread and of the wine, the company acknowledge the deliverance of their ancestors from the Egyptian bondage; they lamented their present state; they confessed their sense of the justice of God in their punishment; and they expressed their hope of his mercy, from his former kind dealings and gracious promises.

"In process of time, when the Jews were fixed at Jerusalem, they revived the celebration of the passover; and as the feast of unleavened bread was connected with it, they added the customs of the latter, and blended the eating of the lamb, and the use of the bread and wine, and their several accompaniments of consecration, into one ceremony. The bread therefore and the wine had been long in use as constituent parts of the passover supper (and indeed of all the solemn feasts of the Jews), when Jesus Christ took upon himself, as the master of his own family of disciples, to celebrate it. When he celebrated it, he did as the master of every Jewish family did at that time. He took bread, and blessed, and broke, and gave it to his disciples. He took the cup of wine, and gave it to them also. But he conducted himself differently from others in one respect; for he compared the bread of the passover to his own body, and the wine to his own blood, and led the attention of his disciples from the old object of the passover, or deliverance from Egyptian bondage, to a new one, or deliverance from sin." . . . .

"The first conclusion which the Friends deduce on this subject is, that this flesh and blood, or this bread, or this meat, which he recommends to his followers, and which he also declares to be himself, is not of a material nature. It is not, as he himself says, like the ordinary meat that perisheth, not like the outward manna, which the Jews ate in the wilderness for their bodily refreshment. It cannot therefore be common bread, nor such bread as the Jews ate at their passover, nor any bread or meat ordered to be eaten on any public occasion.

"Neither can this flesh or this bread be, as some have imagined, the material flesh or body of Jesus. For, first, this latter body was born of the Virgin Mary: whereas the other is described as having come down from heaven. Secondly, because, when the Jews said, 'How can this man give us his flesh?' Jesus replied, 'It is the Spirit that quickeneth, the flesh profiteth nothing;' that is, Material flesh and blood, such as mine is, cannot profit anything in the way of quickening, or cannot so profit as to give life eternal: this is only the work of the Spirit. And he adds, 'The words I have spoken to you, they are spirit, and they are life.'

"This bread then, or this body, is of a spiritual nature. It is of a spiritual nature, because it not only giveth life but preserveth from death. Manna, on the other hand, supported the Israelites only for a time, and they died. Common bread and flesh nourish the body for a time, and it dies and perishes; but it is said of those, who feed upon this food, that they shall never die.

"This bread or body must be spiritual again, because the bodies of men, according to their present organization, cannot be kept forever alive.

But their souls may. The souls of men can receive no nourishment from ordinary meat and drink, that they should be kept alive, but from that which is spiritual only. It must be spiritual again, because Jesus Christ describes it as having come down from heaven.

"The last conclusion, which the Friends draw from the words of our Saviour on this occasion, is, that a spiritual participation of the body and blood of Christ is such an essential of Christianity, that no person, who does not partake of them, can be considered to be a Christian ; 'for, except a man eat the flesh of the Son of man and drink his blood, he has no life in him.'" . . . .

"Neither does St. Luke, who mentions the words, 'Do this in remembrance of me,' establish anything, in the opinion of the Friends, material on this point. For it appears from him that Jesus, to make the most of his words, only spiritualized the old passover for his disciples, all of whom were Jews, but that he gave no command with respect to the observance of it by others. Neither did St. Luke himself enjoin or call upon others to observe it.

"St. Paul speaks nearly the same language as St. Luke, but with this difference, that the supper, as thus spiritualized by Jesus, was to last but for a time.

"Now the Friends are of opinion, that they have not sufficient ground to believe, from these authorities, that Jesus intended to establish any ceremonial as an universal ordinance for the Christian Church.* For, if the custom enjoined was the spiritualized passover, it was better calculated for Jews than for Gentiles, who were neither interested in the motives nor acquainted with the customs of that feast. But it is of little importance, they contend, whether it was the spiritualized passover or not; for, if Jesus Christ had intended it, whatever it was, as an essential of his new religion, he would have commanded his disciples to enjoin it as a Christian duty and the disciples themselves would have handed it down to their several converts in this light. But no injunction to this effect, either of Jesus to others, or of themselves to others, is to be found in any of their writings. Add to this, that the limitation of its duration for a time seems a sufficient argument against it as a Christian ordinance, because whatever is once, must be for ever, an essential in the Christian Church.

"The Friends believe, as a further argument in their favor, that there is reason to presume that St. Paul never looked upon the spiritualized

---

* The extraordinary silence of St. John on this subject is considered by some as confirming the idea, that this evangelist himself believed that the passover, as spiritualized by Jesus Christ, was to cease with the Jewish constitution, or after the destruction of Jerusalem. For St. John did not write his gospel till after this great event. But if he thought the ceremonial was then to cease, he would have had less reason for mentioning it than any of those who wrote prior to this epoch.

passover, as any permanent and essential rite, which Christians were enjoined to follow. For nothing can be more clear than that, when speaking of the guilt and hazard of judging one another by meats and drinks, he states it as a general and fundamental doctrine of Christianity, that the 'kingdom of God is not meat and drink, but righteousness, peace, and joy in the Holy Ghost.'

"It seems also by the mode of reasoning which the apostle adopts in the Epistle to the Corinthians on this subject, that he had no other idea of the observance of this rite than he had of the observance of particular days; namely, that if men thought they were bound in conscience to keep them, they ought to keep them religiously. 'He that regardeth a day,' says the apostle, 'regardeth it to the Lord:' that is, 'He that esteemed a day,' says Barclay, 'and placed conscience in keeping it, was to regard it to the Lord (and so it was to him, in so far as he regarded it to the Lord, the Lord's day): he was to do it worthily; and if he were to do it unworthily, he would be guilty of the Lord's day, and so keep it to his own condemnation.' Just in the same manner, St. Paul tells the Corinthian Jews, that if they observed the ceremonial of the passover, or rather, 'as often as they observed it,' they were to observe it worthily, and make it a religious act. They were not then come together to make merry on the anniversary of the deliverance of their ancestors from Egyptian bondage, but to meet in memorial of Christ's sufferings and death. And therefore, if they ate and drank the passover, under its new and high allusions, unworthily, they profaned the ceremony, and were guilty of the body and blood of Christ.

"It appears also from the Syriac and other oriental versions of the New Testament, such as the Arabic and Ethiopic, as if he only permitted the celebration of the spiritualized passover for a time, in condescension to the weakness of some of his converts, who were probably from the Jewish synagogue at Corinth. For in the seventeenth verse of the eleventh chapter of his first Epistle to the Corinthians, the Syriac runs thus: 'As to that, concerning which I am now instructing you, I commend you not, because you have not gone forward, but you have gone down into matters of less importance.' It 'appears from hence,' says Barclay, 'that the apostle was grieved, that such was their condition, that he was forced to give them instruction concerning those outward things, and doting upon which they showed that they were not gone forward in the life of Christianity, but rather sticking in the beggarly elements.' And therefore the twentieth verse of the same version has it thus: 'When then ye meet together, ye do not do it, as it is just ye should in the day of the Lord; ye eat and drink.' Therefore showing to them, that to meet together to eat and drink outward bread and wine was not the labor and work of that day of the Lord.

"Upon the whole, in whatever light the Friends view the subject before us, they cannot persuade themselves that Jesus Christ intended to establish any new ceremonial distinct from the passover supper, and in addition to that, which he had before commanded at Capernaum. The only supper which he ever enjoined to Christians was the latter. This spiritual supper was to be eternal and universal. For he was always to be present with those 'who would let him in, and they were to sup with him, and he with them.' It was also to be obligatory, or an essential, with all Christians. 'For, except a man were to eat his flesh and to drink his blood, he was to have no life in him.' The supper, on the other hand, which our Saviour is supposed to have instituted on the celebration of the passover, was not enjoined by him to any but the disciples present. And it was, according to the confession of St. Paul, to last only for a time. This time is universally agreed upon to be that of the coming of Christ. That is, the duration of the spiritualized passover was to be only till those, to whom it had been recommended, had arrived at a state of religious manhood, or till they could enjoy the supper, which Jesus Christ had commanded at Capernaum; after which repast, the Friends believe, they would consider all others as empty, and as not having the proper life and nourishment in them, and as of a kind not to harmonize with the spiritual nature of the Christian religion."

Earlier Witnesses protesting against this Sacrament of the Supper.

From John Allen's "State Churches."

"Berenger, who died in 1088, took a more spiritual view of the Lord's Supper than most of the ruling men of his day, though many others agreed with him. 'Christ,' said he, 'does not descend *from* heaven, but the hearts of the faithful ascend devotionally to him *in* heaven. . . . . The true, the imperishable body of Christ is eaten only by the true members of Christ *in a spiritual manner.*' It was a favorite maxim of his, 'Though we have known Christ after the flesh, yet now, henceforth, know we him thus no more.'

"Peter de Bruis, Abbot of Chigny, with Henry, his disciple, and their followers, about the same time, held, not only, with Berenger, that there is no change of substance in the sacrament, but also that it is no longer to be administered. Peter de Bruis was burnt at St. Giles, Languedoc. This was the usual end of such as ventured to dissent from the gross ideas upheld by the priests, and by arbitrary authority in church and state.

"A hermit, disputing in St. Paul's Church (London), about 1306, affirmed that the sacraments then used in the church were not instituted by Christ. John Fox supposes this to have been one Ranulphus, mentioned in the 'Flower of History,' who died in prison.

"The author of 'Ploughman's Complaint' thus writes: 'Ah, Lord Jesus! whether thou ordainest an order of priests to offer on the altar thy flesh and thy blood, or whether any other man may do so without leave of the priest—Lord, we believe that thy flesh is very meat, and thy blood very drink, and *whoso* eateth thy flesh and drinketh thy blood dwelleth in thee and thou in. him; and he that eateth this bread shall live without end. But Lord, thy disciples said, "this is a hard word;" but thou answerest them, "The Spirit it is that maketh you alive; the words that I have spoken unto you are spirit and life." Lord, blessed mayest thou be; for in this word thou teachest us that he that keepeth thy words and doeth them, eateth thy flesh, and drinketh thy blood, and hath everlasting life in thee.'

"'Hocus pocus' is said to have been the mocking phrase of the common people in derision of the Papal ceremony of transmuting the bread, it being a corruption or abbreviation of the words, 'Hoc est corpus' (this is my body).

"Some of the priests confessed that they had so little faith in the transmutation, that they used, at times, to say in derision, 'Panis est, et panis manebis—bread thou art, and bread thou wilt remain.'

"In her early days, Queen Elizabeth, perceiving the falsity of the pretensions of the Papal priests, evaded the questions of her Popish examiner respecting the sacrament, in the following epigrammatic style:

> "'Christ was the word, and spake it,
> He took the bread, and brake it,
> And what his word did make it,
> That I receive, and take it.'

"PHILIP REPINGTON, in his public examination, declared that, as touching the sacrament, he would hold his peace until such time as the Lord should otherwise illuminate the minds of the clergy. He was afterwards, however, prevailed upon to adopt the Romish doctrines, and at length became a cardinal!

"WALTER BRUTE, before quoted, who lived about 1405, had very clear and spiritual views on the communion of the body and blood of Christ. He thus discourses: 'I believe and know that Christ is the true bread of God, which descended from heaven, and giveth life to the world. Of which bread whosoever eateth shall live forever....... By the faith which we have in Christ as the true Son of God, who came down from heaven to redeem us, we are justified from sin, and so live by him which is the true bread and meat of the soul..... As we believe that he is true God, so must we believe that he is a true man, and then do we eat the bread of heaven and the flesh of Christ. *Except we thus eat the flesh of the Son of man, and drink his blood, we have not eternal life in us.*.... But the priests be greatly deceived, and greatly deceive others; for the people believe that they see the body of Christ, nay, rather Christ himself, between the hands of the priests, for so is the common oath they swear: "By Him whom I saw this day between the priest's hands." And they believe that they eat not the body of Christ but at Easter, or when they lie upon their death-beds, and receive with their bodily mouths the sacrament of his body. But since the body of Christ *is the soul's food*, and *not the food of the body* in this world, whosoever believeth doth eat spiritually and really, at any time when he so believeth; and it is manifest that they do greatly err, who believe that they eat not the body of Christ but when they eat with their teeth the sacrament of his body. The priests, therefore, are in great peril, most dangerously seducing themselves and the people.'

"WILLIAM THORP, of Shrewsbury, being examined before Archbishop Arundel, about the same time, as to his faith, thus answered: 'I said to the people, "The virtue of the most holy sacrament of the altar standeth much more in the belief thereof that you ought to have in your soul than in the outward sight thereof. And therefore ye were better to stand still quietly to hear God's word, because through the hearing thereof men come to very true belief. . . . They that come to church to pray devoutly to the Lord, may in their inward wits be more fervent, that their outward wits be closed from all outward seeing and hearing, and from all disturbance and lettings. . . . No one needs to be afraid to die without taking any sacrament of those enemies of Christ (the priests) since Christ himself will not fail to minister all sacraments, lawful, healthful and necessary, at all times, and especially at the end, to all them that are in true faith, in steadfast hope and perfect charity." ' The archbishop and priests were very bitter against him, and he is supposed to have died in prison.

"Ten persons, mostly of Tenterden, in Kent, were compelled, in 1511, to abjure the following among other supposed errors: 'That the sacraments are not necessary or profitable for men's souls; that holy water and holy bread are not better after benediction by the priest than before.' Many others, adhering to their opinions, were burnt about the same time, as obstinate heretics. Elizabeth Stamford, being examined before the Bishop of London, confessed thus: 'Christ feedeth and nourisheth his church with his own precious body,—that is the bread of life coming down from heaven; this is the worthy word that is worthily received, and joined unto man to be in one body with him. Sooth it is, that they be both one, that they may not be parted.

"'This is the wisely deeming of the holy sacrament, Christ's own body; this is not received by chewing of teeth, but by hearing with ears, and understanding with your soul, *and wisely working thereafter*.'

"MARTIN LUTHER, when in his right mind, giving free course to the Spirit, and unbiased by his fear of a separation from the Papacy, could write thus: 'If divers men should use a diverse rite, let not one judge or contemn another, but let every one abound in his own sense; and let us all savor and judge the same things, though in forms we act diversely; for outward rites, as we cannot want them either as meat and drink, *so neither do they commend us to God*, but only faith and love commend us to him. Therefore let Paul be heard here, that the kingdom of God is not meat and drink, but righteousness, peace and joy in the Holy Spirit. And so no rite nor form is the kingdom of God, but faith within us. . . . The better part of every sacrifice, and consequently of the Lord's Supper, is in the word and the promises of•God. Without faith in this word and in these promises, the sacrament is but dead. It is a body without a soul, a cup without wine, a purse without money, a type without fulfilment, a letter without meaning, a casket without jewels, a sheath without a sword. . . . The priests may deny us the sacrament, *but they cannot deprive us of the strength and grace* which God hath attached to it. *It is not their will nor any power of theirs, but our own faith that the Lord has made essential to salvation.* The sacrament, the altar, *the priest, the Church,* we may pass them all by; that word of God, which the bull of the Pope condemned, is more than all these things. *The soul may dispense with the sacrament,* but it cannot live without the word. Christ, the true Bishop, *will himself supply your spiritual feast.*'

" ŒCOLAMPADIUS, at a conference in 1527, says: ' Christ, who said to the people of Capernaum, "the flesh profiteth nothing," rejected by those very words the oral manducation or chewing of his body, therefore he did not establish it at the institution of his supper. There is danger in attributing too much to mere matter;—*since we have the spiritual eating, what need of the bodily one?*'

" So ZWINGLE remarks to Luther, ' Jesus says, that to eat his flesh corporeally profiteth nothing; whence it would result that if outwardly eaten he had given us in the supper a thing that would be useless to us. The soul is fed with the spirit, and not with the flesh. Christ's body is, according to you, a corporeal and not a spiritual nourishment. You are thus reestablishing Popery.'

" WILLIAM TYNDAL, the martyr, declared that it were better to receive neither of the parts of the sacrament than one only, as practised in the Romish Church.[*] It was frequently expressed by him and other reformers, *that the ceremonies of the Church had brought the world from God!* Said they, ' By works, superstitions and ceremonies, we decay from the faith, which alone doth truly justify and make holy.'

"JOHN FRITH, one of the English martyrs in Queen Mary's reign, said : 'The ancient fathers *before Christ* never believed the gross and carnal eating of Christ's body; yet notwithstanding, they *did eat him spiritually*, and were saved; as Adam, Abraham, Moses, etc., all of whom ate the body of Christ, and drank his blood, as we do. They were all " under the cloud," and drank of the Rock which followed them. " That Rock was Christ." Moses also prefigured him by divers means, both by the manna which came down from heaven, and also by the water which issued out of the rock ; nor is it to be doubted that the manna and the water had a prophetical mystery in them.'

---

[*] By thus canvassing the comparative value of the sacrament *in both parts*, or *neither*, it would seem that all could see the utter worthlessness of sacraments.—AUTHOR.

22

"JOHN LAMBERT, another of the martyrs, expressed himself thus: 'God sendeth his grace where and when he pleaseth, either with the sacraments or without them; so that it is at his arbitrament how and when. Moreover, many lewd persons, destitute of grace, receive the sacraments to their confusion; so that I cannot affirm that they give grace; yet in due receipt of them, I suppose and think that God giveth grace, as he doth to all good persons even without them also.'

"The rubric of Edward VI. required all married persons to receive the holy sacrament on the day of their marriage; afterward it was changed to the form now in force, that they should do it on that day, or at the first opportunity afterwards; and required each parishioner to communicate at least 'three times in a year.' This, however, has fallen into disuse. In a letter to Bishop Ridley, Edward states that 'most of the altars in the churches had been already taken down,' and he orders that the rest be removed, and instead thereof, a table be set up in some convenient part of the chancel, for the ministration of the blessed communion, since, contrary to the Popish notion, '*no sacrifice is offered* in the sacrament, and a table is the most suitable to the occasion!'

"Dr. REDMAN, an early English Protestant, being asked in the time of his illness, whether he thought that the very body of Christ was received with the mouth or not, paused and held his peace awhile, and then replied, 'I will not say so; I cannot tell; it is a hard question; but surely we receive Christ in the soul by faith. When you speak of it otherwise, it soundeth grossly.' His friend replied, 'I am glad to hear you say so much. I fear lest that sacrament, and a little piece of white bread lifted up, hath robbed Christ of a great part of his honor.' Then said the sick man, looking upward, 'God grant us grace, that we may have true understanding of his word.'*

"Two French martyrs at Samserre, declaring that the mass was mere superstition and idolatry, said that, to attribute any part of salvation thereto, was 'utterly to destroy the benefits of the sufferings of Christ, and ought not to be named by a Christian man!'

"In a conference between Ridley and Bourne, the former, a well-known and illustrious Protestant martyr, expresses himself thus: 'When you hear God's word truly preached, if you believe in it, and abide in it, ye shall and do receive life withal; and if ye do not believe it, it doth bring unto you death. And yet Christ's body is still in heaven, and not carnal in every preacher's mouth.' Thus he showed that the participation in an outward rite is not necessary in order to partake of the body and blood of Christ.

* In the life of Gregory the Great, it is related that a certain woman, when he gave her the eucharist with the words, "the body of our Lord Jesus Christ preserve thy soul," laughed at the form, and when asked the reason, she replied, because he called that the body of Christ, which she knew to be bread that she had made with her own hands a little while before.

"ROBERT SMITH, of Windsor, another of those who proved by death the sincerity of their Christian faith, was asked at his examination before Bishop Bonner, how long it had been since he received the sacrament of the altar. His answer was, 'I never received the same since I had years of discretion, nor ever will, by God's grace. Neither do I esteem the same in any point, *because it hath not God's ordinance,* either in name or in other usage, *but rather is erected to mock God.*' Bonner replied, 'Do ye not believe that it is the very body of Christ, that was born of the Virgin Mary, really, naturally, and substantially, *after the words of consecration?*' Robert Smith replies, 'I showed you before it was none of God's ordinances, as ye use it; then much less is it God, or any part of his substance, but only bread and wine, erected to the use aforesaid. Yet if ye can prove it by the word to be the body that ye spake of, I will believe it; if not, I will, as I do, account it a detestable idol, not God, but contrary to him and his truth.' After many raging words and vain objections, Bonner said there was no remedy, but he must be burned. Smith replies, 'Ye shall do no more unto me than ye have done to better men than either of us, but think not thereby to quench the Spirit of God, nor to make your matter good; for your sore is too well seen to be healed so privily with blood, for even the very children have your deeds in derision.'*

"JOHN PHILPOT, another eminent martyr, being examined by the Bishop of London and others, protested thus: 'There be two things, principally, by which the clergy of this day deceive the whole realm; that is the sacrament of the body and blood of Christ, and the *name* of the *Catholic Church;* both of which they have usurped, having, indeed, neither of them! As touching their sacrament of the altar, I say now, as I said before, *that it is not the sacrament of Christ;* neither in the same is there *any manner of Christ's presence.* And when they take on the name of the Catholic Church, they are nothing so, but call you from the true religion to vain superstition.'

"Dr. JOHNSON gave it as his opinion, that deviations from the primitive mode in what is merely ritual may be admitted on the *ground of convenience,* and that the Roman Catholics are as well warranted in withholding the cup from the people as the Established Church is in substituting sprinkling for the ancient mode of baptism.

"In the form of communion composed by Drs. Ellert and Neander, for the new evangelical church in Prussia, under the authority of the king, no terms of actual 'consecration' were used, the historical fact only being related that Christ said, 'This is my body,' etc.; 'This is my blood,' etc. Such was the state expedient adopted to reconcile the opinions of the Lutheran and Calvinistic churches. Many, however, contended that this was no real sacrament at all, only a narrative of the transaction; and that in this way, even Jews and Mohammedans might be admitted to communi-

---

* He was consigned to the stake at Uxbridge, in the reign of Queen Mary, *in the year of death,* 1555.

cate. Many conscientious Prussians suffered severely on account of their religious convictions, and especially on this subject of the eucharist.

"And who does not see that if a literal interpretation be given to the language and example of the 'Lord's Supper,' a *supper* should now be strictly observed, and not the use of a sop-cup, or wafer (or crumb of bread) in the middle of the day. But in the eucharist, as in water-baptism, a literal consistency, or imitation, has oft been departed from. The Anglican Church forbids her ministers to administer the communion to any but to such as kneel, under pain of suspension. On the continent the bread and wine are usually received by Protestants while standing, and that weekly or monthly.

"At a general meeting of Scotch Episcopal ministers held at Perth in 1617, one of the articles adopted enjoined the practice of 'kneeling at the communion,' which proved more obnoxious to the people than all the others, being so identified in their minds with the idolatry of Rome that they shrank from it with horror, and great excitement and opposition followed.

. . . .

It is not necessary to continue this record of sacramentarian ritualism on the one hand, and of the protest against it on the other; the true spiritual Israel has waged this conflict with the " Israel after the flesh," in all the Christian ages. The high sacramentarians, as the Greek, Papal, and Anglican Churches, have proclaimed the right of *the embodied Church to institute and decree ordinances and customs, and enforce them ;* and certain it is that no sacrament has been observed for a long period among them without a tedious addenda of senseless mummeries, and superstitious adjuncts; and turning the attention of religious inquirers wholly to the forms rather than to the substance of religion in its regenerating and life-exalting power of love to God and man.

Love and fellowship have been everywhere sacrificed to the *sacrament* and the *form*, however much every age and nation has differed as to what the form should be. Germany was at one time about depopulated by a bloody war for churches and sacraments (see tract, "Results of One War," published by the American Peace Society).* And every nation where

---

* In England, in 1555, and the three following years (in Mary's reign), not less than two hundred and eighty persons were publicly burnt or otherwise executed, chiefly for their difference of sentiment on the mysterious question of the bread and wine; and many more died in prison. This was using the power of state to enforce *a sacrament in the Church!* And of fifty million persons, said to have perished directly or indirectly by the persecutions of the Papal Church, visited upon Protestants, how many of these were not on account of *nonconformity in sacraments?*

See this subject with the connected persecutions lucidly set forth in John Allen's "STATE CHURCHES." from which we have freely copied, and to which we have often referred in this volume.

Christ has been named has stained its soil by the bloodshed and martyrdom of its truest saints for this cause supremely. Did Jesus Christ come to send "a sword," among his followers for such causes? Ah, when shall the churches be truly *Protestantized* and reformed from the whole ritual idolatry of Judaism, Heathenism, and the Papacy? Who will arise to strike down with a mighty arm this illusive idolatry of ceremonies and sacraments?

Who, in Christ's name, will enter the lists to lift the real New Testament baptism from its degradation and subsidized vassalage to a mere formal worship? to sect and schism? and to profitless externals? while the true Anointing, the Spirit of life from God, is eschewed? Who will call all churches from their worthless clamor about the Lord's table, to that true "supping" and "dining" with Christ, to which Christ invites us?

As the Lord's Supper is now ceremonially (as a general custom) celebrated at the "dining" hour, we submit (in concluding this chapter) the following most practical and most sensible thoughts on the "Lord's Dinner," and the *improvement* here suggested, in lieu of the ceremonial supper, and its awakened strifes, as more honorable to Christ, and more beneficent to man. Moreover, the "Lord's Dinner," as thus presented, will surely be found to be an *institution* of the "first resurrection," the "regeneration," or the *New Dispensation*.

THE LORD'S DINNER.

[Extract from a sermon preached to a Presbyterian congregation in Chicago, on occasion of a National Thanksgiving. By Rev. ROBERT PATTERSON, *Pastor of the church.*]

(Inserted by permission of the author.)

TEXT—"Come, and dine:" and context—JOHN xxi. 12, etc.

[A clear and concise view (by contrast) of the kind of sacrament, sacrifice, ritual, and *ordinance* the Lord Jesus Christ would have us observe.]

"Hundreds of volumes have been written, and thousands of sermons have been preached on the Lord's Supper, the symbol of the cleansing and feeding of our souls; but who has ever read a volume or heard a sermon on the Lord's Dinner? So greatly have we neglected this other half of true religion, charity for the bodily wants of our brethren of mankind, that I presume my hearers experience a feeling of surprise that I should read such a text, and that some may suppose I am about to present some innovation on Christian doctrine, or at least to startle you by some novelty. To disabuse your minds of such a mistake, as well as to establish your faith on the foundation of the apostles and prophets, it is needful—

"I. To show you the historical place of the Lord's Dinner, as a Christly exemplification of that union of faith and charity, which ever constituted true religion.

"II. Glance at the extent of our backsliding, and the evils resulting from it.

"III. Exhort to a return to Christ's Christianity.

"I. Christ's exemplary care for the bodies, as well as the souls of sinners, was not now for the first time manifested to the world. His humane charity was displayed at the very beginning of the Church, by his clothing our first parents in coats of skins, probably those of the first sacrifice. The covenant of salvation, with its rainbow sign, is no sooner renewed with Noah, than Christ, taking notice of man's heavier toils in the malarious atmosphere of an inundated world, enlarges his larder with a more generous diet, and allows him the use of animal food—showing thus that religion cares first for the body, and next for the soul. You next find the Lord eating of Abraham's and Sarah's cakes and calf under the tree, and thereafter directing a perishing fugitive African woman and her child to a fountain of water in the wilderness. All these divine examples give us Christ's idea of religion, as a salvation of the body no less than the soul.

"Then you find our Lord taking notice of the straw which the Egyptians withheld from their slaves, counting the blows they inflicted on them, listening to the cries of the bondmen, and coming down to deliver them from slavery; all before he has made any revelation of law, or required of them any return of sacrifice. Moreover, you will not fail to note the daily gospel of manna to feed their crying children, and the quails with which he gratified their appetites, and the fountain of the smitten rock with which he quenched their thirst, and the promised land, flowing with milk and honey, which he bestowed upon them—not from any expectation that they would be won, to gratitude by his goodness, for he knew they would persist in unbelief and perish in their sins; but simply because it is a delight to him to do good, even to the unthankful and to the evil.

"You will not forget, also, when he instituted ordinances of worship, to which he commanded his people to devote not less than one-tenth of the produce of their farms or increase, how little he says about psalms or sermons, and how emphatically he reiterates his commands that the poor and the stranger, and the fatherless and the widow, shall be invited to eat of the sacrifices, and to rejoice before the Lord. The worship of the God of Israel at the great national festivals was more inseparably associated with a public dinner to the poor, than our church services are with prayer and praise.

"This must be remembered when we read all these prophecies of the reign of Messiah, which predict his love for the poor and needy, the plenty which shall spring from the earth in his days, and the feast which he shall spread for all people.

"When he comes into the world he takes his place among the poor, is cradled in a manger, and reared in a carpenter's workshop. We see him looking for a breakfast in the hedge-row, and comparing his lot with the foxes and the birds of the air—doubtless voluntarily enduring these privations that he might the better sympathize with the hungry and the houseless poor.

" His first miracle, at the marriage in Cana of Galilee, plainly disclosed that his religion was to be no *merely intellectual and spiritual doctrine*, but a restoration of *all the blessings of Eden*, a deliverance from the perplexities of poverty, and an enjoyment of social family plenty and happiness in the living earthly home, through the blessing of the Son of man ; and his first sermon assured us that our Heavenly Father, who provides for the lilies of the field and the birds of the air, cares for the food and clothing of his children. The whole course of his ministry followed this beginning. You ever find him preaching the gospel of the kingdom, and healing all manner of sickness, and all manner of disease among the people. When the hungry multitudes fainted around him, he had compassion on them, and twice miraculously fed them with barley loaves and fishes— influenced by no hope of buying their suffrages, for he foresaw and foretold their apostasy, but simply by his natural inborn love of relieving human suffering.

" His preaching corresponds to his practice, and he urges his people to follow his disinterested example in this matter :

" ' When thou makest a dinner or a supper, call not thy friends nor thy brethren, neither thy kinsmen nor thy rich neighbors, lest they also bid thee again, and a recompense be made thee ; but when thou makest a feast, call the poor and the maimed, the lame and the blind, and thou shalt be blessed, for they cannot recompense thee, and thou shalt be recompensed at the resurrection of the just.' No command for any one to endow a college or build a synagogue ever fell from his lips, nor does he glory in the mighty works performed in his name by his disciples ; but you hear him commanding a rich young man to sell his estates, and houses, and horses, and furniture, and give the proceeds to the poor, and rejoicing that salvation had come to the house of the convicted publican who made restitution of his extortions, and gave half of the remainder of his estate away in charity.

" In his last public address to his disciples before his crucifixion, charity occupies the most eminent place, and is enforced by the most solemn considerations. He describes the irrevocable issues of the great day of retribution, not as decided by an accurate knowledge or an intelligent orthodoxy, or even a fervent piety, but by their infallible fruit—a warm-hearted, open-handed charity for Christ's sake. 'Then shall the King say unto them on his right hand, Come, ye blessed of my Father, inherit the kingdom prepared for you from the foundation of the world : for I was an hungered, and ye gave me meat ; I was thirsty, and ye gave me drink ; I was a stranger, and ye took me in ; naked, and ye clothed me ; I was sick, and ye visited me ; I was in prison, and ye came unto me. Then shall the righteous answer him, saying, Lord, when saw we thee an hungered, and fed thee ? or thirsty, and gave thee drink ? when saw we thee a stranger, and took thee in ? or naked, and clothed thee ? or when saw we thee sick, or in prison, and came unto thee? And the King shall answer and say unto them, Verily I say unto you, inasmuch as ye have done it unto one of the least of these my brethren, ye have done it unto me.' Matt. xxv. 34-40.

"We are now, I hope, in some degree prepared to receive the meaning of the solemn scene recorded in the text. As immediately before his passion our Lord concentrated all the great truths of his atonement in the significant symbols of the Lord's Supper,* so now, about to send them forth to the great work of converting the world by his gospel of love, he embodies and dramatically exhibits to his apostles, in the Lord's Dinner, a vivid picture of the other great department of religion, a true Christ-like charity, as their guide in all their intercourse with their brethren of mankind.

"It was at Jerusalem, the holy city, that the Son of God revealed the sublime system of theology to his Church; but the Son of man sought the familiar shores of the Sea of Galilee, where he had wrought so many works of mercy, when he would teach his brethren the lessons of a kindly humanity.

"The Son of Mary, during the period of his lowly life of humiliation, might, despite the halo of his miracles, be expected to feel for the wants which he shared with his followers; but now, that he is declared to be the Son of God with power by his resurrection from the dead, and exalted above the stings of want and death, and associating with the hierarchy of heaven, does he, *can* he, still retain the same fellow-feelings for our infirmities, the same care for our bodily necessities? Undoubtedly! This is Jesus Christ, 'the same yesterday, to-day, and forever.' 'This is now the third time he showed himself after he was risen from the dead,' and on each occasion had eaten with them, or asked them to handle him, and see that he was still the same. The friends to whom he addressed himself are the same humble fishermen whom he had called to make them fishers of men, who had been his companions in the glory of the holy mount, had witnessed his agony in the garden, and whom he was about to commission to establish his kingdom in all the world. It is the last interview between the Lord and the Church, of which we have any full account, and it occupies the solemn position of being the very last recorded by the pen of inspiration—the conclusion of the gospel history; the Holy Ghost thus intimating the solemn significance of the event. Ponder it carefully.

"See the solicitude of the Lord for the success of the common industry of his people, in the kindly familiar inquiry, 'Children, have ye any meat?' He sympathizes with the toiling tradesman. Then behold his willingness to help them, by his superhuman wisdom, to a success they

---

* Query: Was not the supper, now so greatly perverted to an ecclesiastical or sectarian use, by apostles and primitive saints used only to inculcate lessons of charity to the poor, the sick, and the needy also? So it was.

could never acquire by their own toil. For the truth of the other lesson drawn from this acted parable of the success of the gospel fishers of men, we must just take this literal truth for granted, that the Lord is [that is, cares] for the body ; and you behold the recognition of his character, while his person was yet veiled by the mists of the morning, by this well-known care of their bodily welfare. John at once says, ' It is the Lord.'

"But the scene that follows the landing confounds all comment. We see the fire, the fish laid thereon, and the bread; and we ask ourselves, in utter amazement, 'Have those pierced and glorified hands been engaged in these menial offices for his hungry brethren?' and we remember the supper, and the basin, and the towel, and the washing of feet, and feel that it is certainly the same Jesus; but alas! our astonishment proves that we are of a different spirit. And as we think of our so-called *spirituality*, which shrinks from personal labors for the poor, and of our religion, all dogmas and prayers and praises, we blush and feel how far removed from Christ's Christianity is our *correct, cold, supercilious orthodoxy:* and we would fain be excused from eating of this dinner cooked by Jesus' hands. But he will take no excuse; he calls us to ' Come and dine,' and none durst ask him ' Who art thou?' knowing it was the Lord !

"The Church was not slow to learn the lesson thus taught by the example of the Lord. Recognizing him as the great Redeemer of mankind from all the sorrows and miseries of sin, and himself as the messenger of Christ's salvation to the bodies and souls of men, no sooner was the Holy Ghost poured out than Christians rose in a might of charity, which, had it continued, would soon have conquered the world. Rich men sold their estates for the relief of the poor ; no man said that any thing he possessed was his own, and it seemed as if the human race would soon be once again one happy family. The very first ecclesiastical business of the new Christian society was the appointment of deacons, whose sole and special business it was to see that none of the poor were neglected in the distribution of this charity. Paul, the most doctrinal of the apostles, is as emphatic in enforcing charity as the chief of Christian virtues, as John, who leaned on Jesus' breast. With his friend Titus, he risked his life in dangerous journeys, to collect from Christians in distant lands, and of strange tongues, relief for the victims of famine, the poor and suffering at Jerusalem. James, the Lord's brother, writes an epistle expressly to rebuke a tendency to a niggardly orthodoxy, and to pillory faith without works.

"The early churches followed in Christ's footsteps; and when the heathen, terror-stricken by the plague, fled from their dearest friends, leaving the sick unattended and the dead unburied, the Christians, singing their hymns of faith and hope, *nursed the sick, buried the dead, and fed the orphans* thrown by thousands on their care. Thus the gospel was demonstrated a gospel of love.

"For centuries the Christian Church gave great prominence to charity, as the chief part of religion. She found more than half the population of the Roman empire slaves, and emancipated them; forbade the fierce soldier to strike the fallen warrior who asked for his life in the name of Jesus; *purchased captives with the price of the sacred vessels, and set them free,* as the noblest offerings to the God of Liberty; built monasteries and churches, where the oppressed and helpless fugitive might flee for sanctuary; and waved the awful [wand] of the Father of the fatherless in the face of the pursuing robber, ravisher and murderer; endowed these establishments with lands, and taught her people to send them gifts, which she expended in feeding the multitudes of famishing men, women and children, whom the invasions of the Goths, Vandals, Germans and Northmen had driven from their homes to perish; and, finally, laying hold on these very savages, converted and civilized them into the French, German, British, and American churches and nations. [But Popery having at length run to the extreme of making charity and alms, legacies and bequests, without repentance, faith, and a personal righteousness, the substance of all religion, need we wonder that there was at length a great reaction?]

"Need we marvel that the men of an after generation, who having enjoyed the benefit of the battles of the first reformers, took time to hold synods, and councils, and assemblies, and to frame articles, and most formal and minute catechisms and confessions of faith, some of which embrace several thousand propositions, and present a complete body of theology, *should have so utterly forgotten that theology is only one-half of religion, and never have treated of the subject of humanity,* which occupies so large a portion of the Scriptures.

"In a most minute confession of faith, ranging over all subjects, from the eternal decrees to the last judgment, and displayed in more than thirty chapters, there is only one devoted to 'Good Works,' and six-sevenths of that chapter are controversial and polemical. In a catechism designed for the instruction of adults in the nature and practice of the true Christian Protestant Reformed Religion, containing over two thousand propositions, there are only two references to the duty by whose performance men will be judged for eternity. Nor is this awful omission peculiar to the creeds and catechisms of that period. In a collection of the works of the Puritan divines, consisting of fifty-five octavo volumes, and treating of every subject of controversial theology, cases of conscience, and many of the duties of common life, *there is not a single chapter or discourse on charity, and not more than half a dozen casual references to the duty of relieving the poor.*＊

＊ In his inaugural at the University of St. Andrew's [England], Mr. Froude, the historian and lecturer on Papal and Protestant annals, touches the subject of ministerial education. He seems to consider it as too fearfully abstract and ritualistic to meet the wants of these corrupt times. Hear him:—"What I deplore in our present higher education," says this eminent man, "is the devotion of so much effort and so many precious years to subjects which have no

"We need not wonder that a theology thus divorced from charity was speedily rejected by the people, whose instincts have always denied the sovereignty of the intellect, but bowed down willingly to the *supremacy of love.* What cared they to be mocked with unintelligible disputes about election and free will, while the law of the land made it a penal offence for a starving pauper to solicit alms, and forbade the workingman to leave the parish in which he was born, on pain of forfeiting his right to the alms-house, and of risk of imprisonment as a vagrant? Accordingly, the English people . . . rose in utter disgust and loathing, and cast off this heartless orthodoxy, which had shown itself so utterly ignorant or careless of the wants of human nature. Wise and learned in all that pertains to God, it is to this day dumb on the claims of manhood. Need we wonder that when it had been accepted as the standard of religion, as in Germany, England, and New England, and to some extent in Scotland, the reaction to Socinianism was speedily accomplished.

"In Scotland this result was partially prevented by the practical sagacity of the Scottish Parliament, which, influenced partly by a desire to save their own pockets from a poor-rate like that of England, placed the relief of the poor as a charge upon the church, to be defrayed out of the Sabbath collections, and distributed by the elders; which provision, pitiably insuf-

---

practical bearing upon life. Classics and philosophy are supposed at Oxford to be specially adapted for creating ministers of religion. The training of clergymen is, if anything, the special object of Oxford teaching. All arrangements are made with a view to it. The heads of colleges, the resident fellows, tutors, and professors, are generally ecclesiastics themselves. The effect ought to have been considerable.

"We have had thirty years of unexampled clerical activity among us; churches have been doubled; theological books, magazines, reviews, news-papers, have been poured out by hundreds of thousands, while by the side of it there has sprung up an equally astonishing development of moral dishonesty. From the great houses in the city of London to the village grocer, the commercial life of England has been saturated with fraud. So deep has it gone that a strictly honest tradesman can hardly hold his ground against competition. You can no longer trust that any article that you buy is the thing which it pretends to be. We have false weights, false measures, cheating, and shoddy everywhere. Yet the clergy have seen all this grow up in absolute indifference; and the great question which at this moment is agitating the Church of England is the *color of the ecclesiastical petticoats.* Many a hundred sermons have I heard in England, many a dissertation on the mysteries of the faith, on the divine mission of the clergy, on apostolical succession, on bishops, and justification, and the theory of good works, and verbal inspiration, and the *efficacy of the sacraments;* but never during these thirty wonderful years, never one that I can recollect on common honesty or those primitive commandments—Thou shalt not lie, and thou shalt not steal.

ficient as it was, by God's blessing prevented the total divorce of faith and charity there.

"But in England, until the march of Methodism, the name of Presbyterian was synonymous with Socinian; and in New England, Universalists to-day are preaching and teaching in churches and schools founded and endowed by Scotch Presbyterians and English Puritans. In both countries the great majority of the people have turned their backs on the church; and in London, the capital of Christendom, not one-tenth of the people are communicants. Neither these facts, however, nor all the increased activity of the present century, have yet awakened the Protestant churches to any earnest consideration of the subject. In the bookstores of Philadelphia, Boston, New York, Washington, and Chicago, *I have not been able to find a systematic treatise in the English language on Charity, such as French, Italian, and German laymen and noblemen have written.* In a collection of some hundreds of pamphlets, sermons, and addresses, delivered during the past ten years, now before me, there is only one which treats of the duty of beneficence. [Yet they have a plenty of treatises on the sacraments.—AUTHOR.]

"The Tract Society has issued some excellent tracts on the subject, and a layman has called attention to it, as furnishing '*New Themes for the Protestant Clergy;*' but beyond this, the orthodox clergy seem to have concluded that the great business of their lives was to preach theology, and if their people chose to practise beneficence, it was over and above the requirements of the church covenant. During thirty years' regular attendance on church, I have never heard a sermon on the subject of Charity.

"And the people, too, settle down into the belief that a religious experience consists in beliefs, and notions, and feelings, and prayers [and sacraments] merely, and would feel greatly shocked to hear any one narrate such an experience as our Lord enjoined in these passages we have read; yet it is evident that both our Lord and his apostles regarded *this dinner, cooked with his own hands for hungry men,* as not less sacred than the preceding sacramental supper; and that when charity and worship interfere, *worship,* according to him, *must always give way to charity,* as he says, '*I will have mercy, and not* SACRIFICE,' though ministers familiar with the Bible will think and speak of religion *as something different from charity.* [Do they not urge their *sacraments* and put them *in the place* of love and mercy?—AUTHOR.]

"Nevertheless, the divorce of religion and charity is not now and never was complete. The Bible, with its great catholic benevolence, and its graphic and natural style, its biographies, and similes, and parables, was always more read than the theologians. The catechism was forgotten, but the good Samaritan was remembered. Wherever there was true love to Christ, there was always love to the poor for his sake, who had not where to lay his head. So it came to pass that poor, stunted, prickly Cavinism, all neglected and untilled though it was, when the angry blasts of biting controversy lulled, and the sun of revival shone, began to scent the air with fragrant benevolences, and ripened healthful golden fruits of works good and profitable unto men, while the rootless limbs cut off from Christianity by infidel reformers, and planted with wondrous prediction of the miracles they were about to accomplish, *die out before their planters, and wither and are cast into the fire.* Socialism is selfishness—Christianity is charity."

BENEVOLENT INSTITUTIONS BASED WHOLLY ON CHRISTIANITY.

"All our greatest and most beneficial institutions are the real and avowed fruits of Christian faith; not by any means so great or so numerous as they should be, but yet the world would be in an ill case without them. Have you ever seen orphan houses, blind asylums, charity schools, Dorcas societies, city missions, Bible women, medical missions, prison reforms, Sabbath schools, West India emancipation, acting on infidel principles? Does any man dream that our war having been fought, four millions of negroes would have been set free, if the people could have believed the dogma, that fourteen different races of men originally sprang out of the earth, divided into superior and inferior races, united by no ties of common parentage and common redemption, and incapable of equal rights and equal happiness in our common Father's house? Or did ever infidel or heathen nation show such an outburst of genuine charity as when thousands of clergymen and laymen, from love to Christ and country, left their pulpits and offices for the camp, to bind up the wounds of the bleeding, and give the cup of cordial to the sick, to sing hymns of hope by the bedside of the languishing, *to find their famishing enemies,* and feed and nurse them, transmit the last messages to friends from the dying, and point the departing spirit to Him who felt the sharpness of death for us, and thereby opened the kingdom of heaven to all believers? This, and much more than this, was done during the course of the war, avowedly from love to Christ, without pay or fame, by Christians of all evangelical churches; and all felt that it was but a return to the Christianity of the gospels. And so far from this outburst of charity leading to any disparagement of devotion, it is now manifest that the churches and Christians who most actively engaged in these labors of love have been revived by the largest outpouring of the spirit of prayer, and blessed with the greatest success in the conversion of souls.

"The past history of the Protestant churches, then, shows us the suicidal results of dissecting religion into its component parts, and of offering to the world a skeleton of orthodoxy, instead of a living gospel. The present experiments of the Church in the revival of charity, as a revival of religion, encourage us to persevere in the endeavor to retrace our backslidings, and to imitate the example of our blessed Lord in endeavoring to save *both the bodies and the souls of men.* God and man alike disown orthodoxy divorced from charity, and bless the religion of faith and love. Infidels know this, and labor by every art to procure the power over men's minds which the administration of charity to their bodies imparts. But Christian faith is needful to the permanence and success of their charities; and, as they have it not themselves, they frequently seek a partnership with Christians. The proposal is sometimes made as a favor, and a relief to the aged Church. Having failed to relieve the world's miseries, she is invited in future to confine her labors to her prayers and her tracts, her sermons and her psalms, and hand over the work of charity to them, or unite with them in bestowing bodily relief on infidel principles. We reply, that the proposition is officious. Why should they propose to do our business? How do they come to possess a monopoly of humanity? We are men as well as they. We reply, in the second place, that the past experience of infidel philanthropists is not encouraging to those who would seek to raise man's condition by destroying his faith in God's revelation, in Christ's salvation, and in a holy immortality. We reply again, that they grossly mistake the revival of religion, and the power of God's providential education of his Church, if they suppose we will ever again tolerate the divorce of works of charity from the faith which produces them, or own a religion of dead faith. We thank them, however, for the insult, which has roused us to an examination of our principles, and we hope will impel us to such a performance of our duty as will preclude its repetition."

True Religion combines Piety and Charity.

"God's religion consists of a living soul of piety and a working body of charity, fully described in the two great commands, 'Thou shalt love the Lord thy God with all thy heart, and thou shalt love thy neighbor as thyself.' Mere sentimental piety, unclothed in the bodily forms of practical benevolence, has no more influence in this world of ours than those disembodied spirits which, it is said, some where tinkle on tables, and move the tongues of imaginative females, and attempt other equally useful performances; and we know from the words of our Lord that it is treated with equal contempt in the other world of stern realities. But, on the other hand, benevolence toward man can have no origin but in faith toward God, as the common Father of all mankind; nor has philanthropy ever been practised persistently by any save believers in the brotherhood of men. All the liberties, amenities and charities of our modern civilization are merely so many expressions of Christianity, without which they would no more have existed here and now than they did in Britain two thousand years ago, or than they do in Turkey or China to-day.

"Had Christianity been fully and practically taught in Christian lands for the last eighteen centuries, as it was by its Author, these blessed fruits of this tree of life had been much more numerous. There is scarcely a misery of life which might not have been relieved, not an ignorant country which might not have been instructed, and not a savage nation which might not have been civilized, had the time and talent which Christian churches have wasted in theological disputes, AND THE MANY LIVES WHICH CHRISTIAN NATIONS HAVE EXPENDED IN WAR, been employed in the blessed work of doing good to the bodies and souls of men. These two must never be separated in our philanthropic efforts; for the plain reason, that we never meet them separated in actual life. God made man with body and soul, capable of eternal happiness or misery, and both alike redeemed by the sufferings of the body and soul of the Son of God. If you can find a man without a body, you may rationally propose to him a mere theology of the intellect; and if you can find men without souls, they are suitable subjects for the charity of the manger and the stable—a Christless benevolence. But for the mortal men of this world of ours—*so cold and busy, and sickly and hungry*—a gospel of flour and fire-wood, and gospel consolations, of shoes and Sabbath-schools, of hoods and hymn books, of conversion from sin, and *steady work and fair wages*, is the only practical religion.

"Such a religion the Young Men's Christian Association of this city carries to the homes of the poor. Their visitors feed the hungry children of the widow, fill her stove with a rousing fire, tell of Jesus, for whose sake it is done, and invite the children to Sabbath-school and the parents to church and prayer-meeting. They bring the temperance pledge to the drunkard, and kneel in prayer with him for God's grace to strengthen him against the love of liquor. They send the gentle sympathizing Christian woman to the side of the sick sufferer with a bowl of soup and words of sympathy, and a tract or religious newspaper full of soul-comfort; for man doth not live by bread alone, and the sorrows of a soul convinced of sin are not to be lulled by incredible universalisms about the equal love of God for holiness and wickedness. But why occupy time in describing the work which you yourselves are performing; for this work is not done by paid agents, but by the volunteer labor of the members of the churches. It is, in fact, a return to Christ's Christianity, and will ultimately, I hope, engage every member of the Church; for *nothing short of personal labor* corresponds to the example of our blessed Saviour. In the meantime, let those who do not now engage personally in it furnish liberally the means to those who do, and bless God that they may thus express their gratitude to the God of our mercies by a generous thank-offering for the relief of Christ's poor, and God will own it, perhaps, by inspiring you to become the almoners of your own bounty. He will accept and bless it, and will one day say, '*Inasmuch as ye did it unto one of the least of these my brethren, ye did it unto me.*'"

ADDENDA.

CORRELATED MISCELLANY.

CHRISTIANS NON-ACCOUNTABLE TO MAN—WHAT THE REFORMATION TAUGHT.

[From an address of Dr. Schaff before the *Festival of the Reformation*, held at Plymouth Church, Brooklyn, October 31, 1867.]

"I HAVE not time to read these ninety-five theses of Luther to-night; if I did, you would be surprised to observe how recently is the full-grown development of Protestantism. In some of these theses Luther professes great reverence for the Pope of Rome and submission to his authority. In those theses is found a vital element of truth, which proves a living germ of the whole system of Protestant Christianity. It is especially the doctrine of repentance, concerning which Luther teaches that it does not consist simply in outward mortification and penances, but in a change of heart, and concerning Jesus Christ and his cross as the true and unfailing fountain for the remission of sins, to which, if the sinner applies, peace will come to his conscience.

"The Reformation was not a sudden abrupt event; nor was it a part of any declaration on the part of Luther. He was innocently made a reformer. The times made him as he made the times; or Providence, rather, shaped both to each other. And when he affixed those ninety-five theses to the doors of the castle church of Wurtemberg he had not the most distant idea of the incalculable consequences which should grow out of them. I say the Reformation had been prepared long before, not only by the corruptions of the Papacy, but also by the great revival of letters through Erasmus and others, by the labors of the Mystics who were preaching a moral inward religion—a religion consisting in direct union and communion of the soul with God. It was prepared by the activity of Wickliff in England, of Huss in Germany, of Savonarola in Italy, and many like-minded divines and preachers throughout Europe during the fourteenth and fifteenth centuries. It was prepared by many of the devout in the Catholic Church, in the head and in the members. It was prepared by the invention of the art of printing, which preceded it about seventy years, and which alone spread the light of the Reformation with the speed of lightning all over Europe; so that the Reformation of the sixteenth century is only the ripe fruit, the seed of which had been cast and scattered for centuries before in the various parts of Christendom. Hence those ninety-five theses kindled the Reformation all over the Church; they were the signal of the great intellectual and spiritual battle which now broke out all over the Catholic world. It had the same connection with Protestantism that Fort Sumter had to the civil war. It was not the cause but the occasion of the Reformation. The material which was to be kindled into a conflagration was at hand long before. All the causes were prepared through the preceding ages in all the departments of the Christian Church, and hence the extraordinary effect.

"What has come out of those ninety-five theses at the beginning of the Reformation? Simultaneous with that movement of Luther was this Zwinglian Reformation in Switzerland, and Calvinism in Geneva. That was followed by the Reformed Churches of England and Scotland. Then came Puritanism, which was the mover and shaper of the destinies of the New World, not only in religion but in politics. We may say of the Declaration of Independence of 1776, our whole political economy, our self-governing institutions, our civil and religious liberties—they are all the legitimate results of the Reformation of the sixteenth century. The great proclaimers were Luther, and Zwingle, and Calvin, and Knox, and Latimer, and Cranmer. It marked the great epoch in civil as well as in religious affairs. And this leads me to say a few words about the proper principle or moving force of Protestantism as represented by the great reformers of the sixteenth century.

"Protestantism is not simply a negative protest against tyranny and Popery (infidelity likewise protests); but it is a protest on a positive foundation, on the foundation of the gospel of Jesus Christ. The nature of Protestantism, the essence of Protestantism, the principle of Protestantism, is freedom; but freedom only from the restraints of man, from a tyranny of conscience, from all that false teachers had imposed upon man without any divine warrant; it is freedom on the basis of obedience to God and to his holy word. It is that freedom which consists in the cheerful and ready obedience to the divine word and to the divine will. The great Protestant principle is this, the doctrine of evangelical freedom. It brings man into a direct and immediate relation to Christ. The relation of the Roman Catholic to Christ is mediate, through the Church and through an innumerable army of saints. The Roman Catholic, pious as he may be, hardly ever prays directly to Christ, but always through the mediation of the Virgin Mary; while the Protestant Christian always enjoys the privilege of addressing himself directly to Christ; he enjoys a direct and individual union and communion with him. This is the soul and heart, the sum and substance of true evangelical Protestantism; and this is what I mean by evangelical freedom. It is freedom in Christ as required in the New Testament, without the intervention of human traditions. It is freedom to search the Scriptures to see whether they really teach what has been given us by our pastors and parents—the exercise of private judgment concerning those divine truths necessary for salvation. It is the saving power of freedom in Christ, all-sufficient as a rule of faith. Hence theologians teach of a formal and material principle of Protestantism: the formal teaches the supremacy and all-sufficiency of the Holy Scriptures; that they are a sufficient rule in all matters of faith and practice; and the material principle consists in the doctrine of justification by the grace of Christ as apprehended by faith. But both these principles resolve themselves into the one principle of evangelical freedom in Christ.

"Protestantism aims at a universal priesthood and the universal kinship of the human family. This great mission is to be accomplished here on the soil of the new world. America was barely discovered when Luther commenced his reformation, and the name of America never occurs in his writings. It is here and here alone that the idea of a universal priesthood of believers will be ultimately carried out.''

HENRY DICKINSON, of the Society of Friends, also added:

"Martin Luther believed that he was a good son of the Church. He knew not the mighty power that was working within him, when he sought a spiritual benefit (as instructed by the Pope) by creeping on his knees at Rome. How much that man suffered in the earnestness of his purpose, to experience the blessedness of peace with God, and joy in the Holy Ghost, none of us know. It is our privilege to reap the benefits that have been purchased for us by the sacrifices of Martin Luther and others. 'The just shall live by faith,' was wrought out in his spirit. How much that man passed through in his narrow cell at Wurtemberg we can never know; but we may go over the ground in thought and reflection. We reflect upon that journey to Worms—how nothing seemed to make him fear; that crowded assembly of magnates and representatives of the Pope were as nothing to him. He saw him that was invisible, with his mind's eye, by faith. Luther moved on with prayer; the Saviour led him as the divine truth was opened to him; first beginning as the devout son of the Church to sweep away abuses, he went on until, at last, he came to believe the Pope the very incarnation of all evil.''

At the same meeting Rev. S. H. TYNG, Jr., spoke as follows:

ANOTHER REFORMATION NEEDED.

"If there be any fact to which the American people need to awake, it is to the necessity of another reformation, a reformation in every successor of the old Reformation. For, whilst in the Church which I strive loyally to serve, there may be excrescences, developments more pronounced from the inevitable tendencies of liturgic worship, I hold, that in every existing Church of Christ the spirit of Rome is manifesting itself. The effort to invest the Lord's Supper with an excessive dignity *can nowhere be found* in the word of God; it is rendered a sacrament of *distance*, rather than a sacrament of *nearness*. This is Romanism in the bud. And these peculiarities which belong to the church of which I am a member, I claim to belong to every existing Church of Christ. The great need is placed in connection with the great event, and we rally around Luther when we stand true to the principles which he affirmed. Rome is not eternal. Rome is not an organization simply; it is not a ceremony. Rome is in doctrine, and where Romish doctrine is admitted, or where the tendencies of the Romish doctrine are submitted to, there is the need of the united effort to oppose the innovation.

"What is the spirit of the Reformation? Free thought, limited only by the word of God, and abundant confidence and trust in the self-vindicating power of the word of God. I believe that everything which any man can get out of this Bible he has a right to teach, whether his speculations overthrow my theories or not—entire freedom of thought limited by the inspiration and authority of God's sacred book. Then, over and above that, an abundant faith that God can bring forth truth out of this controversy. What is a free pulpit but this? Take the three points which make up the spirit of the Reformation, as it was afterwards developed. First, opposition to the doctrine of the mass, the false use of sacraments. Here is a system which can symbolize itself, typify itself in the crucifix and candle, in postures of reverence before the plain table of the Lord. The true doctrine of the sacrament cannot symbolize itself. On one occasion Francis I., attended by the Bishop of Paris, went to the Church of St. Eustace when a celebrated minister, suspected of a Reformation tendency, was to present his views of the Lord's Supper. He said, amidst the universal silence: 'In your service you say lift up your hearts —you bid them look above this table. You say, here is the memorial; but the One to look to is above!'

"The authority of the conscience, enlightened by the word of God, can be carried out in the same line of thought. Christians are asleep to the tendencies of the Church of Rome. The only way to resist these claims of Rome, which were resisted in the Reformation, and which have been almost smothered, is by an absolute liberty of priesthood—the absolute freedom of thought in the word of God, even although it may betray some persons into absurdity, still the admission of every one to read this Bible as they choose, providing they recognize its authority and its inspiration, and the inalienable right to preach whatever and whenever they please!"

While Drs. Wall, and Geo. Fox, and Robinson, and Gill, and Brewster, and Gale, etc., were laying foundations and defining the boundaries of their diverse churches, placing diversity thus in well-defined sect-form, as we come down the track of time a century or two, we find this same diversity increasing even in the same fold, so that an utter confusion of tongues is now found among the ministers and members of the same denomination.

CONFUSION AMONG PEDO-BAPTISTS.

[Outlines of a discussion in the Presbyterian Ministers' (Monday) Meeting, held at the Presbyterian Hall, Philadelphia, in the summer of 1872, touching the questions, Why are infants baptized? and, What is the duty of the Church relative to those baptized in infancy?]

The writer being present during a portion of this discussion, took notes as follows: The first speaker (name not obtained), whose essay respecting the duty of parents and the Church toward their baptized children called forth the discussion, took positions as follows:

He objected to Dr. Dale's view of the patriarchal baptism of households—as their mode of introducing their children to the patriarchal Church—and insists that the children of believers in all ages 'are born into the Church,' i. e., by their natural birth.

Hence, that baptism only recognizes their relation to the Church. He insists, therefore, that parents should so teach their children that they are members of the Church with their parents, and should so train them that they may prove to be spiritually regenerate from the womb. Baptism, to his view, is but a sign and seal of this prior engrafting into Christ.

He cites from the 'Confession of Faith' in corroboration of his view, the section which declares baptism to be a sign and seal of the covenant of grace, of engrafting into Christ, of regeneration, etc.

Another brother followed, who insisted that, according to the Confession of Faith, grace was not merely *symbolized* (as attained) but conferred according to that clause of the Confession of Faith. Chap. xxviii. sect. v. and vi.

The efficacy of baptism is not tied to that moment of time wherein it is administered; yet, notwithstanding, by the right use of this ordinance, the grace promised is not only offered *but really exhibited* and conferred by the Holy Ghost to such, whether of age or infants, as that grace belongeth unto, according to the counsel of God's own will, in his appointed time.

From this he argued that infants are really introduced into the *invisible* Church, as well as the visible, by baptism: "That is," he says, "the parent may, through sense (this sensible emblem), exercise faith, and thereby the child be regenerated." Query.

Is Popery more *sensible* and materialistic than this? Does it teach baptismal regeneration otherwise than does this expositor of the Confession of Faith? And does the Confession of Faith teach just as this brother expounds? Yet he disclaims the doctrine of baptismal regeneration, still insisting, however, as he adds: "But faith is strengthened through the sense to the child's regeneration, as those of old, seeing one let down in their midst, the sight inspired faith to the healing of the palsied man." So the act of baptism inspires the faith of parents to the regeneration of the child. Note how the fancy of even a wise man may, at the behest of a theological dogma, connect spiritual regeneration with an act that, in itself, has no more relation to such regeneration than any other of all the moral acts of a whole life. Nay, infinitely less connection with it than the after moral teaching of parents and the internal co-working influences of the Divine Spirit. But this speaker further contended that baptism, because of the faith connected with it—or that should be connected with it—was, therefore, truly the spiritual seal of regeneration. The absurdity of all such teaching, respecting baptism as a "sign" or "seal" of spiritual life or of spiritual blessings, may be seen in the light of the truth that works of love, and fruits of a living faith exhibited in the daily life of accountable agents, are alone true "signs" of a regenerated heart—and rituals never; much less a something imprinted upon or done unto an unconscious child by another person. The reverse of this is simply Luther's farcical notion of infantile faith and infantile regeneration. So the twin doctrine of baptism being a "seal" of regeneration is seen to be equally absurd in the light of the truth that, as far as man's agency can give the seal, persevering obedience and love to God and man alone constitute the seal and signet of heart regeneration. The seal that God gives is simply the strengthening, sanctifying, and abiding power of the Holy Spirit.

But this speaker, like the first, who read the essay upon the question, insisted that parents should, from the beginning, treat their children as children of God, not talking to them as though they needed conversion, or necessarily must be converted in after years, but as already redeemed, regenerate, and sanctified: thus to give the child an enlarged view of his relation to the covenant of redemption, and to the love and grace of God.

Now this is precisely what every parent, whether Pedo-Baptist, Baptist, or Quaker, should teach their children, and the one with as great faith in the faithfulness of a covenant-keeping God (a God that keeps covenant with all faithful parents), the one the same as the other. But the conception that your child is regenerate from birth, or because baptized in infancy, is intrinsically more baseless than the conceit of the faithful Quaker, that because he "walks before his household," and "is perfect" in that walk, as Abraham was, therefore he shall find his child growing up to maturity giving constant proofs of a moral regeneration from early life.

The latter has confidence in God's blessing upon consistent and effectual means of grace; the other, if he relies at all upon the baptism, relies upon that which, as a means of grace, is only imaginary, like a trusting to enchantment or magic. Yet of this latter species of trust the Church of England is full. So the Church of Luther and the Church of Rome, ay, and all sacramentarian and ritualistic churches. The writer of this, having never carried his children to the baptismal font, though connected with a church that requires it, has never doubted that children should be treated as children of God from the very first, for they are God's gift, and God's workmanship from the first, and they should never be left to think otherwise than that they belong to God and with his people for a moment, and that Christian obedience, faith, trust, prayer, and the Christian graces, are to be the characteristics of their lives, as much as of any redeemed saint. Thus teaching, the writer has not seen the time when his children, now mature, did not deem themselves a part of the church of which their parents were members, albeit they needed (at a maturer age than infancy) a deeper searching of the Spirit and its baptizing power to qualify them for faithfully and earnestly fulfilling the responsibilities assumed in becoming avowed and covenanted members of the visible Church, in which covenant they now stand.

But the speaker we criticise who teaches that baptism introduces both to the visible and invisible Church—to the visible especially, because adult believers are thus introduced—claims also, that parents and all adult members of the Church should hunt out the baptized children, and, watching over them, should encourage them to come to the Lord's Supper as members of the church with their parents. And he inquires, "Do our religious teachers that instruct children to come? and urge them to come? that they may impress upon them the responsibility of walking orderly and obediently as members of the household of faith, and as having the vows of God upon them? or do they rather surrender them without admonition and watchcare to the Evil One, to spend all their youth in dissoluteness and vice, hoping against hope for their future conversion by some marvellous display of grace countervailing all their parental negligence of moral and religious culture which was promised at their children's baptism?"

We admit there was force in this questioning of those who practise infant baptism, since it surely must be a "vain oblation" to bring children to the font, and then turn them loose in a "wilderness of sin" and to the foster-care of Satan, as it would be no less hazardous for those who do not patronize the font to do so; and if a moral end may be gained by making use of the superstition of Jew or Roman, this speaker was on the right path to turn the baptism of children to some good account. And his proposition to have them (the children) invited to the "supper" before they had formally accepted the church covenant, though a little loose Presbyterian-wise, was probably, for the sake of a moral impression on the "Jews by birth," very expedient, and commendable Christ-wise.

But the first and second speakers differed respecting the reasons for infant baptism, the first not having any definite view on that point, unless it were to obey a command (a legal reason) and to place the children, not in the church, but under its watchcare, as candidates for future membership. The second speaker was sufficiently ritualistic and sacramentarian on the subject. He would have them baptized that they might thereby be born again, and introduced both into the visible and invisible Church.

Another speaker, however (Rev. Phillips), expressed the greatest surprise at the positions taken by both the speakers, either that an infant is a child of regeneration and a spiritual child of God by its natural relation to its parents or by external baptism. He averred that the first of these positions—that the child, by its natural generation, though of Christian parentage, was a child of grace and of God—was more horrible than the doctrine of baptismal regeneration, for it made God's grace and the heavenly birth to be after the "will of the flesh," and the "will of man," contrary to the Apostle John's express teaching in the first chapter of John's Gospel. "Nor," says he, "is the doctrine that they become members of Christ by the sacrament of baptism in its fruits any better." He had left the Reformed (Dutch) Church, because it taught the doctrine of baptismal regeneration, or held to its equivalent, that we are in Christ's Church by the natural birth; and to find these doctrines taught in the Presbyterian Church leads to the inquiry, "Have I bettered myself by the change?"

Dr. Musgrave arose and said: "The whole difficulty is in confounding the visible and invisible Church." He protested against teaching children that they are Christians by virtue of their natural birth, "a most alarming doctrine," he affirms, most dangerous, infinitely worse than that of baptismal regeneration.

Another arose and said that all had departed from the question, which was: "The duty of the Church to its baptized children." Another replied that they must know what baptism is, and what it does, in order to know their duty relative to baptized children.

Dr. Dale argued that the obligation to train up a child in the way he should go rested upon parents, as parents, as much before as after their children were baptized; it arose from the natural relation of the parent to the child, and of the child to the parent. The only question was, and herein was found all the utility of baptism, if any, that it served to impress on the parent the sense of this responsibility. It did not change or regenerate the child, nor did it change its relation to the Church, that it differed from that of any other child in that respect, only thereby the parental obligation might be more thoroughly impressed, and therefore more faithfully fulfilled.

So Brother Phillips took Christ's words, "Born of water and of the Spirit," to refer in the first clause to baptism as a door to the Church's watchcare simply, and thereby to this school of grace.

Thus Drs. Dale and Phillips only appeared to have clear and well-defined evangelical views of the province and design of baptism, on the presumption that baptism is an appointed ordinance of the Church.

But the first speaker (the one that opened the discussion), in his rejoinder to all these comments, refers again to the Confession of Faith, and asks attention to its teachings before brethren cry heresy, or danger, when they declaim against his view of being the "sons of God" by the natural birth and, like the Confession of Faith, he refers to the "elect," as "born" in God's favor, and only introduced to the visible Church by ordinances, and that in their due time and order.

Now in what a muddle do these brethren find themselves by assuming infant baptism to be a duty, an ordinance of God, and referring to the "Confession of Faith" for light, where they only find that they are thrown into an inextricable labyrinth of conjecture without defined moorings when they attempt to follow its requirements and teachings! See the utter confusion that reigned in this meeting: one brother saying we are made members of the invisible Church by baptism; but others saying *we are not!* We are made members of the visible Church by baptism in infancy (or at maturity); (*vs.*) *we are not,* but were members before. We *have* a right to the Lord's Supper because of our (infant) baptism, and (*vs.*) *we have not,* are only candidates for the ordinance. The doctrine that regeneration is connatural or synchronical with the natural birth is very dangerous and false; and (*vs.*) *it is not,* but leads to a proper training of children for God. The doctrine of baptismal regeneration is a great illusion, and fearfully perilous, and (*vs.*) *it is very true and useful.*

The "elect" are regenerated by baptism, or as a consequent of their baptism, while *others are not at all affected* by their baptism. The non-elect are neither regenerated by baptism, either at that or any other time. Thus drifting about, pressing the inquiry, what is the force and import of baptism (infant baptism in particular), without a word of instruction in Holy Writ respecting its obligation, its wherefore, or result, see huge denominations of Christians, learned in ancient and modern lore, agitated like a boiling sea (even in their own folds) by questions on the subjects that never have been and never can be definitively and satisfactorily answered. And these inquiries, what is the duty of the Church to its baptized children? and in what relation do these children stand to the Church? are suffered to puzzle sage doctors of divinity for ages, and so far from approximating to an answer there is, perhaps, in every decade, an increasing diversity of views respecting them. Why not answer these questions by the simplest principle of Christian duty and humble common sense, and say, the duty of the Church, all churches, to their baptized children (or unbaptized), is to seek their immediate conversion to Christ, and enlistment in his service; those of kin to you first, simply because you have readiest access to them, and are accountable to God and to them (at the judgment) for the influence you have exerted upon them. Carrying them to a font cannot increase their need of your moral influence, nor your obligation to exert it: but if you judge that thereby your moral influence may be increased for their salvation, you do not sin in having them baptized, or consecrated without baptism, as many ten thousands have done in all ages. See the customs of the ancient Catharists, and the lately revised Episcopal formula for consecration without baptism. Also note the fact that the Congregational churches, of the West especially, are losing confidence in infant baptism, as a moral power either upon parent or child, or any part of the unquestioned divine law, and are extensively discontinuing the practice, as the Methodist societies have ever granted full liberty respecting it, and baptize more on the profession of their faith than in infancy.

To "hunt out the baptized children" and "watch" over them especially, for the sake of bringing them into your church-fold, very much resembles state church custom, and ritualistic church custom, as witnessed in the record of the Pharisees of old, and of the formalistic Greek, Papal, and Lutheran Churches of modern times; but to "hunt out" sinners, estranged from Christ by wicked works, and enemies to God and to the experience of his love shed abroad in their hearts by the Holy Ghost, very much resembles what Christ sent all his followers to do, and what would most likely bring salvation to our own households and to a world perishing in its sin. The former course (recommended by one of the speakers in the meeting) makes you consistent sacramentarians; the other (seeking all the "lost") makes you consistent Christians.

The latter course solves all the questions respecting rites by one simple principle, love to souls, and if you baptize any, you will do it to move men thereby to glorify God the more in their bodies and spirits, which are his, his by special redemption; and if you baptize not, it may be because you would exalt in their view the moral above a ceremonial law, and recommend, rather, the baptism of the Holy Spirit, which really sanctifies and saves, and makes its recipients truly strong for Christ's work.

But for truth's sake, and for the love of Christ's sake, and for charity's sake, cease receiving unquestioned a ritual law that none can define or expound, and which teaches as the Confession of Faith, chap. xxviii. sect. v., that "although it be a *great sin* to contemn or neglect this ordinance (baptism), yet grace and salvation are not so inseparably annexed unto it as that no person can be regenerated or saved without it, or that all that are baptized are undoubtedly regenerated;" or that "grace is really exhibited and conferred by the Holy Ghost (to those baptized) whether of age or infants, as that grace belongeth unto, etc." Open thine eye, Christian brother, to see the incongruity of teaching that it is a "great sin" to neglect baptism, yet that we may be regenerated and saved without it, and therefore "saved" in a great sin, yet that the "counsel of God's own will confers grace by the Holy Ghost," on both infants and adults receiving baptism, and thus (inferentially) is their "election made sure." May the rising light of a true spiritual illumination lift all churches from the bewilderment of such manifest Augustinian and Papal creeds and teachings.

A CATECHISM COMMENDED TO ALL RITUALISTS AND SACRAMENTARIANS.

Q. During how many centuries of earth's earliest ages was there no ceremonial law? or, at least, none that is left on record?

A. Twenty.

Q. Was not heaven open that angels might "ascend and descend," and saints from earth ascend thereto during all that period?

A. Yes; and Enoch attained to that holiness in his walk with God that "he was taken" and "ascended" to the glory prepared for him before the world was.

Q. When Abraham was commanded to circumcise himself and his offspring, did his personal circumcision render him more a sanctified man than he had been for twenty-four years prior to his circumcision?

A. No, in nowise. The promise that "all nations" should be blessed in him was made to Abraham while in uncircumcision, twenty-four years before he received the law of circumcision.

Q. Why was a more extended ritual law given to Moses than had been given to Abraham, as the law of oblations, baptisms, and sacrifices for atonement?

A. It was added because of transgression, as a partial (yet "weak" and "imperfect") defence against surrounding idolatry, and utter apostasy from God with its attendant corruptions.

Q. For how long a time was this ritual economy to continue?

A. "Until the seed (Christ) should come," through whom all the "gospel" promises to Abraham were to be fulfilled.

Q. Did the gospel promise make any allusion to the land of Canaan, or to circumcision?

A. None at all. It was infinitely broader, promising to the "believing" seed of Abraham "all nations," when circumcision, through prevailing faith, should come to "avail nothing."

Q. Did that covenant with Abraham, which included circumcision and the promise of Canaan, improve upon or enlarge the faith covenant?

A. It was infinitely less valuable than the latter, but was of value as bearing a promise to Abraham and his seed of the "life that now is," while the other was pregnant with the promise of the eternal life and blessedness of the whole Church of the living God.*

Q. Did the ritual "law covenant" hasten the "fulness of time" when the faith covenant could reveal all its blessings in Christ?

A. Nay. It only operated as a preservative during the necessary postponement of the blessings of the faith covenant—*i. e.*, until a Saviour for "all nations" could be received among men, Gentiles as well as Israelites.

Q. The "law covenant" being imperfect, did its manifestation (ratification) in any sense mar or lessen the fulness or value of the faith covenant?

A. No! The circumcision covenant made twenty-four years after, or the "law covenant" made four hundred and thirty years after the promise covenant, served their purpose but could not disannul or render the promise covenant in any respect deficient or "of none effect." If man is unfaithful, "God is faithful, and cannot deny himself."

Q. Did the righteousness of Enoch, Noah, Melchisedek, Abraham, or Moses, come through sacrifices or a law covenant?

A. No. Their righteousness was attained ere they had obeyed or observed any ceremonial law.

Q. Did perfection come to Israel by observing the Jewish ritual law?

A. No. That law was but a preparatory school, adapted to a rudimental education, to be used as a breakwater or shield against surrounding

---

* The lesser blessing (unsought) may, by the divine love, be added to the greater. Solomon asked *wisdom*, the greater blessing; God added "length of days, riches and honor." But "is not the life more than meat" or "raiment?" If Paul "sows spiritual things," is it not "a small matter," though needful, that he should reap (receive) the "temporal?"

idolatry, or as an alphabet and diagrams in learning to read and expound the moral law, which learned, they no longer need the alphabet or the diagrams before used.

Q. Is the moral law, obedience to which is to bless all nations, binding upon all nations?

A. Yes; and ever was, and ever will be.

Q. Was the ceremonial law of circumcision (or baptism) ever binding on any but the children (posterity) of Abraham?

A. No. It was to be the distinctive badge of Abraham's lineage.

Q. Why binding on them?

A. As a distinction between his posterity and other nations for good or evil, so long as that distinction was required in fulfilling God's temporal promises to Abraham; and until the time should come when all other nations should begin to inherit the greater blessings made to Abraham through Christ.

Q. Were spiritual blessings sealed to Abraham's posterity by circumcision?

A. Not at all. The covenant of circumcision was a *recognition* (a "seal" or signet) of Abraham's personal righteousness, without which neither temporal nor spiritual blessings would have been promised; but Abraham's natural posterity, who were without righteousness, received no *spiritual* blessing sealed to them through circumcision: this is self-evident.

Q. On what basis or condition were spiritual blessings promised and sealed to Abraham and to his posterity?

A. On the condition or basis of faith, and that basis only.

Q. Are these spiritual blessings equally the inheritance of the Gentiles since circumcision ceased?

A. Most assuredly. Herein is all the glory and blessedness of the gospel, that it secures the righteousness of both, and all the sequences thereof to all nations equally and alike, irrespective of rite, ceremony, birth, or lineage.

Q. If it had been necessary to extend circumcision to "all nations," would not infinite love have made the circumcision connatural or congenital?

A. This would seem to have been the dictate of mercy and good-will, for why should the human frame be created unworthy to be pronounced "good," and therefore in need of mending by man? Besides, if circumcision were universally extended, it would lose its significance as a badge.

Q. Does Christ give any specific law of externals, to distinguish his people from others?

A. No. None save a godly walk and conversation, manifesting thereby the spirit and mind of Christ; showing thus a death to sin and selfishness, and a *new birth* to holiness.

Q. Is the observance of any ceremony or obedience to any ritual now a moral duty?

A. Nay; save in accordance "as a man thinketh," or is internally persuaded. The correlative external law is wanting, and an assumed obligation to one is the creation of erroneous instruction based on the opinions and commandments of men. Neither circumcision nor uncircumcision, baptism nor unbaptism, eucharistic observance or non-observance, availeth aught, but the cross of Christ, in which alone salvation is found, and saints may truly glory.

Q. What is the fruit of transferring the obligations of the moral law and moral duty to sacraments and externals in religion?

A. It makes void the moral law; substitutes for the true spiritual circumcision a circumcision of no possible value to-day; and substitutes for the true spiritual baptism a cold and worthless shadow or type; and for the true spiritual bread that really comes from heaven that earthly bread that priests assume to consecrate, which when a man eateth, "like one that dreameth that he eats, he awakes, and his soul is empty."

Q. Is the "doctrine of baptisms" in the New Testament one that has exclusive reference to that which is external, or does it centre in that which is internal?

A. The word *baptismos*, which signifies external baptism (which was a Jewish custom), is found in only four passages of the New Testament, viz.: Mark vii. 4, 8; Heb. vi. 2, and ix. 10; while the word *baptisma*, which is transferred to the English Testament by dropping the last letter of the word, is found in the following passages: Matt. iii. 7; xx. 22, 23; xxi. 25: Mark i. 4; x. 38, 39; xi. 30: Luke iii. 3; vii. 29; xii. 50; xx. 4: Acts i. 22; x. 37; xiii. 24; xviii. 25; xix. 3, 4: Rom. vi. 4: Eph. iv. 5: Col. ii. 12: 1 Pet. iii. 21: in all which passages Dr. Dale and Prof. J. W. Beecher affirm that it (being a new word, found first in the New Testament) refers exclusively to religious doctrine, or that baptism which is internal.

Q. Can there be a positive law relative to externals, which yet is undefined and ambiguous, and open to endless "doubtful disputations?"

A. The ambiguity of any pretended law would render it a nullity; and to urge such a pretended law would be but a mockery of the human intelligence and man's moral conscience.

Q. That Matt. xxviii. 19 refers to purifying with water is a mere matter of human opinion (of some); so all the after questions of subjects, modes, administrators, design, effect, etc.; if this be allowed, it opens the way for endless human conceit, human devices, adjuncts, and pretended effects, leading to incessant jars upon the subject. Can we suppose the infinitely wise Teacher intended to tantalize his people by necessitating these worthless queryings about that which is external?

A. It would be infinitely derogatory to his character and aim.

Q. Is there to be found in the New Testament a specific command for infant baptism?

A. Pedo-Baptists do not, and dare not, assert that there is.

Q. Are Pedo-Baptists in accord with respect to the age, the mode, the object, and the relations into which infant baptism introduces its subjects?

A. No. There is a labyrinth of confusion upon the subject (see Discussion at Ministers' Meeting, Philadelphia, 1872).

Q. Are the children of Christian parents born more holy than other children?

A. No. All are born after the flesh, by the blood and will of man; *i. e.*, of the parents. "Behold I was shapen in iniquity, and in sin did my mother conceive me." "Death passed upon all, for all have sinned."

Q. Is sin attributable as guilt to those who know neither good nor evil?

A. This would be infinitely unworthy of God, the Father and Judge of all: "The son shall not bear the iniquity of the father; the soul that 'sinneth it shall die." [The "all" that have "sinned," then, are all those who have reached the age of moral accountability.]

Q. Can imputed sin, or actual sin, be washed away by the waters of baptism?

A. It would be folly to talk about purifying one who is not morally unclean, or to speak of a physical act of any creature as cleansing from moral obliquity.

Q. Does the *faith* of a parent work to the saving of a child?

A. It does not cause God, the infinite loving Father of all, to love one child more than another, or to seek or will to save one child more than another; but the child of the believing parent, increasing in years, and beholding the living faith and obedience of the parent, is thereby constantly influenced, and drawn to the same faith and obedience. The parents' righteousness is the moral lever that God uses to lift heavenward the child; "God also working with them." The needful means of grace may be fatally lacking in the case of the unbelieving parents.

Q. Ought all parents, whether believing in baptism or not, to consecrate their children to God, in their earliest years, and seek their sanctification and eternal welfare from their very birth?

A. Unquestionably they ought, and all considerate and well-instructed believing parents do.

Q. Does God bless children the more because the ceremony of baptism has been performed upon them?

A. No, in nowise; no more than the circumcised Jews were blessed because of their circumcision. The infant circumcised received no credit in heaven for that, nor any spiritual blessing on earth, any further than he "*walked* in the steps" of his believing father Abraham, even in the faith which he (Abraham) had *before he was circumcised.* So with the infant of to-day; God blesses the faithfulness of all parents, circumcised and uncircumcised, baptized and unbaptized, alike.

Q. What is the duty of parents to their children that have been baptized?

A. To train them up in the love and fear of God.

Q. What is the duty of parents toward children that have not been baptized?

A. *To train them up in the love and fear of God.**

Q. What is the duty of unbelieving parents?

A. To consecrate themselves and their children to God; to deem the eternal life paramount to the life that now is, and God's law the "higher law" by which both parent and child should seek to live! There is but one law for baptizer and non-baptizer, believer and unbeliever in this matter.

Q. If baptized children are growing up impenitent, what is the duty of the Church toward them?

A. To seek their conversion, and no less to seek the conversion and salvation of all others.

---

* Giving up children to God in baptism increases no man's moral obligation. It may and may not be a prompter or occasion of his more faithfully fulfilling his obligation. The simple fact of parentage creates the highest possible obligation. No ceremony can increase it. No lack of ceremony can annul it. Let every parent, as for his soul's life, and the soul's life of his child, remember this.

WHAT CAN BE LAW?

Nothing can be moral or unending positive law but that which is intrinsic, essential and universal. All externals must be circumstantial in the nature of things, and when circumstances afford a reason for non-obedience, the *positiveness* of the requirement does not exist. There is, therefore, an utter absurdity in the answer given by *Whitefield, Barnes,* etc., to the inquiry, " Is water-baptism necessary to an entrance into the kingdom of heaven?" "Yes, when it may be had."*

Is it not amazing that such teachers will propose as a condition of entering heaven a "bodily exercise," a "making clean the outside," which *must be wholly dependent on very variant circumstances,* as well as the unending conceits of men who undertake to answer what that baptism is? All the virtue there can be in water-baptism is derived from *spiritualizing* it, on the part of the administrator. And so of the eucharist, or any other mere symbol. The symbol does not sanctify of itself, no more than a pattern makes a garment, or a picture of food feeds the body. Nor can a moral duty be spiritualized, or made of another duty. To feed the hungry, clothe the naked, "bring the poor that are cast out to thy house," and shelter them, is no symbol, and requires no spiritualizing to be known as a duty. So to preach, or sing, or pray, or read the Scriptures, and use direct means to learn and teach the way of salvation to men, requires no spiritualizing; it requires already a spirit attuned and energized of God to the work; *that is all !* And such works are directly and intrinsically useful to those suffering bodies and hungering souls, whether you can explain a symbol so as to make it useful or not! But rites or emblems are of no worth *unless rightly expounded,* and we doubt whether the Almighty is perfectly "well pleased" with most of the expounders of rites and symbols. We doubt whether he would be exceedingly angry if they should let the rites entirely alone, which they have so long used to the mangling and marring of Zion!

Their obligation can be but circumstantial, as we have said, and were safely omitted by the thief on the cross, and many other repenting sinners dying in a prison, a wilderness, or desert, where no *church* administrators of rites are; or among those who, like the "Friends," do not believe in rites. There can be no "positive" obligation in such cases; nor do churches, when torn by internal factions, or destitute of "regular" administrators of ordinances, count themselves remiss for neglecting the "positive" laws!! By such illustrative cases, the impropriety of calling a ritual observance a positive law, and necessary for heaven "when it may be had," is seen.

Suppose that, instead of "tithing mints" and washing the flesh as a duty and a door to heaven, or eating sacramental bread that we may find

---

* Robinson says (p. 303): "Retaining the necessity of water-baptism to salvation exposed the Catholics to almost insurmountable difficulties in finding salvation possible to all past saints. Some of them claimed that Old Testament saints might be cleansed by *spiritual* baptism in Hades. The Gnostics used the term *baptisma* generically. They spoke of eight baptisms, viz.: 1. *Flumenis, i. e.,* of the river; 2. *Flaminis, i. e.,* of fire; 3. *Sanguinaris, i. e.,* of blood; 4. *Diluvium, i. e.,* of a flood; 5. *Moses, i. e.,* unto Moses; 6. *Legalis, i. e.,* of the law; 7. *Christus, i. e.,* unto Christ; 8. *Penitentia, i. e.,* of repentance. AMBROSE, one of the Gnostics, said that 'to will is to do,' in the case of baptism;' making baptism really internal."

Christ, we should all simply repent of sin, and thus receive the Holy Ghost, cleansing our hearts and giving us heavenly bread, and prompting us to all works of faith, love, and obedience—without any explained or unexplained symbols—would we not be as acceptable in God's sight and man's as if we had consented to receive the *badge* and *washing* of a sect?

The Quaker GRELLET could gain a hearing of the Pope himself, when, perhaps, a ritualistic Lutheran or an Episcopalian could not have gained it, and he preached Christ and righteousness and peace unto him. A WILLIAM PENN could gain the ear of King Charles of England, and plead for mercy in behalf of all persecuted dissenters, when, perhaps, no other dissenter could have gained it? A J. J. Gurney could get a hearing in Representative Hall at Washington, where he preached Christ to Henry Clay and Daniel Webster, and other tall senators and representatives of the nation, when no canonically baptized "priest" would have dared to ask such a hearing. So a Quakeress—Sarah Smiley —could get access to a Presbyterian pulpit in Brooklyn, N. Y., and preach Christ there, when it is probable that no other woman in America could have done it.

The baptizers are enclosed in narrower folds than the non-baptizers need to be. God's seal is on the non-baptizers as clearly as on others, and who shall assume that the non-baptizers are not as correct in their interpretation and application of "positive" law and moral law as others? Is it consistent to suppose that the emblem and the thing emblematized are both needed at the same time?

Is the model needed after the building is finished? or the pattern when the garment is already put on? We can have all the benefit of spiritualizing old customs, sacrifices, and symbols without keeping up the customs themselves? We need not circumcise, nor carry a cross, in order to preach the true circumcision and the cross of Christ to men! Those reformers, above named, thought it a great step to give the sacrament of the supper in both parts—the cup as well as the bread—to the laity; and it was, for it ended the scandalous monopoly of the wine-cup by the bibulous priests, who before had drunk the wine, and only gave the minute bread-tokens to the people! It is a great thing oft to even *change* the custom, if all is not made right thereby. To stir up and drain off a part of the filth of stagnant pools is better than allowing utter corruption to remain. Hence, the Protestant view of the sacraments is, in many denominations, better than the Papal; yet a ritualistic, sacramentarian spirit is far too common, and holds too much sway in the Protestant churches.

Zwingle and Œcolampadius thought to save the sacrament of the supper by putting the soul of it (which *they* gave to it) uppermost, *i. e.*, by observing it without an idolatrous trust in it. This was a great step toward reform from the Papal doctrine; yet, as shown by the sequel, it was only to annul the sacrament, or else give it lease of life to live again in the High Church sacramentarianism of Protestant Christendom. The magic or charm of the sacrament was not thus to be destroyed, the evil spirit not thus exorcised. To-day the sacraments are more accounted of by three-fourths of professed Protestants than the preaching of the word, or the life of faith and holiness. If a sacramental meeting once a quarter be attended, it is too oft assumed that all the others may be safely omitted. So, also, the weightier matters of the law are supplanted, as justice, mercy, love, peace, and fellowship among Christians. *They* think that God is pleased with the sacrament even if fellowship is disrupted thereby. And to impose that as a positive law on the Christian Church which scarce any two denominations interpret and practise in a similar manner, whether baptism or the supper, is, evidently, from the very confusion on the subject, "teaching for doctrine the commandments of men."

Teaching thus the Church has swung from one conceit or pretence for water-baptism to another, and from one mode or custom of observing the sacramental supper to another, and it is evident that none can tell what the "great commission" means, if applied to the external baptism, nor how or when, or how oft to eat the bread and drink the cup sacramentally, for no New Testament law defines either. Yet are they lured all the way by a vain imagination of obeying the last command of Christ. So in respect to its object. WALL constantly reiterates that infants come into the regenerated state by baptism. Neander and Gale, more discerning, deny it; and thus have the advantage of Dr. Wall. Albeit these do not deny that this was the doctrine of the early fathers that practised baptism at all. Wall quotes the fathers as fearing that children might come short of heaven through the neglect of their parents in not having them baptized, and himself indorses their fears. Pelagius denies that infants had sins to be purified by baptism, yet, in order that they may be fully fitted for heaven, thinks they ought to be baptized! Baptists deny that unconscious infants can be purified or benefited by being baptized, any more than they can commune and be benefited by it.

Pedo-Baptists think they should be baptized to render their parents faithful, and unconsciously to seal a covenant between the infants themselves and God ; albeit *they are not fitted for communion thereby,* albeit they *are already* partakers of the merits of the atonement to the justification of their natures, corrupted as they were by natural inheritance.

Such is the chaos of thought and reasoning upon this subject, all betokening as dense a darkness and entanglement as those were in who speculated and queried as to what sort of dinner Christ had had brought to him when he said, "I have meat to eat that ye know not of." These baptizers are in as dense a wilderness respecting what sort of baptism Christ enjoined in the great commission ; and they have mistaken it in the same manner.

THE CHARGES PREFERRED.

We charge those who claim to be Christians, and are Jews respecting baptism, with opening the flood-gates of controversy for an unending jar about things to no profit. We charge them with encumbering Christ's Church with an exotic plant, that grows luxuriant in many a sink-hole and morass of moral degeneracy and fleshly corruption, and countenancing an endless twaddle about a ritual law that Christ abolished in his death, and therefore has no actual being save by the commandment of men who have erred through their ritual blindness. We charge them with creating an engine of priestcraft and persecution in the name of a ritual law, and thus feeding fuel to the fires of sectarian strife that rage in the form of intolerance, bigotry, superstition, persecution, and every species of civil and spiritual despotism. We charge them not only with the sin and folly of marring Zion's peace to no profit, but also starving and tantalizing millions who hunger for salvation through the power of the Holy Ghost, by offering them *elemental water* instead of *spiritual life*, and *a stone* (a heart unregenerate) instead of that "bread that comes down from heaven!" And, perchance, Christian reader, these charges stand in all their force against thine own church to-day.

All admit that the symbolic water-baptism is not baptism, without the internal or spiritual baptism from God; that the heart still defiled is not even (canonically) baptized by any outward rite; and that, if the internal baptism has been received, the lack of the external baptism cannot efface it, or render it null or of less effect. *Why not, then, take the* REAL BAPTISM, that makes all hearts one, and leave the other to those who "war after the flesh," and love "doubtful disputations," and cling to their "vain oblations" and ceremonials the closer, the less of the Holy Spirit and of a holy life is required by their ritual observances.

CAMPBELLISM IN MOURNING—LAMENTATIONS OVER THE TEACHINGS OF DR. DALE'S SURVEY OF THE DOCTRINE OF BAPTISMS.

[Extract from the Christian Standard (of Cinn.), March 29, 1873.]

"If *eis* then, after the words *baptiso* and *baptisma*, always introduces the 'element' of the immersion—*i. e.*, that whereinto a thing is immersed—then there will be as many distinct and different immersions or baptisms as there are different elements. [Precisely.] This will fill the New Testament with very many baptisms unknown to the world to this day, till this extravagant conceit came into being. . . . If *eis* always introduces into elements, then no purpose of baptism is anywhere expressed at all. [Right, it expresses state or condition]. . . . All these inevitable conclusions are so monstrous, so fatal [to discipleism] that it is beyond amazement how any thoughtful man can accept them and not shrink back from them with alarm. What sad reality is here? We see Christian, God-fearing men go to the terrible extreme of preferring to accept such monstrous conclusions, rather than give up very lately introduced corruptions of a divine ordinance, which they now love and practise because of tradition from their fathers!"

ANNIHILATION OF THE ORDINANCE.

"According to this novel theory what the use of water in the ordinance is, is entirely unknown in the New Testament. Whether it is to be sprinkled or poured, or otherwise applied to the candidate, or whether he is to be immersed in it, is wholly unknown, and without any authority. [Right, once more.] Whether it is to be put on the head, breast, foot, or any other part, is equally, utterly in the dark, and unauthorized. [Right again.] Furthermore, it is absolutely unknown whether it is to be applied to the candidate at all. If, with this doctrine, a minister pours water in the ordinance, where is his authority for such an act, and where his authority from God's word for applying it at all to the person to be baptized? Not one syllable. [Right again.] To pour the water on the ground, as a libation, is, according to this doctrine, as defensible, as well authorized, and as reasonable. . . . This doctrine then, it is clear, *utterly annihilates the visible ordinance in any form.* . . . And now, in all charity and in the fear of God, we hesitate not to declare, that such a conclusion is worthy of such a bad progress, and of such persistent effort against a divine ordinance, and against a world of light. It is fitting that it should be brought to this last deep shame of an utter annihilation of this blessed, beautiful, exalted ordinance of the Lord. . . This sinful, long-persistent departure from truth in anti-immersion, this bitter war, this insane rejection of all light and proof, has culminated inevitably in this last crowning delusion."

Correctly does the above critic read the result of the declaration that *baptisma* and *baptiso* always introduce the element into which a thing is immersed or baptized, and thus establishes the "divers baptisms" of the law and gospel, of the Greeks and Hebrews, of ancient and modern times. And very clearly also does he see that this doctrine wholly annuls the assumed law for water-baptism in any form, or for any reason whatever. And we most appositely apply his own words, and say, "it is fitting that" that most shallow, superstitious, obtuse, and bigoted idolatry of a rite, should be brought at last to "this deep shame" of an "utter annihilation" of what has ever been a source of unutterable folly, weakness and spiritual blindness to the Christian Church. The light of truth on the subject, as seen above, so begins to shine, at length, that it will be impossible to save that writer's idol, and let him be wise, and before his idolatry becomes utterly nauseating, and a stink in the nostrils of all devout men, evince his prudence and discernment by giving up the worthless idol.

BAPTISMAL THESES—CONCLUSIONS REACHED IN THE FOREGOING WORK.

1. Two baptisms are specially known to the Church, viz.: the baptism of water, which is a symbol, and the baptism of the Holy Ghost. The baptism of the cross is auxiliary to the latter.

2. The baptism of water commenced with Moses. He was the first, as he is the only authorized law-giver that has required it, and the aim of the requirement was evidently partly hygienic, and partly symbolical or typical of the moral regeneration of purifying by the blood of Christ and the Holy Spirit.

3. John's baptism was repentance baptism, and in connection therewith he used the Jewish typical baptism, and therefore he was not the mediator of any new covenant, or new and separate dispensation, but when he preached repentance, and by the word and baptismal sign pointed to the "Lamb of God," he prepared the way for that gospel dispensation or "kingdom of heaven," which was then "even at the door."

4. Christ's baptism, himself assures us, was the antitype of Moses and John's baptism, so far as they were typical, for it is specifically the baptism of the Holy Ghost, or at least, is not completed, without the renewing and sealing energy of the Holy Ghost.

5. Water-baptism, as a religious rite, was ever a symbol of spiritual purifying, and the spiritual baptism alone secures that purifying.

6. The apostles and early Jewish Christians at first continued typical baptism, as they did the passover, circumcision, and other Jewish rites, for an age or more after the legal dispensation was, in fact, fulfilled, and only lingered in a gradual decay and evanishment, as by the Divine economy the kingdom of Christ was supplanting it.

7. Jesus established no new symbol baptism; this was neither necessary, nor consistent with his specifically spiritual dispensation and reign; he simply submitted to the purifying of the law, and to the feasts and customs as a loyal Jew, until the type dispensation should be ended in his crucifixion. Though a priest of his own kingdom, he neither sacrificed nor baptized any but himself, for in him was centred and by him fulfilled all sacrifices, and all circumcisions, and all baptisms.

8. In the Great Commission (Matt. xxviii. 19), Jesus Christ commanded no baptism with water, but a renovation of the nations by the purifying power and influence of the gospel attended by the promised presence and energies of the Holy Spirit.

9. Christ having fulfilled or made provision for the universal proclamation of the saving baptism (into Christ, or into "Father, Son and Holy Spirit"), and for its universal prevalence and supremacy, there is now but "one Lord, one faith, one baptism," that baptism of merging into Christ and into his true Church.

10. Paul, the great apostle of the Gentiles, was not sent to baptize (with water as himself testifies) but having received the Great Commission, and Christ's "anointing" to qualify him therefor, he was sent "to open the eyes" of Jew and Gentile to the truth and "to turn them from darkness to light, and from the power of Satan unto God"—*i. e.*, to enlighten and regenerate them—"that they might obtain an inheritance among *all them that are sanctified.*"

11. All questions and contentions about ritual baptism should only have been incident to an incipient and rudimentary state of the Church while under Moses, or when merging from Judaism to the full freedom of the Christian dispensation. The Church of Christ should have left shadows and types, and pressed on to that perfection in the Christian life which the power and indwelling of the Holy Ghost is able to secure.

12. Regeneration, sanctification, Christian love, Christian union, and eternal life are gained only by the baptism of the Holy Spirit, with all types, and all inter-penetration of a ceremonial law, which is but of the "letter that killeth," left out.

13. Water-baptism may be used, in liberty, if Christians can use such liberty, and not seek to impose their ceremony upon others, as they may use the formula of a creed, or modes of worship, in the same way; but if allowed to abridge Christian fellowship, or crucify Christian love, or observed as a yoke of bondage to a duty, it thereby makes void God's real law of love and charity, of holiness and practical righteousness, and the use of this and other rites in such way *becomes a sin*, which should be repented of and rites omitted until such time as Christians have light or grace enough to use them in liberty and charity.

14. It is a grave and fatal delusion to substitute water-baptism for the spiritual, in the hope thereby of regenerating the souls of men to holiness, and to teach that thus they are to secure eternal salvation.

15. That which is termed the Lord's Supper was originally either the passover or the Christian's "feast of love and fellowship;" therefore Christians should observe it, if at all, in freedom, not as obeying commandment, but as a voluntary act of professing Christ, or manifesting love to Christ, and to our fellow-saints and fellow-heirs of the same grace and glory. So all kings, princes, and the families of the earth make voluntary feasts to manifest kinship, and increase fellowship one with another.

THE CREED QUESTION.

When all Christian believers come to think precisely alike on all religious questions, or, rather, when independent thought, on the part of every Christian, save some priest or pope, has altogether ceased, then, and not till then, can a creed be written by man that shall receive the assent of "all evangelical Christians."

To make creeds tests of Christian fellowship, and bases of Christian or Church union, should never be attempted.

The COVENANT of a Church in which it avouches Jehovah to be Sovereign, Jesus Christ to be Redeemer and Saviour, and the Holy Spirit to be Sanctifier and Comforter, and in which, also, the Church promises to walk in love and faithfulness toward all the household of faith, and holily and unblamably before God and man, is the true and all-sufficient bond of union. No man-written creed can unite all Christians. No such creed is tantamount to the teachings of inspiration. Any number of believers in Christ may unite in the adoption of an uninspired creed; but it is folly to presume that all Christians can or ought to receive and assent to it. A portion of the household of faith may adopt such a creed, expressive of views, by them deemed very important, as having a momentous moral bearing, provided they do not reproach or condemn uncharitably those not adopting it, but hold steadfastly to the principle of unrestricted *Christian fellowship*. There is no divine law requiring all Christians to be in one organization (to assume that there is is Popery), but the divine law does require that all Christians should love and fellowship each other. Yet this fellowship need not be *sacramental* fellowship; that also is Popery or Judaism.

Unrestricted sacramental fellowship is not within the reach of those on earth, still compassed with human infirmities. This vain attempt has served as an *ignis fatuus* before champions of Christian union long enough. Doctrinal views when written in creeds, and set up as a standard to rally adherents, may serve a good purpose, where the truths propounded are momentous, but owing to modifications or variations of human thought all such standards are soon outgrown, and thus in the future (as in the past) it ever must be. Where are the "Schoolmen?" and the "Supralapsarian Predestinarians" to-day? The occasion of church organization on such issues is gone by forever: as soon it will be, we trust, on the question of rites.

A union creed (attempted) should be so written as to accommodate the greatest diversity of belief in the household of faith, that human charity can reach, as near all that love Christ and his cause as practicable. Otherwise, if you desire to express your own view by a specific statement, let every member of the Church you walk with also have his specific statement of faith, and thus in candor and frankness let each have his own creed. He has equal right with thee to the imposition of a creed upon the brotherhood. Most of the pretended union creeds are the sheerest mockeries, expressing the real sentiments or views of the writer, perhaps, but of how many more, it might be hazardous to say. Most of the professed union creeds and church unions (as recently published in the UNION ERA, for example) are simply transcripts of epitomized Congregational and Presbyterian Church manuals. They oft retain, moreover, the crude, tritheistic, and predestinarian statement of two or three

hundred years ago. They nearly all include the Papal law of sacraments, and millennarian doctrine respecting the resurrection and the
final judgment. Yet none dare say that respecting these, the holiest
men Christ has ever called to his kingdom and glory have not, and do
still differ.

Asserting our right to present a platform or statement of faith, such as
the present day demands (in America) which shall also be as near the
untrammelled union basis as our feeble insight can make it, we present
the following:

*Form of Covenant and Declaration of Principles for a local
church or congregation of saints, organized for the purpose of
maintaining Christian worship, fellowship and labors.*

Recognizing the honesty of purpose and right of all existing church
organizations to proclaim each their own faith, to worship God according
to the dictates of their own consciences, to organize churches after the
model of simple or more complex forms, if Christian love be not hindered,
and Christian freedom be not trammelled, and thereby personal moral
accountability is maintained, we choose so to do, and do now unite and
enter into fellowship for Christian labors of love in the field and sphere
where God has placed us, or shall hereafter place us, by mutually pledg-
ing ourselves to the work of Christ, in adopting the following covenant:

COVENANT.

We do now, in the presence of God and this congregation, solemnly acknowledge Jehovah to be our God, and enter into covenant to love and
serve him *forever!* We receive the Divine Father as our Father, our
Friend, and our chosen portion forever; the Lord Jesus Christ in all his
mediatorial offices, prophet, priest, and king, as our only Intercessor,
and Saviour; the Holy Spirit as our Sanctifier, Comforter, and Guide.
We receive the brethren in Christ as our brethren, his friends as our
friends. We submit to the government of Christ in his Church, and to
the regular administration of it in this church in particular, so long as
we remain members thereof. We promise by this covenant to attend
the regular and special meetings of the church, and in all respects to conduct ourselves as individually responsible for the prosperity of the church
and the cause of Christ as connected with it. We promise to religiously
instruct and govern those under our care, to reverence the Sabbath as a
day consecrate to religious duties, to refrain from unnecessary intercourse
with the vicious, from sinful pleasures and amusements, from speaking
evil of others; and to live a life of self-denial and benevolence, consecrating our influence, time and property to promote purity, temperance,
equality, peace, and righteousness among men; and thus to extend the
kingdom of Christ till it shall become universal.

When members are received subsequently to the primal organization
of the church, the ministering angel of the church may change the form
of the pronoun *we* to the appellative form *you*, and then a response from
the church will be fitting, thus:

We then, the members of this church, in view of these your professions
and engagements, do joyfully and affectionately receive you to this communion, and welcome you to this fellowship with us in the blessings of

the gospel, and in the service of our Divine Redeemer. We covenant to love and watch over you, and in Christian fidelity to seek your advancement in the life and likeness of him whose name we bear. And now, beloved of the Lord, let it be impressed upon your minds, that you have entered into solemn engagements, from which you can never escape. Wherever you go these vows will be upon you. They will follow you to the bar of God, and abide upon you to eternity. May you walk worthy of God and of your profession! May the Lord guide and preserve you till death, and at the last receive you and us to that blessed rest, where our love and joy shall be forever perfect! And unto Him who is able to keep us from falling, and to present us faultless before the presence of his glory with exceeding joy ; to the only wise God our Saviour be glory and majesty, dominion and power, both now and forever. Amen.

Have not such a church, and those who adopt with them such a covenant, given ample assurance before God and man, that they are both *sound in the faith*, and acceptable before God in heart and life ?

But if asked for a creed, that a local church might adopt and still hold the church door open to the greatest portion of Christians in any community, we would commend the following, being the basis of fellowship for the Reformed Churches of Italy, as reported by Gavazzi, and we will also present a formula of our own.

CHURCH UNION.

GAVAZZI speaks of the efforts to unite the newly formed Protestant Churches of Italy, which effort resulted in leaving out of their devised creed all mention of those dogmatic and ritualistic features which are ever an apple of discord, and have hitherto defied all attempts at union where they are incorporated. We allude to *sacraments*, and the doctrine of absolute divine decrees of reprobation.

Hear what he says respecting the conflict :

"You cannot imagine how long we had to fight in order to get out of the influence of sectarianism. That was the work of ten years. For when the various denominations would come to Italy, each saying, 'We are the true Church,' the Italians preferred to remain in Rome rather than go into a church they knew nothing about. So we had to get free from this as best we could. We have tried to fight extremes with the word of God, avoiding scholastic theology. We also had a fight against a foreign theology that our hearts revolted at, a theology that teaches eternal decrees of damnation. We had to come simply to justification by faith to be shown by a holy life. We have now a Scriptural Church in Italy, and I stand before you to-day to recommend it to your minds and your hearts and your pulpits."

And here is the condensed, and, as sacramentarians would say, eviscerated statement of *principles*. A statement whose phraseology we would not, perhaps, pronounce, in every respect, the most felicitous, but to us it is amazing that those specified omissions have not been thought of in "free" America's attempts at Church Union. Yet all can see that in a country cursed to the death with Papal sacraments, the only way to deliver evangelical Christians from the incubus was to count the sacraments a dead letter, and leave each redeemed soul to his own Christian freedom respecting these principles.

FREE CHRISTIAN CHURCH OF ITALY.

Declaration of principles. Adopted unanimously in General Assembly at Milan, June, 1870.

"1. GOD the FATHER, SON, and HOLY GHOST, has manifested his will in Revelation, which is the Bible, the alone perfect and immutable rule of faith and conduct.

"2. GOD created man perfect in his own image and likeness, but Adam disobeying the word of God, sinned, and thus by one man sin has entered into the world, and death by sin. On this account, human nature in Adam and by Adam has become corrupt and sinful; and we are all born in Adam with the inclination to do evil, and the inability of doing well what God has commanded; wherefore, naturally, we are all sinners under condemnation.

"3. GOD does not desire the death of the sinner, but that he should come to the knowledge of the truth and be saved.

"4. Salvation comes from the eternal and gratuitous love of the FATHER;—it is obtained through the expiatory sacrifice, resurrection, and intercession of the SON;—it is communicated by the HOLY SPIRIT, who regenerates the sinner, unites him to CHRIST by faith, comes and dwells in him, produces peace in his heart, giving him the assurance of the entire remission of his sins, making him free, guiding and consoling him by means of the word which he himself has given, sealing and guarding him until the day of the glorious appearing of our Lord and Saviour Jesus Christ.

"5. The Christian, redeemed with a great price, ought to glorify God in his soul, body, and spirit, which belong to God, walking in holiness, without which no man can see the Lord. In order to this, he finds strength in communion with him who says to him, ' My grace is sufficient for thee.'

"6. Believers, regenerated in Christ, form the Church, which cannot perish nor apostatize, being the body of the Lord Jesus.

"7. In addition to the universal priesthood of believers, God himself has established in the Church various special ministries, for the perfecting of the saints and the edifying of the body of Christ, which ministries ought to be recognized by the Church itself.

"8. The Lord Jesus Christ will come from heaven and transform our body of humiliation into a glorious body. In that day the dead in Christ shall rise first, and the living who are found faithful shall be transformed, and thus together shall we be caught up in the clouds, to meet the Lord in the air, to be forever with the Lord; and, after his kingdom, all the rest shall rise to be judged in judgment.

"These articles are held to suffice as a testimony of a Christianity purely evangelical, without pretending that there are no other doctrines in the Bible to be believed. It is also clearly asserted that this ' Declaration of Principles ' does not pretend to infallibility. The word of God is alone infallible and immutable. Nor is it looked upon as the cause or title to salvation, but simply as the outward bond of unity in the faith and the banner of the Church."

The government these churches have adopted unites the Congregational and Presbyterian in one, but who would presume to say that this organization will certainly enclose all the Protestants of Italy, or that future changes in the Statements of Principles and Rules of the body will never occur? And who will assume that Scripture will be violated, or benevolence lost sight of, if they do occur?

But among the numerous sects of America the questions of baptism, church order, liturgies and sacraments are the great dividing and hindering causes, and no church or individual advocate of Christian union seems to dare to propose a creed or formula that will hold these at bay, and in proper subordination to soul-freedom in each individual Christian. To friends of organic union in America, we would therefore suggest or propose the following unassuming formula:

UNION ARTICLES OF FAITH.

1. The Bible is the book of God, and is the Christian's standard of faith.

2. God is one: the Father, Son, and Holy Spirit are distinct offices or revelations of the *one* Divine Essence.

3. Jesus Christ, by his sufferings and death, has made an atonement for man, and is now the Mediator between God and man.

4. Moral or spiritual regeneration, *i. e.*, the conversion of sinners from a sinful to a holy life, is a sufficient and only proper evidence of Christian character.

5. The moral law, requiring disinterested love to God and man, is universally obligatory: while all forms, rites, or ceremonials are contingent, deriving their obligation from the circumstances which create their necessity.

6. The sanctification and perpetuity of the Christian Sabbath together with the union of believers in the visible Church are necessary means of grace in all ages; and all Christians within convenient localities should unite their influence for mutual good, and the more successful promotion of the cause of Christ.

7. The door of the Church on earth is to be as wide as the door of the kingdom of heaven; and liberty of opinion and free discussion is ever to be allowed concerning church government, ordinances, and modes of worship; uniformity in these is not to be required, nor expected, except by mutual concession, to such a degree as will secure the harmony and efficient action of the organization.

8. There is no New Testament *ceremonial law*, or law requiring the observance of *ordinances;* the moral law requiring supreme love to God and equal love to man, when obeyed in all moral rectitude, wisdom, and zeal, by each individual Christian, constitutes the sum of all that is "ordained" or required either in man's individual or social capacity.

9. The abettors of iniquity, fraud, covetousness, war, sectarianism, intemperance, licentiousness, or any other form of moral obliquity are to have no place in the Christian Church, nor are they to receive any fellowship or countenance from Christians; moral rectitude, as required by the moral law rather than oneness of sentiment in respect to forms and theories, is the true ground of fellowship and union.

10. There will be a final and eternal separation between the righteous and the wicked; all the followers of Christ are to be exalted with Christ

in glory, and to be advancing from glory to glory. Hence, it is their constant privilege to walk in faith and love while on earth; to be separate in spirit and moral conduct from the unrighteous, and to labor with zeal and perseverance for the advancement of Christ's kingdom and the salvation of man.

Or the following, being briefer, is our preferred

FORMULA OF FAITH.

Recognizing each Christian's right to make "confession of faith," here is ours: We offer it simply as a statement, in succinct form, of those truths which come nearest to being essential truths; such truths at least as must receive recognition by every professing and *visible* Church of Christians. While the Christian spirit, life, and love is the only criterion of character, and the only basis and bond of fellowship, the prime points of our faith are: We believe in

1. One only living and true God.
2. Christ, the divine Mediator and all-atoning Sacrifice.
3. The Holy Spirit (through the truth), our Sanctifier.
4. Moral regeneration necessary for all men.

(a) A holy life its proof.

(b) The visible Church, the sphere where all such should labor and enjoy Christian fellowship.

(c) All contiguous, local churches should be in fellowship.

(d) All regenerated persons should receive and bid each other godspeed in every good work.

5. The Holy Scriptures are given by inspiration of God.
6. The Christian Sabbath and the organized Church are necessary to the moral regeneration of man.
7. The results or sequences of a worthy or unworthy life on earth are interminable.
8. Love toward God and man, with its resultant good fruits, is the essence of religion and the only essential proof of a regenerate state.
9. Obedience to the moral law only, and not to any rites or ordinances of a ceremonial law, may be required of any believer as a test of fellowship or union with the visible Church.
10. For organic church action there must be an intelligible basis of agreement, which is most properly the Church Covenant, and no one that loves Christ, and desires to be a worker with the body organized to promote Christ's cause, should be rejected.
11. Differing views respecting organizations, modes of worship, ordinances, or any circumstantial of external religion, and variance of speculative opinions, should be tolerated in every church, so far as consistent with personal coöperation.
12. No true Christian is a heretic—no palpable violator of God's law is truly orthodox.
13. Supreme love to God and man, with the fruits of peace, virtue, and righteousness, is everywhere, world without end, *the fulfilling of the law.*

We confess that we have no right to impose even such a creed as the above on any body of Christian believers, or to ask any one of Christ's flock to assent to such a creed, either in the aggregate or in the detail, as a condition antecedent to receiving him to Christian and church fellowship; but as those who are not substantially agreed cannot walk and work together in promoting any work of faith and Christian love, and as there is no command or law requiring all Christians invariably to coöperate in each and every department of Christian labor, there can be no harm in a body of Christian believers choosing both their sphere of labor and their statement of faith, provided they do not "set at naught" any that do not choose to work in their sphere, or adopt the same formula of faith.

But let every confession of faith, however variant from the above, nevertheless so diverge that, like the two sides of a right angle infinitely extended, it will more and more embrace the ever-enlarged and varying results of sanctified human thought. Creeds have, conversely, usually been convergent, with the sharp angle pointing toward some of Christ's redeemed flock, who are either pierced or riven asunder, as the point of the angle moved toward them. Some *must be found* on the one or the other side of the sharp point of the angle. Now no Christian or Christian Church organization has a right to trample on the social rights, *i. e.*, the rights and privileges of Christian fellowship, by leaving outside the fold the least lamb in all Christ's flock. If any such lamb be rendered excommunicate or ineligible to any fold, then, Christian brother, that is the one for whose sake *we* should leave the ninety and nine, and go and make alliance with that one in the closest bonds of Christian fellowship, and that *because* he has been "set at naught" of others! Bind your heart and soul to his! Let your sympathies and affections be twined with his, since it is for his honest and unflinching allegiance to his own conscience and to Christ that he is set at naught by the popular, the current, the overspreading church folds. Do this at the cost of the frown, if it must be, of all that have rejected Christ in the person of one of his "little ones." This is, without doubt, Christ's mind respecting the use of creeds.

A FORMULA for publicly consecrating children without baptism has been adopted by a portion of the Reformed Episcopalians of New York, which has also received the approval of the "Baptist Union," a journal advocating the union of all Baptist Churches in one fold, all showing that there is not only inquiry but progress in the direction of asserting Christian freedom from the hitherto excessive bondage to ordinances in the Protestant Church.

THE END.

1540